W9-BAH-052

Oscar & Lucinda

by the same author

fiction

The Fat Man in History

Bliss

Illywhacker

screenplay

Bliss: The Film

OSCAR & LUCINDA

PETER CAREY

Harper & Row, Publishers, New York
Cambridge, Philadelphia, San Francisco, Washington
London, Mexico City, São Paulo, Singapore, Sydney

 For information address Harper & Row, Publishers, Inc., 10 E. 53rd Street, New York, N.Y. 10022.

FIRST U.S. EDITION

Library of Congress Cataloging-in-Publication Data

Carey, Peter.
Oscar and Lucinda.

I. Title.
PR9619.3.C36073 1988 823 87-46125
ISBN 0-06-015903-1

---

88 89 90 91 92 RRD 10 9 8 7 6 5 4 3 2 1

for Alison Summers with all my love

Contents

Oscar & Lucinda

1

The Church

If there was a bishop, my mother would have him to tea. She would sit him, not where you would imagine, not at the head of the big oval table, but in the middle of the long side, where, with his back to the view of the Bellinger River, he might gaze at the wall which held the sacred glass daguerreotype of my great-grandfather, the Reverend Oscar Hopkins (1841–66).

These bishops were, for the most part, bishops of Grafton. Once there was a bishop of Wollongong, travelling through. There was also a canon, and various other visiting or relieving reverends. Sometimes they were short-sighted or inattentive and had to have the daguerreotype handed to them across the table. My mother crooked her finger as she picked up her teacup. She would not tell the bishops that my great-grandfather's dog-collar was an act of rebellion. They would look at a Victorian clergyman. They would see the ramrod back, the tight lips, the pinched nose, the long stretched neck and never once, you can bet, guess that this was caused by Oscar Hopkins holding his breath, trying to stay still for two minutes when normally—what a fidgeter—he could not manage a tenth of a second without scratching his ankle or crossing his leg.

This was obvious to me, but I said nothing. I sat, tense, my hands locked underneath my thighs. In a moment the Bishop would ignore our big noses and many other pieces of contradictory evidence, and remark on our resemblance to this pioneer clergyman. We lined up: my mother, my brother, me, my sister. We had red hair, long thin necks like twisted rubber bands.

My mother was pleased to imagine she looked like the photograph. I would rather have looked like my father. He was not like us at all. He was short, broad-faced, pigeon-chested. He had crinkled eyes and crooked teeth. He laughed and farted. He was a cunning spin bowler. He could roll a cigarette with one hand. He was not like us, and when my mother told the visiting Bishop the story of how Oscar transported the little church of St John's to Bellingen, my father would peel a match with his broad fingernail and look out through the windows to where the great physical monument to his marriage, the Prince Rupert's Glassworks – the roof painted bright red then, in the 1930s – sat high above the Bellinger River.

My mother told the story of the church in a way that always embarrassed me. There was an excess of emotion in her style. There was something false. We must have all known it, but we never spoke about it. I could not have named it anyway. She was the same in church: her responses to the Sanctus (Holy, Holy, Holy, Lord God of Hosts) were loud and showy in their reverence. My father made jokes about many things, but never about this.

My father was jealous of that church, although if you could see it now, it is hard to imagine why. It sits on a patch of flood-prone land beside Sweet Water Creek at Gleniffer – a tiny weatherboard building with a corrugated iron roof. For fifty years it was painted various shades of brown, and then, in 1970, it was painted a harsh lime green. Now it has gone chalky and sits in that generous valley like something on which lichen has grown. It tucks in underneath the long line of casuarinas that mark the course of the river. High above, behind this line of river, the mountains rise sharply to three thousand feet – the back wall of the valley, so steep there are no tracks, although they say there is an old tin mine up there were they planned to hide the women and children from the Japanese during the Second World War. I was away at the time, but it seems unlikely to me. I learned long ago to distrust local history. Darkwood, for instance, they will tell you at the Historical Society, is called Darkwood because of the darkness of the foliage, but it was not so long ago you could hear people call it Darkies' Point, and not so long before that when Horace Clarke's grandfather went up there with his mates – all the old families should record this when they are arguing about who controls this shire – and pushed an entire tribe of aboriginal men and women and children off the edge.

These are the same people who now want St John's removed on a low-loader. They want it taken to Bellingen to be used as a Sunday school.

My father, for one, would have been appreciative. He was, as I said, jealous of it. He did not like my mother's proprietorial attitude to it. Perhaps if the church had been in the town of Bellingen itself it would have been different. But Gleniffer is ten miles away. She would not hear of attending service in Bellingen. They must motor out to

Gleniffer. During the war they used their petrol ration just going to church. We were all baptized there, confirmed there. I was married there. When my father died he was carried ten miles to Gleniffer for the funeral service, and then ten miles back into town to be buried.

My father did not get drunk, but once, after drinking two beers, he told me that my mother walked around the perimeter of St John's like a dog pissing around a fence. But only once did he ever show my mother the intensity of his feelings.

2

The Advent Wreath

There was no torch available for my father because I had dropped it down the dunny the night before. I had seen it sink, its beam still shining through the murky fascinating sea of urine and faeces. My father did not, as he had on an earlier occasion, come out and retrieve it.

So when the lights went off in the storm the following night, he had no torch to examine the fuse-box. Lightning was striking all around us. The phone was giving small pathetic rings in response to strikes further along the line. We thought our fuses were blown by a back-surge in the power system. My father took a candle out on the veranda. The candle blew out. When he came back into the house he did not have the fuse with him.

We were sitting in silence at the kitchen table.

My father said: "Where is the fuse-wire?"

I was ten years old. I sat next to my mother. My sister was sixteen; she sat next to me. My brother was fourteen; he sat next to my sister.

"I used it," my mother said. People described her as a tall woman. She was not. She was five foot six, but she had an iron will and a suspicious nature and this, combined with her power as an employer in the glassworks, was a tall combination.

I could smell the smoking candle. Although my father held this candle, I knew he could not smell it. He had no sense of smell at all.

"*How* did you use it?" I could not see my father. I waited for the next flash of lightning. "How?" He had a hoarse voice. This was somehow connected with the loss of his sense of smell. He syringed his nasal passages with salt water every morning. Often he would ask: "Does it smell?" "It" was his nose.

"I used it," my mother said, "to make the Advent wreath."

There was no note of apology in her voice. Lightning sheeted the kitchen. She had her head tilted in the air in that disdainful pose which, in the family mythology, was said to resemble a camel.

I felt very tense. I was the one who had helped my mother make this Advent wreath. There had been no holly or ivy, but I had found camphor laurel leaves, which are shiny and green. I knew she had not only used the fuse-wire but had taken the wire netting from my brother's rabbit hutches. The rabbits were, at this moment in shoe boxes in the linen press. She did not think that they would piddle. It did not occur to her.

My father lit the candle. He did not approach the table. He did not go back towards the door. He stood in the middle of the room.

"Where is it?" he asked.

"At church," my mother said. "Please, David, sit down."

"Which church?"

"What does it matter?"

"It matters to me."

I cannot explain how frightening this was. My father did not speak like this. He liked life to be quiet. Even when he was dying, he tried to do it in a way that would not upset my mother.

"St John's," she said.

Of course it was St John's. What else would it have been? But for some reason this announcement seemed to outrage him. He clasped his head. He put the candle on top of the Kelvinator where it promptly went out again.

"Oh, Christ," he said. "Jesus, Joseph and fucking Mary."

In the lightning I saw my sister's mouth drop open.

My mother stood up. She never made gentle or gradual movements. She stood so quickly her chair fell backwards. It crashed to the floor. The phone rang—two short bleats, then stopped.

"Kneel," my mother said. She meant for God to forgive my father his blasphemy. We understood her meaning, but we were outside our normal territory. Only "divorce" could have frightened me more, only "sex" been more embarrassing.

"Kneel," she shrieked.

Later we knew she was a bully. But when we were children, we felt too many confusing things. Mostly we wanted her to love us. So we came and knelt beside her, even my brother although he liked to stay up late and talk cricket with my father.

Then my father knelt too.

We stayed there kneeling on the hard lino floor. My brother was crying softly.

Then the lights came on.

I looked up and saw the hard bright triumph in my mother's eyes. She would die believing God had fixed the fuse.

3

Christmas Pudding

There would have been no church at Gleniffer if it had not been for a Christmas pudding. There would have been no daguerreotype of Oscar Hopkins on the banks of the Bellinger. I would not have been born. There would be no story to tell.

This was not a normal Christmas pudding. It was a very small one, no bigger than a tennis ball. It contained two teaspoons of glacé cherries, three dessertspoons of raisins, the peel of one orange and the juice thereof, half a cup of flour, half a cup of suet, a splash of brandy, and, apart from the size, you would not think it was such an abnormality were it not for the fact that it was cooked in the cottage of my great-great-grandfather, Theophilus Hopkins, in Hennacombe, Devon, England.

Theophilus Hopkins was a moderately famous man. You can look him up in the 1860 *Britannica*. There are three full columns about his corals and his corallines, his anemones and starfish. It does not have anything very useful about the man. It does not tell you what he was like. You can read it three times over and never guess that he had any particular attitude to Christmas pudding.

He was a dark wiry widower of forty, hard and bristly on the outside, his beard full, his muscles compacted, and yet he was a soft man, too. You could feel this softness quivering. He was a sensualist who believed passionately that he would go to heaven, that heaven outshone any conceivable earthly joy, that it stretched, a silver sheet, across the infinite spaces of eternity. He steeled himself in the face of his temporal feelings as a Royal Guardsman—a carouser and a funny man when at the pub—must remain poker-faced when flies crawl across his eyelids. He was one of the Plymouth Brethren and he thought—there is nothing mad in this particular bit—that the feasts of the Christian Church were not Christian at all. His problem was his temper, although the word is misleading. His problem was his passion. His body was a poor vessel for containing it, and when it came to Christmas each year it was all he could do to keep himself in check. For the most part he used his passion constructively—he was a preacher and it was his great talent to make his listeners share his feelings. He would not call it Christmas. He would call it Yuletide. He had so convinced his small congregation of farm workers, thatchers, warreners, charcoal-burners, fishermen—all those earnest white-laundered folk who, if they could read at all, could only do it slowly, with a finger on each word—so convinced them that Christmas was not only pagan but also popish, that they went out about the fields and lanes on Christmas Day as if it were any other day. Their Baptist neighbours laughed at them. Their Baptist neighbours would burn in hell.

Oscar was fourteen, an age when boys are secretive and sullen. Yet he did not question his father's views. He knew his own soul was vouched safe and when he read the Bible, aloud, by the fire, he placed no different interpretation upon it than the man who poked the little grate and fussed continually with the arrangement of the coal. They both read the Bible as if it were a report compiled by a conscientious naturalist. If the Bible said a beast had four faces, or a man the teeth of a lion, then this is what they believed.

But on this particular Christmas Day in 1858, they had a second servant where previously they had one. The first servant was the large bustling Mrs Williams who brushed her untidy nest of wire-grey hair with a tortoiseshell brush whenever she was agitated. She had been with the family fifteen years, ten years in London, and five years in Devon. In Hennacombe she brushed her hair more often. She fought with the butcher and the fishmonger. She swore the salt air was bad for her catarrh, but it was—as she said—"too late to be making changes now." She stayed, and although she was not "saved," and they sometimes found her hair in their scrambled eggs, she was a part of their lives.

The second servant, however, was not only not "saved." She could not even be classified as "questing." She was an Anglican who was in the household from charity, having been deserted by her navvy husband and been denied Poor Relief by two parishes, each of whom claimed she was the other's responsibility. And it was she—freckled-faced Fanny Drabble—who was behind this Christmas pudding. She had white bony hands and bright red knuckles and had lived a hard life in sod huts and shanties beside the railway lines the brawling navvies helped to build. Her baby had died. The only clothes she had was a thin cotton dress. A tooth fell out of her mouth on her first morning. But she was outraged to discover that Oscar had never known the taste of Christmas pudding. Mrs Williams—although she should have known better—found herself swept along on the tea-sweet wave of Fanny Drabble's moral indignation. The young'un must know the taste of Christmas pudding, and what the master don't know won't hurt him.

Fanny Drabble did not know that this pudding was the "flesh of which idols eat."

It was only a small cottage, but it was built from thick blocks of Devon limestone. You could feel the cold limey smell of the stone at the back of your nostrils, even when you were sitting by the fire. If you were in the kitchen, you could not hear a word that was said in the tiny dining room next door. It was a cramped house, with low doorways, and awkward tripping ledges and steps between the rooms, but it was, in spite of this, a good house for secrets. And because Theophilus did not enter the kitchen (perhaps because Mrs Williams also slept there on a bench beside the stove) they could have manufactured graven images there and not been caught.

But Oscar liked the kitchen. He liked the dry floury warmth and he carried the water, and riddled the grate, and sat on the table when Mrs Williams scrubbed the cobblestones. He soon realized what was going on. He saw cherries and raisins. They did not normally have raisins. He had never seen a cherry. On Christmas Day it was expected they would have a meal like any other.

Theophilus had called Mrs Williams up to his study. As this study was also Oscar's schoolroom, he heard the instructions himself. His father was quite specific. It was his character to be specific. He paid attention to the tiniest detail of any venture he was associated with.

When he drew an anemone you could be certain that he did not miss a whisker on a tentacle. The potatoes, he said, were to be of "fair to average size." There would be a half a head of King George cabbage, and so on.

But within the kitchen the treasonous women were kneading suet, measuring raisins and sultanas, peeling a single precious orange. Oscar set by the bellows and puffed on them until the kettle sang so loud you could hardly hear the hymn that Fanny Drabble hummed. Mrs Williams went running up the stairs like a dervish whose activity is intended to confuse and distract. She made a screen of dust, a flurry of rags. She brushed her hair on the front step looking out through the dripping grey branches, over the rust-brown bracken, to the cold grey sea. She walked around the house, past the well, and put the hair on the compost heap. Oscar knew that Mrs Williams's hair did not rot. He had poked around with a long stick and found it. It had been slimy at first but you could wash it under the tap and it would turn out, with all the slime washed off, to be good as new. This was exactly how Mrs Williams had told him it would be. He was surprised that she was right. His father did not value Mrs Williams's beliefs. She was not scientific. She said there were men who robbed graves just to steal the hair of the dead. They sold it to hair merchants who washed it and sorted it and sold it for wigs, and curls and plaits. This hair still had bulbs at the end of each strand, "churchyard hair" was what it was called. Mrs Williams lived in a state of constant anxiety about her hair. There were, she insisted, perhaps not in Hennacombe, but in Teignmouth and Newton Abbot, "spring-heeled Jacks" with sharp razors ready to steal a living woman's hair right off her head. She brushed her hair on the stairway and the upstairs study. At each place she collected the hair from her brush, made a circle with it, knotted it and put it in her apron pocket. On the day they made the Christmas pudding she did this even more than usual. Theophilus, being a naturalist, may have noticed. Oscar certainly did.

Oscar was not told about the Christmas pudding, but he knew. He did not let himself know that he knew. Yet the knowledge thrust deep into his consciousness. It was a shaft of sunlight in a curtained room. Dust danced in the turbulent air. Nothing would stay still. When Oscar ate his lunch on Christmas Day, his legs ached with excitement. He crossed his ankles and clenched his hands tight around his knife and fork. He strained his ear towards the open kitchen door, but there was nothing to hear except his father breathing through his nose while he ate.

Oscar had a little wooden tray, divided into small compartments. It was intended to house beetles, or shells. Oscar kept buttons in it. They were his mother's buttons, although no one told him it was so. They were not his father's buttons. There were small round ones like ladybirds with single brass loops instead of legs. Others were made of glass. There were metal buttons with four holes and mother-of-pearl with two. He drilled these buttons as other boys might drill soldiers. He lined them up. He ordered them. He numbered them. There were five hundred and sixty. Sometimes in the middle of a new arrangement, his head ached.

On this Christmas Day, his father said: "You have reclassified your buttons, I see."

The buttons were on the window ledge. It was a deep sill. Mrs Williams had put the buttons there when she set the table.

Oscar said: "Yes, Father."

"The taxonomic principle being colour. The spectrum from left to right, with size the second principle of order."

"Yes, Father."

"Very good," said Theophilus.

Oscar scraped his plate of stew clean. He finished his glass of water. He bowed his head with his father and thanked God for what He had provided. And when Mrs Williams came to the door and asked would he please help her add pollard to the pigs' swill, he went quickly, quietly, a light, pale, golden-haired boy. He thought about his buttons, not about what he was doing.

The two women stood side by side like two jugs on a shelf. One was big and floury, the other small and freckled, but their smiles were mirror images of each other and they held their hands in front of them, each clasped identically.

They had "It" on a plate. They had cut it into quarters and covered it with lovely custard. Mrs Williams pushed her hairbrush deeper into her pinny pocket and thrust the pudding at him. She moved the bowl through the air with such speed that the spoon was left behind and clattered on to the cobble floor.

Mrs Williams stopped, but Fanny Drabble hissed: "Leave alone." She kicked the fallen spoon away and gave Oscar a fresh one. She was suddenly nervous of discovery.

Oscar took the spoon and ate, standing up.

He could never have imagined such a lovely taste. He let it break apart, treasuring it inside his mouth.

He looked up and saw the two mirrored smiles increase. Fanny

Drabble tucked her chin into her neck. He smiled too, almost sleepily, and he was just raising the spoon to his mouth in anticipation of more, had actually got the second spoonful into his mouth when the door squeaked behind him and Theophilus came striding across the cobbled floor.

He did not see this. He felt it. He felt the blow on the back of his head. His face leapt forward. The spoon hit his tooth. The spoon dropped to the floor. A large horny hand gripped the back of his head and another cupped beneath his mouth. He tried to swallow. There was a second blow. He spat what he could.

Theophilus acted as if his son were poisoned. He brought him to the scullery and made him drink salt water. He forced the glass hard against his mouth so it hurt. Oscar gagged and struggled. His father's eyes were wild. They did not see him. Oscar drank. He drank again. He drank until he vomited into the pigs' swill. When this was done, Theophilus threw what remained of the pudding into the fire.

Oscar had never been hit before. He could not bear it.

His father made a speech. Oscar did not believe it.

His father said the pudding was the fruit of Satan.

But Oscar had tasted the pudding. It did not taste like the fruit of Satan.

4

After Pudding

His son was long-necked and delicate. He was light, airy, made from the quills of a bird. He was white and frail. He had a triangular face, a thin nose, archer's-bow lips, a fine pointed chin. The eyes were so clean and unprotected, like freshly peeled fruit. It was a face that trusted you completely, made you light in the heart at the very moment it placed on you the full weight of responsibility for its protection. It was such an open face you could thank God for its lack of guile at the very moment you harboured anxieties for its safety in the world. Not even the red hair, that frizzy nest which grew outwards, horizontal like a windblown tree in an Italianate painting, this hair did not suggest anything as self-protective as "temper."

He should not have hit him.

He knew this even as he did it, even as he felt himself move like a wind through the cabbage-damp kitchen, which was peopled with stiff and silent mannequins. He saw Mrs Williams reaching for her hairbrush. He saw Fanny Drabble raise her hand to cover her open mouth. He knew, as he heard the remnants of the nasty sweetmeat hiss upon the fire, that he should not have struck his son.

Theophilus saw the two blue marks he had made on bis son's neck. They were made by the pincers of his own thumb and forefinger. He regretted the injury, but what else could he have done? The boy had skin like his mother. In a surgery in Pimlico, a Dr Hansen had dropped nitric acid on this skin from a 15ml pipette. Had the boy in the waiting room heard her cry out? She had cancer, and Hansen had removed the growth like this, with drops of acid on her tender skin. What they finally removed was a lump, dark and hard from all this pain. She had died anyway.

He had never struck his son. They had supported each other, silently, not wishing to touch their hurt with words. They were alone in a country where they did not belong. They sat on the red soil of Hennacombe like two London bricks. When the father fell into a brown study, the boy squatted silently, an untidy mess of adolescent limbs, and clasped his father's knee and horny hand. They were united by blood, by the fundamentalist certainties of a dissenting faith, by this dead woman whom they could not talk about directly.

He had thrown her clothes into the sea. He had been half-drunk with anger and grief. He had left the boy in bed and gone running down through the rifle-sight of the combe, carrying her lavender-sweet clothes, not caring to separate them from their wooden hangers. The sea took them like weed, and threw them back along the beach. He dragged them out, searching for a current. The sea rejected them.

It was little Oscar, standing in his flannelette nightgown like a wraith, who finally brought him to his senses.

They had never talked about this with words, but in the silence of their eyes they understood each other and said things that would have been quite unthinkable to say aloud.

Mrs Williams began to brush her hair. She stood, wide and tall, her stomach pushing out against her white starched pinafore, and brushed at that tangled mass of grey frizz which would never right itself. She stooped a little so she might stare out of the seaward window while she did it. Thusk-thusk-thusk. She brushed as if she was in the privacy of her own room. And such was the conviction with which she brushed that she made herself a room, a little glass cage within the kitchen. It had a door and lock and you might not enter.

"Well," Theophilus said. He was riddling the grate of the stove. No one dared tell him he was riddling to excess or making coals go through the grate. A long strand of Mrs Williams's hair fell on his own. He did not feel it. Fanny Drabble saw it but did not dare to lift it off.

"Well," he said, still riddling, back and forth, forth and back, "Master Hopkins, you will be a good helper and fetch up the buckets."

"Let me get them, sir," said Fanny Drabble who was ill, almost to the point of vomiting herself. She knew her tenure to be in danger. She knew it was to do with pudding, but beyond that she really could not fathom. "Oh, please," she said. "Let me go, sir." And she snatched the grey hair off his head. She could not help herself.

"No," said Theophilus Hopkins. He did not notice the hair was gone. He kept on at the grate, in-out, out-in. "That will not be necessary, Mrs Drabble. Master Hopkins and I are going to collect some specimens."

He looked at her then. She did not understand the look she saw. It seemed weak and watery. It did not match the tenor of the voice.

"But, sir," said Fanny Drabble, feeling at last that she was free to stoop and pick up the spoon from the floor, "It be Christmas Day."

It was then Theophilus turned his head enough to look at his son's eyes. It was then that he saw the damage he had done.

"Christmas Day," cooed Fanny Drabble, "and they say the boilers are bursting from all the frost at Exeter."

When Theophilus looked at her he brought a face whose emotions were related to what he had just seen. The face had nothing to do with Mrs Drabble.

"Christmas Day," she said gently, not knowing what she did.

"Some call it that," said Theophilus, standing from the grate. He held out a hand so she must hand him the spoon. She gave it to him. "Some call it that, but none in my employ."

"Yes," thought Fanny Drabble, "and what a black loveless bastard you are."

5

A Prayer

Oscar was afraid of the sea. It smelt of death to him. When he thought about this "death," it was not as a single thing you could label with a single word. It was not a discreet entity. It fractured and flew apart, it swarmed like fish, splintered like glass. Death came at him like a ghost in a dream, transmorgrifying, protoplasmic, embracing, affectionate, was one minute cold and wet like his father's oilskin, so he shrank from it and cried out in his sleep, pushing the tight-bunched flannel sheet into the pit of his stomach, and then sometimes it was warm and soft and wore the unfocused smile of his mother.

In the sea-shells on the beach he saw the wonders which it was his father's life to label, dissect, kill. He also saw corpses, bones, creatures dead. Creatures with no souls. When the sea lifted dark tangles of weed, he thought of jerseys with nothing in their arms. He fetched the buckets from where they had stood since autumn, hanging on the back wall beside the well. He did not like the sea to touch his ankles. He felt the light frizzing froth like steel shackles on his skin. He put his fine hands to the pit of his stomach and stood stock still, his face chalky and carved, like a creature wishing to make itself invisible before the eyes of a predator.

Mrs Williams swooped down on him with pullovers. She made him put four of them on, helping him in her breathless, impatient way, pulling his hair by mistake and getting the sleeve of the first rucked up inside the sleeve of the second, and so on, until he was a sturdy lumpy creature with a big woollen chest.

She did not meet his eye or say anything about the pudding.

"What will happen to her?" Oscar asked.

Mrs Williams was not worrying about Fanny Drabble. She was worrying about herself. She took her hairbrush from her pinny and tried to tidy Oscar's hair. It was as bad as her own. Oscar struggled under the sharp bristles.

"I forbid you," said Oscar, and was surprised that Mrs Williams stopped.

"Then go," said Mrs Williams, handing him the buckets and the coil of rope. "Swim," she said maliciously. She knew he was afraid of the sea. He carried his fear coiled and tangled in him like other boys carry twine and string in their crumb-filled pockets. You would not know he had it. You would think him cheerful, happy, obliging, polite. And he was. He was very religious, yes, but not in a gloomy way. When he talked about God it was with simplicity and joy. He had a face better suited to the master's beliefs than the master himself.

Mrs Williams looked into this face to see the fear. She could not locate it. There was something else, but he would not show her what it was.

This something else was anger.

His right ear was still hot and stinging from the blow. He followed his father out of the front gate (bumping it—he always bumped it) and down the steep and sticky path (counting his steps—he always counted) towards the sea, with his anger held hard against him, like a dagger. He took short steps to make the number of steps right. He carried six metal buckets, three hessian bags, a coil of rope, and the buckets banged against his scratched blue shins. His stockings did not have sufficient calf to hold them up; they were rumpled and mixed with red mud around the shiny brown laced boots. He had already torn the seat of his knickerbockers on a bramble and there was more red mud on his woolly combinations. This was a boy, anyone could see it, whose school books would be smudged and blotted. He slipped and stumbled down the path, counting, in the direction of the sea.

It was not marine biology that led Theophilus down this path to stand chest deep in freezing water. He was a naturalist, of course, and he would collect specimens. But now he was in a passion to bear witness. He dug his nails into the palms of his hands. He pulled himself upright by that imaginary thread he kept in the centre of his skull. He would show all of Hennacombe—his son most particularly—what a true Christian thought of Christmas. His breath was shallow and he bore on his face an expression which a stranger might mistake for a smile.

They were still in the mulch-damp dripping woods between the high downs and the sea, but Oscar could already smell death. It was lying out of sight, neat black velvet mounts of it, a weed named *Melanasperm* washed up beneath the fox-red cliff which gave the hamlet of Hennacombe its name. He could also smell the poisonous salt. He was shortsighted and could not see any more of the sea than a soft grey colour, like a sheet of satin thrown across a pit. But he could hear it already and knew how it would be, lying flat and docile like a tiger sleeping. It would be grey and pearly and would let itself be drunk up by the sand in quiet fizzy laps. But the *Melanasperm* was there to give the lie to this, to show that the sea could pluck free a plant the strongest man could not dislodge, could kill the man himself, push white plumes down his gurgling throat, tear off his clothes and leave them scattered and formless, pale pink things like jellyfish along the white-laced edges of the beach.

He counted the steps. It was habit. He was hardly thinking about it. If he could walk to the bottom of the cliff in three hundred and sixty-five steps, it would be, in some way, he was not sure, good.

He could still taste the plum pudding which had been denied him so violently. His ear ached and burned, and the anger did not diminish. The anger was unthinkable, but it was not a thinking thing. It took charge of him and shook him. He was a rabbit in its jaws. He slid down the red crumbling combe (count that as five steps) clanging his buckets together, barking his knuckles on the gravel-rough clay.

His father was breathing in that way. He wore thick woollen pullovers and a mottled oilskin the colour of burnt toast. Around this he wound belts and ropes to hold his hammers and chisels, his buckets and bags. His father was dark and sinewy, like something made from tarred rope. His father's hair was black, signed with silver fire.

The son's hair was golden-red, wiry, always awry. He stood on the beach (four hundred steps) like an angel, recently landed, his hair buffeted by turbulent air.

"Fill up," said Theophilus. He should not have hit the boy, but how else could he prevent the stuff being swallowed?

Oscar began to "fill up." This involved him standing on the edge of the rust-red rock pool, lowering a bucket, letting it fill, drawing it up, and then pouring water into the buckets his father lashed to himself. As the buckets filled his father would groan with the weight. His groans were comic.

But today Oscar would not look at his father. He was frightened of what these eyes would reveal. He watched his father's mouth instead. He watched it as if it were a sea creature, a red-lipped anemone with black hairy fronds. He stood above the sea as above a pit of hissing snakes.

Then the father walked into the sea. The sea was an amoeba, a protoplasm. It opened its salt-sticky arms and closed around the man. It flowed on to the sand and hissed beneath the boy's boots. He stepped back from it, back above the funereal fronds of *Melanasperm*, back until the cliff was firm behind his bony shoulder blades. The clouds were a soft and pearlescent grey, moulded like sand from which the tide has slowly run out. They were like a lid, sitting tight on the horizon, except to the south where there was a thin swathe of soft gold, like a dagger left carelessly lying on a window sill.

His father was indistinct, an unfocused dark shape, a lump in a dream.

Oscar sat like a stook of sticks, a lean-to of too-long bones. When he hugged himself against his knees, they clicked. He sat with his back pressed hard against the red cliff, his scrotum tight with cold, a leathery wrinkled purse with only twopence in it, the skin tough and thick, like the gizzards of chickens, like the worm-eaten rock where his father stood, with cold water up above his chest, chiselling lumps of rock and dropping them into a wire basket.

Oscar pushed his back hard against Hennacombe Cliff and while the wind brought a small storm of sand to dance around his ankles, he talked to God. He did not do this in the distant and ritualistic way the Anglican Stratton was said to do, with crossing and kneeling. He sat upright. He brought his hands together (one sandy, one smooth) and rubbed them hard as he spoke, unconsciously mimicking his father who, when praying, could be seen to wrestle physically with himself while he tried to hear, amidst all the clamouring costers' voices of his sinner's heart, the pure and uncorrupted word of God.

"Dear God," he said loudly, in a high and fluting voice, "if it is your desire that your flock eat pudding in celebration of Thy birth as man, then show Thy humble supplicant a sign."

He screwed up his eyes and opened them fast. What did he expect? Angels? His friend Tommy Croucher claimed to have seen an angel. He said it was ten feet tall and his mother had seen its head above the milking shed. He took Oscar and showed him what the angel had left behind. There were three small stones which made the points of a triangle. Tommy said they stood for "Father," "Son," and "Holy Ghost." Oscar had not believed Tommy Croucher, but when he saw that the sign was the mathematical symbol for "therefore it follows," he changed his mind.

But on the beach on Christmas Day there was no sign, just the slightest brightening of the golden dagger to the south.

He grunted and rubbed his hands together. His ear was still aching from the blow. The taste in his mouth was vomit, but what he remembered was plums, raisins, cherries, suet, custard made from yellow-yolked eggs and creamy milk. This was not the fruit of Satan. It was not the flesh of which idols eat.

"Dear God," he said, and the straight edge of his teeth showed, "if it be Thy will that Thy people eat pudding, smite him!"

He twisted his limbs around the sandy corridors of prayer. He looked up to see his father almost out of the sea. He struggled to his feet. His knees went click; first the left and then the right, and then he ran, the guilty and obedient son, to help with the little creatures his father had captured, the anemones, antheas with fragile white tentacles, red-bannered dulses, perhaps a sleek green prawn or a fragile living blossom, a proof of the existence of God, a miracle in ivory, rosy red, orange or amethyst.

He ran with his arms flailing, his lower legs kicking out awkwardly. He was not an athlete, but he was at the water's hissing edge when his father emerged, like a matted red-lipped Neptune, blue-nosed, encased in dripping wet wool and shining burnt toast. It was then, as he took the heavy buckets, as he knelt to untie the ropes, that he saw his father had been smitten.

Theophilus's teeth were chattering, his limbs shivering. Red blood came from the wound in his thigh and the instrument, the naturalist's own rock chisel, was still in his hand. Sea water had kept the blood washed away, but now it rose through the blue serge, a thick flower of it, unnaturally bright.

Oscar was no longer angry. He lowered his bucket, frightened of what he had begun.

6

The Anglican Church

The Reverend Hugh Stratton saw Oscar praying. He did not know he was praying. The boy was standing at a kink in the path at the top of the combe with two spilling, brimming buckets hanging from the ends of his long pale wrists. He was praying with his "inside" voice, with his lips still. He was praying that his papa would not die. He felt cold and tight across his chest. The pain in his arms did not seem related to buckets. "Oh Lord, do spare him please, even though he be in grievous error. Let not his blood be poisoned in Thy smiting. Let him not be taken in ignorance. Dear Jesus who died for us, lift the scales from his eyes so he may see true light. Let him not be cast down. Let him sit with your saints in heaven." He did not pray for himself. But thoughts insinuated themselves between the warp and weft of the prayer. He tried to keep them out. They pressed in. He saw his father in a pinewood box with tiny handles. He saw Mrs Williams pack her case. She was going to "The Agency." She had threatened before. He had no money to pay Mrs Williams. These were selfish thoughts. He drove them out. He made his mind as bare as the meeting hall. He began again.

Hugh Stratton could not be privy to this praying. He saw only a boy with buckets. His back hurt. His sciatic was pinched. He had a pain pushing down his thigh, in his calf too. It pulsed in his left buttock and left testicle. He saw nothing admirable in the boy (nothing suggested angels or porcelain to him). His path was blocked by a boy with buckets and he thought nothing about him except that he was the son of the man who had stolen what was left of his congregation. Like smallpox, like plague, Theophilus Hopkins had emptied the pews one family at a time.

The Reverend Mr Stratton imagined that he liked all men. No matter what tribulation he suffered personally, he tried to be fair, to see all points of view. But he could not abide the famous Theophilus Hopkins who had used the musical masculinity of his voice to seduce away his illiterate rural workers and leave him with the gleanings—two families of High-Tory Anglicans and one elderly rabble-rouser who was in rebellion against the Squire. The Easter Offering last year had been two shillings and sixpence halfpenny. A ton of coal cost seven shillings and sixpence.

Hennacombe was the sump, the sink-hole of the Anglican Church. It was a pit. It was a "living," hardly a living at all, in a county where the wheel had come late. It was a place for sledges whose runners had dug the lanes deeper and deeper, further from the sun. He loathed the red mud. It was like heavy glue around his boots and his left leg hurt every time he brought it forward. There were two red-backed hawks riding the updrafts from the cliff. They were not more than a chain away, but Hugh Stratton did not notice them. He edged around the boy who did not move from the path, although the path was narrow. Hugh Stratton was accustomed to disrespect, even hostility. He imagined the boy was deliberately obstructing him.

He was carrying a sack of turnips on his narrow back and leading a lame horse; the horse could not bear the weight. He pushed around the boy. The sack knocked Oscar's shoulder and the horse pushed him back into the furze. Hugh Stratton did not see the boy stumble; he knew only that his back was hurting. He was pleased not to be greeted, to be "not seen" on Christmas Day. Dear Lord, forgive him. May the Lord forgive him and vouchsafe the health of his neighbours when they ate his fowls.

Hugh Stratton was forty years old, tall, stooped a little, with a face which had, from a distance, a pippin youthfulness to it—round cheeks, small pointed chin, a floppy fringe of sandy hair—but which showed, on closer examination, all the fine marks of pain and disappointment that buttered rum could not smooth over. He was an Anglican clergyman in a county with a popular Baptist squire. These circumstances made his position less powerful, and his financial situation more humble, but it need not have been desperate. Even when Theophilus Hopkins arrived from London and stole his congregation, he could have lived reasonably enough—for the vicarage had ten acres of good pasture attached to it. But he had no talent for farming. His wife had more, but not sufficient. She read the journals of the London Agricultural Society. She was in enthusiastic correspondence on the subject of a combined seed and manure drill. But there was no point. They could barely afford the postage stamps, and they were always in crisis with his back injured from lifting or their oats stunted or their sow aborting or, today, their fowls taking ill and dying just when they were plump enough for market. They would have fetched ninepence each. He could not bear the loss, God forgive him—he had beheaded them and dressed them as if they had died healthy. He had broken the sabbath to do it. As soon as the dismal morning service was over he had taken these dressed fowls across to the Squire's mansion, pretending them a gift. He was bartering, of course, but it was Christmas Day and he must pretend otherwise. He went to the kitchen door. They were Baptists. They despised him, not for trading, but for trading on Christmas Day. They knew it was not a gift. The cook gave him turnips as a measure of her feelings. He had hoped for something better, but he had pretended it was an exchange of gifts so he could not haggle. He worried about the safety of the dead fowls. May no illness come to the Squire's house. The Squire wore a tall hat, a high collar, a muffler around his neck. His long grey hair hung over his ears. His eyes were fixed, looked straight before him and shamed the devil. He would not put up with poisoning. He had a broad nose and defiant nostrils. he was rugged, bluff, kind, and he would lay his Dissenting whip across an Anglican's face for poisoning his people.

Hugh Stratton led the lame horse up the steep path, under the bare elms. He saw no beauty in these woods. Through black dripping branches he could see the Norman tower of St Anne's, and to the left a little, the high thatch of the vicarage. It had grey rock walls with lichen, stonecrop and moss, but he was no longer the clever man just down from Oriel, charmed by the rusticity, the peace, the little sundial in the garden which bore the legend "To serve and to rule." He knew the thatch was full of rot and the walls were seeping. It was money he thought of, and how to get it.

7

Stethoscope

The stool had three legs and stood against the sloping, flaking white wall of the attic in which Oscar slept. It was a sparsely furnished room, with just an iron cot, a rag rug, and a small spirit lamp. But it was a dry room, too, and it had a sweet, sappy smell which emanated from its ancient aromatic timbers. The stool was made from Devon oak and, while generally dark, was polished to a honey colour at its knees, the point at which two hundred years of hands had picked it up, swung it, set it down, always within this one cottage.

In the mornings Oscar stood on the stool and hoisted up his nightdress so that his father could listen to his chest with the stethoscope. He had never questioned why the stool was necessary, not even now that he had begun to question other aspects of his papa's practices. He stood on the stool. He hiked up his flannel while his father tapped at him anxiously, like a young and inexperienced man called to check for deathwatch beetle. This would happen first thing, as soon as he woke. He would have his bladder full. Sometimes his penis would be hard, sometimes not. Having no interest in the function of a hard penis, he was not embarrassed.

When Oscar lifted his nightdress, his father observed the ginger hair growing around the genitalia. He observed this with a naturalist's eye, but not only. He did not like the appearance of the hair. With the hair came the great difficulty of life.

The stool was also used when Oscar slept, late at night, when Theophilus's eyes were tired and his fingers cramped from writing. His study (it was also Oscar's schoolroom), was across the way, at the top of the staircase, and at two in the morning he would remove his shoes and come across, lifting his feet so as not to attract splinters, in his dainty yellow socks. Then he would lift the stool and place it, very quietly, next to his son's bed.

He sat and listened to him breathing.

In the morning he would listen with the stethoscope. The lungs were clear. They were always clear. He would hear himself say, "Clear as a bell," but it gave him no peace, for God had told him there was something wrong with the boy. This voice he heard may not have been what you would call God, but let it rest. You may have another word for all the things both Hopkinses (father and son) called God. It does not matter what you call it. For Theophilus it was God. It was his fear, his conscience, whatever you want, but it was clear to him. In any case, the boy had his sister's chest. The fluid in her little lung sacs still gurgled in the blocked drains of Theophilus' waking dreams.

When he sat down on the little stool he would draw up the eiderdown until it touched Oscar's little chin. The nail-bitten hand would then push the eiderdown away and Theophilus would smile and, in spite of his anxiety, he would not try to push it up again. His son had a white flannel nightdress and breath like warm milk. There was nothing to indicate the boy's troubled state of mind; for he now believed his father was in error, that he was wrong, not merely about puddings, but about many other things beside.

Theophilus, however, had no doubts about the life hereafter. It was this life he worried over. He feared his son would be "taken." He begged God to spare him. No voice came back. He would bear it if he must. If his God covered him with boils like Job, he would bear it. God took his daughter Sarah, his son Percy, his beloved wife. He had not been able to bear it, but he had borne it. There was nothing unbearable. The teeth of lions, the torture of martyrs, was a flea bite in the face of eternity.

He thought himself a weak man, a sensualist.

Sometimes he wished only to lie on the bed and embrace his son, to put his nose into his clean, washed hair, to make a human cage around him, to protect his bird-frail body from harm; and what pride, he thought, what arrogance that would be.

For Oscar was already given to God. He was one of the elect. The mysteries of salvation had been divinely revealed to him. He had laid hold on Christ and would not be cast into hellfire. All this had been vouchsafed him.

And when he made himself think this last thought, Theophilus would feel the tension leave him. The muscles in his chest and upper arms would go soft and his breathing would become deeper and more regular. In his mind's eye he saw his own blood oxygenating, turning a deep and brilliant red. He stretched and felt the blood tingle in his hitherto clenched fingers.

What a miracle Thou hast wrought.

He bent over his son and kissed the air above his forehead and then walked on tiptoe in that slightly exaggerated and silly way that men like Theophilus, normally gruff and bustling about their business, adopt as a sort of dance to celebrate their most tender feelings.

8

Pagan Signs

This was in Devon, near Torquay. To pretend—as Theophilus did—that this was almost tropical, is like referring to a certain part of Melbourne as "the Paris end of Collins Street." It is quite reasonable if you have never been to Paris, but once you have been there you can see the description as nothing more than wishful thinking.

When I visit Devon I see nothing tropical. I am surprised, rather, that so small a county can contain so vast and indifferent a sky. Devon seems cruel and cold. I look at the queer arrangements of rocks up on the moor and think of ignorance and poverty, and cold, always the cold.

But Oscar had not yet seen the Bellinger River and he shared his father's view that they were privileged to live in the "almost tropics." It did not matter that he was chased and mocked by the sons of fishermen and farmers, that the Squire's cook's son made him eat a stone. This was an earthly paradise. They read London papers one day late. They gloated over myrtles and fuchsias unburnt by frost.

Half Theophilus's congregation still believed that the sun danced when it rose on Easter morning, and many claimed to see a sheep dancing with it. This was a county where cockerels were still sacrificed at the winter solstice. Theophilus had himself recorded a wassailing where a naked boy was sat up an apple tree and made drunk (he thought) on toast soaked with cider. He had not come in search of pagan darkness. He had come to study the marine zoology, but now he was here he would bear witness to the miracle of the resurrection. He was dismayed, often, at the depth and complexity, the ancient fibrous warp, the veinous living wefts, of the darkness that surrounded him.

When he found pagan signs scratched on his path one morning, he recorded them in his notebooks, thus:

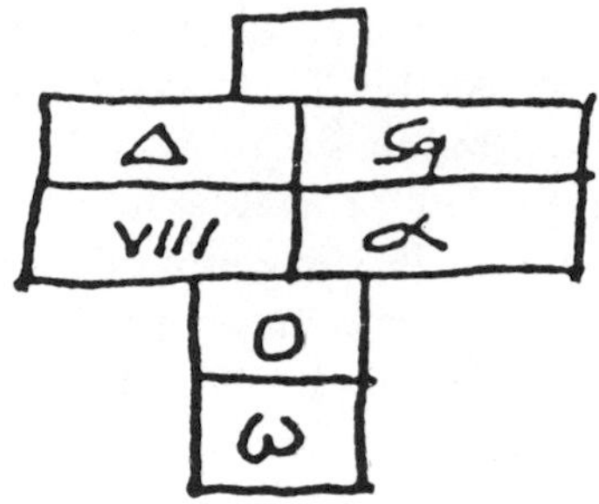

Theophilus imagined he recorded this in a scientific spirit, and even if he was meticulous in rendering the exact proportion of the sign, he was not a dispassionate observer. The sign frightened him. And just as he had seen a mockery of the crucifixion at the wassailing, he now saw a heathen assault upon the sanctity of the cross.

He could not leave it. He must tilt at it. But where to tilt he was not sure. He walked all the way to Morley, briskly, imagining he would find someone in the public house. It was Bargus he had in mind, he who had been a warrener and was now the sexton. But when he entered the Swan at Morley he found it completely empty. He turned around and walked back, four miles across the fields.

Theophilus was agitated at the time he had wasted. He was completing the illustrations for his *Corals of Devon*. He must produce two drawings every day, to meet his deadline. Today he had done no drawings, except this sacrilegious symbol. He was out of breath when he climbed over the stile at Hennacombe and saw Bargus sitting on the little stone bridge which was built acoss the stream there. He did not think himself a superstitious man, but this "coincidence" unnerved him.

Theophilus gave Bargus credit for some kind of power, which the old man would have been surprised to know. He was over seventy years old, short, broad-chested, with red cheeks and a snow-white, shovel-shaped beard. He was one of those men whose great business in life it is, a matter more important than any other, to be liked, and in this he had been generally successful.

When the gentleman thrust the notebook at him, he took it. He looked at the drawings of the markings, and then he looked at the other drawings as well. He admired the felicity of the sketches of ferns, furze, early violets, sweet oar-weed and then, smiling, but puzzled, he gave the book back.

"Very fine," he said, and then set about stuffing his pipe. He had intended to save his last twist of tobacco for the inn, but he was discomforted. He did not know how to take the fellow's death's-head grin. He had never seen a grin like this. He thought, stuffing the pipe, "Why would the fellow grin at me in such a way?"

He looked up, squinting a little as if he might bring the meaning of the other's smile into focus. It was getting cold quickly now the sun had gone. He made some comment about this.

"So," said Theophilus, tapping his book, stamping the mud off his boots on the stone bridge, still grinning all the while. "You can make no sense of this?"

"Nor hide nor hair."

"It is the Holy Cross?"

"Oh, aye," said Bargus, who had thought it looked like a children's game, "I do not doubt it."

Theophilus bid him an abrupt good day. He did not believe a word Bargus said. He was a pagan. He liked to lead a coffin three times around the granite cross at St Anne's. He had walked before the coffin with his blue eyes blazing, his spade held out from him and down. When he said he did not understand, Theophilus saw this as certain proof he did.

But Bargus—who was now walking slowly across the path to the

Swan at Morley with his pipe still unlit—was not the one who had made these signs, and Theophilus put away his notebook without guessing their true author.

Mrs William's suspicions were better placed. She was walking to the post office at Morley—this was two days later—when she came across another set of what were now known locally as "witches' markin's." She was rushing noisily along, a big-bummed, white-aproned figure on a long red hill. She wore the apron everywhere. In Morley they called her "Nurse." She did not mind the title either.

Oscar was with her, counting the steps to the village. He walked alongside her, a little behind, scratching the line of their journey with a pointed stick.

Mrs Williams was never comfortable standing still. She found it nigh impossible. She had jumped and jiggled insider her mother's womb and she had jumped and jiggled ever since. But when she came across these markings, she took a good long pause.

She would not have noticed Oscar's face, would not have thought about it at all had he not suddenly began to dance back and forth across the symbols, at once scratching at them with his dragging heel while he tried—the two aims were contradictory—to hop across them.

"Hopscotch," he said shrilly.

Then she looked at his face. It was scarlet. His cheeks were flat, his top lip long, his lips drawn as if on a string. He would not meet her eyes and she suddenly felt very queer.

9

Throwing Lots

It was Oscar, of course, who had made the "witches' markin's." They were a structure for divining the true will of God.

The △ stood for Theophilus who, in turn, represented the revelation as understood by the Plymouth Brethren and all that strict system of belief that Oscar had, until now, accepted without question.

This was the sign that said you could go to hell for eating pudding.

"Sq" was for the Baptists, being an abbreviation for the Squire who was their local representative. He had grown up believing the Baptists damned. But perhaps the God who smote his father looked upon the Squire with favour after all. The markings were a way of asking the question directly.

The VIII was the eight from Henry VIII and was a coded reference to the Reformation, a glance at the incredible possibility that the Catholic Church was not the creature of the anti-Christ, but the one true Church. Later Oscar feared his code was too obvious, so he added an X to make this square read XVIII.

The α was code for "A" which stood for Anglican. He almost did not put it in at all, but there was nothing else to put there in its place. He knew the Church of England to be most powerful in the world outside, but in Hennacombe it was an object of pity. No one could consider the Reverend Mr Stratton a suitable guide for the difficult path to salvation. He could not even pluck poultry without tearing its flesh. When Oscar had made these four squares, he added a "tail" of two more squares to make his system look like a child's game. He put a zero in the first square because it was nothing, and an omega at the next because it was the end. And then seeing he had the alpha and omega of Revelation 1:8, a quotation made by accident, he knew it was *not* an accident at all, and that what others might call chance or coincidence, he knew to be the word and blessing of God.

At the head he made another square and left it empty. This was a form of reverence.

The first of these markings was the one his father had recorded in his notebook. Oscar had made it on the little path leading above the western side of the beginning of the combe. He had made it, shivering, just near an old wooden bench, its slats half-rotten and overgrown with ivy. It was afternoon, about three o'clock, and the day already nearly drowned by darkness. A northern gale was blowing, but it was not this that made him shiver. He felt himself, quite literally, teetering on the edge of eternity. Old leaves rushed across the path, formed parties, were sundered and scattered. He was fourteen years old. His mind was filled with death, damnation, paradise. He marked out his system with a special yellow stone he had chosen from the millions on the beach. He should have been washing the milk pail in the stream below. He could hear it rattle on the rocks as the wind caught it. He worked with the special stone. It was no more than an inch and a half long and shaped, as his face was, a little like a heart. He was not aware of this coincidence. He did not, in any case, accept the notion of coincidence. He squatted, drawing, moving backwards, his teeth chattering.

When he had all the symbols down he stood with his heels against the omega square, facing away, towards the smell of the sea.

He then said these words from the Book of Judges, silently, without moving his lips: "And he said unto him, If now I have found grace in Thy sight, then show me a sign that Thou talkest to me."

There was rain in the wind now. It stung his face. He took his yellow stone, his "tor," and threw it over his shoulder.

It landed on alpha.

He stood, with his shoulders bent, peering at it. He stood for a long time, his heart heavy. It could not be true. But it must be true. If it was true, he could not live in his father's house. He must live in an Anglican house. He stooped quickly, picked up the stone, and put it in his pocket.

He wore a long oilskin coat, of the same burnt-toast material as his father's jacket. But being cut down from something else, the pockets were close to the ground. He tried to get something from one of these large pockets, but it would not come. He walked, awkwardly, his hand still in his pocket, down near the hem, and perched himself on the edge of the ivy-covered seat. He heard the milk pail tumble further down the stream. He tugged at the pocket. A rolled-up handkerchief came out. He retrieved this. Next there was a pencil, and finally a bulky notebook.

As the rain was now heavy he undid the front of his oilskin and held it out—this made a sort of tent within which he could record the result. He wrote: "1st Monday aft. Epiphany: Alpha." Then he put the book, the pencil, the tor and the ball of handkerchief back into his pocket and, having scrubbed at his "hopscotch" markings in a desultory sort of way, rushed down the bank to rescue the milk pail. He scrubbed it out quickly, shivering, and climbed the slippery mulch-soft bank to the path.

He ran home, counting. He had to pass the Anglican vicarage. His knees clicked. He made faces against the click and the rain. He wished to be home by the fire in the clean, lime-cold cottage where his father and he frightened Mrs Williams by discussing famous murders in calm and adult detail. They were closest then. Afterwards his father would give him a sharp hug and rub his beard across his cheek, making him giggle and squirm. This was called a "dry shave." It was an expression of love.

But God had chosen alpha. There was no way he could talk to his father about this.

It was one hundred and twenty-five paces from the markings of the Anglican privet hedge. The hedge was patchy and broken like the beard of a sick man. Oscar caught his breath there. Through the hedge he could see the back of the house where the Anglican and his wife were trying to kill a pig with no help from a butcher. The pig should have been killed in the weeks after All Hallows, not now. They stuck it in the cheek. The pig shrieked. Oscar's face contorted. The Anglican took the pig sticker from the Anglican's wife; his hands were red, not from blood, from mud, from slippery red mud from the wet pig. The clergyman stabbed a number of times. His face was screwed up more than Oscar's. At last the boy heard the rattle of wind from the pig's windpipe. He unclenched his hands and saw that his nails had made crescent moons in the fleshy part of his palms.

It was not possible that these were God's servants. And yet they must be.

"That the Lord called Samuel: and he answered, Here am I."

The Anglican could not have heard, but he saw him, somehow, standing there.

"Go away," said the Reverend Mr Stratton. He threw a muddled fir cone at him. "You horrid child, go *home*."

Oscar went home and hid his book.

10

False Instruction

Oscar had his new divining "tor" in his pocket.

This was not the yellow "tor" he had begun with, but a new one, a red oxide of a colour his father would (should he be given a chance) have told him was *caput mortem*, or death's head. His father appropriated everything by naming it, whether he was asked or not. He had discovered the yellow divining "tor." He had come out on to the flagstones by the cellar door when Oscar was bathing. (It was the custom that they bathed outside, in all weather. It was intended to strengthen the constitution.) Oscar was pouring cold water from the big zinc ladle, huffing, puffing, rubbing his narrow chest and stamping his feet. There was a peg on the wall where Oscar was meant to hang his clothes. He preferred to lay them on the lip of the well. His father came out to wash, saw the shirt and knickerbockers on the well, picked them up, hung the shirt on the peg, and proceeded to go through the pockets of the knickerbockers. This was not prying. There was no such category. His father examined all the little pieces his son had collected in the day. He held them between thumb and forefinger, as if they were the contents of the gut of some fish he wished to study.

The notebook was hidden, but he found the yellow "tor." For reasons he did not explain he placed the "tor" in his pocket. He did not say that he was "confiscating" it. He expressed no opinion. He slipped it into his dressing-gown pocket and it was difficult to know if he were absent-minded or censorious. Oscar, feeling himself blushing, turned away, presenting the walls of his bony shoulder blades.

Nothing was said about the "tor" in prayers.

On the next morning the stone was on the breakfast table. It sat at his place, an accusation. Oscar's heart raced. He thought himself discovered. He was wearing a greasy jersey of a type that fishermen in that area wear. Suddenly he was very hot inside it.

"A pretty stone," Theophilus said, after Oscar said grace.

"Yes, Father."

"Where did you find it?"

Theophilus was sprinkling sugar on his porridge. He had a sweet tooth. He sprinkled sugar quite gaily, giving no sign of the terrible anxiety that gripped him. There was something wrong. Something terribly wrong. He had taken the stone, pathetically, so he might be close to the boy. But now he could not think of anything to say. It was a stupid question he asked, but he had no other.

Oscar did not want to answer the question. He felt it was not innocent. Even if it was innocent, he could not tell him. With this very stone, God had told him that his father was in grievous error.

His father would not tolerate any questioning of his faith. He imagined God spoke to *him*. Oscar was moved to pity by his misunderstanding. But he could not, not even in his imagination, find a way to tell his father why he had been smitten.

Every day Oscar had thrown lots. The tor continued to land on $\propto$ and not on Δ. He wished he were a pig, that he had no mortal soul, that he be made into sausages and eaten, and released from the terrible pressure of eternity. He could not even look his father in the eye.

His father asked him where he had found the stone. Oscar did not know what he meant. He stirred his tea. The window beside the small roiund table was steamed up. Outside, the brown bracken was drowned in fog.

His father did not seem to notice the lack of answer, and yet his eyes were strange. Dear God, lift the scales from his eyes. Lift the scales from his eyes *now*.

"Do you know the name of the colour?" his father asked.

Oscar did not wish it named. He was angry at his father for what he was about to do.

"It is Indian Yellow."

"Thank you, Father."

Mrs Williams filled the toast rack, one slice in every second space, according to her master's strict instruction. She found it painful to be with them. She made a remark about the fog. They did not answer her. One of Croucher's ewes had been taken by someone's dog in the night, but this news had no effect. She had been with them in the days when they were a complete family, not this awkward lurching thing with one of its limbs cut off, out of balance and bumping into things in broad daylight. They were painful to be with. She went to the kitchen where she could not hear them.

"It is called Indian Yellow for a very good reason," said Theophilus, taking a slice of toast and testing it, squeezing it between thumb and forefinger to make sure that it had not, in spite of the careful racking arrangement, become soggy. "For a very *interesting* reason."

Oscar looked up, but was embarrassed by something in his father's eyes. The look was soft and pleading. It did not belong in that hard, black-bearded face, did not suit the tone of voice. Oscar knew this look. He had seen it before. It was a will-o'-the-wisp. If you tried to run towards it, it retreated; if you embraced it, it turned to distance in your arms. You could not hold it, that soft and lovely centre in his father's feelings.

"I name it Indian Yellow because it is the same colour as the pigment in my colour box named Indian Yellow and this is made by a rather curious process. From pee-pee," his father said.

Oscar looked up. His father made a funny face. Pee-pee was the intimate word. It was odd that he said "pee-pee" in a place he would have normally used "urine." Oscar looked down, away from the demands of his father's eyes.

Dear God, let him see.

But he knew his father would not see. He was filled with stubbornness and pride and could not hear God's voice.

Dear God, do not send me to the Anglicans.

"From the pee-pee of cows that have been fed on the leaves of the mango tree."

The tablecloth was white. The yellow stone sat on it, beside the little green sugar bowl. It was named Indian Yellow and was now useless. Oscar did not bother to put it back in his pocket, and Mrs Williams, when she was cleaning up slipped the stone into Theophilus's aquarium.

A week later Theophilus discussed pee-pee again, although this time he used the proper word for it. This was in connection with a particularly large agaric he had sketched last year and of which was now preparing a finished illustration. He called Oscar from his Greek composition and the boy, pleased to be rescued from his smudgy work, was also wary of what was required of him. He could not allow himself to love his papa. He held his feelings away from him, at arm's length, fearful lest he be flooded with pity.

"Of course you know," Theophilus said, "that witches eat this plant."

Oscar felt the new tor heavy in his pocket and held it hard with one ink-smudged hand. He wanted to scream at him: *Your soul is in danger. You are wrong.*

His father was close and familiar, so familiar he would not have described his face to anyone. He was a shape, a feeling, that thing the child names "Pa." He was serge, formaldehyde, a safe place.

He was not a safe place. Not any more.

"They drink the urine of someone who has eaten the plant." Oscar did not look up. "They are in communication with the devil or, in their state of intoxication, imagine they are."

The stone in his pocket was heavy, too heavy. His hand locked around it so hard he could not let it go. The muscles around his neat little jaw reflected the spasm in his hand. His safety was in God.

The beloved of the Lord shall dwell in safety by him; and the Lord shall cover him all the day long, and he shall dwell between his shoulders.

"We have several witches in the area," Theophilus said. He felt he was talking in a fog. His son would not look at him. "I think it is true, that there are witches nearby?"

Oscar touched the edge of the cartridge paper his father was drawing on. It had a sharp edge but a soft velvety face.

"Do you think this is true?"

"Yes," said Oscar. He looked up and was frightened by the eyes.

Beware of prophets that come to you in sheep's clothing, but inwardly they are ravening wolves.

"Yes, I think so myself." There was a pause. Oscar heard his father sharpen his pencil. He smelt the sharp, metallic smell of pencil lead, the sweet, sappy smell of wood shavings.

"There is evidence," Theophilus said, "around the lanes, that the agaric eaters are out. You have seen the markings?"

"Yes."

Theophilus then did something which was completely out of character—he described something he had not actually seen. In his desperate desire to have his son's loving attention, to feel those amethyst eyes rest unanxiously upon his own face, he repeated something said to him by Smart Jack, the warrener who called at the cottage to sell his rabbits and discuss scripture.

"There is a blank square at the top," Theophilus said, "where they sacrifice a goat. They decapitate the poor creature and leave its head upon the square as a mocking image of Our Saviour."

And they shall turn away their ears from the truth and be turned into fables.

Oscar saw his father raise the glass of cold black tea he always sipped at while working. The mouth moved open a fraction. The tip of his tongue showed. Oscar saw the father whom he loved, but he also saw that person most reviled by Theophilus Hopkins—an agent of false instruction.

Oscar's hand clenched round the stone. The tendons in his neck showed the strain of the grip.

He pulled his hand out of his pocket and opened it in front of his father. There!

Theophilus took the stone from the ink-stained palm. The stone was warm. He placed it on the cartridge paper and turned it over with his pencil.

"*Caput mortem,*" he said.

Oscar burst into tears.

11

Apostasy

The Baptist boys made him eat dirt. They made him sing songs he was not allowed to sing. They showed him engravings of a pagan statue from the Crystal Palace. They put coarse mud on his skin because they could not bear it so soft and white.

He was not from "here." He was from "there." He did not like the sound of his own voice. He tried to change it, to make it soft and leafy like Timmy Croucher. He said "fayther" for father, but not at home.

How small his world was. He did not mind it small. He would have had it smaller still, have been a mole or a badger. He preferred the tangled forest of oak and elm which separated the high downs from the sea. Here he might stand still for hours, in a day-dreaming trance no wind could cut, examining dead leaf, leaf mould, spores, fungi, white indeterminate life—something without a soul that looked like spilt flour. He posted letters to his mother in a hole in a tree. Timmy Croucher, a large-boned, olive-skinned boy with soft hair on his lip, devised special prayers; they conducted their own services and argued about the nature of hell. In the bulging, spiky map which marked his territory, this was the larger part. The map did not include the village. He went there, but only when instructed, and with Mrs Williams for a guard if he could arrange it so. He had as firm a sense of territory as a dog, and when he moved across the terrain outside his map, across the Downs to Morely, for instance, he moved jerkily, running, his knees clicking, out of breath with a pain in his side.

He did not wish to leave the shelter of his father's home. He had no ambitions to see the world, to take part in the great adventures of Empire. This empire existed beyond the myopic mist. Somewhere there were "Disraeli" and "Lord Russell" and "Lord Elgin." He could not imagine them. He knew Mrs Williams, Timmy Croucher, Smart Jack.

He had seen the Anglican minister and his wife, but they had no place in his life. It is true, of course, that Hennacombe was built around the Anglican church of St Anne's and its vicarage, but the hamlet was like a tree in which the heart wood has rotted out. There was no heart, only a place for dust and spiders. And yet this was where God wished him to go. When he would not listen to the stone, God repeated the message again and again. α = Anglican.

Thus, God said: "Go." There was nothing attractive in this idea.

He promised God he would go before Good Friday. He celebrated Easter, in bad faith, amidst the white-smocked Plymouth Brethren. He read them the lesson God said: *"Thou hypocrite."*

Easter came, but did not come. The flower buds of the wild cherry were still tightly sealed on Easter Sunday. This was on 24 April, almost as late as Easter can be. It had never happened before that there were no wild cherries on Easter Day. There was no pussy willow either. This was called "palm" in Hennacombe, and used as palms on Palm Sunday. So there were no palms for Palm Sunday. Nor were there primroses for Easter Day. There were not brimstone butterflies. The swifts did not arrive. This also was a sign.

The weather frightened him. It was this that drove him to apostasy.

He did not allow himself to know what he was doing. While the Brethren sang their long and doleful hymn—it was the second Sunday after Easter—he slipped quietly out of the meeting-house door. He had no more in his pocket than a threepenny bit and a soiled handkerchief. He walked beside his father's house and heard the door slam as Mrs Williams came inside from the garden. He could see the square tower of St Anne's below him, a little to the left. It was deep in shadows, hemmed in by leafless trees. It was not an attractive destination.

He was fifteen years old, nearly sixteen. His feet were tight inside his boots. His pale wrists protruded from his sleeves—they looked a foot long. He took a path, but not the one that led most directly to St Anne's. He tried not to think about what he was doing. He said a little prayer, but the words were like bricks—he placed them carefully, slowly, one after the other—to keep out the nightmare images that had leaked into his waking mind—his papa's face burning in the hellfire.

He could hear the Plymouth Brethren singing. They pulled out the words like taffy pull. "Dear Lord," he prayed, "I am only fifteen."

The path forked. The left path ran down into the combe, and therefore led more or less directly to St Anne's. He took the right fork which led to Man's Nose and up on to the Downs.

He looked down, watching his brown spit-and-polish boots, the red gravel, the dead margins of the path. He thought of summer, of hawthorn white with blossom, the sloe, the maple, the guelder-rose with its snowballs, the glossy, heart-shaped leaves of bryony. He was hurt and aching for bright evenings. He saw the gentle enquiring motion of his papa's malacca cane as it blessed the pretty dog-violet, stitchwort with its thousand white stars, dog mercury, rose campion.

He thought: I will never be happy again.

He blew his nose and looked briefly, but with curiosity, at what came out. He put his handkerchief back in his pocket. The path was almost at the sea. He did not like that part of the path. He turned, and began to run down the path in the direction he had come, towards St Anne's. He took a new path. It went down through a dark coppice. There were blackbirds, like flutes, but he did not hear them. There was a thing like a dry pea rattling inside his head. The way was tangled and overgrown. He pushed through. He stamped down the thick stems of briars. His breath started to come with difficulty. He tripped and stumbled. And when he emerged on the high bank which looked down on the Reverend Mr Stratton's vegetable garden, he did not even follow this path any longer, but slid down on his backside and landed, heel first, in the shallow ditch beneath it.

He reached for the threepence in his pocket, intending to flip it. But the coin was lost. There was a tiny hole in the pocket. He stopped a second, looking at the overgrown stone wall, breathing hard.

He was caught between bank and wall. He could have edged around and found the stile, although had he done so he might have hurt himself, for the stile was ancient, its timbers rotted with the damp, unused since the time of the previous incumbent. But Oscar was too impatient in any case, and he now flung himself at the wall as a fear-weak soldier may, in despair, go over the top of a trench, his body awash with urgent chemicals, teeth clenched, mouth already open in a yell.

He clawed at the rock, scraping off both skin and lichen. He got a boot up, slipped, tore his trouser leg, then got a better purchase and was up on the ragged top looking down on tomato seedlings, brown soil, and brimstone butterflies. He was already launched when the Reverend Mr Stratton came running, a garden spade in his hand. The clergyman cleared the beds, one, two, three. He was fortunate his paths were wide and allowed for one long pace between. He had not run like this since sports day at Eton.

The seedlings already had their stakes in place beside them. This made a barrier the clergyman could not easily cross. He was on one side, the young intruder on the other. They looked at each other, both breathing hard.

"You, boy!" said Hugh Stratton.

Oscar's mouth was open. The seat of his breeches had been torn when he slid down the bank. He thought the clergyman looked like some sort of vegetable picked too long ago. He could smell the alien odour of what he knew must be alcohol. He assumed it was from the exotic ritual of the eucharist.

The clergyman walked around the tomato bed. He should not have run like that. It had made his back hurt horribly. The sciatic nerve sent a pain like toothache up both his legs, pulsed through his aching testicles, took possession of his buttocks.

"You, boy, go home to your father."

"I cannot," said Oscar, taking a step back on top of the new lettuces.

"Get off my lettuces," said Hugh Stratton. He took a step forward. This was a mistake. It forced Oscar to take another step backwards, into one more lettuce.

"I am called," said Oscar.

It was some time before he could make himself clear.

12

To Serve and to Rule

Mrs Stratton was not a don. She could not have been, for while the constitution of the university would permit entry to a fourteen-year-old boy (with his pocket full of string and dried-out worms) it could on no account matriculate a woman. Yet Mrs Stratton had the walk for it. Her whole body expressed her calling. She had a walk you can see today in Magpie Lane and Merton Street. The dynamics of this walk are best appreciated if you place a three-foot-high stack of reference books in your imaginary walker's extended arms. From here on it is all physics. You can resolve it with vectors—the vertical arrow indicating the mass of the books, the horizontal one the propulsive force of the moving body. It is obvious. You can see immediately why the body of such a person tilts forward at 60° to the horizontal. It is the books, or the propensity for books that does it. And when you see the height of the stack it is also clear why such people always lift their head so high. You thought it myopia, but no—it is the height of the imaginary books they must look over.

Mrs Stratton's father had been a don (but only briefly—there was controversy). He, however, did not have this walk. Her mother, of course, had never been a don, but neither did she walk with her body on the incline. The daughter, it would seem, had made her walk to suit herself. To see her walk up the steep red lanes of Devon was to see a person out of her element. She was awkward, so awkward that no matter how much you liked her you would not invite her to play a set of tennis. She belonged in Oxford, not in Hennacombe, and yet she did not realize it. She carried with her, as she plodded in mud-caked boots up the lane, a combination of doggedness and well-meaningness, so that when she lifted her head and jutted her long jaw at you, you could not allow yourself to feel irritation or see anything as unpleasant as stubbornness; you saw, rather, the determination to succeed in spite of any handicaps.

Her father had been a rector with a large glebe in Buckinghamshire which he had farmed himself. She had liked the farming life, all pitching in at harvest time—curate, parson (although not the dean) the tenantry and farm hands and all the young women, regardless of their rank, all with big white bonnets to protect their much-praised complexions from the sun. She liked this just as much as she liked life in the drawing room where her conversation was every bit as intellectual as was suggested by her walk. Her father was fond of saying that Betty would "make a useful wife." And although his assessment of usefulness was quite correct—her husband might have starved without her—she was an old maid of twenty-eight before the future vicar of Hennacombe came to claim her.

What had alarmed the previous young men was not her enthusiasm for the stooking at harvest, but her passion for discussion of the larger issues that beset the Anglican Church in the ever-widening wake left by the Oxford Tractarians and the Wesleyan schismatics. There were those who disliked her passion because they thought theology was not a woman's business. And others still who thought her voice always a fraction too loud for the drawing room. Of these, of course, some rightly belonged in this first group, and one should also record that there were others who, whilst personally repelled, felt drawn to care for the owner and protect her, just as they might a blind person forever bruised by bumping into walls. But there were also young men who were fascinated by her conversation. They were not necessarily in the minority, although they tended to lack staying power, suffered a bright and fast attraction and an equally quick fatigue. These were the ones who called two or three times in quick succession, and then not at all. These were the young men who came to the conclusion that she was, although clever, quite spoiled by being argumentative and contrary, and whatever position they put up themselves Miss Cross would see it as an Aunt Sally she must quickly lay low. If her suitor took the Evangelical position she would feel herself drawn to the Latitudinarian; or she might just as easily come out in favour of Enthusiasm and the Evangelical, easily, that is, if her suitor revealed Puseyite tendencies. She was quite capable of putting a formidable argument in favour of the doubtful aspects of the Athanasian Creed and then, without bothering to trouble her friend with so large a difficulty, knock it down herself. Her father's dean, a dry old man who did not like his botany to be disturbed, likened her behaviour to that of a large and enthusiastic child who will spend five hours on building a sandcastle simply in order to knock it down again. This was unfair, and not just because the dean's mouth was prim and puckered when he told it (assuming the same drawstring pursing as when he recalled—this, always, on the third brandy—the pubic hairs a famous lady novelist had left behind in the deanery bath). It was unfair because Betty Cross had no position, belonged to no party, advocated no schism, and cared only to find out what the "truth" might be. She sought for an absolute and could not find it. She had no prejudice to anchor herself to and was as unaware of this as of her walk.

Fortunately, that is, for Hugh Stratton who was doing his Greats at Oriel in 1838. He came down to Buckinghamshire in Michaelmas terms to see his friend Downey who was playing curate to Betty Cross's father while secretly translating the early gnostic gospels. Hugh was much taken with Betty Cross and did not tire of her.

It was his opinion—and he was not shy of expressing it—that the dean's eldest daughter had presented him with vistas, with possibilities that the distinguished Fellows of Oriel—good men, famous men—had not made him aware of. He whirled before the wind of her contrary mind, spinning like a top. He was not offended by her donnish walk, the loudness of her voice, the fact that she had large hands and that they had freckles on them already. She was large-boned, but this was not the sort of thing he noticed, either to desire or dislike. He had no eye for the physical at all and could meet you four times and still not recognize your face. It was this, a serious disability in a parson, which accounted for the uncertain smile he would bestow on total strangers, ready to broaden if responded to, snatched back if not. So he did not notice the freckles. He knew she had flaxen hair, but if he had been asked the colour of her eyes he would have had to guess. He saw her face, in memory, with that gentle formlessness, all the details made soft by feeling, with which a one-year-old is said to perceive its mother. He saw her ideas though, in profusion, like a garden. In a garden no one argues about which is the true flower, and so it was, he imagined, with her ideas and arguments. He did not see then (and did not see ever) that she would be a professional liability to him, that she would so distress succeeding deans and bishops, that the pair of them would be tucked away like two ghastly toby jugs given as a gift by a relation who may, someday, visit. The toby jugs cannot be thrown away. They must be retained, in view, but not *quite* in view. Hence: Hennacombe in the bishopric of Exeter.

The Strattons had no children and, given the chaste nature of their embraces, had no reason to have any. They thought this a civilized arrangement. They had reached it, with relief, on their wedding night and felt no temptation to change their minds. Mrs Stratton felt no sense of loss. She was happy with almost every aspect of her life, more happy, she thought, than she had any right to be. She was forever refreshed by the countryside, the sea, the seasons. She was out and about. She had her periodicals to read and an intelligent man to talk to, but she also liked to be with country folk, and she liked to seek the opinions of warreners and shepherds, thatch cutters and farmers' boys. She was poor, of course, so much poorer than she had ever expected, but somehow this terrible thing, this most dreaded thing, had not been as she might once have imagined it. So many of the people they lived amongst were poor. The young boys hereabouts grew up wearing their older sisters' dresses and no one thought to laugh. If her husband had been happy she would have judged life perfect.

But Hugh did not like their poverty. He fretted. He would blame the Squire as a Baptist or Theophilus Hopkins who was always standing in the sea. He could be reduced to crying like a child for no more reason than a patch of damp on the livingroom wall. He worried at the thatch, and had a tin in which he put coins that would, one day, pay the thatcher. He wrote special prayers to the Almighty in order that the Easter Offering might be substantial, that the aphids stay away from the tomatoes, the wheat not have rust. Her point was that it had always been like this, that the Squire was a boor, the walls had been damp, etc., etc., dear Hugh, and they had survived. This was not a good argument to use. It made him worse. He took her around the house pointing out *new* mould and *new* rot. By the sun-dial ("To serve and to rule") he lay down amongst the rank grass and wept. He begged her to give up the subscription to her Oxford and London periodicals. She would not. He ranted at her. She said she would rather eat turnip for a month, have no shoe leather and sell the horse. He said they might have to. She said nothing about the cost of sherry he would soothe himself with later.

This was the same man as represented by the symbol α, the one whom God told Oscar was his chosen servant. The emotions that moved the chosen servant were, when he at last understood Oscar's intention, far more complicated than those immediately summoned by the loss of two young lettuces.

Hugh Stratton flicked his straight fair hair back out of his eyes and plunged his hands deep in his pocket. He made a small motion, a bob, a nod, a genuflexion. And then he turned and led the way through the wide maze of garden paths, indicating his guest should beware of the fallen rake, the rusting fork, the half-dug cesspit with the crumbling edges. And while, predictably enough, one part of him was in despair that there was a new body to feed and clothe, there was another part of him in blazing triumph – he had a soul, a theological refugee. He walked fast, with long strides, and the pinched grey look on his face was made only by the pain of the sciatic nerve. He did not go to the back door or the front, but to the kitchen window through which he was accustomed to handing hens' eggs and vegetables to the cook. He knocked loudly and impatiently and brought Mrs Millar away from a tricky moment with the custard.

"One more for dinner, Mrs Millar," he said. He could not help himself. He smirked.

"He has his own," she said, "at home."

"He shall have his own, Mrs Millar," shouted Hugh Stratton, but joyously, recklessly. "He shall have his own with us. The oblong napkin ring shall be his."

She would not normally have let that pass – calling a ring an oblong, but she was confused by his mood. She leaned forward, pretending to examine the boy, but really trying to smell her employer's breath. It was the smell of custard, however, that intervened and, without excusing herself, she withdrew and slammed the window shut.

13

Raisins

This was the second time in his life he had seen raisins. He removed them from what they claimed was "shepherd's pie." He laid them side by side, along the borders of the dinner plate. The plate was painted with pagan scenes. He began to obscure the images with raisins. It was not calculated. He was in too much distress for calculation.

The first time he had eaten raisins was in that so-called "fruit of Satan"—the Christmas pudding.

All the muscles in his narrow chest were tight. He grasped his knife and fork and tried to stop his sense of smell from operating. The air in the vicarage was sour. He had never been anywhere so alien. It seemed there was not a thing his hand might brush against that was not sticky with damp. He had been taken to see the view and his hand had accidently touched the antimacassar on the big maroon couch. The damp made it feel like a dead thing. He snatched his hand away, repulsed. He pulled a face. This was noticed. He blushed bright red while his hands burrowed into the dry-breadcrumb corners of his jacket pocket.

But the nest-smell of the Strattons' house was worse than its damp. It was like a gloved hand pressing your nose into the pages of a musty book. When he entered the room the smell had risen and settled on him like aphids on a rose bush. Books, papers, newspapers, leaned and tottered all around him, not always on shelves, either, sometimes like towers built straight upwards from the floor.

The three of them sat down in chairs and faced the yellow evening light. Oscar felt himself choking on regret and melancholy.

He imagined this room must be the Anglicans' drawing room. No one else in Hennacombe had a drawing room. But then, from the corner of his eye (he could not devote his whole attention for he was being interrogated about the health of his father's poultry) he saw the Anglican servant at the big reading table. She was removing newspapers and periodicals and stacking them on top of the paper towers which lined the walls. She thrust others into cupboards which looked—except that there was paper where there should be linen—like receptacles for soiled bedclothes. When the table was clear she put a tablecloth on it and began to lay it with cutlery.

When they had learned all they could about Theophilus's cockerels, Mr and Mrs Stratton placed him at the head of the table and sat on either side of him. This seemed wrong to him, but almost everything was wrong. There was not sufficient light to make out the oriental deities (for that was how he misunderstood the willow pattern) and, more particularly, the so-called shepherd's pie which seemed like a thick layer of potato with a thin sauce underneath. It had a most peculiar taste—curry—but never having tasted curry he did not know it.

It also contained raisins. He did not know what this signified, but in spite of the Christmas pudding that had led him here, the raisins felt wrong to him. You do not stop being one of the Plymouth Brethren in five minutes. He placed the raisins across the pagans' faces.

It was important that he eat everything on his plate, that much was made clear to him. When he had finished everything but the raisins, Mrs Stratton leaned across and put another large spoonful on his plate.

"Thank you," he said. He wished he had never come here.

"They are only raisins," said Mrs Stratton, beaming at him through the gloom.

"*Only* raisins!" snorted Mr Stratton. "At four pence the pound and *only*."

"Yes, my darling," said Mrs Stratton whose father had sent the raisins (finest Elemes) together with a whole tea-chest full of other items he classed as "necessaries," on the train from Oxford. "He is probably unfamiliar with them. Are you familiar with raisins?"

"Oh, yes," said Oscar. "Yes, I am." He was pleased to have such a simple reason for not eating raisins. He begged her silently to remove the plate from him. He sipped his tea. He smiled painfully at Mr Stratton who also tried to show good will.

Mr Stratton was tense. He clicked his fork against his empty plate and took a sip of what Oscar realized must be "drink."

"Have you ever seen an orange?" Mrs Stratton asked. She had a pretty face, Oscar thought, with large soft lips and pale, gentle, blinking eyes, but everything about her was bigger than it should have been.

"Yes," he said.

"Jolly good!" she said, and leaned back, folding her hands in her lap as if oranges were why he was there.

He ate more of the nasty food.

He thought: "They are Thy servants, Lord."

It would appear that neither of the Strattons knew what to talk to him about. Mr Stratton tapped his plate with his fork and had more of his "drink." Mrs Stratton asked him about various fruit and then described for him a little church in Torquay which was being restored by some followers of Dr Pusey. There were to be a number of altars in the church apart from the high altar. Each altar was to have its own dresser and wardrobe in its sacristy. She asked Oscar what his view was on this subject.

"I do not know, ma'am," the boy said in misery. He knew an altar was a place where heathen sacrifice was made. It was all he knew about the term. He knew he must eat his raisins, otherwise his plate would not be taken from him. They were waiting for him to eat the raisins.

The raisins had become a symbol of a Christmas pudding. He knew he should eat them. He could not bring himself to do it.

"So you draw the line at altars," Mrs Stratton suggested. "Well, I don't know—Hugh, I really don't—don't know that it is incorrect to do so, for really there is so much that we have accepted unthinkingly, and if you will call it a communion table instead, I, for one, will not call you a fanatic."

The boy moved a raisin sideways on the rim on his plate. He looked so very unhappy.

Mrs Stratton smiled. "Really, you know," she said, "it is a nice distinction. Don't you think so, Hugh?" And having begun her speech so confidently, she now ended on a breathless and rather supplicatory note, bowing her head.

Mr Stratton suddenly took Oscar's raisins.

He speared them, one, two, etc., with his fork. He did not speak until he had finished eating them.

"Do you think your pater will come rushing around here?" He stared at Oscar belligerently.

Oscar could not hold his gaze. He was not comforted when Mrs Stratton patted his hand.

"Threatening me?" asked Mr Stratton.

Until this moment Oscar had not thought about the immediate future at all. He had his mind on eternity. He had thought merely to do that which was unthinkable. Had he permitted himself to think about his father's actions he would never have had the will to climb the fence into the Anglican garden. But now, imagining his father arriving here, angry, threatening Mr Stratton, his heart lightened.

"Yes," he said, "I expect so." And when he saw the effect of this on Mr Stratton, he felt suddenly very powerful. He was the object of his papa's care and love. Of course his papa would come. He was only a boy and the matter would be taken from his hands.

He smiled at Mrs Stratton, even though he knew that a smile was out of keeping with the seriousness of the question.

"Threats will do his cause no good," said Mr Stratton. He picked up the bell and shook it. He was, it seemed, impatient that Oscar's plate should be removed by Mrs Millar. He topped up his "drink." "You can tell him that from me."

"You thought to stay *here*?" said Mrs Stratton, her eyes suddenly filled with alarm, looking from Oscar to her husband and back again. "Hugh?"

Mr Stratton, quite without warning, grinned at her. Mrs Stratton chose to attribute this grin to sherry.

"Yes, ma'am," said Oscar.

"But what will your poor father do?" said Mrs Stratton. "Think of the terrible pain you will cause him, to know his son is here with us, not half a dozen chains away."

Oscar's eyes were brimful of tears. He scratched his head. He looked around the room (a little wildly, Mrs Stratton thought).

"I know, ma'am. He will be very sad."

Mrs Stratton heard the West Country accent where the Baptist boys had heard only London. She thought, not for the first time, how expressive it was. When Oscar said "sad" she felt an immediate response, as if to a reed played in a minor key.

"Yes," she said, "most sad."

"I know, ma'am, I *know*, but he is in *error*, you see."

"But still you will go home to him," she said, but looking at her husband whose intentions she had not divined. She expected to see his face twisted in anxiety about this matter. Money would be a trouble for him, that most of all. She was surprised therefore to see his grin transmogrified into a beneficient smile.

"But still," said Mrs Stratton, continuing to look at her husband. "Still you shall go home to him." She added: "Hugh?"

"Oh, no," said Oscar, and he banged his hand upon his knee in an agony of agitation. Beneath the banging hand, his knee rose and fell, his foot drumming the Turkoman which made Hugh Stratton–in spite of his triumph–think about the rot in the floor joists.

"I *cannot,*" said Oscar, still not crying, but the face so frail, so white, pulled into furrow lines by the clench of the fine little jaw. "No matter how I yearn to."

"But surely," she said, "surely your father loves you?"

"Yes, yes, most dreadfully." the tears had come now, but the boy had not lost control. Mrs Stratton extended her napkin a little and then, not having the offer accepted, withdrew it. She extended a hand to his shaking shoulder but did not feel she had a call to be intimate. He looked alien to her now, like a praying mantis–those long thin limbs shaking with agitation, the raw scratched hands wiping the triangular face. She thought this and still felt great compassion.

"I also love him," said Oscar, with some effort.

The gooseberries and custard were then brought in by Mrs Millar who was surprised to see Mr Stratton serve the boy himself. He doled out excessive quantities of custard. It was not like him to be so generous towards a guest. Mrs Stratton also observed this custard-ladling with interest.

"I could not otherwise."

"Otherwise?" said Mrs Stratton. "Please have sugar if you wish."

"Otherwise than to love him." He accepted the very small handkerchief which Mrs Stratton gave him. He had never seen anything like it; it had fragile lace around its edges. He blew his nose thoroughly and judged the lace a poor material for such a task. "But the dispute is not personal so much," he did not know what to do with the handkerchief ("Keep it, keep it," said Mrs Stratton), "not so much personal as theological. You see," he said, "he is not saved."

"What a remarkable boy you are," said Mrs Stratton.

Oscar, in spite of his agony, felt pleased to accept this compliment and he tucked it away carefully just as he now tucked away this hard warm ball of wet handkerchief into the depth of his pocket. He *was* a remarkable boy.

"But, Oliver," said Mrs Stratton, "we cannot steal you from your father, even if we wished."

"It is not Oliver," said Mr Stratton (rather smugly, thought Mrs Stratton).

"What is it, then?"

"It is Oscar," said Mr Stratton.

"Oscar?"

"Yes."

"What an extraordinary name," said Mrs Stratton.

"I am named after an old friend of my father's."

"Was he a foreigner?" asked Mrs Stratton, but her mind was not on her interrogation. Her husband had unsettled her. She did not understand his face. It bore a calm and powerful look it had not shown for years. He was very still, and this stillness was perhaps the source of his power. In any case it was most unusual.

"He was English, ma'am. It was he who lifted the scales from my papa's eyes."

Mrs Stratton had lost interest in Oscar's namesake. She addressed her husband directly on another more urgent matter, not worrying that what she had to say was of a private nature.

"Hugh, the cost."

"The boy is called."

"In what sense, Hugh?"

"He is called to Holy Orders," said Hugh Stratton. "He must go to Oriel. I am to coach him for his Articles."

Mrs Stratton pressed her hand against her bosom, not lightly, but hard, to press her heart into stillness. "You have had three glasses," she said.

"Quite right," said Mr Stratton.

"Tomorrow we might talk about it properly," said Mrs Stratton, cocking her head on one side and looking at her husband.

"Quite so," said the Reverend Mr Stratton, rising from his dining chair. He was a little unsteady at first and then he appeared, as he stretched himself, to be of a springier and more athletic type than previously. He flicked his hair back off his forehead. "I think," he swung his arms backwards and forwards, expanding his chest, "that the best plan would be for Oscar to go to bed."

Mrs Stratton looked at her husband's smile. It was lovely, and rather boyish, as if he held roses behind his back, or if not roses, something rarer, some genus hitherto unseen in this part of the country.

14

Trials

Men and women with lanterns crossed fields sown with winter oats. Sleepy children were raised from bed to pray by cold hearths. The three Croucher men, Timothy, Cyrus and Peter, came to Theophilus and offered to take the boy back by force. They were big men with barrel chests, arms like blacksmiths'; they carried big wooden staves which they thumped on the floor to punctuate their conversation.

Mrs Williams silently sided with the Croucher brothers. She would have paddled his backside with a hairbrush and had him in his bed before the hour was up. But her employer sent the Crouchers away asking "only" that they give up their precious sleep for prayer.

Mrs Williams was tired. She wished to sleep. Her employer seemed to expect her to pray beside him. It was a hard floor and no prayer mats, not even the piece of felt she used when scrubbing.

Her master prayed loudly. He prayed self-importantly. He prayed as if he were the centre of the universe, as if the only reason the son had run away was so that God could punish the father. He begged God to punish him in some other way. He begged him loudly, continually, but Mrs Williams thought he sounded like a duke talking to a king and not the "poor sinner" he claimed to be. Mrs Williams was fifty-five years old, too old for this sort of nonsense. If she had been God she would have given him a thwack across the earhole and sent him to bed.

At fifteen minutes past eleven, the two Anglicans came, bringing red mud and the smell of the taproom into the little limestone cottage. She was permitted to get up from her knees then. She made them tea, but they did not stay long enough to drink it. She was required for more praying, and then she was not—Mr Hopkins rushed out of the house without a lantern. She sat and waited at the kitchen table and after five or ten minutes the wind brought his voice to her: he was praying, loudly, on the beach.

The last time she had seen this hysteria was when the boy's mother passed on. On that occasion she had tried to calm him. On this occasion she went to bed.

15

The Vicarage Kitchen

It was true that Lucy Millar did not like her kitchen. It was not a kitchen at all. It was a large pantry into which some previous vicar had moved the stove and sink and, presumably because there was no room to do otherwise, had left behind all the shelves, cupboards and tables which make a kitchen a proper place to be. It was not that the Strattons had not been apologetic. They had, on the day she arrived (with all her references tied up with ribbon), drawn it to her attention. Mrs Millar had been charmed by Mrs Stratton who gave all the appearances of being a firm and practical woman. She could remember her now, her indignant, "Look at this!" when she poked a large finger at the tattered bellows, or tried—she had to give up—to open a minuscule window to the gloomy north. She begged Lucy to imagine how splendid the other, original kitchen would have been before some interfering clergyman had wasted good money squeezing the stove and scullery into the pantry.

Mrs Stratton acted as though none of this was her responsibility. She commiserated with Lucy for having to spend a lovely summer inside a "dreadful pantry." She paid her only sixpence the week and sometimes, although Lucy had four children and two old parents to keep out of the workhouse, only threepence or fourpence, depending on what was available. Lucy was cross enough to spit in the soup.

She was always cross. She was walking here across the Downs at five in the morning or half-walking, half-running home again at eight at night. She could not count the reasons she might have to be cross.

There were a hundred inside the kitchen itself, and she made her family tense and unhappy by listing them. It was a litany they had come to dread. They bowed their heads and ate their soup.

Today she was even crosser than usual. They had brought that silly Theo-dogus, Theo-whatshis, to sit at her table and they knew—or Mrs Stratton did—or should if she didn't—that this ruined her entire method of working. Because the other room, the old pantry, was so small, she always tried to do as much work as possible at the big table in the original kitchen. She had two tubs in which she washed dishes, and she would prepare all her ingredients in advance, all these little bowls and chipped cups set out across the table—an egg yolk in one, chopped chives in another, the chopped meat soaking in a herby sauce which took the smell out of it, and so on and so forth. She liked this big room. It was as generous as the other was mean. Alone in all the house it was dry. It had a window to the south which often took the brunt of storms in winter but through which you could see—she kept the privet trimmed herself to allow it—calm blue water, and a touch of the red cliff that gave Hennacombe its name.

But then Theo-holius had sat himself down and ruined her day. The place for such visitors was in the book-musty room she called the pigsty (although in public she said "drawing room" like everybody else). He did not belong here.

"Are you saved?" he asked her, first off, no introduction. She told him to mind himself. She had a leg of lamb she wished to bone. But there would be no hot-pot if this man with staring eyes did not eat and go. She went into the so-called kitchen and made dough for the scones. This was not for the lunch, but the tea Mrs Stratton liked to give for the Old Men (although the Squire looked after them anyway and Mrs Stratton had no business to give away what she could not afford). She needed the big table to make the scones, but Theophilus had the table so she tried to make do in the pantry, using the back of the wooden breakfast tray. She balanced it on the top of a stool and had to kneel to roll the dough across it. But the tray slipped and the dough fell. She said nothing out loud. She scraped the dough off the floor and carried it to the little window to examine it. She was a thin, nervous woman with dark sunken eyes and brisk movements, but she was, while she examined the dough, very still. She was thinking, weighing up, knowing the fuss that would be made if they found her dough in the bucket for the hens. She pushed the dough together and sat it on the tray. Then she went to the doorway where she surveyed the mournful man. He did not see her. As she watched, he sighed.

She was too cross to be sympathetic. She could see the shadow of Mrs Stratton as it moved across the other side of the little kitchen window. The glass was of a rather poor quality, opaque and filled with bubbles, but Mrs Millar knew Mrs Stratton was waiting for her scones. She sprinkled the dough with flour, kneaded it, and soon the cinders from the floor were hidden. But still she did not like to make her scones from it. She left it to stand, in limbo.

She took the leg of lamb from the meat-safe. It had turned a little green, but she had seen worse meat in this household. She took her best Sheffield, a lovely knife she had brought with her to the job—and just as well, too—and sharpened it. She set the dough aside and washed the tray and, once again, balanced it on the stool. Then she took the leg of lamb and rested it on the tray. She did not approve of using the tray for cutting meat, but she had no choice. She knelt and began cutting. It was such a lovely knife, and very sharp. She laid open the leg to the bone, taking pleasure in her skill, and the noise, in which she could hear the faintest tearing, even though the cut was razor sharp.

It was then that she heard the Evangelical groaning, the sort of noise a sick man might make in his sleep, but not, please God, when he was awake, at her table. She listened for a minute or two, her head on one side, like one of the Rhode Island Reds which would not—she had definitely decided—eat the scone dough. Then she laid the leg of lamb down, placed the knife carefully beside it, stood, and went to look.

She had seen him before, of course, but she had never—odd as this may seem, given that he lived so close and they they both used the same lane every day—ever seen him so close. He was a queer one all right, as you might expect of someone who did not hold with dancing. He was hard and wiry with ebony eyes. He sat bolt upright, his eyes clenched shut so tight it made his top lip twist up beneath his nose. He was rubbing his hands together as if they were fighting each other, as if the right hand wished to snap the wrist of the left. His lips, as she watched, began to move. The lips did not belong with all this rigidity. They were thick and red and passionate. It embarrassed her to look at them.

She made a noise, quite loud enough to hear. It indicated her disgust. If he heard it, she did not notice. She turned her back, and, having considered her scone dough again, went back to work on the lamb. It was so unfair. She could hardly bear the unfairness of it, that she must kneel here, with her knees hurting while he had all that table to himself. He thought himself humble for doing so. She had heard his big important voice. "The kitchen will do well enough."

She resumed her work on the lamb. Then, because she was angry and the light was poor, and because she had to balance the lamb without putting pressure on the tray, she cut deeply into the cuticle of her index finger. There was a quick blooming of Turkish Red, a perfect circle which quickly ran to seed. It left great hot splashes across the tray and on her apron.

"Damn God," she said loudly, spitefully.

The noise in the other room stopped, and when she went in there to find a bandage, she noted that he was watching her with interest.

"So," he said. It was a deep voice, the thing people normally mentioned about him first. But she had heard the voice already and was not surprised by it. It was the note it struck that shocked her—bright, triumphant, quite out of keeping with the anguished hands.

"So, Cook, you have cut yourself."

She did not understand this triumph, because she did not share his belief, i.e. if you were sick or injured, if you broke a leg, for instance, it was to punish you for sin. He had heard the Damn God and seen the cut, but he had the order of events quite wrong and thought the cause was the effect and vice versa.

She tore some strips of linen to make a bandage. She did this on the table and although she did not apologize for doing so, her heart beat very fast indeed. She could hear Mrs Stratton fussing with the unbrella stand in the passage, straightening up the sticks and umbrellas for no reason other than that she was waiting for her scones.

Mrs Millar brought the leg of lamb to the big table. She was bright with defiance. She placed it at the other end of the table from Theophilus but she did not look at him. She worked with her head bowed, standing up. She was occupied in this when the son arrived. She had seen him before last night, quite often, from her window. He was not like any other boy in Hennacombe. She thought him like a girl with the manner of a grown man. She had often heard him in the laneway singing hymns and she had no great opinion of his voice.

Mrs Stratton came bursting in straight afterwards. She had been interfering with the poultry. She was carrying a bowl of eggs and probably had the one from the broody hen. She would be better off building a proper roost and providing shelter from the wind-driven rain. Mrs Stratton put the eggs on the table and winked at Mrs Millar who, whilst pleased enough by the wink and even more pleased not to be sent into the pantry, suffered another wave of irritation. She sighed, and closed her eyes. She could not put off the scones any more.

"Papa," she heard the boy say. The voice swept from tenor to alto.

He was at that age. She sprinkled flour across the table and began to roll dough. She was well aware that the flour was sprinkled on what could be regarded as her guest's territory. She felt specks of cinders in the dough, felt them through the wooden roller. She wondered what such peculiar people would say to one another.

16

Job and Judas

Everything about his papa was so familiar and sweet that he briefly forgot the circumstances that brought him there, only that he *was* there. His strongest desire was to rush and embrace him, to push his face against the rough blue serge which could contain the faintest odour of formaldehyde or, if decorum would not permit this, then at least hold those two strong hands which were always marked with some scab or cut from his work with rocks and sea.

He felt he had been mad, infatuated with something not quite wholesome. He wanted to be somewhere good and dry and in that moment, at the kitchen door, the two qualities seemed synonymous.

He saw his father stand. He heard the chair pushed back. He registered the interest of the servant. He thought his papa about to take the matter out of his hands, that he would simply open his arms—the good shepherd, the father of the prodigal son—and sweep him to his bosom, press him into the good honest cotton of his shirt, bid him come home, away from all these musty smells to the lovely ascetic odour of floor polish, the smell most readily associated, in Oscar's mind, with sanctity.

And his father did embrace him. But he held him out, and away, in a tight grip that vibrated with a possion Oscar could not correctly read. It felt as if his father were moved more by love than anger, and yet he also wished to act sternly. Oscar imagined it was because of the servant. he was embarrassed that a stranger be a witness to this interview. His papa obviously felt the same. they both looked expectantly at the servant. The servant picked up her knife and the blood-red bone scraps and left the room. But in a moment, before father and son could be seated, she was back again with a scrubbing brush. When the scrubbing was done, they imagined themselves free of her. But no, she was back, dusting another corner of the table with flour. She began to roll out dough, with no show either of apology or hurry. Then Mrs Stratton burst in carrying eggs and saying Mrs Millar would make them breakfast. But Mrs Millar, it appeared, was insolent and would not do as she was bid.

They were painful with each other, aware that they must bare themselves before strangers. On any less fraught occasion they would have walked out into the garden, or down along a lane, but the father had lost his normal sense of authority and the boy was just lost and waiting to be led.

There were two places set. Oscar's was marked with a white napkin and a silver ring. The ostentation of the silver ring would be offensive to the father. Oscar saw this and was ashamed. He was a Judas. His alphas and deltas had no weight in the face of this. He would be kissed, even forgiven, but he was Judas. When he was back in his own home, his happiness would be marred for ever. He would never be asked to read the lesson to the Brethren.

"I have prayed for you," his papa said.

Oscar looked at him, and then down. He was ashamed of what he had done to his father's eyes—yellow whites, red veins, a red contusion in the corner of the left eye. he had caused this torture. There was a cut on the forehead, sand glued to his beard in two places.

Lucy Millar cut the scones into squares although she knew Mrs Stratton liked them stamped out round, but there was no time for Oxford tricks today. The Holy Hypocrite was whispering to his son. He held him oddly, by the finger, and leaned across the corner of the table. The boy should wipe his nose. She looked away.

"You are travelling down the tide of time," his papa said. The voice was tangled, all wound around on itself like toffee. To Oscar's ear, this voice was a thing that had lost its bones. It was soft and floppy, without conviction.

But when Lucy Millar heard Theophilus speak, she felt a strange feeling, not unpleasant, at the back of her neck. She greased the tray.

"And you have chosen—or so Mr Stratton has, last night, informed me—to throw away the chart your Lord has revealed to you. What a dreadful thing it will be when Our Lord says, on the Last Day, "Come, ye Blessed," and says it not to you."

Mrs Millar goose-pimpled all over.

Oscar was embarrassed by his father's lost authority. He wanted to free his finger from his grasp but did not know how.

"It is not as if you have been tempted, and given in to temptation," Theophilus said.

Oscar did not listen to the words. It was the tone he heard. He thought: He is in error, and he knows! He felt pity, but also anger.

"It is not a weakness of your flesh," Theophilus said. "A weakness of the flesh is soon conquered. It is an arrogance of spirit. You must listen to the voice of God."

His son had a smudged red mouth and green eyes that looked at him as though he were a stranger. He could not bear this lack of love. He rubbed his beard. Sand fell on the table. He brushed the sand on to the floor. He thought: Oh Lord, how have I offended Thee?

"I have listened to the voice of God, Papa."

He was frail-boned like a girl, thought Mrs Millar, and tangle-footed. His voice squeaked and farted and had no authority. His face showed his feelings like a pond that wrinkles in the slightest breeze. And yety, bless me, he could be a magistrate. She picked up the tray of scones and rushed them to the oven.

She came back to ask about their breakfast. It was too late for a fuss. She would offer them some tea and toast. The father was asking the boy: "Then why are you here, child? Why are you sitting in a household of this *type*?"

The boy was a fidgeter. His trunk twisted against the wooden rungs of the chair and his hands, in his lap, were at war with each other. His legs kicked the table. But although everything he did with his body usggested a sort of panic, his eyes were calm. Mrs Millar saw something in him which would make her defend him against all the c oals Hennacombe would heap upon his head, something she could only name as "good."

She asked them about their breakfast. She offered them things the household could not afford. She would do them kippers, eggs, she would coddle some if they liked, or fry some in pork fat with a slice of bread. She felt moved to offer the boy gifts, but they looked at her and ignored her. This seemed to her to be arrogance on the father's part, and she was mostly right, but the son was also imitating the father. She went to make them toast, cutting the loaf thin.

When she returned with the toast the thing she was struck by was the sinews—the father's, the son's, both of them—they were showing taut sinews along their necks. Tears ran down the father's cheeks and were lost in his beard. She imagined he was imploring his son, but she was wrong. He could not implore. He could only endure.

Oscar had just, at the moment, realized the extent of his father's self-absorption. All this, everything that Oscar had done and felt, was seen by his papa as something God was doing to his father. Oscar was merely an instrument of God's wrath.

He would not be invited to return home.

He could hardly breathe. HBis stomach hurt. A panic struck him and bound him still. He lifted his head oddly high, like a child drowning, and it was *this* that made the sinews stand out on his long neck.

They took their napkins and unfolded them on their laps. The air was wet with tears.

"I will not order you home, Oscar. I will pray for you each day."

"I will pray for you too, Papa."

And then they were both crying, and Mrs Millar placed toast in racks in front of them and filled their cups with tea. They sat isolated from each other, no longer connected by hands, and wept, bowing their heads as if it were a form of prayer.

17

Scuffed Boots

It was known about in Teignmouth and Torquay. Mrs Stratton heard it discussed at Newton Abbot markets by two women whom she judged were hardly Christians. On Sundays the Baptists from Babbacombe, walking to chapel at the Squire's, now chose to take the longer route via Hennacombe so they might observe this new phenomenon: the Plymouth Brethren congregation kneeling and praying outside the Anglican vicar's broken-down front gate. There was not trimmed grass for them to rest on. There were blackberries and nettles, but this did not stop them. They flattened an area like cattle seeking shelter from the wind. The way they knelt, so still and neat, you would not think their knees were pierced or ankles bleeding. The men wore red handkerchiefs and some of the women scarlet shawls, and although you would see one or two dark suits, the menfolk were mostly in their smocks. Here and there you might notice a blue smock with a pattern of white thread on the breast, but most of the smocks were a brilliant snowy wite. They were all abloom, like a garden, and nothing suggested pain.

The Baptists filed past them silently and did not speak until they were round the corner of the lane.

The Plymouth Brethren never announced what they were praying for. The Reverend Mr Stratton imagined it was for his downfall, but those who kept this vigil knew that the Reverend Mr Stratton could not be saved. It was Oscar, little Oscar, they were praying for. Big men with white beards, young women with snow-white bonnets – they screwed up their faces and furrowed their brows. There would be great rejoicing in the Lord's house when this one sinner returned to the fold.

The Anglicans, walking briskly past, noted only that Theophilus was still not present. There were not many Anglicans, just the four. They knew, as everyone knew, that Theophilus disagreed with this praying, that he believed the boy had been taken from him because of his own pride. It was his sin that had done this, and it was for him to be punished and no one else. He could not approve of kneeling amongst blackberries, but no-one believed it was his fault at all.

Hennacombe thought Oscar unnatural. It could not accept what it might have accepted from a more robust boy. A sturdy young fellow, already a fisherman at sixteen, might come to blows with his father and even bloody his nose. This would not be welcomed, but no one would gather in gateways to pray because of it. There would be no detours on the way to chapel either. But Oscar was so girlish, so harmless, so gormless and it was this – this harmless, heart-shaped child's face which made it so unnatural. He was like a goblin or a devil in a story – what other being appears with the body of a child and the voice of a man? They would give him no credit for filial feelings, although, of course, he was boiling with them. He suffered the pains adults imagine reserved for them – those lonely, murderous, ripping feelings that come with the end of marriages or the death of babies. He was free from the disciplines of his father's house, and although it might be reasonable to hope that he would feel some lightening of his soul now that he no longer lived in a place where music and dancing, poetry and puddings were all seen to be the work of the devil, this was not the case at all. His world did not open, but rather closed, and he was trapped inside the vicarage with nothing to take away his bewilderment and grief. He was angry that his father should abandon him in such a place. And yet how could he blame his father? He suffered stomach-aches and three times peed inside his bed.

He did not like the Strattons' house. He did not like its damp, its mould, its sour smell of rotting thatch which became confused, in his later memory, with the idea of failure and disappointment. The Strattons were kind to him, but it was a tense household. He did not understand it. It was full of clocks that struck hours when there none to strike. It was nervous and on edge, and although he was certainly coached in the Articles, the two most common subjects were money and the Bishop of Exeter. No one said he was a burden on the household, and yet he could not help but be aware of it. Each night he prayed to God to give the Strattons money, and sometimes thoughts leaked into his prayers, like coarse newspaper leaving its imprint on something clean and white, and because of these thoughts God must know he wished to be somewhere else.

His map shrank. The myopic fog descended around its boundary fences. Outside this border he could see the soft fuzzy massings of the Plymouth Brethren's smocks. He brought the full force of his guilt to those silent unfocused faces. He imagined hooded brows, twisted lips, judgemental eyes. He wondered if he had been tricked by the devil. He skulked inside the vicarage and hid behind the privet. He pretended an interest in gardening so that he would not have to accompany Mrs Stratton when she went out on to the fuzzy Downs to distribute largesse (withered carrots that she could not really spare) to those Baptists whom she insisted on claiming as "our little flock."

On an errand to the post office he saw a large white shape which metamorphasized into Mrs Williams and than chased him with a stick.

Once, above Combe Pafford (sent to find Mr Stratton who was, anyway, lying snoring in the bed upstairs) he met his father carrying buckets. This was later, around the tenth Sunday after Trinity. They had not seen each other in over two months. There was a strong wind blowing. It pushed against their mouths and left them stricken, winded. His father had shrunk. He seemed a good three inches shorter. The skin beneath his eyes was like a wound that had healed—it was ridged and livid. He had white dry spittle caked on the corner of his mouth.

His father stopped. He put down the buckets. Oscar did not look inside them. He knew the delicate tentacles of anthea were now forbidden him and he would not learn the names of these or see them through the microscope.

"Hello, little Oscar," his father said.

"Hello, Papa."

"I pray for you, little Oscar. Do you pray for me?"

"Yes, Papa."

Theophilus attempted a smile, but it could not hold firm and was sucked back under the shelter of the beard. He nodded, stooped, picked up the buckets and set off along the path towards his cottage, and such was the wind that, although he had seemed to approach silently, the sounds of his clanking buckets as he departed tortured his son's ears for longer than seemed possible.

Theophilus knew that his son now assisted the Anglican at the so-called Eucharist. He wore a red cassock and white surplice and held the silver salver of blessed wafers. This image haunted him, continually. There was not an hour when he did not see it ten times, in detail, in his mind's eye. But now, above Combe Pafford, he carried away the vision of his son's boots. They were scuffed and scratched and gone white at the toes. They were not cared for. The lace of the right boot had been broken and had not been replaced—it was tied up in a mean little knot three eyelets short of the top.

18

The Thirty-Nine Articles

"When you are before the Provost of Oriel," said Mr Stratton, "it will not be pleasant like this." He gestured around the area of grass he had scythed. Indeed, it was pleasant. It was the third Sunday after Trinity and warm and sunny. If there were thistles in amongst the grass they did not show. The sundial was at last rescued from its wilderness and showed the hours. Butterflies cast light, lop-sided shadows. Mr Stratton lay on his rug upon the grass and shaded his eyes with his hand as he peered towards Oscar.

Oscar sat on a straight-backed chair. He had been invited to share the rug, but he preferred to sit with his face in shadow.

"It will be pleasant in its own way," said Mrs Stratton who had stood up again and was pacing up and down–she could not seem to help herself–inside the hedge. "It will be pleasant in its way. You will take tea."

"It will be pleasant," agreed Mr Stratton, "but they have not forgotten Dr Pusey, you know. They will be rigorous in their examining."

"They will be rigorous," agreed Mr Stratton, "but they will not–surely not, Hugh–expect a parrot."

Mr Stratton grunted–his back was bad–he could not find a good position. "At Trinity, perhaps."

"But not at Oriel."

"No."

"And he must not expect, Hugh, it will be like his catechism. He must know the land around the subject, as it were. Do you understand me, Oscar?"

"Yes," said Oscar. His trousers were cutting in between his legs. He was growing out of the clothes he had arrived in. House martins flew to and fro above his head to their nest inside the gable of the house.

He did not like it when Mrs Stratton started talking, as she often did, about the "land around the subject." When she spoke like this she would–she was doing it now"–begin to pace. Oscar saw this land in his mind's eye–it was full of swamps and ditches. There were areas of tall grass and thick mist. You could get lost in the land that Mrs Stratton was so keen for him to enter.

He wished only to believe in the Thirty-nine Articles of Faith. He was ready to believe in them as he believed in the Bible. And when Mrs Stratton wished to drag him out into the marshy "land around the subject" he would sit up straight in his chair and stretch his face into a smile.

Mrs Stratton picked up her big blue skirt in one hand as she strode across the rough, scythed grass. She did not seek to confuse her husband's pupil. She merely wished to question whether divine grace is directly *given* or whether it must be *sought* from scripture. Her husband sipped barley water. The pupil smiled at her attentively. Mrs Stratton was very happy.

Oscar's smile was a mask on his face. He tried not to hear a word the woman spoke. She brought doubt and argument. He wanted only certainty. He blocked her out. He silently recited the Athanasian Creed, the Nicene Creed, the Apostles Creed.

Mrs Stratton galloped across the "land around." She sought the high ground, then abandoned it. She plunged into ditches and trotted proudly across bright green valleys. She set up her question, then knocked it down–she argued that her own question was incorrect. She set alight to it and watched it burn. Divine grace, she now proclaimed, was neither sought nor given.

Oscar's face hurt from smiling.

Mrs Stratton walked as far as the quince tree and then came back to proclaim that divine grace was to be *proposed* by the Church and *proved* by the individual. She argued brightly with her husband on this point, waving her hands up and down as if conducting music.

Oscar found it almost unbearable, and yet–it was obvious–the Strattons were enjoying themselves immensely. Mr Stratton called for Mrs Millar to brew fresh tea on three occasions and did not once worry about how much they had left and how long that might last.

Mrs Stratton said that we must use our judgement in the determination of doctrine.

She also said it was a sin to doubt.

She also said that doubt was the highest state for a Christian.

Oscar held on, like a frightened boy on a high mast in a big sea.

19

Christian Stories

My father, my mother, my brother, my sister and I believed the following:

The miracle of the loaves and the fishes.

The miracle of the virgin birth.

All those miracles involving the healing of the sick and the driving out of demons.

We believed Jesus raised Lazarus from the dead.

We believed God spoke from the burning bush.
We believed Moses' rod turned into a serpent.
We believed Aaron's rod turned into a serpent.
We believed the river turned to blood.
We believed God sent the plague of frogs.
We believed God sent the plague of lice.
We believed God sent the plague of murrain.
Of boils.
Of hail.
Of locusts.
We believed God took the first born of the Egyptians.
We believed the story of Jonah and the whale.
We believed Lot's wife was turned into a pillar of salt.
We believed God parted the waters of the Red Sea.
We believed Jesus walked on the Sea of Galilee, that he turned water into wine, that he rose from the dead and ascended into Heaven.

We had none of the doubts of the 1860s. At Christmas we made a star of Bethlehem from cardboard and silver paper.

20

Palm Sunday in New South Wales

They did not have proper palms at home in Exeter. But in Parramatta there were two kinds of palms with which to decorate the church and Elizabeth Mullens, ten years old, just arrived in the colony, was excited.

The children from the Sunday School were to decorate the church. This was not the custom at home. It was the custom here. They waited in the street while the men unstrapped the palm leaves from their cart and threw them on to the street.

There was Letty Savage, the daughter of Dr Savage, and her two younger brothers. Letty Savage had held Elizabeth's hand and already told her two secrets. There was the Mayor's son, a small pale boy and very quiet. There were two pretty daughters of the clergyman. They were all from good families, and all well behaved. They stood still by the cart, but not too close, and did not talk and giggle.

Elizabeth would never know why she did what she did. It was excitement. It was getting ready for Easter in such warm sunshine. It was wishing Miss Ahearn, the Sunday School teacher, to know that Elizabeth knew all about Palm Sunday.

When the cart drew away she picked up a palm leaf and waved it. She was not boisterous, rather tentative in fact. She waved reverently, as if she were in Jerusalem on that day.

There was a man–she could see him, would always see him–with a broad black beard and small jug ears, riding a little fat-bellied horse down Church Street.

All she meant to do was lay the palm beneath the horse's feet.

"Hosanna," she cried–afterwards her voice would sound shrill and silly in her memory–"Hosanna in the highest."

All her life she saw what happened: the horse rearing, the man's mouth open, the dreadful trajectory. The noise his head made was as definite as a walnut cracking.

21

Lucinda

The doll was purchased from the jam jar, or one of the jam jars, for in the earth-floored hut in New South Wales in which Lucinda Leplastrier was born there were a great number of jam jars, some of them visible, some of them not. The less important ones–thick, dumpy, heavy with ha'pennies and farthings, squat toads, unkissed by silver–sat on the twisted mantel beside the heirloom clock. There were two of these, the bluish one for the plate at church, the scratched green one for stamps and jam and other luxuries; these jars were never full. But there were other taller jars tucked away behind the cast-iron stove, and several others inside the wattle and daub walls, their exact location hidden by the dried mud and one would think, looking at the place, that this particular piece of mud was a part of the daub, or, even if you arrived when it was fresh, that it was nothing but a draught hole her papa had filled as he had filled so many others, with old newspaper and mud.

There were jam jars hidden behind the handsome books her mother dusted—always in the middle of some other task (making white sauce, cutting up the soap into square cakes on the central table) a flick of a rag, whisk, whoosh—a lizard's tongue licking the white clay dust off Carlyle, Dostoevsky, Seneca, Dickens, Tolstoy, John Stuart Mill, and the novels of her old friend Marian Evans behind whose affectionately autographed books there lay an ash-smelling jar fllled with pennies and even threepences. This was the birthday jar.

It was from this birthday jar that the doll had come, and sometimes it seemed it was against her mother's wishes—for she was often sharp with Lucinda when she held the doll against her breast—and yet sometimes it seemed the doll must have been her mother's idea, for her father would, when he was tired or depressed about their lack of headway with the farm, or the ignorance of their nieghbours, tease her mother about her love of luxury. This meant the doll. There had been no other luxury.

The doll was her ninth birthday present. It had come in a ship across the world, just as her mama and papa had. She was very pretty with bright blue eyes and corn-yellow hair. Her cheeks were as smooth as china, and cool against your neck on a hot day. The doll had been purchased by Marian Evans who had gone in a coach to a great exhibition, especially to buy it. And that time Lucinda—much impressed by what she called the "expedition"—did not know what an exhibition really was, but it later occurred to her that the doll must have come from the building she was to so admire in her adult life—the Crystal Palace.

On the day she took Dolly to play over on the back creek, she wrapped her in a white crocheted shawl that she took, without permission, from the Baby Drawer. She wrapped the doll in the shawl because she knew—although her brothers had all died before they were old enough for her to remember them clearly—how it was you should treat a babe in arms.

"There is a nasty wind blowing," she told the doll. Her mother did not approve of her speaking with dolls. Had she heard her, she would have said it was "limiting." Her mother, however, was not there–had been called to help "the poor silly girl" (Mrs O'Hagen) have a baby, and Lucinda–who clearly remembered the last occasion Mrs O'Hagen had given birth–knew there would be no more lessons today.

To reach the back creek one had first to cross the other creek–really it was a river–behind the house. There were stepping stones across this creek, but they were wobbly and awkward and shifted their position after every rain. She wore her wellingtons. She also carried the glue-pot she had "borrowed" from her father's workbench, thus establishing beyond doubt that the incident that took place when she finally crossed the twenty-acre paddock and reached the place where tea-coloured water ran across a bed of yellow sand, that the operation she there performed could hardly be seen as impulsive. When her mild and careless father, in a most uncharacteristic temper, called her "secretive" and "wilful" he was only in error to the extent that he did not really believe what he was saying.

It was a bright clear winter day–quite warm when you were sheltered from the wind–with small white clouds like old men's faces scudding across the sky.

Lucinda clambered up the crumbling riverbank and set off across the pasture to the back creek. She was short for her age–counter to her mother's early hopes and expectations. ("She has big feet!" Elizabeth had written triumphantly to Marian Evans; but nothing came of it.) Her steps were small and measured, fast, but not hurried. In truth she was nervous and excited. She had never been to the back creek by herself before and although no one had actually forbidden her, she knew she would be refused permission if she sought it.

The back creek had once been the main creek, until, in the big rains of 1821, it quite suddenly changed its course. So the Mitchell's Creek beside which the Leplastriers had built their hut was a new Mitchell's Creek and the trees that grew there were no more than thirty years old, whilst the back creek contained a richer, tangled growth of old gnarled trees where you could see the scars the blacks had made cutting barks for canoes and other implements.

It was dark under the trees by the back creek and the water was stained with fallen leaves and moved slowly. Light came in motes from the ceiling of the canopy and there were small birds which lived on the ground and made alarming scuttling noise in the undergrowth right next to you. It was Blackfellow territory.

Lucinda placed her doll on a springy khaki-green tussock, the glue-pot on some dust-dull river gravel. She then collected twigs and bark

She elected to build her little fire competently. She arranged two rocks on which the glue-pot would sit. She had wax matches in her pinny pocket. She lit the fire and watched it, squatting with her bent knees cloaked by the calico pinafore. She had a thoughtful, intelligent face—a high forehead, perfectly arched and clearly defined eyebrows, a mobile, slightly thin but prettily bowed upper lip, which betrayed—by its constant contraction and expansion—her enthusiasms, and a full lower lip, which would one day suggest sensuality but now, set against her large, heavy lidded green eyes, made the false promise of a wry, precocious humour. Her hair was reddish brown, more brown than red except here, by the creek, where a mote of light caught her and showed the red lights in a slightly frizzy halo.

She did not like her hair. It dragged and snagged on her mother's tortoiseshell hairbrush. Both her mother and father had straight black hair through which a comb could pass as if through water. She loved the way the strands of their hair lay so neatly, side by side, like pen lines. She had assumed—until her father had gently disabused her—that her own hair would change when she grew older, that the brush would one day cease to pull and the hairpins might at last have her as neat as she was meant to be.

Indeed the sole purpose of this illicit journey across the back paddock was all to do with her admiration for straight black hair. It was her plan to give a present to her doll, and while the glue-pot began to give off its comforting and distinctive aroma, one inextricably linked (like the smells of bran, pollard, tweed, apple peelings and ink) with her father, she took the doll in her lap and began to pull the hair from its head.

The hair was like her own—curly and frizzy to touch—but blonde, of course, where hers was frizzy brown. She pulled the hairs out in little tufts, grimacing and screwing up her eyes.

"Oh, do be *still*," she said. "If you squirm and slide you'll only make it worse."

She placed the hair in an envelope on the back of which was written the name of John Bell, a Fellow of the Royal Society, and the man—by the by—responsible for Abel Leplastrier having such a large entry in the *Encyclopaedia Britannica*.

Soon the envelope was fat and spongy and the doll's head was not bald and shiny as she had imagined but sticky and brown with a substance a little like a hessian bag.

"There," she said. "You see. it wasn't so bad."

But she felt a little frightened, not only of what she had done, but of where she was doing it. She looked around her, peering into the deep shady tangle of bush.

"I like the blacks," she told the doll loudly, "I like them better than the Mayor of Pparramatta." But she had lost some of her earlier composure and when she reached for her other envelope—the one in which she had the hair her father had trimmed from the percheron's black tail—her hands grabbed and her fingers pecked and, quite suddenly, nothing would go right.

The glue ran down the doll's face, across her wide blue eyes. She used the shawl to wipe it clean, but the glue would not come off and then she saw she had made a nasty brown stain. She tried to wash this in the creek.

As for the hair—she had seen, in her mind's eye, how it would fall. She had seen it clearly, often, particularly after she had said her prayers and was drifting into sleep. But now the hair did not behave as she had imagined. It lay flat and sticky, matted together. She laid the doll down flat on the gravel bed and thought how she should now proceed. She rubbed her neck and forehead and left brown marks there. Then she coated the doll with more glue and this time she pushed the hair on in handfuls. What fell loose she pushed on again. It did not look how she had imagined, and although a part of her was alarmed, another part was thrilled by the great change she had wrought in Dolly who was—as if by magic—a different person, a native of a land where maps were not yet drawn. Her father would know which one, and if did not, then, why, he would make believe.

She was not prepared for the upset she created. There was no bread and butter when she brought her doll back into the hut in the late afternoon. Indeed, finally, there would be no supper. Dreadful things began to happen around her. Her mother slapped her leg. She had done this once before. Her mother had passions; she recovered from them quickly. But her father had no passions, did not shiver and shake. He was steady and even and never fussed, even when he lost the mail from Home somewhere in Parramatta. Her father saw the doll. She held it up to him. He drew himself up, he opened his mouth, he shuddered, he threw their best serving dish across the room where it nearly broke a burning lantern. Lucinda held her doll up in the air. Her mother threw a frying pan through the open doorway. She threw it so hard it clattered down the boulders on the creek. These missiles were not directed *at* her, but the air was filled with a violence whose roots she would only glimpse years later when she lost her fortune to my great-grandmother and was made poor overnight. Then she wondered how much the doll had cost.

"Why?" they asked her. "Why?"

And all she could say, through her tears, was that she wanted her Dolly to be neat.

This was not an event one would easily forget, and Lucinda did not. And yet, paradoxically, when she came, as a young adult, to think about her own neatness, a habit she was always at war with herself about (suggesting as it did a great construction, a lack of generosity) she somehow failed to realize that it must have been with her from a very young age. She did not remember how great a virtue neatness had been held to be in her early childhood. This early childhood was always "quite normal" in her recollection. She imagined that her neatness was something she had "caught" from her mother after her father's death, for then Elizabeth, left alone to farm, became like a caricature of her former self and would demand neatness in the most ridiculous degree.

It was—as we have seen—not so; although her confusion of memory may be explained by the curious coincidence that the death of her papa also involved hair, and when she thought about the death she would always see a sticky black mess of hair like the one she had made herself at the back creek so many years before.

On the Saturday before Palm Sunday in 1852, her papa was thrown off his horse in Church Street, Parramatta. He cracked his crown and was dead almost immediately.

Mr Chas Ahearn brought the body out to Mitchell's Creek in a wagon borrowed from Savage the grocer. He had wrapped a gaudy checked blanket around her papa, tucked it in tight around the sides and it was when this was undone that Lucinda, clinging to her silent mother as someone might clutch hold of a tossing log in a flooding river, saw the hair which would now grow for ever—matted, sticky, suffocating—in the gloomy undergrowth of her nightmares.

It was only after this, so Lucinda remembered, that they suffered the disease of neatness.

Elizabeth Leplastrier believed, as many still believe today, that you can tell everything you need to know about a farmer's skills by the condition of his sheds and fences, and whilst this may be true enough in a way, it became, for Elizabeth, such a tenet of faith that fences and sheds were attended to in preference to sheep and wheat and, on one occasion that was soon notorious in the district, amongst

Protestants and Catholics alike, Mrs Leplastrier chopped down a Bartlett pear, a ten-year-old tree, healthy and fruitful in every respect, because she could no longer abide it standing out of line.

These small madnesses were not much beyond what one might term extremes of character, and although they had an effect on Lucinda, it was not exactly the one she imagined. It was not that she "caught" them, but rather that she came to feel herself inhabiting a cage constructed by her mother's opinions and habits, one she could not break free from. She longed to stretch and fracture whatever it was that held her in so neatly, and when one considers the personality of the young woman she became, it is easy to see the push and pull of these unresolved desires. There was, in Lucinda Leplastrier, she who became known as the "Glass Lady," a sense of containment, of order, a "clean starched stillness." But the stillness was coiled and held flat. Like a rod of ebony rubbed with cat's fur, she was charged with static electricity.

22

Elizabeth

Oh, you are a witch, she thought, a wicked, loveless witch. God save you, Elizabeth Leplastrier told herself, God save your wretched soul.

She bit the inside of her cheek, bit it good and hard so that she tasted blood inside her mouth.

"Clear the table," she told Lucinda who was still perched on her cushioned chair at the kitchen table.

He is dead, Elizabeth thought. She took off her pinafore and folded it neatly as she watched the wagon come down the track, waited for it to slip and lurch at the bog-hole. It was Savage-the-grocer's cart and there were men, six of them, all clinging to it, all black angles of knees and elbows, like vultures. The sun had not gone yet, but the shadows were long and there was a chill in the air.

Her husband's horse, that silly, nervous, prancing horse, trotted behind. Pandora she was called. Was ever a beast so aptly named?

You fool, she thought. It was a stupid horse to buy. I said nothing to you, God knows I should have. Why did I bite my tongue? I let you spend thirty pounds on a horse, a *horse*. And now you have gone and killed yourself.

I will go Home, she thought. There is nothing for me to stay for. God save me. Do not think these things.

She rubbed her hands together. They were dry and horny. She thought: I am an essayist. I am an intellectual. I should not have hands like these.

Dear Lord Jesus, do not let him be dead. He has broken his arm, he has fractured a collar-bone. When she thought of broken bones she was not angry with him. She loved him. She would miss him.

But now the men and their wagon were at the gate of the home paddock and turtle-necked Chas Ahearn was fiddling at the gate and she could see ("Hurry, Lucinda, clear them away. Kettle, kettle—put the kettle on") that there was someone in the cart wrapped in a yellow and black checked blanket. She saw Ahearn look her way. The sun had gone. It was very cold. She shivered. She thought, I have wasted ten years in New South Wales to be rewarded by this moment. The silly man has widowed me. But when she saw Ahearn's face as it turned to her—pouchy-eyed and turtle-slow—grief came on her. It was like a punch in the stomach. It caught her hard and winded her. She steadied herself against the daub-dusty wall, her mounth wide open, her hand patting her neat, braided hair. A great gust of grief blew down her open mouth, so much air she could barely stand. She was a sail. A great hard curve pushed inwards inside her guts.

The wagon had Mr Savage's name in gold letters on its black slabsides. Someone had misspelled "vicuals." The killer horse bent its head to eat, but there was no grass here, you stupid beast.

Chas Ahearn imagined the woman had not understood her plight. She held out her hand and shook his. She smiled, a little vaguely, but she was known to be aloof and also quite eccentric. Only the furrows on her high forehead suggested any understanding at all. As the men brought the body from the cart and laid it on the kitchen table, she made a fuss about his boot being lost.

Elizabeth was thinking about London. She thought: There is nothing to keep me. I am quite free. The reason I must stay exists no more. And then she bit the inside of her cheek so hard that the morrow would find it infected and she had to gargle salt water for a month before it passed.

But it was true, she had no reason to be in New South Wales. She did not care for farming. Farming was her husband's concern. He was a soil scientist but secretly romantic. It was he who had such dreams of country life and she who was careful not to pry into the wells from which these desires sprang lest she find something so foolish she would cease to love him altogether.

Elizabeth Leplastrier was Elizabeth Fisher—*that* Fisher—whose great passion in life was factories. In London, this passion had been something of a joke. (She is that person Carlyle refers to in his correspondence as the "Factory.")

Like her daughter after her, the diminutive straight-backed woman was a great enthusiast and it was said that there was not an object, idea or person she could not "lasso" and drag into the stable with her hobby horse. She had seen industrialization as the great hope for women. The very factories which the aesthetes and romantics so abhorred would, one day soon, provide her sex with the economic basis for their freedom. She saw factories with nurseries incorporated in their structure, and staffed kitchen, fired by factory furnaces, that would bake the family dinners the women carried there each morning. Her factories were like hubs of wheels, radiating spokes of care.

When her husband became enamoured of New South Wales, Elizabeth thought about it only in terms of her obsession and she saw, or thought she saw, that innovations of the type she promoted would be more easily made in a place where society was in the process of being born. And, besides, they could slough off the (for Elizabeth) uncomfortable weight of an inherited house in Sloane Square. They could, at last, *use* their capital. And it was this—and only this—that lay behind her enthusiasm for the colony. She would have her factory. She saw it in her mind's eye, not as something fearful and slab-sided, belching smoke from five tall chimneys, but as others might see a precious mineral. It emanated light.

And yet somehow it did not happen like this. She let gentle passive Abel somehow persuade her that it would be wiser, in the short term, to invest in these twenty thousand acres at Mitchell's Creek. It was a bargain. It was a bargain made them poor. It was a bargain that—this was not clear immediately, but it became clear soon enough—prevented the factory, which he had *promised* they would lease in Parramatta, ever being more than a dream. She had had better dreams in London.

She did not know how angry she was until that odd collection of men came down the track on the Saturday before Palm Sunday. And then she thought such bright and bitter thoughts that it occurred to her, in passing, that the devil had taken possession of her soul.

She berated Chas Ahearn for having lost her husband's riding boot.

The hut soon filled with the smell of Irish. Damp fustian, stale wool-wrapped skin, the warm, mouldy smell of her neighbours. There was old Mrs Kenneally with whiskers on her chin who tried to persuade the widow she should cry. She would not cry. She would rather slap someone. (God save me, she thought, vouchsafe my soul.) Mrs Kenneally tried to persuade the rigid little woman to drink rum, but she would not even unclasp her hands to hold the glass. The O'Hagens and the MacCorkals took possession of the body—this was later, when it was properly dark—and they set up candles and lanterns and washed poor Abel on the cold grass outside, but politely, modestly, and all the time singing in high keen voices, as alien as blacks. And they, too, came, the blacks. They stood on the edges of the lamplight amongst the wattles by the creek.

As her daughter was to be, so Elizabeth was now, and not merely physically. In the face of grief, she became energetic. She made decisions. In the face of guilt and uncertainty, she became definite. Now she gave orders. They were obeyed. The MacCorkal boys, the smallest of them taller than six foot, brought chest and trunk across from the hayloft in the barn. It was now around nine o'clock at night. There were people everywhere, but Elizabeth, although a socialist, had no friend to talk to. She had only the neighbours who cooed around her, were alien and gentle, brought her a pot of stew, milked her cow, stacked her pumpkins against the veranda, offered to take her butter in to Parramatta to sell.

Elizabeth became a door her daughter could only press against. She would not wear black. She announced it that night. She maintained her resolve on the cold and widowed morrow. They neither of them wore black, not even to the funeral, the first ever burial at the cemetery—it was only a paddock with two cypress trees not four foot high—at Gulgong.

They were all set to go Home. It was this Elizabeth would discuss with Lucinda, and nothing else.

"We must not give in to grief," she said. "This is what your papa would expect of us."

But it was anger, not grief, which was her dominant emotion. It lay there like a poacher's trap ready to snare the unwary. Lucinda learned to step around her very carefully. Mr O'Hagen also knew to tread carefully but his knowledge of the territory was insufficient.

Mr O'Hagen was short and barrel-chested, of a height and build so close to Abel Leplastrier that—Elizabeth remarked this—it was uncanny to think that Abel's entire wardrobe would end its days half a mile further upstream.

Mr O'Hagen was a young man, and although he had six children, he was no more than twenty-six. He was polite and shy and would not let himself take an entire wardrobe but most have each item pressed on him, one at a time. On this night he could accept only a waistcoat and a pair of boots. He took his leave. To him, no doubt, it seemed an ordinary leave-taking. He stamped his boots (it would leave mud, but never mind, never mind) and said it was a good time to be selling the land "for you ladies won't be having to worry your pretty heads about such things as harvest."

Now that is all he said.

But Lucinda, who was lying in her bed, knew it would cause trouble, and when Mr O'Hagen had gone her mother came and had her rise. She must dress in a hurry. She was not to worry with hair brushing, but just to rise, girl, and quickly, quickly.

It seemed then that they were staying. They were not going Home. This was as a direct result of Mr O'Hagen's comments about "pretty heads." They unpacked—there and then—the crates they had so carefully packed. They carried them back to the barn themselves—six trips by lantern light. In the hayloft of the barn, Lucinda shivered while her mother delivered a long tirade against Irishmen. She did not like the way they treated their own women, or the assumptions they made about women in general. The Irishmen had been beaten and humiliated by the English soldiers for so many centuries that they must, like farmyard poultry, turn around and find a weaker creature to strike at themselves. She said all this on the edge of the loft, with her legs dangling into the pit of the night. There were mice there already, come to eat the feed. They had not been there before, and Lucinda remembered the sour smell of mice as if it were the smell of failure itself. Her mother said the Irishmen had their women walk after them with their heads bowed like prisoners of war.

"We are not going to leave this country to the Irish," she said, "so look smart, my girl, and help me here."

Sometime after midnight they burned the rest of Abel Leplastrier's clothes. They made a bonfire on the river bank, and that was how the two women came to farm Mitchell's Run at Mitchell's Creek.

23

A Square Peg

Lucinda did not know her mother well. This was not what she imagined. All her life she dusted and polished the fiction she had made as a child: that they were "intimates," like sisters. In her memory there was always laughing and hair brushing, and tickling and cuddling. And there had been, it is true. They had fished for blackfish and waterlogged earthworms, been bitten—simultaneously—by bull ants, swum in the creek with their white singlets ballooning around them like sheets puffing up in a copper on washday morning. They had run shrieking and giggling from O'Hagen's silly dribble-mouthed bull and read to each other on frosty winter nights while the wallabies thumped the hut. All these things really happened, but if they were remembered so vividly it was because anxiety and bad temper had been far more common. As Elizabeth came, in her bitter heart, to loathe farming, the more private she became.

The more she hated it, the more she fought to prove she could do it well. She feuded with Michael O'Hagen ovedr his fencing, not merely his habit of using wattle and other timbers that soon rotted, but over the lazy doodling lines these fences ran across, the land. She berated the MacCorkals for neglecting their thistles. She rode to church in Gulgong with her hair clipped short, like a consumptive, and dressed in a style the congregation thought hilarious. Her letters to Marian Evans are filled with her spleen. She finds New South Wales "venal, materialistic, corrupt, and when not corrupt, plain damn stupid."

> "I have spent sixteen years [she wrote] ruining my complexion so it would make you weep to see it now—freckled, dry, with a raw red spot on my neck that will not get better. I have not read a book, none save the Bible and the Book of common Prayer, in four years. I can only occupy my mind with money, a way to outwit the stock agent I know is cheating me, whether I might do with one hired Irishman

instead of two, a clever construction for our feed bins which will–it *is* quite clever–drown the mice who plunder me. And this, which I have done to myself, I can tolerate, but what I have done to my pretty little Lucinda, I cannot bear to think about. She is so *happy* that I am, often, irritated that she should be blind enough to be so. Yet it is I who have made her blind, I who have kept her away from Parramatta and isolated her from every neighbour and member of the congregation who might, by sopme casual comment, reveal to her how society really is. I fear my maker will judge me harshly for what I have done, but, dear Marian, *I could not have been otherwise.* My daughter lives in a fairy world I have made for her, and they would not tolerate her in open society in New South Wales where they hate women like us with a passion you would not believe without seeing their angry resentful little eyes. It would chill you, Marian, to walk down a street in Parramatta. All this is my great achievement as a parent, that I have produced a proud square peg in the full knowledge that all around, to the edges of the ocean there are nothing but round holes. We must return home.

"I know farming bores you, although you are polite enough to only admit this very occasionally. However my latest farming news, I suspect, will prove an exception and unless I exaggerate your feelings for me, will have you clapping your strong and sensible hands together and crying: At last!

"I have said some wicked things about poor Leplastrier's "bargain" land purchase, but now, with the poor man unable to witness his vindication, I am about to reap the benefit. There is, as he always said, enough land here for five good farms and the prices are sufficient to make even the sanest woman (a creature I could not claim to be) quite giddy. In short: I shall sell. I am to have Ahearn, my very Low Church solicitor, over so he can arrange to have the place surveyed. That is how it is here–solicitors are great dogsbodies in this colony and it is no great shock to find them owning an inn, reading the lesson, and serving you three yards of muslin in their lunch hour. Once I am surveyed, I shall–God give me strength to tell my daughter–sell.

"I give up, Marian, I retire, not quite defeated."

By the time this letter arrived in Bayswater Road, its writer had contracted Spanish influenza.

While Oscar Hopkins read Greats at Orie, Lucinda Leplastrier nursed her mother. Dr Savage (no relation to the grocer) came out from Parramatta to be told he was not needed. The Reverend Mr Nelson came from Gugong and found himself criticized for the ostentation of his vestments. Lucinda nursed her mother alone. She was two years older than Oscar—seventeen—and sensible and able, but no amount of praying or sponging, no broth or poultice could do anything to give ease to the red-faced, sweating woman whose only thought was that the harvest be brought in before it was ruined.

It had already been brought in. Lucinda carried a whole stock and placed it by the bed. A stock was not enough to persuade her. She was dying, but did not say so. She fretted about the unharvested wheat. She had visions of canker and rust, mouldering stocks with Parramatta grass growing through their hearts. The fence posts went loose like bad teeth in decaying gums. They lay at odd angles. She straightened them. She tamped new soil around their bases but butcher-birds alighted on them and sent them crooked.

She could not speak.

The stocks turned into blacks. She knew they were not real. They were ghosts. They stood in the stubble-slippery fields keening.

She had been implicated in something terribly wrong. It was hot and her thirst could not be slaked. It was Epiphany. The O'Hagens were already burning stubble and laying blue strands, like a pipe smoke, across the foothills of the mountains. She could smell the smoke. She thought it was summer, and the MacCorkals had "dropped a match" again. It made her twist her limbs in anxiety. She turned and turned on the bed and the stocks turned into blacks, and the blacks into stocks, and the stocks into blacks. Leplastrier had made this bed. Such a fussily made bed. How could a man who could kill a black man with his rifle make such a stupid, romantic bed? A knowingly rustic bed made with saplings and greenhide. Her husband had been a secret admirer of Dante Gabriel Rossetti. Rossetti was a reactionary fool. She thought of sarcastic jokes about Rossetti and his women, but she could not say them. In any case there was something more important. She needed a pen.

Such a small word. Possibly she could say it. Lucinda's face loomed. Such a dear top lip, but her paternal grandmother's frightful hair. There was a noise of blow-flies. Pen—such a tiny word. It became a bead, a small black bead in her mind. Then the bead was stuck in her throat. It had been rolled in butter to ease its way. But then it had fallen on the floor.

Oh, curse the earth-floored huts of New South Wales.

Now the bead was covered with dirt, with sand; it stuck in her throat. She had made a mistake. She had made a truly dreadful mistake. She had given in to Ahearn so as not to damage his male pride. With a pen she could still change this mistake, but the word would not come. It stayed in her throat, unsaid, a small red pea coated with sand, dropped into the oesophagus.

Damn you, Rossetti.

Elizabeth Leplastrier died without attempting to amend her mistake, not realizing the mistake was not hers—if it was a mistake—but one made by those men who made the law. It was because of the law that Lucinda could not control her inheritance until she reached the age of eighteen. And even if Elizabeth had known herself to be dying—as distinct from signing a will—there is little she could have done to change it.

She had not gone to see Ahearn about a will. She had been intent only on subdividing her land. She wanted, she said, to "slice and cut it as much as possible." These words, and the tone in which they were delivered, so alarmed Charles Ahearn that, sensing incipient insanity, he started talking about a will.

Elizabeth wanted only to rescue her daughter and take her back to London. She had no time for wills and then, when the earnest old goose showed himself so stubborn—oh dear Lord, he was a *plodder*—she saw it would be faster to get the will done so she could have his full attention on the subdivision.

She was about to sign the will when she saw that it prevented Lucinda coming into her inheritance until the age of thirty. Chas Ahearn was worried—he had such an ugly Adam's apple and a long neck like a plucked chicken skin and because he was "worried" there was movement in this quarter—he was most concerned, he said, about unscrupulous chaps who might prey on a young heiress. If Elizabeth had read his letters to the paper on such matters as the profligacy of the Parramatta poor, she might have had a more precise idea of the man she was dealing with, but she saw it only crudely—what an old fool he was. She said she would have no stipulation about age at all, and then he began to huff and blow. He started to "madam" her. He referred to Lucinda as "girlie." Elizabeth rebuked him and then felt so sorry for him that she began to think only about how rude she had been and stopped listening to what he was saying. Thus she accepted eighteen as the age of Lucinda's inheritance, not realizing that this was the best the law was prepared to allow her. She signed and watched impatiently while Chas Ahearn carefully sprinkled sawdust over the wet loops of ink. She certainly did not imagine she would be dead not long after Lucinda's seventeenth birthday.

So it was because of the law—not because of the "mistake" which tortured the dying woman—that the preposterous Chas Ahearn became the trustee of Lucinda's affairs for a full six months. He was not a bad man. But he was, in matters of money as much as in public morals, a stern, even a strict man. He was a conscientious Christian with a great fondness for the parable of the talents. He was a big man, but soft and awkward, with his hips wider than his shoulders and his head craning forward myopically from the neck. He had a belly which he covered with woollen cardigans. He sat gold spectacles on the end of his big nose. He had thin strands of hair—a finite number, almost possible to count—on his pate. He had mutton-chop whiskers. He wheezed.

Mr Ahearn could not budge Lucinda from the hut itself. She was a strong girl, and grief-stricken. He was sixty-two years old, and no longer well. He called in two Irish labourers and gave them a crown (which he later debited to the estate) to remove their new mistress to his jinker and thus ride with him—four of them in a light vehicle built to carry only two—into Parramatta.

24

Mr Ahearn's Letter to the *Parramatta Argus*

A correspondent has lately called attention to such nuisances as "polluted water," public bathing, and a few other annoyances. I wish, if it should be convenient, that he would take a stroll now and then through the beautiful park of this town. It appears to me his graphic pen would describe what I cannot attempt otherwise than what is conveyed by broadly hinting that the details are too disgusting to be fit for publication.

We have seen so many of the appliances and requirements of

civilized society in this town in the shape of Oxford-educated clergy, French-speaking schoolmasters, intelligent magistrates and aldermen, that it can scarcely be credited that the Domain of Parramatta is being made such a haunt of infamy that no respectable lady, no innocent child, can venture to walk there morning, noon or night–it was no later in the day than three o'clock when, in taking a walk through the public park, that I saw the outrage which, I already said would be unfit to describe.

The parties in question are of that class of society which have ample means to avail themselves of all the advantages held forth by education and religion: they would be the least likely, judged by appearances, to turn public vagabonds. I hope, by calling your attention to the infamy through the columns of your journal, that the laws of society are not be outraged without exposure to public reprobation. Yours, etc., C. Ahearn, Parramatta.

25

Mrs Cousins

When Mrs Cousins opened her door to Mr Ahearn she had, not ten minutes before, finished reading his letter to the paper and while, in her own parlour, she had been pleased to imagine exactly what this "outrage" might have been–just a little daydream, nothing harmful to anybody else, and if it recalled an occasion in her own past, then that was her business–but seeing the man himself, like a baliff bursting into her dreams, she felt a hot flush of panic. Certainly Mr Ahearn did not come to her door in the manner of one paying a polite call. He knocked ten times, loudly, slamming the knocker like a man grown self-important with a warrant, and when she rushed to open up she found him standing there, sweating, puffing and blowing, holding his topper in hands which were–she observed this particularly–shaking slightly. Mr Cousins had sweated like this in the two years until his death, but the cause in Mr Cousin's case had been Morton's Rum whilst Mr Ahearn was known to be a Rechabite teetotaller.

Mr Ahearn said almost everything he had to say on the doorstep. He said it all clearly enough, but Mrs Cousins, trying to connect what he was saying with what he had written, took a little while before she understood him properly. He told her how the girlie (he did not say which one) had met with a "tragedy" and how he must "expedite"—he liked to use this word and it was noted by many, Mrs Cousins included, who had never heard it before—the matter of her estate. The "poor little girlie" was to be rich. Her late mama had wished the estate subdivided and he must carry this through immediately while he had the power to protect her interests. In the meantime it was most important (he could not stress this enough) that she be accommodated correctly, so if Mrs Cousin's establishment was full he would beg of her that she arrange for one of her young ladies to be accommodated elsewhere for the while. Miss Leplastrier, he said, still standing on the doorstep and twisting his beaverskin hat in his big hands, was most in need of Christian, nay, *Anglican* accommodation.

Mrs Cousins invited him into her front room and—it being dim on the south side at this time of day—lit a lamp.

Mrs Cousins was a handsome lady of forty—dark-haired, pale-skinned, almond-eyed and—it was often remarked, although the observation was true more of opera than life—rather Spanish in appearance. She had a tiny waist which she was proud of but, being these days wary of being thought to advertise her charms, chose not to emphasize. She dressed well, but rather austerely. Her hair was tightly coiffured and had you accidentally touched her shoulder you would have been surprised to find that it, too, was tightly put together, as if all its muscles had been drawn into a mat. And yet, for all this tightness, the excessive rigidity of her spine, Chas Ahearn might have seen (he did not) that when she lit the lamp she revealed, as she set it on the piano top, the shadow of a willowy, more supple person. The supple person had once lived in Bendigo, Victoria, and had followed the dictates of her heart more than Bendigo judged wise or proper. In Bendigo she had been taught, most painfully, the value of propriety. She came to Parramatta to apply her knowledge.

She listened to what Charles Ahearn said. And although she had once been a woman with a weakness for handsome men, she did not see Mr Ahearn (as one easily might, without being excessively cruel) as ugly. She responded to his dolefulness and solemnity. The effect was soothing, safe, like a good woollen worsted from Bradford.

And only when he wished to be reassured on the Anglican question did she feel agitated. She straightened her spine and put her shoulders back.

Mrs Cousins believed in the resurrection of the dead and life everlasting. She had not been baptized in any church but attended the Church of England in Parramatta as though it were her right. It troubled her that she took communion without being confirmed. This was a sacrilege. She tried to live a Christian life, but this was perhaps not enough. She did not know how to correct the matter. She would wake in the middle of the night and think about it—suddenly all cold and damp with fear. And when Mr Ahearn mentioned the matter she was alarmed almost as much as if she had seen a face in the street from Bendigo. But she showed—apart from this excessive uprightness in her posture—none of this to Mr Ahearn. She poured him tea and assured him that she could accommodate the young lady without evicting anyone, that Miss Leplastrier would indeed attend an Anglican church and that she would see her steered carefully through the difficult shoals of Parramatta society.

But when the orphan materialized wearing bloomers, Mrs Cousins was overcome with an urge—it was visceral, self-protective, a thing of muscle and blood, nothing as rarified as an idea—to put her hands on the girl's shoulders and push her back down the steps.

26

Bloomers

Amelia Bloomer had come to London in 1851 with her famous "rational costume." It was, as everybody knows, a pair of baggy trousers surmounted by a short skirt. It was worn in Melbourne quite early, but it did not seem to catch Elizabeth Leplastrier's attention until she actually saw a woman wearing the new rational dress in Church Street, Parramatta, in 1858.

Here, at last, was an antidote to the "obscene bustle" and the "crippling crinoline." From this time on both mother and daughter dressed in nothing else, and if this occasionally caused offence to street urchins in Parramatta, what else could you expect?

Now Mrs Cousins knew nothing of Amelia Bloomer. She knew only what respectability required and this was not it. She took the girl up to her room and was dismayed to discover, in the suitcase the labourers had so gracelessly packed for her, another seven outfits of the same design in different colours. On the pretext of taking them for laundering, she removed the lot of them. She did not understand Miss Leplastrier's commitment to the fashion any more than she understood her hair (she assumed the short cut was the result of sickness). She called a dressmaker. Miss Leplastrier did not want a dressmaker. She was small, but wiry and determined. There were tears, locked doors, much upset in the house. Mrs Cousins was beside herself. The girl tried to rip the flouncing off her dress as an ignorant animal will tear the bandage from its leg. She would not go to her mother's funeral in a bustle. Mrs Cousins *could not* give back her bloomers. The girl did not go to the funeral, which was a small and sad affair in any case. She howled in her room all that day. You could hear her howling from the street. One of the young ladies, a Miss Knight from Surrey in England, left on the packet for Sydney and refused to pay for her accommodation from the date of Miss Leplastrier's arrival.

From that time Lucinda ate in her room. This had never happened in Mrs Cousins's house before. It had been requested but never agreed to. Now she acquiesced and did not want the situation changed. When Miss Leplastrier emerged from her room at last, she was wearing bloomers. She had stolen them from the laundry and then, back in her room, locked them in her suitcase. It was impossible to introduce her anywhere. Mrs Cousins told Mr Ahearn all this. She went to his offices and spoke with him. She had not intended to weep, but weep she did. She feared for that more precious and fragile asset: her reputation. She wanted the young woman to be accommodated elsewhere. But Mr Ahearn spoke about the Good Samaritan. He recited all eight verses to her, ending thus: "Then said Jesus unto him *Go and do thou likewise.*"

Mrs Cousins promised to continue.

But Lucinda did not know what to do in Parramatta. She tried to behave well, but as long as she would not wear the bustle it seemed no one would behave well towards her. She sat by her mother's grave until it was judged morbid and she was taken away. She then decided that she would go back and live on the farm. She announced this to Mrs Cousins who was so relieved that she did not, as she should have, prevent her departure. She mentioned the dangers of larrikins and footpads and blacks, but without ever believing it would change the stubborn young woman's mind.

It was only three miles. She was there within the hour. There were no footpads and the only people who troubled her were shearers who called rough things to her from high on their farting horses.

She found surveyors with mattocks and axes clearing a sightline through her dew-bright orchard. Sweet white broken wood glistened in the sunlight. The axes stopped. They stared at her – a girl in emerald-green bloomers carrying a suitcase through the wet winter-grey grass. They smiled, having no idea how her heart raced, or what anger she felt – all the curdled love, the rage at death, look at the thistles in our pasture! – all focused on them in their blue shirts and bright white moleskin trousers.

She hated them. It is the hate you reserve for a thing that can hurt you. There was a long-handled pitchfork standing in a pile of rotting mulch inside the orchard fence. She walked towards it. God knows what she might have done if Chas Ahearn, finally alerted to his client's escape by a guilty Mrs Cousins, had not come galloping up the road from Parramatta in a jinker too unstable for such a high-speed chase. She turned to watch him work his way from one paddock to the next, straining and stretching at each gate, and, when he was at last beside her, at the top of the dam above the orchard, he was so out of breath that he could not speak but only lower himself from the jinker and press a sheaf of papers into her red-fingered, brown-mittened hands.

And that is how Lucinda learned of her mother's betrayal, in a wheezing rush. Her suitcase, which she had held firmly by her side, she now stood carefully in the long wet grass. She took the plan of subdivision and tried to understand it. Mr Ahearn's breath whistled in her ear. The men were watching her. One whistled "The Wearing of the Green."

"This is not my mama's signature," she said.

Mr Ahearn did not answer. He smiled at her. It was inadequate. It was his way of showing pity.

The dark man chopped a branch from the pear tree. He did it lazily, holding the axe in one hand. In the other hand he held a long white stick.

"In six months time, I could order you," she said. Her voice was small, her shoulders rounded, and her eyes could not even hold his, but slid off and down to the scarred red earth her papa had found for her.

I could *order* you," she repeated, but she had no confidence.

Mr Ahearn steeled himself. He felt as he had once when, having run over a fox terrier, he had been forced to deliver the *coup de grâce* to the writhing, crippled creature. He did what he knew was right, which was to continue and not flinch.

"You will thank me, one day when you are older."

"Who has the cow?"

Mr Ahearn blinked. "You will be wealthy," he said, "at least you have that consolation."

She heard him. It made no sense. "The cow is stolen," she said, crying.

"Dear little girl," he said.

Her feet were wet and cold. The light was clear and sunny, but with no heat in it. It had the sharpness of a dream. The butcherbirds lined up and sang on the fence posts. The axe rang out again. The poultry had been stolen too, and all Mr Ahearn would say was that she was wealthy. She walked to the hut, carrying her own case. He followed her, wheezing, getting further and further behind. She remembered all this vividly, all her life, but what she did not recall were the circumstances which meant she could not have done otherwise. She imagined she had been too weak, had given up her farm too easily, had let herself be bullied into exile.

There was a square of sunshine on the wooden step. She narrowed her eyes against it. Inside she saw (although she tried not to see anything but what she had come for) that someone had folded the blankets on her mother's bed.

The jam jars were still tucked in their hiding places. She would have counted them, but she did not wish to be seen, so she opened her case and rolled up each jar in a different garment, stuffing a sleeve down a glass throat to stop spillage and noise. Then she walked back out into the sunshine and allowed herself to be persuaded into the jinker.

On 7 May 1859, the five farms at Mitchell's Creek were sold at auction.

On 10 May Lucinda Leplastrier turned eighteen.

On Ascention Day she travelled on Mr Sol Myer's steamer down to Sydney. She would also blame herself for this "flight." She often imagined her life would have been happier had she stayed, perhaps bought part of Mitchell's Creek herself, but the older Lucinda forgot that the younger one had an itchy impatience to grasp what her mother called "the working world," a term which made the daughter see vague and rather frightening pictures like the ones engraved on N. G. Nixey's Stove Black: factories, smokestacks, soot, the Empire.

On Ascension Day she wore a Garibaldi hat and a dress with a bustle. She had her jars of coins wrapped up inside her case and a bank draft for the entire sum of her fortune in her green-beaded, netted purse.

27

The Odd Bod

It was Wardley-Fish's opinion that Mr Temple, his tutor, was a low-grade suck-up. And it is not unduly psychological to imagine that it was this, the tutor's smarminess, which made Wardley-Fish so completely "forget" to attend the breakfast in the tutor's rooms. He did not merely forget it in the morning. He forgot it the night before—ten minutes after discussing it with his would-be host—when he instructed his scout to bring him a breakfast of Yorkshire pie, plovers' eggs, grilled turkey leg, pickles, and a large tankard of ale to wash it down. And it was only when he had eaten this breakfast—there was mustard too, but I forgot to mention it—and had settled himself in front of his grate and had called for a second tankard that he "remembered" he had promised to breakfast with his tutor.

"Blast," he said.

An odd word for Wardley-Fish. It was the sort of word he might use if he imagined God was listening.

In any case he did not look cynically or self-critically or even self-indulgently at his "forgetting." The psychological view did not occur to him. He did not interpret in any way at all. He gazed out through the drizzled glass to the vague outline of the roof above the second quad and reflected that his scout would by now be in the buttery drawing his ale. It was too late to stop this, so he would wait for the ale, drink it, and then consider what he should do.

Wardley-Fish did not go in for interpretation. It made him feel uncomfortable. This was the tutor's passion, a passion almost the equal of his interest in anyone whose father was in *Debrett's*, had a thousand acres or a seat in the Cabinet. Mr Temple's breakfasts made Wardley-Fish turn silent and sour. He would become taciturn, and then sullen. He would glower around the room, imagine insults, and go away convinced that every undergraduate in Oriel knew him as stupid, good for nothing better than a third and a living in the corner of some High-Tory bishopric.

At length the scout brought him the ale. Wardley-Fish barely saw him. Only after he had left did he think of him and only because, due to some olfactory echo, he caught a delayed whiff of urine and knew the frantic little fellow had been running too fast again—he had splashed one of his slops buckets on his trouser turn-ups.

When he had finished his second tankard he decided what he had known he would decide all along, i.e. to hell with Temple and his claret-stained whiskers. He would find his friend Bishop and go shooting at Oxley. He then noticed it was still before eight, and that Bishop would be asleep. He therefore had the scout bring him a third tankard. There were races at Epsom today. This also had slipped his mind. It was the drizzle outside the window and the promise of a heavy track that made him think of it at all. Now all the lethargy was gone. There was nothing more important than that he get to Epsom for the start of the card. Bishop would be no good for this. Bishop was a boring chap to go to a race with—his passion was for animals, not mathematics. No, it was West he would want. West had become a puritan of late, but could be talked around. He had the gambler's disease, and all his theology did was make him less comfortable with himself. As for Wardley-Fish, he had been corrupted from birth. He was his father's son. He got his pomade and slicked down his hair. He was a good-looking young man with broad shoulders and a strong neck. He kept his fair beard neatly trimmed so it did nothing to hide the strong line of his chin, the attractive mouth, or the distinctive mole on his cheek. He smiled at himself with satisfaction. He lifted his tankard, tried to quaff it in one gulp, spilled ale on his beard, did the job in three, wiped the froth from his moustache, shouted for the scout to tell him he would not require the usual full commons at lunchtime, and ran—his hands still in his pockets—down the stairs and across to St Mary's Hall where he hoped he would find West.

He was about to mount the usual staircase when he remembered West had taken better rooms across the way. He had trouble finding the scout for this new staircase and when he did he was in such a hurry that he misunderstood him. He heard a "two" instead of a "one." In any case, when he banged his cane on the "sported" door he was banging at the wrong address.

Wardley-Fish banged hard. He wondered what illicit activity might make West lock up like this. He banged furiously. He made a couple of deep indentations which are probably still there, beneath the paint they apply at Oriel every twenty years, layer on layer, like papier-mâché until the doors take on a slightly melted look, like chocolate left above a fireplace.

He heard the door being fiddled with and gave it two good hard thwacks and then he saw: not West, by Jove. No, it was the Odd Bod.

The Odd Bod peered around his only partly opened oak, blinking, nervously.

Wardley-Fish understood the reason for this nervousness. The Odd Bod had had water poured into his bed because he did not run along the towpath in support of the Oriel crew. On another occasion his room had been made the venue for a rat hunt. The rats were delivered by someone knocking just as Ian Wardley-Fish had knocked. These rats were perhaps in a bird cage, perhaps in a basket, most likely in a sack. They were dumped on the floor, released, and then attacked by men with hockey sticks. The Odd Bod, meanwhile, had stood on his bed, his lips moving soundlessly.

Wardley-Fish apologized. He had no wish to cause the poor little beggar any more fright. It was West he wanted. He tried to explain this, but the Odd Bod was stepping back, inviting him in, although—it was quite obvious—he was still confused and nervous.

Wardley-Fish had never seen an Oriel room so bare, although it was not just cold empty space between objects that defined its worrying personality. It was like stepping into a cell in, say, Spain—some country you had never visited. There was nothing familiar, nothing one would expect at home, no port on the mantel, no rugs, no paintings of game or romantic girls soaring high on swings. There was a bed, a very plain desk, a hard ash chair with a straight back. It was scholarly, and yet not—there were few books on the shelves. It was neat, but there were what one could only call "heaps" of things scattered here and there—papers, clothing. There was a brown felt-covered board leaning against one wall on which the Odd Bod had tacked charts: all manner of scholarly information drawn into small square boxes. The boxes were most precise. The information inside the boxes was smudged and spidery, the work not of an academician but of a small and muddy beetle. On the mantel was displayed a wooden tray, tilted on an angle, like a display of fishing tackle in a high-street shop. Wardley-Fish had heard about this tray. It was famous as far as Trinity. The tray contained his mother's buttons.

There was no fire in the grate. The remains of a very bleak breakfast was on the tray. Wardley-Fish was shocked. The Odd Bod looked so frail and white, so obliging and yet so lonely. He wished to be kind to him in some way but could not think now.

"I say, Odd Bod, do you like a flutter?" And then, having offered this, he regretted it. He would not feel comfortable in the Odd Bod's company. He would not like it to be known.

Oscar was trying to provide his visitor with a chair. He heard "flutter" and thought it pertained to heart, to nerves, to upset, and indeed the banging on the oak had frightened him and he had only opened it to save having it torn down once more. And yet, meeting the ale-breathing Wardley-Fish, he was only half-cowed. Wardley-Fish belonged to a fast set, none of whom were very bright. Oscar, who had not until now been academically distinguished, still judged himself to be *above* this lot of wealthy gentlemen. He was fearful, superior, and also touched by the large man's awkward kindness. He pushed the chair towards his visitor. "What flutter, Fish? If it is slang I am not yet familiar with it."

Wardley-Fish sat, then saw his host had nowhere to sit, and so stood himself.

It was ludicrous to imagine the Odd Bod would have a flutter. He had no cash to flutter with. Further, he was of a very literal and Evangelical persuasion. Evangelicals were always most upset by gambling. Wardley-Fish edged towards the door.

But Oscar was so delighted to see his visitor's obvious good intentions that he was determined to make a friend of him. This was an exercise of pure will. It did not feel natural or easy.

"Please, Fish, explain to me."

Wardley-Fish stood still. "It is all connected with the racetrack," he said reluctantly.

Oscar nodded.

"You know what a racetrack is?"

Oscar perched on the edge of his bed so that Wardley-Fish might be persuaded to sit. (This succeeded.) "A track," he said, "where one conducts athletic contests."

He then smiled, or produced a bud of a smile, a tightly compressed beginning. Fish found this oddly attractive.

"It is for horses," Wardley-Fish said.

"Fancy," said Oscar, and smiled again. The smile could have been misinterpreted as knowing.

"The contests are held between horses. Odd Bod, you really do know, don't you?"

It was the smile that made Wardley-Fish imagine he might be having his leg pulled, but the smile was produced by nothing more than the pleasure of an unexpected visitor. (He wondered if he should light a fire irrespective of expense.)

"And which part of this race involves the flutter?"

There was too much to be explained. The gulf was too great. Time was getting on. If West was not here, he must be upstairs. If he was asleep, he would take time to wake up. Wardley-Fish was overcome with impatience. It made him sound gruff: "A wager, a bet, a flutter." He stood up. Then he felt he had been rude. He had not intended to bark like that. "You know what a bet is," he said, this time more softly than he had meant.

"Actually," said Oscar Hopkins, "no, I don't."

Wardley-Fish saw that this could go on all day. He did not wish to hurt the chap's feelings (he had a tender face and seemed as though he would be easily hurt) but neither did he wish to miss his day at the track. "You give money to chaps and if the horse you like is the one that wins, why then, they give you double your money back, or treble, or whatever."

"Bless me."

"Do not mock me."

"No, Fish, no. I swear to you. It is new to me. I thought you would have known, for what is called my "ignorance" seems to be a popular topic in this college. I was raised very much out of the way, in a little village in Devon. We were concerned with botany and marine biology."

("And buttons," thought Wardley-Fish, but kept his face straight.)

"We did not go in for fluttering, but I must say I rather like the sound of it."

All of this was most disturbing to Wardley-Fish. He felt as if he were involved in something wrong and he wished only to stop it. "Now look here, Odd Bod."

"Perhaps you could call me Hopkins."

"Yes."

"Odd Bod has an unpleasant ring to it. You would not expect to find that sort of name used in a Christian college."

The dignity of this request had an effect on Wardley-Fish who apologized, although he was eager to leave, more eager than before.

"Perhaps next time you were intending to visit a racetrack, you might care for some company."

Wardley-Fish assured him that he would, he most definitely would.

He then made his escape and ran up the stairs to West's room where he received a most uncalled-for lecture on the evils of gambling from a man who had, a week before, in the paddock at Epsom, attracted comment by the size and rashness of his plunging

Wardley-Fish left West in a thoroughly bad mood. He hated to go to the track alone. There was almost no point. He thought of inviting the Odd Bod and then dismissed the idea. The Odd Bod had no money. He would have to lend it to him, and then it would be lost. It would be an embarrassment. Also: he appeared so young. He had ginger down on his cheeks, not even a beard. Also: gambling was an offence for which one could be rusticated.

But Wardley-Fish hated going to the track alone and so, at the bottom of the stair, he turned and went back to Oscar's door.

Only later, on the train to London, did the Odd Bod confide in him that he, Wardley-Fish, had been sent by God, that he had been prayed for, that he was an agent of the Lord, that the "flutter" was the means whereby God would make funds available to Oscar.

Wardley-Fish sucked on his cold pipe and felt at once alarmed (that he had chosen a madman as companion) and remorseful (that he was about to corrupt an innocent).

He lent my great-grandfather five sovereigns. Not knowing the ways of gentlemen, Oscar wrote him a receipt.

28

Store up Treasures for a Future Day

As they came off the train at Paddington, Wardley-Fish started to make a fuss about a key he thought he had misplaced. He used the sort of language Oscar was accustomed to hearing from village boys in Hennacombe. It was not the style he expected from a young man who would soon be called to Holy Orders. He did not "blast." He "damn'ed." He "criminee'd?" The key was of great importance but he did not explain why. He found it, finally, in his fob. It was a plain key with a brass tag. The number 35 was engraved in the brass. Oscar imagined it was the key to a room. He did not expect a locker. He had not been to Paddington since he was eight years old, and did not know about railway lockers anyway. He was, therefore, most surprised to see Wardley-Fish open a cupboard door with the key. There were someone's clothes inside.

Still Wardley-Fish did not provide an explanation. He sent away a woman trying to sell him lavender. He gave Oscar his beaver to hold. Then, with no show of embarrassment, he slipped off his frock coat and stood there, in public view, in his braces.

Then he reached into the locker and removed a folded garment which revealed itself to be a loud hound's-tooth jacket with a handkerchief like a fistful of daffodils rammed into a rumpled vase. He put this jacket on, smoothed it down a little, and then returned to the locker from which he conjured a stout stick, a checked cap and a long overcoat with dried mud on its hem.

When he had these items arranged about his person he retrieved his beaver and his frock coat from Oscar, placed them carefully inside the locker, snibbed the door shut, and slipped the key into his hound's-tooth pocket. He smiled at Oscar who, in spite of his confusion and shock, could not help but be affected by the happy and satisfied air of his friend.

"Turn around," said Wardley-Fish, and, when Oscar hesitated, put both his hands on Oscar's narrow shoulders and did manually what could not be achieved with automatic.

Oscar found himself facing a large mirror advertising Vedemma Curry Powder. Blue and yellow Indians in turbans bowed to each other all the way around the border. In the centre of all this obsequiousness stood Oscar Hopkins and Ian Wardley-Fish.

"By Jove," said Wardley-Fish, thumping his stick on the pavement. "Look at us. What a splendid pair of scoundrels."

Oscar, who had not changed his clothes, was puzzled to be included in this definition. He cocked his head and tried to assess his appearance critically.

Wardley-Fish saw the Odd Bod cock his head and bring his hands up to his lips, rubbing them together, like a praying mantis. He had been offensive to the Odd Bod. He had not intended to.

"Come," he said. "We're late."

Wardley-Fish ran quickly and Oscar had no choice but to follow. They must find a coach to get them up to Epsom. Wardley-Fish tore through the Saturday crowds hoping all this huff and puff would drive the insult from the funny little fellow's head. But, dear me, it was true. Had not the Odd Bod, having just arrived at Oxford, wandered up and down the High Street without cap and gown without the bulldogs ever once thinking they should apprehend him? They had mistaken him for a grocer's clerk, perhaps, but never once did it occur to them he was a gentleman. You could not say the fault was with his tailor, for he had no tailor. His trousers were three inches too short and his frock coat was something left over from the time of Dr Newman. And, indeed, this last assessment was an accurate one, for the frock coat had belonged to the Reverend Mr Stratton and its poor condition was produced not merely by its considerable age but by the vicar's habit of stuffing windfalls into his pockets whenever the chance presented itself.

They found a carriage and hired it to take them to Epsom. They were both excited, Wardley-Fish because he loved the races, and Oscar for so many reasons—because he would soon have money to pay his buttery account, because he was in London and the streets were filled with people, horses, carriages, ladies in bustles, children with hoops, men with three hats worn one atop the other, barrowfuls of pears and apples, a golliwog on stilts, tall houses with brass letter-flaps set into their front door.

They passed a theatre with crowds milling outside its door. Oscar asked if it was, indeed, what he imagined it to be.

"Have you never been?" asked Wardley-Fish.

"No, never."

"Would you like to go?"

Oscar hesitated. He saw the theatre with two sets of eyes, one his own, but one his father's. The second set saw the theatre steeped in sin.

"My father boasts that he has never read Shakespeare," he said.

"Do you think that is peculiar?"

"Not at all. Would you like to go?"

"Yes."

"Good," Wardley-Fish struck his stick hard on the floor of the coach. "Then you shall, Odd Bod. I shall take you myself. I shall ensure it. I shall guarantee it," and he began to sing in a rich baritone:

"Oh, I like the track, I love the track,
'Tis torture sweet
'Tis the scourge, the rack.
'Tis the scourge, the rack.
But I love the track, aloo alack,
I love the track, alack."

For a while he sang songs, offered his flask, thumped his stick, but after a while he became quiet and sat with his chin in his hand looking out of the window. Oscar, in order to cool his overheated system, took out his little traveller's Bible and began to read it. He was thus engaged, in the second chapter of Revelations, when a great, "Halloo," from Wardly-Fish made him jump.

"What are you reading, Odd Bod?"

Oscar held up the Bible. He was irritated. He did not like being called Odd Bod at all.

"For heaven's sake, man, we are going to the track."

Oscar did not see the source of conflict.

"Then put the thing away," shouted Wardley-Fish.

"Do not call the Holy Bible a 'thing,' Fish. It is a blasphemy."

"Oh, Odd Bod, you are odd."

"My name is Hopkins or yours is Queer Fish." He stared at Wardley-Fish defiantly, but the Bible in his hand was shaking. He put it on his lap so it would not show.

"Is it true, Hopkins, that you are a literalist?" said Wardley-Fish quietly, politely, unexpectedly.

Oscar was grateful for the Hopkins. "And do I believe that Balaam's ass really spoke to him in a human voice? Yes, of course. Although I hear at Oriel that I am quite out of fashion and everyone would have me believe that Jonah was not swallowed by the whale, that the mother of our Lord was not a virgin, and all this from people who have sworn their acceptance of the Thirty-nine Articles of Faith."

"So the ass really said: "I am they good and faithful ass. Why have you therefore smitten me thrice?" The ass spoke like this, to a man, in Greek?"

"I doubt it was Greek. Have you ever seen a starfish? Under the microscope, in cross section? Do you not think God created the starfish?"

"Of course," and Wardley-Fish who had, until that moment, been unscrewing his brandy flask, now screwed it up again and slid it back into his pocket.

"Then having Balaam's ass speak, even in Greek, would be a comparatively easy thing to achieve."

"And do you accept the doctrine of eternal damnation?"

"Yes, of course."

There was a silence then. Wardley-Fish looked out of the window. Oscar, feeling the business not yet finished with, waited with his Bible on his lap.

"Do *you* accept the doctrine?" he asked at last.

"Yes," said Wardley-Fish, but he stayed looking out of the window and it was not until Epsom Downs came into view that he was able to rally himself.

He turned to Oscar with his face bright, but also serious. "Just five minutes," he said, "and when we are on the track do not rattle your sovereigns like that or you will shortly discover you do not have them. There are pickpockets everywhere. Also, when you get there the undertakers will be on to you. You are exactly the sort of chap they are waiting for. They can smell you. They will be full of advice for you, how you should lay a sov or two on such-and-such, but they only sell stiffs so you need not waste your time with them. Do you understand? Good. Now the next thing is to avoid behaving like a plunger. Plungers," said Wardley-Fish (who had, so little time before, been pleased to have the appearance of a scoundrel) "are a nuisance to everyone. West, the fellow on your staircase, is a plunger. They are the opium-eaters of the track. They are fools and madmen and are the reason the track is so discredited. All they have is a sordid appetite for gambling. That is West all over. He starts with a couple of sovs. It comes up trumps. Then he dabs it all down on the second and he has lost the lot."

"Please tell me what I should do." Oscar was being polite. he had no intention of following earthly directions. But Wardley-Fish was so serious and tense that Oscar wished, with the salve of politeness, to ease whatever it was that gripped him.

"Firstly we will make a quiet entrance to the ring. Dressed as we are we will attract no attention. We will keep our own counsel, Odd Bod. We will ask no one's advice and when it is offered we will not respond. No one shall induce us to have a bet on a 'real jam.' "

"Jam?"

"An alleged certainty. A jam. We collect our information from our own sources. We keep to the system. We *store up treasures for a future day*. Now this is the system. We never back the favourite. We back and second and third favourites. We never bet on a race when the betting is odds-on or even." This advice continued without a break. Most of it made no sense to Oscar at all. In spite of which he stayed calm and happy. He was pleased to see Fish so scientific and careful about his gambling. He was surprised by his responsible air. It did not match his reckless yellow handkerchief at all. It clashed with his hound's-tooth.

"If you wish to win five shillings in a day, then you must invest five shillings on every race. I am writing all this down for you. If you are to make some money you must adhere to this. Are you listening to me?"

"Yes," said Oscar, and tried to concentrate.

As they arrived outside the track, Wardley-Fish took a large swig of his brandy. "I am damned, of course," he said. "But Mr Temple and Mr Foulkes both argue that it cannot be eternal."

Then he looked up and saw the Odd Bod. He was smiling, but he was not listening. His green eyes were too large and bright.

29

Epsom Downs

It was almost Ascension Day but there was a piercing wind and a low bruised sky. Oscar hunched his shoulders forward as if he wished to roll up his thin body like a sheet of cartridge paper. His temples hurt with cold. The tip of his nose was red. He was so excited he could barely breathe. He took long ungainly steps around the mud and puddles, lifted his head at the scent of pipe tobacco and horse dung, brandy and ladies' eau-de-toilette.

He had never been anywhere like this before. It seemed incredible that this—an entire kingdom—had existed all the time he had lived In Hennacombe. It seemed even more incredible that red-cliffed sleepy little Hennacombe could now exist at all, so much did the racetrack expand, like a volatile gas, to take up every available corner of the living universe. He saw mutton-chopped bookmakers with big bellies ballooning out against their leather bags of money. At this very moment the sea was fizzing across the sand. How good it was not to be near it. The Baptist boys threw stones at rooks somewhere in the myopic haze upon the moors. But he was here. He thought of Mr Stratton, of the damp, long, gloomy room where he and his wife would shortly eat their lunch, and although he was fond of them, and prayed that they might be granted happiness, he preferred to be here, bumping shoulders with gentlemen in grey toppers.

And then he thought of his father, and he stopped the train of thought, uncoupled the engine from the troublesome carriages and reversed at full speed in his mind while, with his body, he pressed urgently forward, following Wardley-Fish towards the next row of stables where he would—in the straw-sweet alleys of this wonderful new world—obtain what he swore was "first-rate information."

Oscar knew this was not first-rate information at all. He was till more Plymouth Brethren than he liked to think, and the way he looked at the man who brought this information was not, to ny substantial degree, different from the way Theophilus would have looked at the same individual. He was a stunted stable hand with the whiskerless face of a boy. He was pinched up around the nose and eyes and suggested with all his talk, guv'nor, about which horse would "try" and which would not—the vilest stench of corruption.

Oscar thought this fellow damned. He would no more listen to his advice than he would invite the devil to whisper in his ear.

And yet Wardley-Fish seemed to see none of this. He nodded eagerly and clucked wisely. He leaned towards the ferret-faced informer and Oscar suddenly saw that he was so eager to believe that he would believe anything at all.

Wardley-Fish did not appear to be a man who had worked a system. There was no longer anything systematic about him. He was in the grip of a passion which made him, literally, overheat. He was quite pink above the collar and red on the cheeks above his beard. His earlobes were large and fleshy and now they shone so brightly red that Oscar was reminded of the combs of the fowls he had decapitated for Mrs Stratton.

Wardley-Fish unbuttoned his overcoat and, by plunging his hands in his pockets, held the heavy garment out away from his chest. He looked like a rooster. He jiggled sovereigns in his pockets just as he had instructed Oscar not to. The stable hand looked towards this noise expectantly. He suggested that Madding Girl was a "jam."

Oscar knew this information was worth nothing, but had he shared this opinion with Wardley-Fish it would not, of course, have been listened to. For this was what Wardley-Fish most enjoyed about the track—the whispered conversations, the passing of "tips for tips," the grubby low-life corners, the guilt, the fear of damnation, the elation, it all dissolved together in the vaporous spirit of his hip-flask. He took off his overcoat and gave it to Oscar.

"Come on, Odd Bod, we will be just in time to see them in the paddock."

They ran then, Wardley-Fish in front. He had big buttocks and thick thighs. Oscar could imagine him sitting on a horse. He ran heavily, but quickly. Oscar came behind with his knees clicking painfully, his borrowed coat flapping around him, and was—with his wild red hair in its usual unruly state—such a scarecrow that some aging Mohawks called out after him. He did not mind. He was intoxicated.

This intoxication was quite different from Wardley-Fish's. Oscar had no guilt at all. He knew that God would give him money at the races and thereby ease the dreadful burden that the Strattons had placed upon themselves. Now they would be released. God would do this just as He had told Moses to divide the land between the tribes of Israel: "According to the lot shall the possession thereof be divided between the many and the few." The Almighty would be Oscar's source of "information."

"Look at her," said Wardley-Fish when Madding Girl was brought into the ring. Madding Girl was in a lather of sweat. It had a white foam inside its hind legs. The horse showed a peculiar look in its eye.

"Look at her," said Wardley-Fish. He took Oscar by the coat sleeve and dragged him so quickly forward that Madding Girl reared, danced sideways, turned, and then backed back, perhaps deliberately, towards them so they had to step back into the whiskered crowd or else have their feet crushed.

"Look at the backside," said Wardley-Fish.

It was difficult to avoid it.

"That, Odd Bod, is the first thing to look at in a horse, and when the track is wet, it's a day for a powerful bum like that one."

Oscar remembered how lonely and lacklustre he had felt this morning. He had been cold, and miserable. Now he was warm inside Wardley-Fish's coat. He was a boy comforted by the sweet-sour wrappings of a larger man, the tweed-pricky armour of an elder brother, uncle, father. He was "looked after" and was content—in the mud of Epsom—as a dog curled inside an armchair.

He grinned at Wardley-Fish.

"See. You have caught the germ," said Wardley-Fish who saw in the grin the symptoms of his own hot condition. "You should not be here. I am corrupting you."

But Oscar did not feel at all corrupted. God had already spoken to him. Sure Blaze would win this race. Tonight he would have the money to pay his buttery account. He would buy long woollen socks and send two guineas and some coffee to Mr and Mrs Stratton. Perhaps he could open an account at Blackwell's. He would like to purchase his own copy of Mr Paley's *Evidence*.

"Look at you," said Wardly-Fish. "You look like a grinning scarecrow."

Oscar frowned. He had no sense of humour about his appearance. In fact he never had any real idea of it. He thought himself "quite plain and average" in build and physiognomy, and as for clothes, he now imagined himself quite reasonably, if humbly, dressed.

"Of course," he said at last, "I am wearing your coat. Doubtless it creates an odd effect."

Wardley-Fish looked at the Odd Bod's wild red hair, his neat triangular face, his earnest praying-mantis hands clasped on his breast and—just when he began to laugh—saw that Oscar was not joking. The Odd Bod imagined himself quite normal.

When they pushed through the crowd towards the paddock, Wardley-Fish was still laughing. He could not stop himself. He laughed while he made his bets. Oscar watched him, smiling. He thought the laugh to do with betting. Wardley-Fish placed his bets in total disregard for the system, going from bookmaker to bookmaker, laying everything on Madding Girl with tears streaming down his face.

My great-grandfather watched him long enough to see how a bet was made and then, selecting Perce Gully, he laid three guineas on Sure Blaze at 9–1.

My great-grandfather won his first bet. In the case histories of pathological gamblers you find the same story told time and time again.

30

Covetousness

When Mr Stratton entered the comfortable rooms of his Oxford friends—and he was better connected than you would think, and better liked than you might imagine—he was like a dog in front of a fire, having crawled into a chair it knows forbidden it, but lying there anyway, farting, wheezing, affecting deafness. How he loved Oxford. How he loathed Hennacombe. How cruel was the contrast between them. He did not think his distinguished friends any better than himself. H drank their brandy with a clear conscience. He ate like a horse and allowed himself to accept small "loans"—a crown or two, nothing substantial, although Mr Temple liked to claim it would have been sufficient for an Oxford mansion had Stratton not frittered it all away on train tickets. Once he had been differentiated from his friends by his tendency towards High Seriousness. Now he was "poor Stratton" and they made the little loans as marks of gratitude, that it was he, not they, who had allowed himself to be mired in Devon by means of an unfortunate marriage—for it was Betty Stratton (the daughter of the controversial don) whom they blamed for the poor chap's predicament.

Hugh Stratton was not an Oxford Scholar but was a Scholar of Oxford. And as lonely civil servants in Hong Kong may know more about the goings on in Knightsbridge than anyone who really lives there, so it was with Hugh Stratton and Oxford. When he brought Oscar up to undergo his interview with Hawkins (the Provost of Oriel) he was also able to bring the news of a certain controversy about the election of Merton Fellows, which had travelled to Hennacombe more quickly than it had across the slippery red cobbles of Merton Street.

Yet for all this intimacy with Oxford and its colleges, Hugh Stratton felt himself cast out. He could not so much as enter the echoing gatehouse of Oriel, could not even glimpse the lovely bright grass of the front quad, without thinking, "I cannot stay."

He emerged into the quad and felt all the eyes of Oriel's windows looking down on him. His shabby clothes proclaimed him a poor clergyman with no place here. He had red mud caked on his trouser turnups and the gentlemen of Oriel, encountering him as he cut across to the chapel, averted their eyes from him, but not so much, he imagined, as not to note the fine red capillaries that had begun, just this year, to show on his nose and cheeks.

When he brought Oscar through these portals he stopped him here, in the middle of the path across the quad, to tell him that he was jealous of him. But as he did it with a wistful smile upon his face, Oscar had no way of guessing the extent of it. The young man understood him as he might understand any older man pining for his youth. He did guess the jagged edges of this jealousy which had lacerated Hugh Stratton, more on every day that passed, none more than at this moment when they stood inside the quad. One would stay. One would be cast out.

But jealousy was not the only serpent stirring the muddy waters of Hugh Stratton's unhappy soul. He could attempt to lay it by admitting it, but the other he could not even admit—the dreadful guilty truth was that he had made no provision for the cost of this education. When his wife had raised the question he had waved his handkerchief as if it were nothing but a march fly to be sent away. "I have told you. He can be a servitor."

"But have you written to Hawkins on the matter?"

"I would not pester the *Provost* with such a matter."

"Then pester Temple or Fisher, but pester someone, dear Hugh, don't you think you should?"

He never did it and now he found there was no possibility of Oscar paying his way by taking a servitor's position. Oriel already had enough young men who must, if not sing, then wait a table for their supper. If Oscar was to be a servitor he must wait his turn. In the meantime the bursar was assuming that the Strattons would foot the bill. Mr Stratton had not enlightened him, but it was out of the question. So when Hugh Stratton, continuing his interrupted walk across the rain-bright quad, led his protégé into that lovely little vaulted chapel where he had once—fair-haired, apple-cheeked—been so admired for the purity of his voice, he was not merely miserable with jealousy, teetering on the edge of grief, but also guilty about this financial matter, a thing he should not, so he felt, have to be guilty about at all. He had intended to take Oscar on a grand tour, a three-hour event he had, when imagining it, expected to be a pleasant experience for both of them. But now he had a blinding headache and he turned back at the door to the library and bade his protégé good bye and good luck.

To Oscar, Mr Stratton's moods would always be a mystery, so much so that he had ceased to try to fathom them. He knew that his mentor had planned to dine with his friend Mr Temple, but now, it seemed, he was going to the railway station. It had begun to rain again.

"Your father must take responsibility," the clergyman told Oscar as they sheltered in the gatehouse. "He cannot go scot-free."

Theophilus, unlike Oscar, would have the benefit of a full revelation of Mr Stratton's thoughts on this matter, but he would not pay a penny towards sending his only son into the everlasting hellfire, and said so, plainly, not only to the pinched and put-upon clergyman, but also (in a passionate letter) to his son whom he implored to flee before it was too late.

So it is in this context that one must understand the delivery of the coffee (the gift from Oscar after Sure Blaze's victory) to the vicarage at Hennacombe. Never have eight ounces of coffee produced such an electric effect upon a constitution. Not four days after the fragrant little parcel had its twopence worth of stamps pasted on its smudged face but Oscar, looking out of his window and down into the St Mary's Hall quadrangle before sitting down to his breakfast, saw none other than his patron, fastened up in his long black coat, limping (an accident with an axe) but limping *quickly* in the direction of Oscar's staircase.

He thought: my papa is dying. And indeed so convinced was he that his greatest fear (that his father would die without their reconciliation) had become a reality that he began immediately to fetch his big brown suitcase out from its hiding place in the window seat. He had this in his hand when he answered the Reverend Mr Stratton's sharp, beak-like knock.

The Reverend Mr Stratton had one of those faces that take some time to arrange themselves for the business of the day. In the mornings he could be expected to look tired and irritable. His colour, at this hour, was normally poor; his skin had no tone; the folds of his face—thin vertical lines like surgeons' scars on either side of his mouth—were deeper, more pronounced. But on this morning his face was ahead of itself—it was flushed and tight, and the eyes had all the secret life (and yet none of the wateriness) they normally took from a sherry bottle.

He did not say good morning, or explain how it was he happened to be in Oxford at that hour. Rather he took the empty suitcase from Oscar's hands, seemed surprised at its lightness, and then put it down outside the door. He had no "intention" in this, unless it was that, in the midst of his confusion at being greeted by a young man holding a suitcase and, finding the suitcase empty, he judged the thing ready for the boxroom and put it in the passage where the scout might attend to it, although if this was what he thought, he did not know he thought it—his mind was aswim with imagined conspiracies; there was no room for a suitcase.

Hugh Stratton said: "You have paid your buttery bill."

This was not said in a spirit of congratulation but, rather, accusation. He shook his head slowly, as if he were at once exhausted by but resigned to this example of the young man's treachery.

Oscar was, by now, quite accustomed to Hugh Stratton's fretful moods, but they had not lost their power to disturb him and he was, as usual, reduced to a sort of paralysis, knowing that almost anything he said would make the matter worse.

When Mr Stratton unbuttoned his coat Oscar held out his hand to take it from him, but the offer was not accepted. Mr Stratton draped the old-fashioned black gaberdine on the end of the bed.

"And drinking coffee," said Mr Stratton, walking over to the table the scout had spread for breakfast. He lifted the lid of the tea-pot as if it were a clever disguise for secret luxuries.

"Oh no," said Oscar, "not coffee," and looked unhappily at the cold tight skin that was forming across the top of his porridge. He was hungry. It was his normal condition.

"Not?" said Mr Stratton. He squinted at the student, and then down into the pot. "Not?"

"I hope you received *your* coffee."

"Oh, yes, we *received* it," said Hugh Stratton, meaning nothing in particular by his emphasis on *received*, wishing only to give the impression that he knew what tricks were being played, whatever they were.

"And very nice too," he said, "forgetting" his wife's request that he pass on her especial thanks for so thoughtful a gift.

"How are things in Hennacombe?" asked Oscar.

"I bring a question from it. It is this: do you have an income? Because if you do, young man, you have deceived me."

"Oh, no, Mr Stratton, please."

"Please nothing," said Mr Stratton. "I would take it very ill if you had tricked me. No, thank you, I would rather stand."

"I have not tricked you," said Oscar, pushing the hard-backed chair back against the breakfast table. "You have been too kind to me to deserve trickery."

"Then how do you send me coffee? Explain that. It is fifteen years since I could afford coffee, and now you, a poor creature who did not know his Athanasian Creed two years ago, a pauper who would *beg* to be made a servitor, now you are so gracious as to send me this luxury with no explanation."

"Dear Mr Stratton, it was because I love you both. I meant no offence."

At the mention of "love" Mr Stratton blinked. "And now I hear your buttery bill is paid," he said.

"I marvel at the sources of your intelligence," said Oscar, meaning to flatter, then panicking in mid-sentence when he saw it could be construed as rude.

Hugh Stratton stopped blinking. "I know everything," he said. "If you walked to Kidlington to say your prayers then I would hear about it."

Oscar thought: He knows I have been gambling. Then he thought: No, he does not.

Mr Stratton had the subject firmly and would not let it go but then, it seemed, neither did he know what to do with it. "I am losing my health and my sleep worrying about how you may be supported here. I have written letters to the men whom I have previously asked to donate funds for the restoration of St Anne's. This is not wise of me. It damages me. It is a fine old church and I fear I have done its cause a great disservice. And then you send me coffee."

"Also: I pay my buttery bill. Surely this makes your worry less onerous?"

"But how did you make money?" asked Hugh Stratton, screwing up his face and tucking his chin into his neck. "Where did it come from? Is it from your father?"

"No, of course not."

"Do not 'of course not' me, young man."

"Dear Mr Stratton, I only wish you not to worry. God will provide for me."

The Reverend Mr Stratton struck his brow with his fist. "Do not, I beg you, be so simple."

"Perhaps I am simple," said Oscar stubbornly, "but I should like to take responsibility for my own bills. I would wish you to worry no longer."

"Your father is paying."

"I swear to you he is not," said Oscar who was due to leave for Epsom in fifteen minutes. Wardley-Fish's binoculars sat on the ledge beside the breakfast table, but they were of even less consequence than a suitcase.

"Then how," the clergyman hissed, "are you paying?"

Oscar felt obliged to tell the truth, was about to do so, but then he thought: He will take the gossip back to Hennacombe and use it against my papa in some way.

"You are up to no good," said Hugh Stratton. "for all I know you are a member of a betting ring. There was one in my time, three Hons too, and they were all of them sent down. You must promise me you would never be involved in such a thing. I am raising money for my little church's restoration in Oxford. I cannot have my name brought low."

"My dear patron," said Oscar, allowing himself to touch Mr Stratton on his rigid shoulder, "there is no need for such a promise."

There were heavy steps upon the stair. Oscar thought: It is Fish. But the steps passed on. It was not Fish.

"No need," said Oscar, "at all."

Hugh Stratton narrowed his eyes and stared fiercely at his protégé. If Oscar had not known him he would have imagined himself hated, but in a moment the gaunt face became loose and floppy and a small pink tongue came out to dampen the dry white corners of the mouth.

"You are a good boy, Oscar," he said. "You must not think that I imagine otherwise."

31

Ascension Day

There was something wrong with Lucinda's dress. She did not know what it was, but it attracted attention. She had no confidence in the stupid fashion which bespoke mincing and vapidity. But her own judgement was of no use in the matter and she had purchased in accordance with the preferences of Chas Ahearn and his lavender-water wife. Even now, on the day of departure, they would not let her be but shepherded her, the one huffing and blowing, the other wobbling on her ankles and complaining about the dangerous timbering on the wharf. People stared and she assumed it was the dress. A larrikin threw a rock to fright her with its splash. She was in a fright anyway. She needed neither larrikins nor Ahearns to make it any worse. She had her inheritance, her parents' lives rendered down as whole sheep are rendered down to tallow, something living and breathing that has become reduced to a piece of paper, a bank draft she could carry in this silly beaded purse and which, in the words of Mrs Ahearn, would "have you married in a jiff, and to the best in all the colony, a judge, a governor, yes, indeed, I mean to say."

Mr Ahearn thought that wishing for a governor went too far. Mrs Ahearn thought not. Their excitement made them quite insensitive to the feelings of the young heiress whose eyes were slitted to contain her anger. How dare they. They would dress her up in silly frippery and never once think how her Papa and Mama had worried and fretted over every penny. This money did not belong to them, or to her either. The money was stolen from the land. The land was stolen from the blacks. She could not have it. It was thirty pieces of silver. She would give it to the church. Indeed, she tried. She made a written offer to the Baptist Church but the minister, instead of accepting, visited Mr Anglican Ahearn and together they conspired that she should keep it. And she wished to keep it. She was alone in the world, orphaned, unprotected. She trusted nothing so much as she trusted that money, which she wished, fiercely, passionately, to keep, even while she tried to give it away. There was no one she could talk to about her feelings. She was pinned and crippled by her loneliness. In the afternoons she lay in her bed. There was a spring coiled tight across her chest. She held her arms straight and rigid by her side, like a trap waiting to be triggered.

Lucinda Leplastrier was leaving Parramatta and going to Sydney. She was going against the most passionate advice, but she could not bear to be in Parramatta any more. Everyone wished to steer her this way and that, have her sit down, stand up, while all the time they smirked and thought her simple. She thought her simple. She thanked her God in heaven that she had money and was not at their mercy. And now there was this one final series of misunderstandings and she would be gone. Her crinoline cage bumped and swayed against the pressure of Mrs Ahearn's wobbly-ankled perambulations. Everyone encouraged her to see this crinoline as an "improvement." She thought them ignorant. The impracticality of the garment made her angry. She also had a silly hat. No wonder they stared at her.

Mr Ahearn had it into his head that she should on no account travel down to Sydney with the *hoi polloi* aboard the packet. He was one of those men who must always deliver you safely to his friend, his associate, his colleague. If you are going to Woop-Woop, he will know the bank manager of the Australasian or the dog-catcher or Jimmy Jones, the sergeant of police. As for Sydney, he was not quite so knowledgeable, but he had a letter of introduction to Petty's Hotel and to Mr James d'Abbs the accountant–a funny little chap, but somehow a relation of his wife. And Miss Leplastrier certainly must not travel on the packet steamer, but with his good friend and trusted client, Sol Myer, who was taking nothing down to Sydney but cold white cauliflowers and would, in any case deliver her gratis to the Market Street Wharf where there were none of your predatory types you found at Semi-Circular Quay waiting to prey on foolish young ladies.

The foolish young lady's face hurt from false smiling.

It was Ascention Day and you could feel the winter lying like a snake along the water. Lucinda's hair had been spared the scissors for three months and now that it had grown to a length her custodians judged more ladylike, Mrs Ahearn had pulled it up tight on her head and secured it with pins and clips. But pins and clips would not work. They had never worked. Her hair was a sea of little snakes, each one struggling to insist on its freedom. She patted her prickling neck feeling as the first wisps of hair escaped. The pins were merely ineffectual, but the patented clips grabbed at her. They dragged and stretched the hair at the roots. Lucinda could not understand the logic: how one's hair must be grown long in order to be pulled up short. Her nose and cheeks felt far too prominent. She wished her hair released so it might stop her headache, so her features might be softened, but no, it was not allowed. She got, instead, the Garibaldi hat and Mr Ahearn's little joke–he pretended to be much amused by ladies' fashions–that it looked like a pimple on a pumpkin.

Lucinda, imagining the expression referred to her red cheeks, was mortified, but Mr Ahearn had liked the expression for its sound, not its verisimilitude–the hat was not too small, nor her cheeks too red. He was a silly puritanical man who wished to show that he cared for her, but had no proper way of doing it, and his attempts resembled his wife's wobbly walk–all that bumping and shoving when all he intended, as she did, was solicitude.

It was already noon, late for a weekday market trip, but not for a

Saturday when there was a night market in Sydney. The cauliflowers would be sold under gaslight. But there was no heat in the sun and the shadows of the ramshackle timber warehouse behind the little party seemed, to Lucinda, to be filled with the most hostile and uncaring cold. There was a smell of bad fish and a confusion of noises, steam whistles, human voices, the heavy thwack of river timber against wharf iron rings. There was a dinghy caught beneath the wharf and in danger of being sunk by the rise of the tide. There were boatmen calling for its removal, and others, in mid river, jockeying so they might take their turn at the busy wharf. Sol Myer was the subject of abuse for not shifting his boat on. There was now a rush to have Lucinda aboard. She hurt her ankle jumping down. There was no time – thank God – for tears, embraces (she thought of that cardiganed stomach – it was as repulsive as a governor's) or recriminations about her actions.

She stood straight on the deck with her arms by her sides.

Chas Ahearn could not see the expression on her face. When she saluted him, as formal as a sentry, he did not know how to take it. A barge carrying a shining black donkey engine now blocked his view. It was a large engine and when the men gathered around it to effect its transfer to the wharf, he completely lost sight of her. In any case, it was only a very small smile, and it is unlikely he would have seen it from that distance.

32

Prince Rupert's Drops

There was a small roofed section on Mr Myer's boat, but it seemed that this was more intended for the shelter of the engine than the driver and, in any case, it was decorated with so many oily cans and rags that she thought it better to pretend an affection for the bracing air beside the cauliflowers.

A thin sheet of cloud began to materialize in the sky – the smoke from burning hedgerows on farms along the banks – and it was soon so general that the river, in response, assumed a pearly yellow sheen. She had never been on a boat before. She had never been to Sydney. She sat on a rough packing case in the bow, her hands in her lap, shivering.

Sol Myer, like all of Chas Ahearn's clients, knew the story of the tragedy. He saw the way she held herself – the straightness of the spine, the squareness of the shoulder. He had not missed the irony of her last salute, but he was most conscious of her dignity, of her solitariness – both qualities being emphasized by her small stature – and he felt, as he did not often with strangers, that he knew her.

He would like to give her something, a gift. It would give him pleasure. He imagined it, his face creasing. But he had nothing except cauliflowers, and these, look at her, she was stealing from him in any case.

She sat so straight, such a good back, such a proper back, a back you would trust in any crowd, and there was her hand – a different animal entirely – scuttling off down, a tiny crab with its friend the snake, gone stealing little florets of cauliflowers.

Sol Myer started giggling. You could not tell a story like this. A story like this you could only feel.

The river journey was picturesque, with so many pretty farms along its banks. Lucinda could not look at them without feeling angry. She looked straight ahead, shivering. It was cold, of course, but not only cold that caused this agitation. There was a jitteriness, a sort of stage fright about her future which was not totally unpleasant. She dramatized herself. And even while she felt real pain, real grief, real loneliness, she also looked at herself from what she imagined was Sol Myer's perspective, and then she was a heroine at the beginning of an adventure.

She did not know that she was about to see the glassworks and that she would, within the month, have purchased them. And yet she would not have been surprised. This was within the range of her expectations, for whatever harm Elizabeth had done her daughter, she had given her this one substantial gift – that she did not expect anything small from her life.

It would be easy to see this purchase – half her inheritance splurged – on the first thing with a FOR SALE sign tacked to it – as nothing more than the desire to unburden herself of all this money, and this may be partly true. But the opposite is true as well, i.e. she knew she would need the money to have any sort of freedom. It is better to think about the purchase as a piano manoeuvred up a staircase by ten different circumstances and you cannot say it was one or the other that finally got it there – even the weakest may have been indispensable at that tricky turn on the landing. But of all the shifting forces, there is this one burly factor, this strong and handsome beast, i.e. her previous experience of glass via the phenomenon known as *larmes bataviques* or Prince Rupert's drops.

You need not ask me who is Prince Rupert or what is a *batavique* because I do not know. I have, though, right here beside me as I write (I hold it in the palm of my left hand while the right hand moves to and fro across the page) a Prince Rupert drop—a solid teardrop of glass no more than two inches from head to tail. And do not worry that this oddity, this rarity, was the basis for de la Bastie's technique for toughening glass, or that it led to the invention of safety glass—these are practical matters and shed no light on the incredible attractiveness of the drop itself which you will understand faster if you take a fourteen-pound sledgehammer and try to smash it on a forge. You cannot. This is glass of the most phenomenal strength and would seem, for a moment, to be the fabled unbreakable glass described by the alchemical author of *Mappae Clavicula*. And yet if you put down your hammer and take down your pliers instead—I say "if," I am not recommending it—you will soon see that this is not the fabled glass stone of the alchemists, but something almost as magical. For although it is strong enough to withstand the sledgehammer, the tail can be nipped with a pair of blunt-nosed pliers. It takes a little effort. And once it is done it is as if you have taken out the keystone, removed the linchpin, kicked out the foundations. The whole thing explodes. And where, a moment before, you had unbreakable glass, now you have grains of glass in every corner of the workshop—in your eyes if you are not careful—and what is left in your hand you can crumble—it feels like sugar—without danger.

It is not unusual to see a glass blower or a gatherer scrabbling around in a kibble, arm deep in the oily water, sorting through the little gobs of cast-off cullet, fossicking for Prince Rupert's drop. The drops are made by accident, when a tear of molten glass falls a certain distance and is cooled rapidly.

You will find grown men in the glass business, blowers amongst them, who have handled molten metal all their life, and if you put a Prince Rupert's drop before them, they are like children. I have this one here, in my hands. If you were here beside me in the room, I would find it almost impossible not to demonstrate it to you, to take my pliers and—in a second—destroy it.

So it was a Prince Rupert's drop, shaped like a tear, but also like a seed, that had a powerful effect on Lucinda Leplastrier. It is the nature of these things. You can catch a passion from them, and the one in question, the first one Lucinda saw—at an age when she had dimples on her knees—was a particularly beautiful specimen, twisted red and milk-white glass from the damp brick island of Murano. It was sent to Abel Leplastrier by his great friend John Bell, FRS, the author of the enthusiastic piece in the *Britannica.* And Lucinda, entering Sydney on her bed of cauliflowers, would have reason to remember the day it arrived, eight years before, in Parramatta.

The post-office steps were made from wood and there was a great fat swathe of sunshine spilled across them. It was winter and the sunshine was welcome. She could feel it through the cotton of her dress. The packet steamer had just arrived from Sydney. Her papa sat beside her on the step. He had Mr Bell's parcel. It was this that took his attention and he could be no more bothered by the complaints of the owners of passing skirts and trousers (sour-smelling wool, velvet with mothballs) than by the demands of all the other mail from Home; these last he threw into his sugar bag.

His hands were like his body—board strong—but they were short-fingered and surprisingly delicate in their movements; they attacked Mr Bell's parcel like a pair of pale-bellied spiders. Pick, pick. Red sealing was shattered. Brown paper was torn in such a way it could never be reused.

Lucinda pressed close against her papa. She liked the rough feel of his jacket on her cheek, all the hairy smells of bran and tweed and apple skins. She saw the Prince Rupert's drop emerge from its nest of wrinkled paper but mistook it—ooh!—for a humbug or a sally twist. She reached out her hand, but her father held it from her.

"No," he said. He did not look at her. He read the letter which accompanied it.

Her father made a noise—a little moan—and jumped to his feet. Lucinda stood also.

"Stay, Lucinda."

She felt herself shot through with dread. She did as she was bade. She sat on the steps. She cradled the sugar bag in her lap for comfort, and watched her father run away from her. Down the steps he went, two at a time, pushing past brilliantined clerks and bent-backed lags. He sprinted—a broad man with short legs—across Church Street. he raised his arm and hurled the glass at the sandstone wall of the magistrate's court. A policeman rose from his chair on the veranda of the court. He watched as her papa picked up the glass humbug. The policeman called out something over his shoulder and another policeman—a thin man with a grey beard almost as wide as his chest—came out to join him. Together they both stared at her papa who, without knowing himself observed, now walked back across the rutted street, fouling his boots on steaming ox dung, wiping them clean on a surviving patch of tussock grass. The thin policeman went back into the court. The other policeman resumed his seat. Her papa trudged up the steps and—no longer smelling quite so sweet—sat beside her. He put his hand into his jacket pocket, and produced his clasp knife. His hands were trembling. He had difficulty setting the knife the way he wanted it—with the largest blade pulled out just a fraction. He looked at Lucinda and gave a gruesome sort of grin. Then he put the tail of the Prince Rupert's drop between the blade and handle and forced the blade hard home.

The drop shattered, of course. It sprayed like brown sugar across the post-office steps, sprinkled a young widow's bonnet, dusted the black whiskers of a flash-looking man in nankeen breeches. There were other affected. There was much brushing and head turning, and perhaps there would have been trouble, for Parramatta could still be a violent place, but when these who had been so rudely assaulted located their assailant, they found him weeping; and not only him, but the solemn little girl beside him. They could not know—how could they?—that while the father and daughter had tears in common, this single effect was produced by two quite different causes.

For Abel Leplastrier had been given, in John Bell's letter, an annotated index to the event he had just witnessed. The glass was by way of being a symbol of weakness and strength; it was a cipher for someone else's heart. It was a confession, an accusation, a cry of pain. It was for this he wept.

Lucinda was moved by something much more simple—grief that such a lovely thing could vanish like a pricked balloon. But her feelings were not unlayered and there was, mixed with that hard slap of disappointment, a deeper, more nourishing emotion: wonder.

It was very more-ish.

It was her mother who provided the second Prince Rupert's drop. This did not arrive unexpectedly, but was sought out by advertisement. The cynical interpretation of this was that Elizabeth Leplastrier, although careful with pennies, would not be denied what her husband and little girl had experienced. The more generous explanation is that the little girl had not stopped talking about it and her mother decided she should have one for her ninth birthday.

It turned out to be a great extravagance, and Abel sulked and made the cynical interpretation.

They "let it off" on the steps of their hut. It was early, with the sun just slanting through the criss-crossed needles of the casuarinas which lined the creek. There was dew on the grass and their boots were wet from it. The *larme batavique* caught the light and gathered it in like molten metal straight from a glassworks' glory-hole. It withstood her father's hammer and her mother's axe. And then Lucinda—it was her birthday, after all—took the needle-nosed pliers and snapped—it took a grunt to manage it—the tail.

Fireworks made of glass. An explosion of dew. Crescendo. Diminuendo. Silence.

There are drugs that work the same, and while I am not suggesting that our founder purchased the glassworks to get more drops, it is clear that she had the seed planted, not once, but twice, and knew already the lovely contradictory nature of glass and she did not have to be told, on the day she saw the works at Darling Harbour, that glass is a thing in disguise, an actor, is not solid at all, but a liquid, that an old sheet of glass will not only take on a royal and purplish tinge but will reveal its true liquid nature by having grown fatter at the bottom and thinner at the top, and that even while it is as frail as the ice on a Parramatta puddle, it is stronger under compression than Sydney sandstone, that it is invisible, solid, in short, a joyous and paradoxical thing, as good a material as any to build a life from.

33

Glassworks

The glassworks at Lanson's Wharf in Darling Harbour were the first in Sydney. There was nothing pretty about them, no suggestion of the molten mysteries which took place within, no light from the glory-hole, just a smudge of black smoke against the cold chalky sky. It would have been easy for Lucinda to have missed them, easy for any number of reasons. The first is that Lanson's Wharf was behind the Market Street Wharf, and had the latter not been crowded with a tangle of punts, barges, and a steamboat (the cockney pilot of which was taking picturesque exception to a Chinaman moored in a dinghy) Sol Myer would have brought his load of pale-stemmed cauliflowers alongside and Lucinda would never have travelled the extra distance up into the throat of Darling Harbour where the glassworks lay waiting. And even then it would have been so easy for her to have ignored them. There was nothing in their architecture to separate them from their neighbours.

The little steamer shuddered, cleared its throat of a clot of smoke, and pushed past the tangle at Market Street. The sun was low but had not yet been blocked by Pyrmont. It bathed the eastern bank of Darling Harbour which is also—for those of you not familiar with Sydney—the backyard of the city. Where there was white it shone. Where there was sandstone it turned a soft and lovely pink. But for the most part there was no white or sandstone showing, only coal and rust and these drank the light like sand takes water.

Sol wiped his engine's copper piping with an oily rag and made the rag steam. Lucinda picked at a cauliflower. She did not much like the look of Sydney. A wine bottle floated in water that rippled with a rather satanic beauty: mother-of-pearl; spilled oil from a steamer. There was a stink, like tallow rendering, but perhaps this was only Sol's rag on the hot copper pipe. Sol rubbed the glass of his pressure gauge with another filthy rag which was different only in that it came from a nail high on the right, now low on the left. He was not satisfied with the result and used his elbow. He looked over his shoulder—a Chinaman was being fetched out of the water. He thanked God for Chinamen. It was a bitter joke he could make only with himself. He continued up into the pinch of Darling Harbour.

They passed the jumbled mud-smeared logs of Walter O'Brien's Colonial Timber Mill just as the sun dropped beneath Pyrmont. They passed beneath the peeling walls of MacArthur's Flour Mill; it was a grey weatherboard structure, tall and thin, and leaning sideways at an angle.

The waterfront seemed clogged with logs, iron, sheets of corrugated roofing, abused timber with giant bolts rusting in it.

Lucinda was afraid. She felt very small. She wished Sol Myer would suddenly demand that she act her age and return to Parramatta.

Her arms, beneath her cape, were goose-pimpling. She wound a cotton scarf around her face and blew into her hands. Sol swung the wheel and, as the boat came about, she saw these words: Prince Rupert's Glassworks. The board that bore the words was weathered and faded—lime green against a poison blue.

The works were all in shadow, like a stranger's face under a hat, and not any more inviting because of it. You could not see what it was, how it was made, how it was put together. There were sheds, a chimney with black smoke. It could have been a blacksmith's, were it not for the crates of bottles.

These glassworks were for sale. There was a sign that said so, not a new sign, but more recent than the one that said Prince Rupert's. They looked intimidating, almost evil. Very well, she thought, if that is what it is to be. She made this decision without understanding that there existed, within this city, places with trees and grass and flowers.

Sol brought his craft into the wharf, sliding it gently through the smaller craft, like a careful hand amongst bobbing apples. Lucinda stood up. The crinoline cage swayed. She moved along the edge of the boat self-consciously. She felt all the wharf looking at her, but she was wrong. She took her own case down from the cabin roof. It was heavy with books. The case banged against her thigh and bruised it. She did not know anything about Sydney. She did not know how to engage an omnibus or a hansom cab, what they cost, where they went or how they were stopped. She paid Mr Myer sixpence for the journey. He gave her a cauliflower and then, in a bristly rush, a kiss on her cold cheek. He delivered her on to the wharf amongst hessian bags and steel-wheeled trolleys. Two Chinamen, one wet, one dry, were slinging heavy parcels on to long cane poles. Lucinda walked like someone unused to shoes. She struggled up the hill from the wharf with her suitcase banging against her right side, a cauliflower clutched in her left hand. The suitcase put her skirt cage violently off centre. This is how she arrived at Petty's Hotel. At first they thought her at the wrong address. She placed her cauliflower on the desk and asked them, blushing brightly, if there was a reliable library close to the hotel.

She had decided to study glass.

34

After Whitsunday

The Reverend Dennis Hasset, vicar of All Saints in Woollahra, was pleased, having received the letter to invite L. Leplastrier to discuss his queries on the "physical properties and manufacture of glass." Not Lavoisier, Leplastrier, but a Frenchman doubtless. Lavoisier was a scientist famous for gases. Lavoisier, anyway, was dead. Dennis Hasset was flattered none the less.

It was the day after the Whitsunday baptisms—fourteen babes-in-arms and the father of Morton the grocer. He had planned an idle day and this inverview was an indulgence. He readied himself for it with a self-consciousness he found amusing. He placed around his study those learned magazines in which his work had appeared, did it in such a careful way (a self-mocking way, too, but that is not the point) that the wandering eye of a guest could not help but fall upon them. He could thus display himself like a case of Tasmanian Lepidoptera, with polished pins through his nose and earlobes. He could lay down the journals like a manservant lays out vestments, and even while he laughed at himself for doing something so childish, still approached the matter with the utmost particularity.

"You see, Monsieur," he told the empty room, "it is like this." Like what? He did not know. He placed two large red split logs on the fire and went to sit behind his desk while the first red splinters spluttered and ignited.

The study was dark, but not sombre, and the desk he had placed across one corner looked out on to a bright, cold vista: a curl of yellow road swirling through two lines of eucalyptus and then out of sight. Behind this was a two-inch brushstroke of ocean. He was burning lamps at midday, four of them. He had them dotted here and there to balance the brightness of the window. The Reverend Dennis Hasset found all this very satisfying. He placed his hands on the red leather top of the desk, regretted the round stain left by a glass of claret, but was pleased to remember that the claret, a Bechyville, had been a good one.

He was a tall, well-made man in his early thirties. His face could almost be called handsome, and often was, for he gave his companions such a sense of his deep interest in them that they easily overlooked those heavy eyebrows—joined across the bridge of his nose—that marred his looks. He had dark curly hair, elegant side-whiskers, a slightly long face and a dimpled chin. His natural complexion was a step short of olive, although an increasing fondness for claret made it redder than the season could explain. But claret or no, he was one of those people who—should you lay a hand on his arm, say, in comradeship—you would find to be of a surprising hardness: surprising, that is, to you, but not to the twenty-four boys at St Andrew's day school whom he coached in Rugby.

He was a bachelor and he would have said it was not by choice, that he wished nothing more in his life than a wife and children, and yet the truth—which he acknowledged now, adjusting the level of the lamp on his desk so that it cast a low and golden light on the cedar surround of the leather top—was that he had become so particular in his habits that it would have taken the most impossible charity for him to permit, good fellow though he was, his beloved to alter either the number of lamps or their intensity. Was that the truth? Or was it what he feared to be the truth? Did he not enjoy the company of women? Would he not, as they said, "adjust"?

It had not taken him long to discover that the women were by far the most interesting of the two sexes in the colony, although you would never imagine it the case if you met them with their menfolk present. For then they affected the most remarkable vapidity. But alone, or with their own sex, they revealed themselves as scientists when it came to the vectors of the human heart.

Besides—and he knew this himself—he was a vain man. They admired him and he liked to be admired. He liked to stretch his big body on their chintz-covered settees and accept another tea. He enjoyed this all a great deal and it would have been reprehensible had he not, at the same time, observed the little beetle of pride, the insect of lust, the segmented undulating caterpillar of conceit. So even while he stretched a leg to reveal a black wool ankle he was describing himself to himself, just as he might press his eye to his microscope and detail the mandibles of a colonial dragonfly. This was his great strength. It was his great weakness, too, an excess of detachment from his own life.

He knew he was clever but not distinguished, influential but not powerful, or if so only in the most indirect way through the fathers who took an interest in the rugby-playing of their sons.

Waiting for Monsieur Leplastrier, he arranged a piece of glass cullet on his desk, a large clear piece, like a great chunk of diamond, clear enough to make optical glass, made from the fine leached sands of Botany.

Glass was his enthusiasm but not his passion, and while—for instance—he had enjoyed giving his lectures ("Some Surprising Properties of Glass") to the East Sydney Mutual Improvement Society—the newspaper report of which had, he presumed, drawn the impending Leplastrier to him—he did not care sufficiently. There was something missing from his engine. It could not sustain the uphill grades.

This quality, however, was represented in plenty by the young lady who was being admitted to his household at this moment. The Reverend Dennis Hasset did not hear the doorbell. He arranged the cullet on his desk, turning it half a degree so that a ray of morning sun was refracted, just so, to strike (he giggled at the cheap theatricality) his framed degree from Cambridge. He was so taken by this preposterous showing off that he did not notice the "Miss" instead of the "Mr" when his guest was announced.

"Jolly good, Frazer," said Dennis Hasset. "Show him in."

He was surprised, of course, to find Monsieur Leplastrier in skirts, but he was not shocked. He was delighted. He made his petite visitor blush by continuing to call her monsieur and it took a while before he saw his insensitivity, and then he stopped it.

She sat opposite him. She was very young, but he could not tell exactly how young. Her manner, in many respects, was that of a woman in her twenties, although this impression was contradicted not only by her small stature, but in the way her confidence—so bright and clean at the beginning of a sentence where every word was as unequivocable as the unsmudged lines of her perfectly arched eyebrows—would seem to evaporate as she began, not quite to mumble, but to speak less distinctly, and her eyes, which had begun by almost *challenging* his, now slid away towards bookshelf or windowledge. There was also the charming, rather European way she gestured with her hands—they were very flexible and she could bend her palms right back from her wrists, her fingers back at another angle again—and there was something in these gestures, so ostensibly worldly, so expressive, even expansive which, combined with the shyness which her shifting eyes betrayed, gave an impression of great pluck. Dennis Hasset was much touched by her.

She wore an unusual garment: grey silk with a sort of trouser underneath. Dennis Hasset—no matter what his bishop thought—was not a radical, and this garment shocked him, well, not quite shocked, but let us say it gave a certain unsettling note to their interview, although the discord was muted by the quality of the silk and the obvious skill of the dressmaking. These were things he knew about. The garment declared its owner to be at once wealthy and not quite respectable. She was "smart," but not a beauty. There was about her, though, this sense of distillation. Her hands and feet were quite dainty, but it was in her face that he saw this great concentration of essence. It was not that her eyes were small, for they were large. The green iris was not a deeper green, or a brighter green. It was clear, and clean and, in some way he could not rationally explain, a great condensation of green. The eyes were gateways to a fierce and lively intelligence. They were like young creatures which had lost their shells, not yet able to defend themselves.

The mouth was small, but there was no suggestion of meanness, merely—with the lips straight—determination or—when they were relaxed and the plump lower lip was permitted to show—a disturbing (because it appeared to be unconscious) sensuality.

She wore a wide-brimmed grey hat with a kingfisher-blue feather which was, although "dashing," not quite the thing. Her hair—what one could see of it—was brown, less than perfectly tidy. This lack of care, when every other part of her was so neat, and pressed, produced an unsettling impression. The hair seemed wilful. It did not occur to him that her hair was, as she would put it, "like that."

In any case, he knew he had met a remarkable young woman, not his type, but unlike anyone he had known before.

"Of course," he said, pouring the leaves from Lucinda's first cup of tea into the little maidenhair fern he kept for just this purpose. "Of course you must, dash it."

He gave her a lot of milk, more than she liked. (It was in deference to her youth, which he felt he must insist on.)

"But you understand that although I write a pamphlet or two, I really don't know anything about the manufacturing process. I might look at a glass factory and see no more than you might."

Lucinda felt quite hot. If he would not help, she would go to the accountant whom Chas Ahearn had recommended. She would pay the accountant. She would write him a cheque and have him employ a man for her who could do what she required. Or was this man actually in the process of helping? He spoke less directly, more playfully, than she was accustomed to. Her mother had been proud to call a spade a spade. They had despised "shilly-shallyers." The tea was worse than Mrs O'Hagen's. The room was too hot. She was confused to end up with a clergyman when she had begun with a small pamphlet titled "On Laboratory Arts," a practical guide to glasswork in the chemistry laboratory. She had written to the printer who had supplied her with the address of the author.

She did not think of clergymen as practical people. Mr Horace (at Gulgong near Mitchell's Creek) had managed to chop off three fingers while trying to kill a sick hen. This man seemed to be confirming her prejudice, to be taking *pride* in confirming his uselessness.

"So I must warn you," he said, "that while I have adequate theory—in fact you have your saucer resting on it—I have no knowledge or experience of the commercial side."

"Then you cannot help me."

"On the contrary," he declared.

He saw her adjust to this. She did not say thank you, but rather: "The vendors must not know me as a woman."

"And why not?"

"They will act strange," she said, gesturing with her flexible fingers and palms, letting her eyes roll away. (Should she pay the clergyman for his labour?) "It would occupy you a great deal," she suggested. "There would be books—wouldn't there?—to examine." (He cannot be poor, she thought, if he burns four lamps on a sunny day.)

"Yes," he agreed, "a great deal to do. But the object is a lovely one, is it not? It is the object we should celebrate.

He stared at her so excitedly that she looked away, blushing crimson. When she looked up again he saw her eyes had hardened in some way. She lifted her chin. She sat straighter in her chair.

He had been misunderstood.

Dennis Hasset hurried to correct the situation. He spoke about glass. He showed her a large lump of cullet, like a little piece of glass rock. She knew nothing, nothing at all. Thousands of pounds to spend, and she knew nothing about it. He insisted she handle it. From his drawer he produced a piece of waterglass. He rang for Frazer and had him bring a beaker that they might dissolve it. He showed her the green glass of Melbourne, that colour being produced by iron oxides in the sand, and let her feel the pure white grains of Botany where one could find a good three feet of fine leached sand, its impurities washed away by centuries of rain. From this Botany sand you could produce the lens for a telescope this clear while—here, he showed her, held the two lenses side by side so she might compare—the lens from Hallet's of London had a faint yellow tinge to it, by no means desirable.

Lucinda thought this Botany lens quite lovely. She took a small lace handkerchief, one of her mama's, from her purse so she might hold the lens without contaminating it. And even when the vicar told her it did not matter if she smeared it, she would not touch it with her naked fingers, which were—she was too aware of this—damp with excitement.

Soon he had all manner of things arranged across his red leather desk. These were not placed with the artfulness whereby he had decorated his study in preparation for the French professor. No, here were particles of glass. A square of poison blue made that colour by the addition of lead oxide. A melted lump of common "beer" in the shape of an old man's face. He said it was the image of his bishop. He said his bishop did not like him, and she would see this in his expression. She saw it was true. He showed her a glass brick, the sole survivor of his compression tests. Lastly, of course, a Prince Rupert's drop which its owner offered to demonstrate.

"No, please. You must not."

"Why must I not?" Dennis Hasset was astonished to find himself peeved. For a moment he disliked his visitor. He did not like the directness of her eyes. He took exception to her tone. He fished in his bottom drawer, looking for some pliers. He found a screwdriver he thought might do, and then he rejected it because the performance would have been inelegant and—besides—he knew she was right. This did not improve his temper. "*Why* must I not?"

"Because you know what will happen," the girl said simply, "and so do I, and when it is gone you can't look forward to it any more." And then, seeing in his face some of the temper for which he was known—"Oh." She did not say it, but shaped her lips as if she had.

"Oh?" he asked, but in a belligerent sort of way which he watched, himself, with surprise, as if to say, Ah, so this is how I feel.

"Mr Hasset, I am so very sorry."

He felt himself seen through.

"Miss Leplastrier, there is nothing to be sorry for."

"I came to you for help. You were kind to me. I began to argue with you about the disposal of your own possessions. Probably I am jealous of you."

"Surely not." He shut the bottom drawer and placed the Prince Rupert's drop on the blotting pad in front of him.

"Yes, quite jealous." She wished to look down, to bow her head, but she would not let herself.

Dennis Hasset saw the eyes become excessively bright, like stones placed in water. She wore an odd smile, a neatly tied bow which only just kept the trembling parcel of the face together.

"And why," he said, leaning forward, feeling clumsy, seeking levity, and therefore imitating the accent of an Irishman. "And why," he said, "would that be now?"

His brogue was perfect but she did not know that the Irish were such figures of fun that to duplicate their speech was cause for mirth. She knew only that the men walked in front while their women followed behind like prisoners.

"I am jealous because the drop is yours, not mine. Because, more than that, you can enter the glassworks."

"Through the main door, just as you may."

"But I cannot, don't you see? They will not treat me with anything but the greatest condescension. And, besides, I would be made into the creature they imagined I was. Do you understand me?"

She held him with her eyes. She was a child. She was not a child. Her eyes were clear and steady while her voice amplified the slightest trembling in her lower lip.

He was held by the strength and touched by the frailty. "No," he said, "I do not understand you."

"By the way they looked at me, by their perception of me, they would make me into the creature they perceived. I would feel myself becoming a lesser thing. It is the power of men."

"But I am a man."

"No," she said, too impatient to let him develop his argument. "Of *men*, men in a group, men in their certainty, men on a street corner, or in a hall. It is like a voodoo. Do you know a voodoo?"

"Yes," he said, impressed, not caring that Frazer had come to signal the arrival of lunch to which he had invited three distinguished ladies of the parish and a Mr Jenkins, newly arrived from Edinburgh with a letter of introduction. He waved away his gesticulating servant. Lucinda imagined a fly. It was not the fly season.

"You are appointing me your proxy, then," the clergyman said, "is that it?"

"You are making fun of me, and most likely there is justice in that. I am being cowardly," she nodded her head, but the nod was for herself, not her listener. "It is obvious to anyone that I am being cowardly, but I have thought about it and it seems I must work within the limitations of my character."

"I was most certainly not making fun of you."

"You would have every right . . ."

"Whoa, Dobbin!" cried Dennis Hasset.

Lucinda stopped.

"You wish to buy a factory to make glass. 'Tis a simple enough matter. Is that it?" He smiled. The smile did what the Irish accent never could have.

"Oh, yes, it is!"

"And you need a little help."

"I *do* know factories, you see," she said leaning forward. "We—I mean my dear parents, when they were alive—inspected many of them, and I am well aware that they are most usually foul and frightening places, but I do not wish this to put me off. I will face it, of course."

"I will be there in a moment, Frazer," said Dennis Hasset. "Yes, yes. Don't worry about him. No, stay, please. Soon, soon, though, I have clergyman's business to attend to. Not nearly so amusing as glass. But yes, I will help you. I did not know you half an hour ago, Miss Leplastrier, and I will tell you I am surprised to hear myself say 'yes' with such enthusiasm, but upon my word I do believe I am looking forward to the exercise. We will need to co-opt, of course. I have a friend, a very clever chap called Dawson . . ."

"I have more than ten thousand pounds."

Dennis Hasset, who had risen to his feet to conclude the interview, sat down again, his face animated by a quite remarkable smile. "The deuce you do."

"I only wish to invest half in this venture." She was apologetic, sorry she had mentioned the sum. She was only a girl. She had done nothing to deserve such a sum. She imagined she saw censure in his eyes.

"And the rest?" he asked, plunging into the questionn before his natural politeness could restrain him. If he had "more than ten thousand pounds" he would leave the confusions of the Church tomorrow.

"As for the remainder, I am being cautious."

"Miss Leplastrier, you are being quite the opposite. You are being admirably reckless. When we began our little meeting I imagined it would be my stern duty to warn you off your passion. Now it seems to me that you possess it—I mean the passion—and you would be a fool to squander it on anything less. And I will tell you, too, before Frazer comes to cane me for disobedience, why it is that I will so willingly assist you."

"Because you have an affection for glass," suggested Lucinda. "Surely," she spread her neat little hands above the desk on which the glass curios still rested, "you made your motive most apparent?"

"You are unduly confident. No, it is not because I am amused by glass, but because you have a passion. It is the passion I am helping you for. I am a cold man warming himself in front of someone else's fire.

"But surely a passion is not an admirable thing?"

"A dangerous thing," allowed the clergyman who was now sorting out his little objects, the square of blue, the cut yellow, the melted beer with the face of a bishop, the glass brick, the phial of sand, the Prince Rupert's drop, placing them all in their correct places, folding his journals, clearing his desk in preparation for less interesting work, remembering his afternoon christening, his football training, his choir practice, his evensong, the sermon to be written, the penknife to be purchased, the paper for the sermon to be cut in the way he liked it, the size of a postcard. "A dangerous thing," he agreed, remembering also that he had only two days before the "inquisition" on his recent sermons. The Bishop thought him a Latitudinarian. He wished he had that much faith.

"I am jealous of your passion, Miss Leplastrier. I will enjoy helping you to exercise it."

"But you will help me to exercise it carefully, I trust." She stood also, collecting her mother's gloves and purse. "You will stop me from coming to harm with it, for I am very young and as yet know nothing of the world."

She held out her hand, like a man. He hesitated, then took the hand and shook it. It was very warm. You could not help but be aware of the wild passage of blood on the other side of its wall, veins, capillaries, sweat glands, tiny factories in the throws of complicated manufacture. Dennis Hasset looked at the eyes and, knowing how eyes worked, was astonished, not for the first time, at the infinite complexity of Creation, wondering how this thing, this instrument for seeing, could transmit so clearly its entreaty while at the same time—Look, I am only an eye—denying that it was doing anything of the sort.

35

A Betting Ticket

As Oscar slit open the long blue envelope and found it "empty," he smiled, imagining that the Reverend Mr Stratton had sealed it at the dining-room table. This was, as Mrs Stratton liked to remind him (forcefully, apologetically), a dangerous habit because he would have all his letters jumbled up amongst the pudding dishes and the sherry glasses and there had been at least one instance of a letter to a bishop being dispatched to a gossipy friend and—it was here that serious damage was done to Hugh Stratton's career—and vice versa.

But on this clean summer morning it at first appeared that the envelope, rather than containing the wrong letter, contained no letter at all and had not Oscar, who was more cautious than his jerky impulsive manner might suggest, held it up to the light, he would not have detected the most unpleasant message Hugh Stratton had slipped inside.

It was this: a betting ticket, Oscar's own betting ticket, not Hugh Stratton's. It was issued by John Rush, Bookmaker, c/o Tattersall's Club. There was more than one series of marks on this ticket. The first was the fat pencilled scrawl of John Rush's hunch-backed clerk who had bet Oscar 8–1 against a filly named Nigger Princess. After this there were some other marks in a finer pencil: the notations Oscar made on every losing ticket—punter's code for such things as position at the start, condition of the track, and what, if any, unexplained phenomena (acts of God) had prevented his scientifically calculated victory. In the case of Nigger Princess, she had been boxed in at the rails and never found her way clear. Had you been able to decipher these notations you may have gathered this fact was in some way Oscar Hopkins's fault.

The winning slips, of course, were all kept by the bookmaker's clerk, but the losing ones were all carried back to Oxford and ordered as meticulously as he had once ordered his mother's buttons. Their contents were transferred to a smudged journal ruled up with careful columns and the tickets themselves were held in a series of small manila envelopes in a shoe box marked *Private* which was kept in Oscar's bottom drawer.

How this betting ticket came to find its way to Hennacombe was a most unpleasant mystery. Oscar, who had, until this moment shown a lightness, evan a jauntiness in manner as he sat himself at his little table, was now prickled by a hot and suspicious sweat.

It was a violation. It suggested other violations, other secret and improbable intrusions. Mr Stratton had said: "If you walk to prayers at Kidlington, I will know about it." As he turned over the betting ticket and found the clergyman's tight black hand there, this no longer seemed hyperbole.

Hugh Stratton wrote this on the betting ticket: "Can I assure your father that this is not yours? Or can you, instead, assure me that such a game can indeed be played for profit?" It was signed H.S.

It did not occur to Oscar to label Hugh Stratton mad; that his mentor should attempt to blackmail him surprised but did not shock him. His pity for the clergyman enabled him to forgive this and all the other peevish and petty acts he continually committed against all those who came into his orbit. It was Hugh Stratton's nature that, as he became more seemingly unlovable, he was loved the more.

But what did shock Oscar was that this very private piece of paper should be spirited from his room to be used as ammunition against him. Who was the thief? Had Hugh Stratton himself paid one of his "flying visits" while Oscar was safely in tutorial? He did not know. He also saw it did not matter.

Oscar fetched his pen and ink and—without thinking that Hugh Stratton was, once more, responsible for making his porridge cold wrote:

> My dear Mr Stratton, how excited I was to receive today one of your rare (and therefore much looked forward to) epistles, and how disappointed I was therefore to discover that it was not what it appeared to be, that you had sealed the envelope, and thereby excluded what we had both wished you to include. I am sure the good Mrs Millar has, by now, discovered the letter amongst the dinner dishes and I enclose a stamp in order that it might be sped on to me and I may hear how things go in Hennacombe and how the fund for the restoration of St Anne's progresses. Professor Arnold asked to be reminded to you and said something about a borrowed book but I am afraid

> I have forgot the message and, if this makes no sense to you, I will go and ask him again in order that I may deliver it more faithfully. My fondest remarks to Mrs Stratton. Your, etc., O. Hopkins.

From that date Oscar left his betting tickets at the course and all the while he was at Oxford, wrote his form records in a code decipherable to no one but himself.

As for Mr Stratton, he believed every word of Oscar's letter. It was neither right nor fair that a gambling student should make him feel so soiled.

36

Une Petite Amie

Lucinda did not really want a factory. She was frightened of it. She walked down to Sussex Street and watched working men emerging from the mills and wharves there. She was repulsed by them just as she was moved by them—the condition of their trouser turn-ups, the weariness of their jackets. They were alien creatures. She watched them as through a sheet of glass, as we, a century later, might look down on the slums of Delhi as a jumbo jet comes in to land. She could not know that she would, within two years, beyond the boundaries of this history, be brought so low that she would think herself lucky to work at Edward Jason's Druitt Street pickle factory, that she would plunge her hands into that foul swill and, with her bands boiled red and her eyes stinging, stand on the brink of the great satisfaction of her life.

But at this time (1859) her hands were white and dry. She pitied the workers their poverty and weariness. And yet there was a way they looked at her that made her fear and hate them. It was her age, her sex, her class. She knew it. She knew it as well as you do, but the knowledge did not make it any easier for she was, so to speak, contracted to proceed. It was the factory, she felt, that gave her the entrée to the vicar of Woollahra's home. It was glass that gave her this comfort. And as a result of her meeting with Dennis Hasset a kind of a reduction, an intensification, took place so that whilst, previously, the town of Sydney had been wide and windy, the streets rude with larrikins and so many "proper" people prepared to hoot and laugh and point at anything outside their narrow experience of life, and the whole place a-clatter with hooves and rolling iron and such a wide and formless canvas of spitting, coughing strangers that she could not endure an hour without the onset of a headache, and even though the library in George Street (her chosen retreat) had reassuring walls of books, busts of Voltaire and Shakespeare, it remained a cold, green, formal place, the territory of glowering men in high collars who might—this happened, too—"tsk, tsk" to see here there—so she remained, even amongst her books, a foreigner, friendless, without a map, until, finding the vicar of Woollahra almost by accident, the world shrank back around her.

Only then did she allow herself to see how frightened and lonely she had been.

Having discovered that glass was the medium wherein a friendship could flourish, she did not intend to let it go. Her need was such that the lamps stayed burning in the vicar of Woollahra's study until an hour better suited to an illegal Pak-Ah-Pu parlour in George Street. Such an offence would not go unremarked in Sydney, although had you brought this to her attention she would have asked that you refrain from patronizing her. She was her mother's daughter. She felt that she and Hasset were above the "ruck and tumble." They were business associates with business to discuss, manufacturers combating chemistry, philosophers with philosophy to deal with. They must study the musty journals of the Prince Rupert's Glassworks as silently as detectives investigating forgery. There were also sample bottles. My bottles, she thought. Blue, amber, clear; bottles for acid, pickles, poison, beer, wine, pills, jam, bottles with vine leaves, laughing jackasses, flowers, gum nuts, serpents and PROPERTY OF imprinted on their underside.

Years later when she remembered how she and the vicar had looked at bottles, with what abstracted superior curiosity they had examined them, so removed from the loud and sweaty business of sauces and pickles and jams, she judged her young self harshly and forgot how much of what she would become was already there. She was neither as ignorant nor as innocent as she would later imagine she had been. But she did enjoy handling these bottles, and she could not see how one could be judged "improper" for staying up late at night to do so. She was not ashamed, not of this, not of, sometimes (usually, often) falling asleep in the leather armchair beside the fire where she would, some time later, be woken with a mug of cream-rich cocoa. She clasped her hands around the mug and looked into the fire, wishing only that she did not have to travel the moonpale clay tracks to her hotel.

The girl did not know enough to care about the opinion of bourgeois society, but Dennis Hasset had no such excuse. He knew better, but gave way—although not without a certain amount of irritation—to the clearer demands of his protégé.

Lucinda had the habit of arriving at any time that suited her. She always apologized. She always hoped she did not inconvenience or interrupt, but such was the way she tilted her chin that she did not appear apologetic at all. He would come back from giving a lecture on "Common Salt," say, at a Mutual Improvement Association, and find her sitting by his fire in his study, or reading a book at his desk. It was true, as he often said from the speaker's lectern, that he saw education as a ladder standing on earth and reaching up to heaven and that to every high and glorious position there was a way from every condition of life, but he would not, just the same, have suffered anyone else reading his books as Lucinda did. She removed his crenulated leather bookmarks and put them back too early in the story. He would ring for a sandwich and only after he had waited too long for it would he discover that Cook was busy making apple pancakes for the girl who was now ensconced, reading, in the dining room.

And yet he thought her, against all this evidence, to be quite independent. On the nights she was absent he imagined her reading at Petty's Hotel; he had no suspicion that she had—as a lonely cat will always present itself at more than one back door—also found a place in Mr d'Abbs menagerie.

Mr d'Abbs, as you will recall, was the principal of an accountancy firm, and supposed to be an associate of Mr Chas Ahearn. Lucinda had consulted Mr d'Abbs in secret because she was unsure of Dennis Hasset's business acumen. She lacked the courage to tell the vicar of Woollahra that she had sought this second opinion, that she had, as a result, been invited home to dinner and eaten goose at the long dark table beneath walls crowded with landscape paintings of the country Mr d'Abbs dubbed "Paradise." On those nights when she judged that Dennis Hasset had had enough of her, this is where she went, to sit with Mr d'Abbs, Mrs Burrows, Miss Shaddock, Miss Malcolm and Mr Calvitto. She liked to be with people.

Dennis Hasset's diary shows Lucinda's arrival in his life. It records the first meeting – the thirty minutes allocated Monsieur Leplastrier on the first Tudsday after Whitsunday, and, thereafter, a great number of red slashes across previous appointments, committee meetings particularly (St Andrew's Building, Ragged Schools, Hot Breakfasts for the Poor) but also the Zoological Society, a dinner with an old friend, and even a vestry meeting which was shifted three times within a month. He could never refuse her, and although he often imagined that he would, on the next occasion, send her packing, he never did. He was thirty-three years old, a grown man, but he was no match for her. Besides – and this surely is the heart of it – no matter how irritated he might be to see her sitting so proprietorially in his study chair, he always felt invigorated by her company, and when she fell asleep he sat contentedly opposite her and smiled while she snored.

But he knew his behaviour was reckless. It was not consistent with his character. He wished success, and comfort. He hoped he would end his days in a bishop's palace with an intelligent dean to work beside him. And yet he drove this girl – biologically a mature female of the species – drove her himself to Petty's Hotel on three, sometimes four nights a week. She was rarely there before midnight, and often it was two a.m. when he rang the bell for the night porter. This night porter knew the young lady was also a friend of Mr d'Abbs. He found the situation amusing. But when this night porter winked at Dennis Hasset, the vicar was so tickled by the man's scurrilous misunderstanding, that he chuckled all the way home, sitting up on the box seat where his servant should have been, a parson in a parson's clothes in a city given over, at this hour, to footpads and the push.

Before August was properly started, Bishop Dancer had him in to give him what he liked to call a "caning." They did not like each other, anyway. The Bishop was a hunter after hounds, a High Tory with no tolerance for the subtleties of Whig theology. This was not the first of their disagreements. There had been a fierce fight about a sermon in which Dennis Hasset had argued against eternal damnation by suggesting (You are not there to *suggest*," the Bishop had roared) that it was ridiculous to postulate a God with a less well-developed moral sense than our own and that damnation was, therefore, unthinkable. The Bishop would not waste his time arguing the point. Hasset was not to preach this Latitudinarian rot. When the vicar said he was not a Latitudinarian, the Bishop's face became as purple as his surplice.

The Bishop began this interview provocatively. He did not imagine himself provocative. Rather he saw himself as understanding – he came right to the heart of what he thought the problem was: "Of course, Hasset, we all have our *appetites.*"

Dennis Hasset did not imagine himself unduly fastidious, but he found this way of approaching Lucinda Leplastrier quite disgusting. She was a milk-breathed child he watched over when she slept by his fire. For a moment his handsome mouth looked as if it held a putrid oyster, but only for an instant, and Bishop Dancer did not notice.

The bishop was one to talk about appetites. He was a great fellow for hanging game until it was maggoty. Dennis Hasset tried to make him see the nature of his relationship with Miss Leplastrier. He spoke well and honestly. The Bishop nodded, rubbing his big hands across his high, bald dome, let his tongue show between his teeth, screwed up his eyes.

"Then post the banns," he said, with perfect misunderstanding.

"No, no," laughed the vicar of Woollahra, "we are too queer a pair to contemplate."

"Well," said Bishop Dancer, who was sick of trying to understand what the man was saying, "you would be wise to marry someone."

"Indeed, yes."

And on that puzzling note, the interview ended. The Bishop imagined he had instructed the vicar to give up his *"petite amie"* and the vicar thought he had satisfactorily explained the innocence of their relationship: they were too queer a pair to contemplate.

37

A Game of Cards

Later, when she knew Mr d'Abbs's house well—and she grew to know it very well indeed—she could smile at how she had perceived it, how she had exaggerated it in her mind, stretched and tangled it until it was a palace, a castle, the sort of home a peer might have, stretched out along the shores of Rushcutters Bay.

It was not nearly as grand as she had, in her country innocence, imagined it. But it was the sort of house that leads to exaggeration. It was a ball of string. An untidy confusion of passages and stairs, the sort of place where you are always arriving where you do not expect. There are long gloomy passages leading to bright alcoves containing nothing but a pair of uncomfortable chairs with dusty antimacassars. You go looking for the library and find yourself in a large laundry where the cememt floor is covered with piles of tangled sheets. You look to retrace your steps and find yourself in a garden where terraced paths lead down—via steps whose treads are far too high—to the harbour. The hydrangeas are clipped for the winter and there is a gardener with rum on his breath (and odd socks on his feet) who offers to show you the scars on his back, the droppings of a wallaby, the scratchings of a bandicoot or a leech which he will pull inside out with the aid of a twig—"T'only way to kill'un missus."

The house taught Lucinda almost as much about Mr Ahearn as it did about Mr d'Abbs. It was obvious that Mr Ahearn had never seen the house. It would have offended him in every way imaginable. He would have thought it to be wasteful, ostentatious, unchristian. He could not, Lucinda realized, know Mr d'Abbs at all, and yet such was his desire to deliver her to "the right hands" that he had pretended acquaintance of a man he had only heard of.

Mr d'Abbs was a small man of forty years and very particular and precise in all his movements. He dressed expensively, artistically. He favoured serge and corduroy in olive green or navy blue. His ties were wool or even silk. He liked a walking stick, although he had no limp. He had a small smile, quite ironic, and it twisted his thin moustache and made him look not quite respectable. He enjoyed being thought of in this way—it was no commercial liability in Sydney—and yet it was not the truth at all.

Mr d'Abbs was married and had three children, and yet it seemed this family was insufficient for his needs. His wife was small and pretty. Everyone remarked on her smile and her golden ringlets. Lucinda was immediately drawn to her. She wished to sit and talk quietly with her, but it was not a house of quiet talk and Mrs d'Abbs would sit at table with anger in her eyes and, more often than not, excuse herself halfway through the pudding. And perhaps it was because of this, because the marriage was so unhappy, that Mr d'Abbs liked to collect people around him and assemble them, not just one night a week, but every night, in his drawing room.

Lucinda could not have imagined a room exactly like it, and although she had read descriptions of many grand rooms in novels, there was nothing in her literary experience which prepared her for the carelessness of Mr d'Abbs house, the way a rug might be thrown across a gilt-backed couch to hide its bursting innards, the length, the breadth, the scandalous quantities of dust, the giddy electric view of the crags and battlements of the eastern shore of Rushcutters Bay. Within this grand expensive tangle danced the pristine Mr d'Abbs. He was a honey-eater amidst raging lantana, a lyrebird scratching the sticks and leaves of its untidy bower.

Neither Elizabeth Leplastrier nor Mitchell's Creek had prepared her for this sort of habitat. You do not find this sort of character in a milking shed, and this was something of which Mr d'Abbs was himself aware. He would stand at his favourite place, his back against the gloss-doored bookcases, a glass of good French cognac in his hand, and look around his wonderful drawing room and not quite believe that it was him, Jimmy Dabbs, Ditcher Dabbs's boy.

The walls of his drawing room were crowded with pictures of every style and quality. They were crammed and jammed into every space available—water-colours with dusty glass in front of them, oils with grand gilt frames, chromos of masterpieces, caricatures, a colour engraving (from the *London Illustrated News*) showing Lord Elgin marching into Peking, a crude pen rendering showing blacks attacking a settler's cabin. He propped paintings by Sir Arthur Gibbs, RA against the skirting board so that they could make way for the landscapes of his new discovery, Mr Calvitto, who was, at this moment, standing out on his veranda gazing out into the evening gloom of Rushcutters Bay. Mr Calvitto had a commercial interest in promoting the Tuscan wheat varieties, which he claimed to be immune to the rust disease that still plagued the colony. But he was also an Italian, an artist, an atheist, and these were all interesting things to be. Mr d'Abbs was pleased to hear him talk about anything he chose to talk about. Mr d'Abbs did not have a lot to say himself, not now. He would rather smile and nod and be amazed at the turns life can take. And in this last respect he shared more than he knew with his new protégé, Miss Leplastrier, although he found her, for all her obvious pluck, uncommonly dull. Later in the evening, he knew, she would come out of her shell, but this was no use to him now. She made him feel a little stiff, and it was not how he liked to feel. She had taken a chair next to Miss Shaddock who was doing her needlework beside the little walnut table. He understood Miss Leplastrier was unhappy. She was an orphan, of course, and new to Sydney. He winked at her. She looked away.

Lucinda sat with her hands in her lap and presented a perfect wall to the room. No one could have guessed her feelings, which were so contradictory it is a wonder she could contain them without fidgeting.

First: she was, like Jimmy d'Abbs, amazed to find herself in such a place. The room, with its tangle of paintings and rugs, its odd mixture of fastidiousness and sloth, suggested more complex possibilities in life than she had previously imagined, and while it offended her carefully inculcated senses of order and restraint, it was also most attractive.

Second: she was grateful to Mr d'Abbs for his kindness, and she would continue—no matter what evidence arrived to say she should not—always to be loyal to him on this account.

Third: she was disturbed by Mrs d'Abbs whose eyes she found continually glancing in her direction. She now wondered if she had done something to offend.

Fourth: she did not like the way Mr d'Abbs had held his children—out, away and at a distance as if they were, even when bathed, too sticky to be encouraged to affection.

Fifth: she felt very lonely. Mr d'Abbs's friends made her feel alien. Miss Malcolm, Miss Shaddock, Mrs Burrows, Mr Calvitto—they were polite to her, she thought, but were in no hurry to have her a member of their circle.

Sixth: she was disturbed to find Mr d'Abbs and Mr Calvitto irreligious. When Mr d'Abbs winked she pretended not to see him.

Seventh: she would rather be in her own bed, drifting into sleep. This territory, between sleep and waking, was her only real home and it was this she sought in Dennis Hasset's armchairs.

Eighth: she was waiting for Mr Calvitto to come in from the veranda so the real business of the evening could begin.

They were waiting for Mrs Burrows to leave so they could play cards. Mrs Burrows would not leave until Mr Calvitto was ready. Mr Calvitto was admiring Rushcutters Bay as it appeared in the evening gloom. Although he was a recent arrival in the circle he had already formed a friendship with Mrs Burrows although no one could speak clearly about what this friendship amounted to.

Mrs Burrows, a vocal supporter of the American rebels, was the widow of an army captain who had been killed by blacks in the "Falls" district near the head-waters of the Manning River. Lucinda did not like her at all. She had reprimanded Lucinda on the subject of the blacks. Mrs Burrows would have them given "bye-bye damper," bush bread made from strychnine-poisoned flour. She knew this was extreme. She liked to be extreme. She was one of those who claimed no white man should be hanged for shooting blacks in self-defence. Her opinions suited her face which was red in the nose, drawn in the cheeks, pinched. She was a critical woman and one would not have expected her to have a friendship with Mr Calvitto, on the grounds of atheism alone. She was so strongly against card-playing that they must all wait before they could play. But here she was, meekly waiting for an atheist to return from the veranda so she could announce her intention to go home.

Then they could play cribbage. Lucinda pressed herself back into the wing-back chair. It was doubtless sinful, but she did like cribbage. She liked it very much indeed. She found herself, during the day, looking forward to the game as she might not so long ago have looked forward to golden-syrup dumplings. When she played cards she was not dull or angry. She laughed. She looked prettier. She could feel her own transformation. People smiled at her.

She was moved by playing cards in a way she could not explain even to herself. She had a feeling, not the same, but similar, to when they fought the grass fire on Bishop's Plain—that line of people, men, women, children, with their sacks and beating poles, even nasty old Michael Halloran, but all lined up in the choking smoke. Cards was not like this, and yet it was. They were joined in a circle, an abstraction of human endeavour.

But now she was lonely, and aware of her isolation, and everyone's isolation one from the other.

There was a Dutch lamp—it was made from black iron filigree and had a gracefully shaped white mantle—above a round walnut table with three legs. Beside this table sat Miss Malcolm, the governess. She was a pretty young thing, or had been not so long before. On the other side of the table sat Miss Shaddock with her needlework. While Miss Malcolm was light and wispy in her nature, Miss Shaddock was dark and heavy. And while Miss Malcolm gave the impression of greater innocence than her age would agree with, Miss Shaddock gave off an odour of foreboding, as if whatever venture was discussed must come to an unhappy ending.

And yet Mr d'Abbs, leaning against his case of books, was obviously so contented, so pleased to have the company of Miss Shaddock, to value her every bit as much as Mr Calvitto who was now—Lucinda could hear his leather soles squeaking—beginning to stir from his reverie on the veranda.

Mr d'Abbs collected people. It was his passion. It was a distinction that Captain Burrows had been killed whilst bravely defending isolated settlers, that Miss Malcolm was the sister of a tenor, that Miss Shaddock's needlework had been presented to the Prince of Wales. Every now and then Mr Horace Borrodaile would drop in. Once he had brought Mr Henry Parkes (Mr d'Abbs still held his IOU). Here was Mr Calvitto, now, standing at the open door and speaking authoritatively about the landscape.

Lucinda did not listen to Mr Calvitto immediately. There was a cow bogged in the mangrove mud flats below the house. No one in the room thought to rescue it. It was not their cow. They were waiting for Mrs Burrows to leave so they could play cards.

"Shouldn't we do something about the cow?" she asked Miss Malcolm, but Miss Malcolm, although she looked at her, did not seem interested in what she said. Lucinda was indignant, but did not know what to do. No one would look at her. She felt a great sense of boredom, of purposelessness, sweep over her. The beast bellowed. It knew it would die. Its own kind would not help it.

"Yes, yes," Mr Calvitto was saying to Miss Shaddock, "but it is not a Christian landscape." Mr Calvitto had sunken eyes and a doleful countenance. He had black curly hair and a strong, wiry black beard. At the back of all this, like lamps placed at the back of a long room, one was aware of his eyes glittering. He was like a man who had been robbed of something precious and is waiting for others to see the injustice so they might restore it to him. "It is not a Christian landscape at all."

"You are not a Christian," said Miss Shaddock, her voice shaking as it always did when the conversation took this turn.

"That is not the point, Irene," said Mrs Burrows.

"God made all the landscape," said Miss Shaddock. "Surely you believe that, Mildred?"

"Of course," said Mrs Burrows but turned to Mr Calvitto.

Lucinda was impatient this this conversation sould continue. It was hypocritical to proclaim your Christianity whilst this suffering continued. And yet she knew what Mr Calvitto meant. She had felt it herself, and her mind drifted to the back creek. In this place the water had been dark and still, brown from tannin, cut by church-like motes of sunlight. Here she had plucked her doll bald. Here she had wept when her papa died. Here she had seen two blacks standing as still as trees. She was sixteen years old. She held her breath. There were two more. Another two. This was in the years when the blacks of

Parramatta were defeated. Their trunks were brown with mud, cracked like iron bark. She was frightened, not that they would hurt her, it was a bigger fear than that. She turned and ran, ran across the flat green pasture with plovers shrieking above her, ran out into the sunlight where the yellow sap-bright fence posts, peeled of slippery bark, with round shiny backs and rough straight sides, were lying in a higgledy-piggledy pile on a bed of stringy bruised bark.

She knew what Mr Calvitto meant. You could feel it in the still shadows along watercourses. She felt ghosts here, but not Christian ghosts, not John the Baptist or Jesus of Galilee. There were other spirits, other stories, slippery as shadows.

She would have liked to say so. She was capable of ordering her ideas and her thoughts and presenting them properly, but she knew that only Mr d'Abbs would welcome it. He was standing there, leaning against his bookcases, swilling his brandy balloon. He looked at her and winked again as if to say: "What a jolly show Calvitto makes. What fun, eh?"

The beast in the mangroves bellowed. Lucinda thought: I should not be here.

"What I do not understand about you, Mr Calvitto," Miss Malcolm said, "is how you live." She did not say "without faith" but everyone understood the meaning of her question.

But Mrs Burrows began to rise, and whether this was intended to prevent the answering of the question or no, this is what it did. She made a small exclamation of pain, holding her bony back. "Your business would be more prosperous," Mrs Burrows said, "if you were earlier in bed."

Did this mean that Mrs Burrows knew about their gambling? Miss Malcolm turned her head a sharp, fast ten degrees to catch Miss Shaddock's eye. Miss Shaddock's eye remained steadfastly on her needlework but her white plump neck turned slowly red.

"Stay the night," said Mr d'Abbs. "I will have a bed made up for you."

"Please," said Mrs d'Abbs who had, until now, remained still and silent, her knitting in her lap (it always upset Miss Shaddock to see how *slowly* Mrs d'Abbs knitted)—they were, none of them, none except Lucinda who was new and did not count, sympathetic to Mrs d'Abbs. "Please *do* stay."

"Thank you, no, Mr Calvitto will drive me home."

"We will deliver Miss Leplastrier to her hotel." said Mrs Burrows, arranging her shawl.

"Oh, no," said Lucinda looking for Mr d'Abbs for help. "Not yet."

Mr d'Abbs raised an eyebrow. Miss Shaddock looked over her rimless spectacles, frowning. There had been too much passion in this outburst.

"Mmmmm," said Mrs Burrows. It was a technique she had. It suggested she knew things.

"We are not right for you," said a great booming male voice from the doorway. "We are below you, Mrs Burrows. You would not be seen *dead* with us. And who can blame you?"

"Nonsense," shouted Mr d'Abbs, obviously very pleased.

"You think me a scoundrel," said the newcomer to Mrs Burrows who, whilst departing with Mr Calvitto, managed to look at once severe, but also pleased to be teased in such a way.

"Fig, you are a rogue," said Mr d'Abbs, making a face at the pink-cheeked bald-headed man with the tight, round little paunch. The face, a crumpled-up grimace, begged Mr Fig to be quiet for just a moment.

"Has the second sitting begun?" asked Mr Fig, winking hugely and miming card shuffling while Mrs Burrows was helped into her coat.

"You must away," he said to Lucinda, wagging a finger and sucking in his cheeks in what was a very poor imitation of the woman who was now—at last, Miss Malcolm's shoulders lost their tense edge—leaving the house. "This is a madhouse," said Mr Fig with relish.

Mrs d'Abbs stood up. She tucked her knitting in the hatbox she used for that purpose. Lucinda did not hear what she said.

"Accepted, Henny," said Mr d'Abbs to his wife.

Lucinda was sorry that Mrs d'Abbs should slink away like this, put her arms around her breast, round her shoulders, and be so apologetic with her body while all the time—anyone with half a soul could see it—her eyes were filled with a grey and watery fury.

She did not like the things that happened in her house. She therefore had a right to put a stop to them. Her husband had an obligation to support her. If he were one quarter of the good fellow he pretended to be, he would feel it to be no sacrifice. Yet even whilst Lucinda was incensed on Mrs d'Abbs's behalf she also acknowledged that she wished to play cards, to empty her purse upon the table, and therefore she must be one of those whose will kept Mrs d'Abbs's shoulders rounded, for if she stood up straight she would, surely, send Miss Malcolm off to prepare her lessons for the morrow, Miss Shaddock home to her rooms in

Macquarie Street, and tell Mr Fig to return when he was sober.

Mrs d'Abbs, of course, did none of these things. She kissed her husband on the cheek and nodded and smiled agreeably before taking herself off to bed.

Lucinda rose from her chair and went to Mr d'Abbs who was removing the cards from their hiding place in the bookcase.

"Are you feeling lucky?" he asked her.

"Indeed, yes,' said Lucinda, 'but the poor beast is most unfortunate."

"Fig," called Mr d'Abbs, "you should hear the names you are being called."

"No, no," said Lucinda, laughing. "Mr Fig, it is not true. There is a beast caught in the mud flats."

"Yes?" said Mr d'Abbs.

"I wondered if perhaps you might send a man to free it."

Mr d'Abbs looked at her and blinked. Lucinda was embarrassed. She had offended him in some way, but could not see ow.

"I will see to it immediately," said Mr d'Abbs, but although he smiled, Lucinda did not feel easy.

"I hope I have not spoken out of turn."

"Of course not, of course not." But the truth was that he could not bear to be given what he thought were "orders" in his own home and although he went through an elaborate mime of leaving the room to order Jack the gardener to attend to it, he did no such thing at all.

38

A Duck to Water

"Ha-ha," Lucinda said. "You have beaten me, Mr Fig."

"I have, Miss Leplastrier," said Fig who had recently appeared in the "Ethiopian Concert" at the Balmain School of Arts. Then he had aroused much mirth with his impressino of a nigger ticket-taker, but now he rounded his vowels and rolled his r's. "I have robbed you blind," he said. "I have bailed you up and relieved you of your doubloons and ducats."

"Beaten," said Lucinda, "but I promise you I am not defeated."

Mr d'Abbs liked Lucinda now. He liked her pluck, the way she laughed. He liked her plump lower lip, her sleepy eyelids, the feeling that she would be capable of the most unspeakable recklessness. Her upper lip was almost irresistible as it stretched and tightened—it was a charming little twitch—whenever she was excited.

"Shall we all take a trip together?" he said. He was less calculating that he might appear. He gathered the cards in across the grey blanket he had spread across the walnut table for their game. "Harry Briggs has brought a steamer. He will hire it out to us. We could take her up to Pittwater."

"Oh, yes," said Miss Shaddock. "Oh, I do so like Pittwater."

Miss Malcolm stared at Miss Shaddock with a dreamy, dazed, slightly contemptuous expression. Mr d'Abbs understood what secret this expression advertised. Soon he would be forced to dismiss Miss Malcolm from his service.

Miss Leplastrier took the cards from Fig and shuffled them. Two weeks earlier she would have spilled them everywhere, but she had taken to the game like a duck to water. He found it both comic and endearing to see a pretty woman shuffle with the finesse of a croupier in a club.

It was ten minutes past two o'clock. Lucinda was not in the tiniest bit sleepy. She took a sip of lukewarm cinnamon punch and began to deal another hand.

Miss Malcolm yawned.

"Have you had enough of cards?" asked Mr Fig, but would not address the question directly to Mr d'Abbs.

"Oh, please," said Lucinda, "let us play one more hand."

"You have already lost three guineas," said Miss Malcolm. Her tone was not friendly. She looked at Lucinda with the same heavy-eyed contemptuous expression she had bestowed on Miss Shaddock.

"One more," declared Mr d'Abbs, looking at Miss Malcolm through visibly narrowed eyes. "A chance for Miss Leplastrier to win her money back."

Lucinda dealt a card to Miss Shaddock. It slid across its fellows, and sailed through the air. Miss Shaddock snatched at it but sent it flying towards Lucinda. It bounced off Lucinda's shoulder and fell at her feet. Lucinda leaned to pick it up.

She did not allow herself to see the suit of the card, but she did see that Mr Fig had taken off his boot. He had his leg stretched beneath the table. His stockinged foot was somewhere in amongst Miss Malcolm's skirts. Lucinda noted it with far less degree of shock than might be thought likely. She thought only: My mama would think this household horrid. She answered the question about her losses.

"One more game," she begged.

"Like a duck to water," said Mr d'Abbs.

Lucinda knew she woud win this hand because she had dealt it. She knew she could control the cards with the strength of her will and there, now, here, the proof: four red threes and a two of spades. She could discard the spades and have a king. She would do this now. It was not a king. It did not matter. She would win anyway.

I am rich, she thought. I can do what I like. It is only pennies. It is only a little fun. My mama would not condemn me to loneliness for ever.

Tomorrow she would have won or lost, but whatever happened, happiness would be denied her. She could be happy now, not then. For if she won, she would know herself a robber. She was already rich. She had wealth she had not earned. To wish for more was sinful, greedy. But if she lost, it would be worse. Then she would feel not remorse, but terror. Her money was her cloak, her armour. She was a miser, counting it, feeling panic to be parted from it. She knew this already. She would go running to the Woollahra vicarage with her tail between her legs. She would read her Bible and attend Evensong. But now she was drunk on the game and only wanted more of it. The cards were sharp and clar, their blues pure ultramarine, their reds a brilliant carmine like the hearts of popish effigies. She saw the expression in Miss Malcolm's eyes. She heard the beast bellow from the mud flats. She patted her neck and felt her palm licked by loose, untidy flames of hair. The sight of her! It would drive her mama to a brushing frenzy, but Lucinda did not care about anything except cards and how to get the next hand moving.

"Come," she said, "look how attractive I can make the stakes."

And she emptied the contents of her purse—the equivalent of sixteen jam jars—on to the blanket.

Mr d'Abbs was amused and pleased. He was about to pigeon-hole her childlike and then she looked up and he caught the clear green challenge in her eyes and then he did not know what it was he felt.

39

Personal Effects

Mrs Burrows did not like to be needed too much. It put her off. It was this which was the impediment in her relationship with Mr Jeffris, not the fact that he was a clerk employed by Mr d'Abbs. Where Mr Calvitto had cold eyes and would allow himself to show no passion, Mr Jeffris had an incendiary nature which one felt to be only just held in control. Tears sprang easily to his tortoiseshell brown eyes. His hands were often clenched or thrust hard in his pockets. He was a stranger to irony and sarcasm. He was as direct as a knife. And apart from his great passion for the widow of Captain Burrows, his great obsession in life was that he should be an explorer of unmapped territories. He was not tall like Burke, or well educated like Mitchell. But you could not hear him talk and doubt that he would finally triumph.

Mr Jeffris was really very handsome. He had a great mane of coal-black hair, a high forehead, finely shaped full lips and fierce, animated dark eyes. He was neat, precise, self-critical. He was the youngest son of Covent Garden costers and dedicated to his own improvement. He was, in almost every respect, a perfect match for Mrs Burrows, except that he needed her.

Mr Calvitto had passion, but it was of a different type. It was as cold as a windowpane in a warm room. It was this she trusted. She liked a little distance, the emotional equivalent of what Captain Burrows, always billeted up-country, had provided her with in miles.

The difference between Mr Calvitto and Mr Jeffris is best illustrated by their reaction to that small tin trunk which Captain Burrows's commanding officer had labelled "Cpt. Burrows—Personal Effects."

The trunk contained a pair of gloves, some letters from Mrs Burrows, an envelope containing certain cards depicting Cossacks, and sixteen leatherbound diaries containing maps, descriptions of journeys, raids against the blacks, and small pen sketches of various bivouacs, river crossings, etc.

Mr Calvitto, on being invited to inspect the diaries, told her plainly that her husband had no talent with the pen. He made disparaging remarks about his English composition and drew her attention to the dashes which Captain Burrows used instead of commas and full stops. He did not end there. He read a sentence out loud and made it sound ridiculous. He showed her how the "settler's hut attacked by blacks" could not help but fall flat on the ground the minute the sketch was complete.

Mrs Burrows, like Mr Jeffris, believed in "improvement." Mr Calvitto offered "improvement" in large dollops, or at least that chastisement which Mr Burrows had learned to be the precursor of improvement. And although she twice slapped his face in response to things he said, she could not help but be spoiled for Mr Jeffris's enthusiastic response.

Mr Jeffris arrived on Tuesdays and Thursdays with his own writing paper and pen. He wore an old-fashioned box-pleated jacket in the style of his hero, Major Mitchell. He sat down at the gate-legged table in the parlour and transcribed from Captain Burrow's diaries. He had a neat, graceful hand with certain flourishes of his own invention. He did not make rude faces about the little brass gewgaws and porcelain knick-knacks with which Mrs Burrows had decorated the room. Mr Calvitto, on the other hand had, on first being alone with her in her house, told her bluntly that she had no taste. He had picked things up and put them down. She had been standing in the parlour. She had a small porcelain elephant in her hand. He had been opposite her, with his back to the window. He had his top hat in his hand.

She had the elephant in her hand when they kissed. Later she found it on a dressing table.

When Mr Jeffris admired this elephant, he put himself on her level, and this level was not high enough. Paradoxically, his natural affection for the elephant made her as fond of him as of a friend survived from early childhood.

Neither Mr Jeffris nor Mr Calvitto realized what a peculiar state Mrs Burrows was in. She gave no appearance of being anything but in control. Her period of mourning was over and her widow's weeds given to a charity, but she was still rocked and buffeted by the wake left by Captain Burrows's murder, the news of which had reached her in three successive waves.

First there had been a polite letter of condolence delivered by a major. Then there had been the newspaper reports. Burrows had been hacked with axes the blacks had stolen from shearers on the Manning. He had been thrust through the neck and eyes with spears.

And then, when she was still gapsing, the personal effects arrived. Amongst the diaries was an envelope containing sixteen picture cards, numbered one to sixteen, like the cigarette cards little boys collected. Each card bore the title "Rape by Cossacks." She was not shocked by the coupling there depicted (or less shocked than she might have imagined), nor by the exaggerated male genitalia, but rather the combination of this with sword and scimitar, with hacked breasts, with women's mouths screaming wide with pain, eyes bulging with terror, and not even this, horrible as it was, but the question as to why Captain Burrows, who had liked to nestle his head sleepily at her breast, should carry cards like this upon his person.

She could not get these pictures out of her head. They disturbed her and frightened her. There was no one she could speak to about them. And when she laid them out, like a hand of patience, on the gate-legged table on a Tuesday night, she was not in her normal mind at all.

When Mr Jeffris arrived, she took his coat and led him to his normal seat. He saw he was to sit down. He sat. She held his coat and watched him while he studied the cards.

"Do they please you?" she asked.

"*Please* me?"

She looked at him, with his slippery pretty lips half-opened. She did not need to hear his answer. She saw his eyes. He was not in control of himself. He was *frightened* of what he had seen. This was no use to her at all. She was already frightened. What use was it for him to be frightened, too?

She gathered in the cards and put them in their envelope. She refused to discuss the matter with him. He was concerned for her. She liked him to be concerned. But she did not like the timidity. She had always though him a brave man, strong, manly. She now began to say frighful things to him, in a perfectly ordinary way. She talked quickly; breathlessly, it is true, but this had been her style before. She straightened out the white tablecloth on the gate-legged table and said that the blacks should straight away be poisoned.

She did not know why she said these things.

It did not occur to Mr Jeffris that she was not well, for the views she was expressing were only different from much opinion in New South

Wales in that they were unambiguously put. He was, himself, fearful of the blacks in the Manning and the Macleay. It was likely he would one day have to confront them himself. He attempted to explain their behaviour to Mrs Burrows, not so much to calm her as to still, through explication, his own anxiety. These blacks, he said, were the most murderous of all, having been dispossessed of their lands and driven into the dense, tumbled country of the "Falls." They had their backs against the wall.

But this sort of talk did nothing to ease Mrs Burrows. She did not hear the words, but smelt something she would name as "unmanly." Her cheeks got hot spots on them and her face took on a chiselled look, pointed, clenched around the jaw, with tendons showing in her neck.

She talked of calling out the army, of a final all-out war against the blacks. Mr Jeffris replied, but what he was addressing was only the thin, sharp ice on the deeper puddle of Mrs Burrows's argument in which blacks, the Cossacks and Captain Burrows all took on the forms of fish with teeth like knives.

Mrs Burrows did not feel safe. She said this often, but was not understood.

When she returned from Mr d'Abbs's with Mr Calvitto, she resolved to show him the cards also. It was all that was on her mind while they disported in her bed. She placed them on the little night table where she would put the tea things afterwards. She made the pot which they then drank—it was their custom—sitting up in bed.

It was then that she gave Mr Calvitto the envelope. He lit a cigarette and blew a thin trail of smoke into the air. And then, in the manner of one performing a wearisome duty, he opened the envelope and looked at the cards, one by one, occasionally sipping his cup of tea, occasionally inhaling smoke from his cigarette. He nibbled at a biscuit. He said nothing.

Mr Calvitto was dark with long wiry muscles, black hair which grew all over him in small tight whorls. He was lean like a racing dog. He had a long, thin, hooded penis which now, as he turned one more card, rose visibly beneath the sheet.

He looked at her and smiled, an unsugary expression, not weak, as austere as whisky with no water. She pressed herself against him, shivering, as once, in the potteries of Stratford, she had pressed wet clay against a plaster mould.

She would be a plate, God save her. Let the aproned decorators paint dancing Cossacks around her rim, or dead blacks like spokes around a poisoned water-hole.

40

Not in Love

The vicar of Woollahra was not in love. She was not pretty enough for him to be in love with. She was also too young. She was not "suitable." A great deal of this judgement about suitability was a function not of his assessment of his personal needs but of his highly developed social sense.

Sydney (or that tiny part of it he knew as "Sydney") would not think her suitable. And he liked to be liked. He did not like, although he though himself a radical, to feel himself outside the comfort of the fold. He did not like to be criticized. And yet this was what was now happening to him all the time. No one—barring the Bishop—said anything to his face. But he could not accompany the girl to the waiting room of a solicitor-at-law without feeling, even amongst the clerks and message boys—this social shiver. He did not know about Jimmy d'Abbs and the games of cards, and yet he knew—without naming it for himself—that there was something. He saw the signs, just as you can posit, from the whorled skin of the sea, the presence of an unseen rock.

Three weeks ago Sydney did not know her, and then only that she had put a cauliflower on the front desk at Petty's Hotel. Then it was remarked—this was before she abandoned the crinoline Mrs Ahearn had made for her in Parramatta—how oddly she dressed. And then they switched and said how well.

She played cards with Jimmy d'Abbs *et al*. But afterwards she took tea with the vicar of Woollahra. It was as if she had broken some law of nature, been ice and steam at the same instant—the two activities were mutually exclusive.

The vicar of Woollhara then took her shopping and Society, always feeling shopping to be a most intimate activity, was pleased to feel the steam pressure rising in itself as it got ready to be properly scandalized—its pipes groaned and stretched, you could hear the noises in its walls and cellars. They imagined he had paid for her finery. When they learned this was not so, that the girl had sovereigns in her purse—enough, it was reported, to buy the priest a pair of onyx cufflinks—the pressure did not fall, but stayed constant, so that while it did not reach the stage where the outrage was hissing out through the open valves, it maintained a good rumble, a lower note which sounded like a growl in the throat of a smallish dog.

Society—if you call it that, Lucinda would not—did not know what to do. It could not *tolerate* to see the two of them together, and yet it was in some way tickled. It squirmed and grimaced and hooted with derision to see him move with such a confident and manly stride, as if nothing were wrong. It could not have been funnier if he had walked beside a billy-goat and called it sweetheart. And as for "her"—she swung her arms. Indeed she did. Like a toy soldier. This might not have been so irritating if she had not walked beside "dear, good Dennis Hasset." Let her walk like this beside Jimmy d'Abbs or Harvey Fig or the Italian atheist. Let her drink wine and dance with them, and jolly good luck to her, in this life at least. But let her not walk in the places where Miss Barley Wilkes or Miss Harriet Crowley might more rightfully, and virtuously, tread.

They watched the handsome vicar of Woollahra like a sleepwalker on a window ledge. He went with her to Jimmy d'Abbs's office to discuss the purchase of a glassworks. Even then he did not get it. He emerged as innocent as he went in. His friends tried to speak to him but he would not hear them. On this account he broke off relations with his friend Tom Wilson, the professor of classics at the university, the man he liked to call "the only educated man in Sydney." This happened on the very day the glassworks were finally purchased and when, in theory anyway, his association with Miss Leplastrier should end.

His "friend" Wilson had turned out as small-minded as the rest. He had claimed Miss Leplastrier stayed up all night gambling with "types" like Harvey Fig. This made Dennis Hasset's hands into tense claws and he cried out: "Agggh." He had reached a state which he could call "unhappy." He wrote the word on a piece of paper, then tore it up and threw it in the fire. It seemed to him, swivelling back and forth on his squeaky chair, that he had been, until his offer to assist with the purchase of the Prince Rupert's Glassworks, a mostly happy man. And he soon became nostalgic for the time he could sit reading alone in his study, or feel his long, athletic form being admired as he stretched across the pleasant slippery chintz surfaces of Mrs Wilson's armchairs. And even if there were moments—like this one—when he could sit alone in his study, it was not the same as hitherto.

Anger, like a blow-fly, had been let into the room and buzzed against the sunlit glass. He did not understand this anger. He thought it all his, but a great deal of it was Lucinda's. She carried an intensity, a nervous tension, with her. She could not sit in a hitherto peaceful armchair without your being aware of a great reservoir of energy being somehow, against all the laws of physics, contained. Even when she was not here, he felt her restlessness. And he was angry—although it was unchristian of him—that this one calm corner, the place in his life where he might be free from the demands of parishioners had now been stolen from him. He could not concentrate on his Dickens or his Wilkie Collins. He was irritated, even whilst praying. If Lucinda was sitting in the house, he would wish her gone. If she was not, he might sit in a small chair by his window, looking constantly up the dusty road, wishing—he did not think it right to pray for it—for the plume of dust that might herald the arrival of her hansom.

But on the evening of the day he had ended his friendship with Tom Wilson, he did not need to wait for her. She arrived promptly at dusk, in order that they might celebrate the purchase. She was on time, but they were somehow not synchronized. They did not feel the way they were meant to. Lucinda had that fearful, tight-chested sensation she experienced after she had lost too much money at her cribbage. But *this* feeling was not caused by anything so doubtful, but by something which should be morally uplifting, i.e. the purchase of a factory. She was expected to be triumphant. She tried to be.

Dennis Hasset was still living the hurt of his argument with Professor Wilson. He was sick at heart, and angry. He poured dry sherry for a toast but launched straight into the story. It gave his voice a hard metallic edge and his eyes, although he did not intend it so, looked balefully, accusingly at Lucinda who could not, in the face of this, bring herself to sit down. She stood upright as if it were she, not Wilson, who was in the dock.

Dennis Hasset was inclined to forget Lucinda was only a girl, just as he was also inclined to forget she was not a child. He told her what was said about her.

Lucinda held her shoulders square and smiled. Her upper lip became very thin, but otherwise she did not show him how hurt she was. She could not see why she should be hated so much. She *could* see, of course. They did not like Mr d'Abbs because he laughed and had a little fun, because he wore a velvet smoking-jacket and was Christian enough not to be frightened when an atheist sat at his table. But she could also *not* see. She felt so small and weak in the face of the moving water-wall of hatred.

She should be sorry that Mr Hasset had argued with his friend. It was her responsibility. She should care for him and nurse him in the loss, just as she should properly celebrate the purchase she had begged him negotiate on her behalf. She raised her glass and smiled in a way she now knew was attractive. It involved a pursing of the lips, sleepy lids around the eyes. She knew, because she had performed it for the mirror, that it gave her a humorous, dare-devil appearance.

But the room was cold. The curtains were drawn. The glass, greenish stuff from Melbourne, seemed black—and being an excellent conductor it wasy very cold to touch. She stood behind it. She imagined herself a portrait suspended in the gloom.

"Well," she turned. "I must go."

She had not known she was going to say this. She looked at Dennis Hasset's face. His mouth slightly open, his forehead suddenly carved by two deep clefts of frown.

"We are having beef," he said. He put his glass down. He put his two hands together. She felt his misery come out to swamp her. She could not bear his disappointment. She could not look at his face and feel its pain.

"I am so sleepy," she yawned.

All she could think was that she must play cards. She was a despicable person. Then she was despicable, and that was that. But she must go. She told a number of lies, one after the other, teetering above each other, a house of cards, all constructed in order that she might abandon the vicarage and fly—as fast as she could down the Glenmore Hill—to the house in Rushcutters Bay where they would lay a hand of shining cribbage across a grey wool-covered table.

41

If He Ask a Fish, Will He Give Him a Serpent?

Notting Hill, you may not know it, derives its distinctive street plan from the racecourse which finally bankrupted its developer, Mr John Whyte. And while it is true that four years at Oriel had not only given Oscar a passion for racehorses, but produced sixteen smudge-paged clothbound notebooks in which were recorded not the thoughts of Divine Masters, not musings on the philosophy of the ancients, but page after page of blue spidery figures which recorded—you could not sit on your backside at Oxford and collect data like this but must travel, by train, by coach, by foot, so that a map of your journeys would be a spider web across the south of England—the names of horses, their sires and dams, their position at last start, the number of days since the last start, the weight carried at the last time, whether they were rising in class, or falling in class, who was the owner, who the jockey and so on, and so while he had this great passion (it was more extensive than I have suggested—his system of weighting would require a bigger book than Pittsburgh Phil's) and had wed his father's scientific methods to the sweating, mud-stained bride of racing, he had come to live in Notting Hill totally in ignorance of the fact that a ghostly imprint of a racecourse lay over its streets.

He did not hear the thunder of two-year-olds down Lansdowne Road. He did not see mud fly in the right turn on Stanley Crescent. He saw the name of Ladbroke, of course. You cannot miss a Ladbroke in Notting Hill. It is there on Square and Road and Terrace. But Ladbroke's was not yet a famous firm of London bookmakers and if the street names were coded messages from the future, Oscar did not know how to read them.

He came to Notting Hill, or so he insisted, only because he was familiar with the area, or the more genteel part of it. He had been accustomed to staying at the Wardley-Fishs' town house in Ladbroke Square, an address the Queen's physician, being unaware of the piggeries a mile away in Notting Dale, and having visited, presumably, on a day the wind was blowing from the south-east, had claimed to be the most salubrious in London.

Oscar, being permanently in London, could no longer expect to be billeted at Ladbroke Square, which was, in any case, closed down again, with the servants left starved on half-pay and no scraps of fat to sell off at the back door while they waited for Lady Wardley-Fish to decide she was, once again, bored with the country.

Oscar's accommodation was on the south side of the Uxbridge Road, a block away from the rattle of the omnibuses and wagons and coaches. He had become a schoolteacher, and had a room in the third-floor attic of Mr John Colville's School for Boys. He was a Reverend Mr and chose to wear the collar but at this moment you would not know whether he wore it or not for he was lying in his bed, fully clothed, with the sheet clenched between his neat white teeth.

His disgraceful shoes—scuffed quite white around the inner heels—lay where they had recently fallen, the right one on its side on the black floorboards, the left standing upright with its toe curling upwards. You could not need to be a cobbler to know my great-grandfather's shoes were too big for him.

The room was cold. There was a grate but it was empty. The brass kindling box was shut but it did not serve to hold kindling in any case, but those letters, written in Theophilus's tight, small hand on an inexplicably expensive crisp white bond, which served to lacerate a conscience which was already as unhealthy as Sir Ian Wardley-Fish's liver.

He knew he was vile. His eyes were wide, staring at the sloping attic ceiling which bore brown marks like an unsavoury old mattress. It was the sabbath. The bells of St John the Evangelist had stopped some ten minutes before but the note for the day was declared more exactly, it seemed to him, by the stench of pig fat being rendered by the dangerous inhabitants of Notting Dale.

Greyhound Row, where Mr Colville's school was situated, was genteel and quiet. Only the whisk-whisk of Mrs Fenn's straw broom broke the silence of the sabbath. Mr Fenn, the tailor, had his freshly painted bright green shutter firmly closed. The butcher's shop next door had a bright brass hasp and staple threaded with a heavy black enamelled padlock. Mr Brewer—he whose establishment was next to the butcher's—would, on this day, sell no cheese, no corn, no paper cones of boiled sweets and was, this could be relied on, in his pew with his family at St John's.

The Swann Inn, near the tollgate, was firmly closed but Oscar, lying in his bed above Mr Colville's empty school, could see the smudge of Brickfield's smoke across the yellow sky. He could hear the barking dogs. It was a great place for dogs, for dog-fanciers and dog-stealers. Certain individuals also wagered on the dogs.

He had become vile. The vileness was perhaps the product of the shape of Notting Hill, that he was made by this map, or chose the map without knowing he was doing it, was drawn to it like iron filings towards the magnetic horseshoe shapes of its street plan. Ever since his association with Wardley-Fish he had come to Notting Hill, and ever since that time he had been vile.

He did not blame his friend for this. His friend gambled no more.

Wardley-Fish had a parish and worked hard on his sermons. And in any case it was not the gambling which was vile. Through gambling, imbued with God's grace, he had managed to feed and clothe himself. It is true there had been hard and hungry times when he felt himself alone and lost. (One bad spell in 1862 lasted from after Easter almost up to Trinity.) But although he had lost he was, as they said at the track, "ahead." He worked hard. He travelled to Newmarket and Newbury, Catterick and Sandown Park. He collected his information and classified it. Indeed, you could look at his results and say he did it all himself, without God's help. But this was not how Oscar saw it. He saw God's hand everywhere about—bookmaker's favourites boxed in at the rails, carried off at the turn, interfered with, broken down, playing up at the barrier and particularly the case of the 2–1 favourite Sailor Boy who—he had this from Jim Clements, the jockey—held his breath from the top of the straight in the two-year-old handicap at Newmarket and thus allowed Desire to win at 33–1.

He also bet without his system. He had lost money to Magsmen and Macers. He had bet on dried peas, spinning tops, and the progress of ants along a gold-tipped walking stick. He had played cribbage for two or three pounds a game. But he had never bet from greed or avarice. The state of his coal scuttle, the condition of his shoes, all attested to that. He would only bet for a proper godly purpose.

It was not gambling itself which was vile. What was vile was his passion, the extraordinary excitement he felt, the appetite which made him place a bet on every race on the card, not because it was wise, but just so he could maintain his frenzy and cheer home his chosen beasts until he was almost too hoarse to make himself understood at the railway ticket counter. What was vile was the need that took possession of him at a moment like this when he knew that, at this very instant, in Notting Dale, they would be gathering their dogs together.

He shifted his bite on his sheet.

No matter what godly purpose his gambling was turned towards, it was not godly to pursue it on the sabbath.

This business with dogs was evil. It was Wardley-Fish – though not, dear Lord, his fault – who had taken him to this place. Oscar had been shocked, but excited too. There was the dangerous smell of the city poor: musty cotton, fustian, toasted herrings. Men sat in rows on benches with their dogs. Later, when the clock was running, they would cry out, but at first, when they were just entered, there was a curious quiet about the men and their dogs. They stroked and patted. There was a soft cooing like a dove house.

They all looked towards the pit. It was not a very large pit, about six feet in diameter, and painted a bright white. In the middle of the pit was a dark grey mound. The mound was soft, moving. The mound was composed of rats, clustering together, crawling over each other.

The men cooed.

Then they stopped. They shifted on their seats, spat, coughed, said something softly to a neighbour or called out a raw-throated joke.

A fox terrier was placed into the ring. The fox terrier was called Tiny. It wore a woman's bracelet for a collar. It took the rats one by one, picked them up like fruit from a bowl, broke them while the clock ticked and the men roared so loud you could not hear your companion speak to you.

On the day he first witnessed this, Oscar would not have believed he would ever be tempted to bet on such a thing. But the temptation came, not because he wished to see creatures put to death, but because it was a sabbath and there was no other betting to be had. Betting was like this: a monster that must be fed.

He bit his sheet, and wondered, as he wondered often, if it might not be this, his need to feed the monster, that lay behind the scrubbed face of his seemingly Christian desire, i.e. to accumulate money in order to dare the formless terror of the ocean, to bring the word of Christ to New South Wales.

And yet the monster could not be the motive. For when he had made the commitment – two years before he lay in bed fretting over rats – he had imagined there would be no money to raise.

The Church Missionary Society would pay his fare. He would need a sun-helmet (3s) and, apart from that, only a piece of cellulolid (10s) to overcome his panic of the sea.

42

Called

Wardley-Fish did not like the people that he knew. They bored him. He imagined them as sturdy beasts grazing in a dense and matted pasture, chewing, swallowing, regurgitating at one end, plopping at the other. Naturally he did not show them what he felt. He acted jovially, even fondly, and what he showed was not exactly false – he felt all these things in a distant sort of way – but were certainly greatly magnified. He worried about his father's bleeding face, and he laughed at his brother's stories about the poacher he had netted in a pit-trap. He could ride with them all day and drink with them all night – they were round and comfortable in every part, and not a sharp edge to cut through the cushions of complacency.

And this was the quality that he valued in his embarrassing friend – that he was itchy and angular in every sense, and whatever there was to disapprove of, you could not put complacency on the list.

There were so many things about the Odd Bod he did not approve of, phobias, fetishes, habits of mind so alien that they could not even be accounted for by the peculiar parent who, no matter how alarming he might be in his belief ("Are you saved, Mr Wardley-Fish?"), was at least neat in his appearance. But the son, no matter how the bookmakers pressed their wads of beer-wet currency on to him, would not spend money on his appearance. He had no money of his own. This was his view. The Lord saw fit to grant him money for his education, and it would be sinful to use this for gratification of what was, so he imagined, nothing but wordly vanity. Thus he bought his clothing from stinking stalls run by the Jews in Petticoat Lane, his shoes from a scrofulous pedlar who had nothing else to sell but a few herrings and a green silk handkerchief, an old-fashioned kingsman probably pick-pocketed by his grandfather.

This mode of dress seemed to Wardley-Fish to be conceited. And when, for instance, he found the gawkish Odd Bod, excluded from

Cremorne Gardens because he had not made the slightest concession to fashion, he was momentarily enraged.

Wardley-Fish had on his white waistcoat and dresscoat. He had spent a lot of time on the waxed ends of his moustache. He stepped down from the hansom, a little late admittedly, and found his friend standing placidly in the splendid doorway whilst the porter glowered behind him. The Odd Bod had made no effort with his dress at all. It was he who had suggested this rendezvous. He knew what sort of place it was. Yet he made no effort. His coat was threadbare. His red hair was more alarming than usual, having developed a corkscrewing forelock to equal the flyaway sides. The porter did not understand that his appearance was a symbol of his incorruptibility. He had, therefore, refused him admittance.

The Odd Bod stood gazing across through the park, his white hands clapsed upon his breast, a bemused smile on his face, waiting patiently for Wardley-Fish to set it right for him.

The thieving cabby wanted half a crown and Wardley-Fish was too irritated to argue. This stance of Oscar's looked so like a pose. He could not believe it was not, at least partly, a pose. And yet he could not doubt the Odd Bod's integrity, or not for long. For he had seen him, on more than one occasion, discard that portion of his racecourse winnings he regarded as surplus to his needs, shove blue five-pound notes into some parish poor-box because he had enough for himself for the present. His jerky charity did not stop there, for there was a red-nosed clergyman from his own village who was also a recipient of bulging registered envelopes of currency which, from all that Wardley-Fish could judge, produced many emotions in the donee, but none of them having much resemblance to gratitude.

Oscar's holy profligacy infuriated Wardley-Fish, and yet it was exactly these acts of charity that he most treasured in his friend, and he could never make his mind be still about the question, which was like one of those trick drawings in *Punch* which have the contradiction built in so that what seems to be a spire one moment is a deep shaft the next.

He took his friend by his shiny, threadbare elbow and propelled him before him, past the porter, into Cremorne Gardens. It was five o'clock in the afternoon, an hour at which the tide, so to speak, was already turning, and the clientele, having been for the most part respectable during the day, now seemed to transmorgrify—the guard changed within the space of thirty minutes—into something more glamorous and dangerous.

Oscar allowed himself to be propelled. He was pleased to have no choice. He felt luxury engulf him and the sensation was at once soothing and abrasive. A table loomed. He unhooked his umbrella from his arm and put it on the back of the chair. He removed the rolled-up parcel from his breast p;ocket and placed it underneath the table. He did all this without hurry, and when he sat down it would not have been apparent to a stranger that he was agitated. He had come here to make a very frightening decision. He smiled brightly at Wardley-Fish. He raked his hair with his fingers, pulled in his seat, placed his evangelical elbows square on the table. He gave all the appearance of being, dress apart, like a tourist come to Cremorne Gardens to have a look, but not a taste. He admired the room, the globed gas brackets, the pendant lustres, the high mirrored panels with ornate mouldings, the couples without wedding rings to explain their obvious intimacy.

"What a splendid place," he said.

But Wardley-Fish could feel the Odd Bod's agitated feet tapping beneath the table. It was not just feet. It was also fingers, drumming on the chair. The surface of the table assumed a nervous kind of energy. You could experience anxiety merely by touching it.

Wardley-Fish ordered champagne. He could not afford it, but neither could he bear the nerves beneath the marble. He would need the one to cure the other.

"How enticing it is," said Oscar.

Wardley-Fish thought none of this straightforward. The Odd Bod was in his "holy" pose and talking at a tangent. He was admiring in order to criticize, being dazzled so that he might thereby lacerate himself for being there.

"You do remember," Wardley-Fish said, "whose idea it was we meet here?"

"Mine!" said the Odd Bod, watching the champagne being poured. You could feel his quivering energy in the floor and table. It felt like a trout feels on the end of a line—all the energy of a life forcing its patterns on to inert matter.

Wardley-Fish had been looking forward to Cremorne Gardens. It had existed as a soft, unfocused promise on the edge of his consciousness. He had not intended to "do" anything, but he had already seen the most delightful creature enter. She was an "actress." She had creamy skin and a tangled artifice of golden hair. She wore ten yards of watered taffeta. He gulped his first glass of champagne and watched it filled immediately. The table had stopped vibrating.

He looked up to find the Odd Bod's pale green eyes waiting for him.

"Fish," said the Odd Bod.

Wardley-Fish felt depressed.

"Fish, I have spent a good deal of the afternoon with the Church Missionary Society."

"Yes."

"And they will have me if I wish."

"What for?"

"I enquired about New South Wales."

Wardley-Fish put down his glass of champagne. He did not look at the Odd Bod. He reflected that there was no natural sympathy between glass and marble.

"Do you hear me?"

"Do not drum the table. It is very irritating."

Wardley-Fish slid his glass three inches to the right, then back again. Oscar folded his red-knuckled hands around each other as if they were a puzzle he could not properly resolve.

When Wardley-Fish spoke, it was very quietly and softly. "There is no need," he said, "for you to frighten yourself with such ideas."

But Oscar, when he replied, had his voice in that tight and scratchy register. "I *must*," said the Odd Bod. It was like fingernails across a blackboard.

"So why have we come here?" asked Wardley-Fish, leaning back and folding his arms across his white waistcoat. "Are you to drive the money-changers from the temple, the pretty whores across into the park?"

"It is a lovely place, Fish. I am very comfortable here."

"Then relax, dear Odd Bod, and do not drum and squeak and fidget. You will be back in college tonight and it will not be nearly so much fun."

They were quiet for a monment. Wardley-Fish fussed around with his cigar as he tried to nip its end with a new patented device that did not seem to work as promised. Oscar watched him, with his palms flat on the table.

"But I have changed," Oscar said when Wardley-Fish had his smoke alight, "look at me. Look at what I have become."

"Oh, *strike me,*" roared Wardley-Fish. He pushed his chair back. He did not care that he made a bellow in such a quiet place. "You have not become this," and he waved his hands around to indicate the sort of trappings that did not exemplify Oscar's personality. "You are tiresome, Odd Bod. You have only one conversation, and it makes no sense. You belong no more here than you belong anywhere. Odd Bod, you must realize, *you do not fit.*"

"Speak quietly."

"You do not fit. You are wonderful. You are perfectly unique. Do you feel you 'fit' in Oriel?"

Oscar looked down into his glass. "I have my friends."

"Who?"

"Pennington, Ramsay."

"Pennington, is a drunk and a Puseyite. Ramsay fawns on anyone who looks at him. And do you have friends in Hennacombe? Do you fit there?"

Oscar's eyes looked hurt and troubled.

"Neither do you fit here. You are not corrupted. It is an impertinence to suggest that you are. You do not have to travel to New South Wales for a penance."

"And you?"

"And me? Oh, I 'fit.' I daresay I 'fit' all too well." Wardley-Fish leaned across and took the Odd Bod's hand. He shackled the wrist. "But you showed me that I might be saved." His smile was fixed. Oscar could feel the big hand trembling. "So do not," he whispered, "start pretending you must cross the world to save your soul, because I tell you it is not true. You must not leave. And anyway," he took back his hand and relit his cigar, "you cannot."

Oscar was enfolded in blue smoke. He blinked and waved his hand while a slow smile budded on his lips.

"And why can I not leave?"

"Because you cannot bear a little *agua*. You could not sail as far as Calais."

Oscar leaned down and picked up a little wrapped cylinder from amongst his papers on the floor. This he unwrapped slowly, smiling all the time at his friend. What he then held up was a flexible material which was transparent, but not so clear as glass. On this material were drawn those lines which my mother imagined represented latitude and longitude.

"What is this, Oscar?"

Wardley-Fish rarely called him Oscar. There was a sibilant sadness in the name which now made its owner pause before answering.

"It is known as celluloid, and is pretty much what it appears to be. But you see I can make these marks on it, and I can carry it around. It is very light and handy."

"This will cure your phobia?"

Oscar then explained his plan for viewing water through the celluloid. He could view it one square at a time, thus containing it. What was terrifying in a vast expanse would become "quite manageable."

Wardley-Fish did not trouble himself with the theory. His friend was talking too much, too fast, in too high a register. It would not work. Only desperation would make a man believe it would.

"Has it ever occurred to you," he said when Oscar had finished and was rolling away his celluloid, "that what you call your 'phobia' is really the Almighty speaking to you?"

"Don't mock me, Fish."

"As a matter of fact I am very serious."

" 'Yea, though I walk through the shadow of the valley of death'—no, Fish, if my soul were clear, I would have no fear—'Thy rod and Thy staff comfort me.' "

"But has it occurred to you that what you call a phobia may be God telling you that you must not go near the water?"

"Very clever, Fish."

Wardley-Fish shrugged. The extraordinary woman had found herself a companion. The Odd Bod was pushing a florin across the table to him. He picked it up, then put it down. "You wish me to flip this?"

"Thank you, Fish."

"You know I only flip my own coins." He pushed the florin back across the table and searched in his own pocket. His handsome face was suddenly weary, pouchy around the eyes.

He found, at last, a penny. He flipped the coin, lethargically, as if he had not guessed that he was tossing for his friend's destiny. It was a dull and dirty penny he sent spinning through the air.

"Call," he said.

The Odd Bod had gone pale and waxy. He had his hands clenched tight together on his breast. He was moving the fingers in the trap of the hands. He looked like a praying mantis.

"Call," said Wardley-Fish, but loudly so that blonde-haired women turned to stare. The penny slapped against his palm.

"I cannot, Fish. You know it."

Wardley-Fish turned the penny on to the back of the wrist. He kept it covered with his right hand. "Why not?" he asked.

"I am frightened," hissed Oscar. "You know I am frightened."

"Then why do you do such things to yourself," smiled Wardley-Fish, "Come, dear Odd Bod, and—"

"Heads," said Oscar.

Wardley-Fish sighed. He lifted his hand to reveal the head of Queen Victoria.

The Odd Bod's face was ghastly, a mask carved out of white soap, and you did not need to be a mind reader to know that God was sending him to New South Wales.

This happened on 22 April 1863. My great-grandfather was twenty-two years old.

43

Leviathan

My father, I think I said before, was a swaggering little fellow, a cunning spin bowler, a smoker of matchstick-thin cigarettes, a practical joker. He was small, but he was proud that he stood straight with his shoulders back. I saw him fight Hector Thompson, a man twice his size, on the deserted forecourt of Carl Foster's service station. He had him down, crumbled, winded, with a bleeding lip, before anyone in the pub across the road had a chance to realize what was happening.

But when it came to celluloid, my father was a coward.

The celluloid was most definitely the property of my mother. It was the same piece Oscar had brought to Australia in 1864, and was certainly the first sample of that substance introduced to the ancient continent. Perhaps it was the first synthetic long-chain hydrocarbon in the southern hemisphere. This was something my father, being a chemist by training, pondered over, but only once out loud. My mother would not hear him speak of it, and not because she was silly, but because she understood as women often do more easily than men, that the declared meaning of a spoken sentence is only its overcoat, and the real meaning lies underneath its scarves and buttons.

When my father spoke of the scientific history of celluloid (which, having a diploma in industrial chemistry, he was entitled to do) she felt that he was contesting her ownership of its original use, its meaning, its history.

And she was right. When my father said "long-chain hydrocarbon," he was saying: "I am right. This one's mine."

But my mother would not let him have it. The celluloid was hers. The meaning of it was hers. The lines ruled on it were—I was brought up on this—lines of latitude and longitude. She would lay the yellowed, scratched material across a Shell road map and explain to us how it would have worked.

She became emotional, as she often did, when discussing the past, and because she wished Oscar to be a "missionary" and a "pioneer Anglican," we gew up imagining Oscar travelling out on steerage, on a clipper ship, crowded in amongst poor immigrants. We imagined our great-grandfather with his map and celluloid, his Bible, his Book of Common Prayer. We saw him—even while we squirmed in embarrassment before my mother's holy-toned recitation—conducting sad funeral services for babies lost, a toothless sailmaker stitching up a sad little parcel in canvas, and young Oscar, his hair flaming red, his milk-white skin burnt raw, squinting into the antipodean sun with the ultramarine sea swelling up above him.

My father surely knew what kind of ship it was Oscar sailed on. He knew its name, and if he knew its name he probably "looked it up." In any case, he said nothing about the *Leviathan* which was no more a clipper than the celluloid was a grid of latitude and longitude.

The *Leviathan* was 690 feet long, 83 feet wide and 58 feet deep. The Ark (if one allows the cubit as 20.62 inches) was 512 feet long, 85 feet wide, and 51 feet deep. This coincidence was not lost on Oscar who "discovered" the *Leviathan* two weeks after his fateful evening at Cremorne Gardens.

At this stage Ishmael Kingdom Legare's controversial liner was undergoing one of its crises in the Tyneside shipyards and it was thought the company would go bankrupt. These uncertainties were nothing to Oscar. He ignored them. He saw only that this was the ship he must travel on. It was unsinkable. *Punch* wrote that a man might travel from Southampton to Sydney and—so vast were the dimensions, so multitudinous the passages, alleyways, gangways, etc.—that the poor chap—although he might dance till he had no shoe leather, and dine till his buttons burst—might go all that way and never find his way to that most simple essential of an ocean voyage—a porthole with a view of the sea.

This was just the sort of ship that Oscar required. It had twin hulls (in case of icebergs), a cellular deck, and the capacity to carry its own coal for the journey.

Oscar Hopkins travelled to Australia not as my mother imagined but in the greatest luxury. And while he appeared, to those around him, to be so unworldly as to take no notice of this aspect of his journey, to be insensitive to the pleasures of "portières of carmine silk," one should remember that Oscar chose *Leviathan* just as he chose Cremorne Gardens. Someone who had grown up in the limestone austerity of Theophilus's house could not be oblivious to either.

The Church Missionary Society, of course, would not pay his fare on anything so grand. That he should have the nerve to suggest they should produced a certain degree of ill-feeling which he did not notice.

He would pay his own fare. Only God could provide so large an amount.

He bet on dogs and horses.

In his heart of hearts he did not know if he was good or bad, holy or corrupt. He bathed in cold water when there was hot available. He went without coal when he could afford to buy it. He met with Wardley-Fish on Friday afternoon and drank pink champagne.

44

A Bishop's Son-in-Law

Wardley-Fish would have dearly loved a little flutter. But he had a curacy in Hammersmith, a fiancée, an impending wedding, and this combination of circumstances had meant that he had not only been forced to abandon his apparently "questionable" address near Drury Lane—no one seemed to think there was anything "questionable" about him coming here to live in the same house as his future wife—he had also given up the sporting life. There were good reasons to give up, but he would have liked to have had just an hour at the Holborn Casino, say, or even better, at Epsom. And he would have liked to do it with his hooting, embarrassing friend. However, they were grown up now, and he was a handsome fellow engaged to a bishop's daughter.

His fiancée, Miss Melody Clutterbuck, did not know that Wardley-

Fish would, in a moment, use the Bishop's coach to pay a visit to the loathsome person he always made such fun of. She understood this friendship to be almost finished. She had put the prickly subject from her mind, or almost, for there was always the anxiety that the ship the chicken-necked madman had chosen to go to Australia—that this ship might somehow (*The Times* said it quite likely) never get built. She could not hear the *Leviathan* discussed (as it lurched from stasis to crisis in the City) without seeing my great-grandfather's praying-mantis head and his ridiculous long white wrists extruding from his grime-polished sleeves. Not being privy to the history of the unlikely friendship, she imagined the Reverend Mr Hopkins to be a bad influence, and although this misunderstanding made her fiancée most uncomfortable he lacked the courage to set her right. She had no sympathy for the Odd Bod and to learn, for instance, that he sat beside an empty coal skuttle because it would be wicked to spend his winnings on his own comfort—it was this which was presently agitating Wardley-Fish—would merely have confirmed what she knew already: that the silly little Evangelical was as mad as May-butter.

After all the jokes he had made at the Odd Bod's expense, Wardley-Fish could not have justified himself to her. There were things he could not explain, and this was one of them: why he should tiptoe down the staircase of her father's house with a pretty cane basket containing "things" wrapped in cast-out tissue paper. His fiancée was with her mother at early service in Knightsbridge. There was only the Bishop to contend with. The Bishop—no stickler for the observation of the sabbath—was in his study cataloguing what he called his "brimborions and knick-knacks" by which he meant certain items of the loot that Lord Elgin's victory had flushed out of Peking. The Bishop's focus of attention was intense. It was most unlikely he would hear. But just the same Wardley-Fish came down the stairs so slowly he made them groan and creak unnaturally. He reached the gloomy patch at the bottom of the stairs where black umbrellas hung like flying foxes from their cedar stand. In a moment he would be safe and out of the door towards the stables, but before the moment arrived the Bishop—intent on fetching the crackle-glaze vase from the drawing room—had flung open his study door and stood not two feet away.

"Ho," he said.

It was not fright. The Bishop did not startle easily. It was a form of shyness, of politeness—the two men were always nervous with each other. They were each anxious to demonstrate goodwill. The Bishop was in his shirt sleeves. He had his cut-down glasses on his stuby nose.

He held a stack of pink index cards in his hands.

"Apples?" he said jovially, and grabbed. When the hard irregular shape benath the tissue told him that it was not an apple at all, he was embarrassed. He felt he had walked into his guest room and found his guest unrobing. He did not know what to do, whether to carry on as normal, or to place the object back in the basket and retreat into his study. He looked at Wardley-Fish with his bushy eyebrows pushing up beneath his furrowed brow.

"Coal," said Wardley-Fish, but only because he did not have the nerve to stay silent.

The Bishop pushed back the tissue paper and, indeed, it was as the young man said. The Bishop crumbled some between his thumb and forefinger and put it to his nose and smelt it, but once he had done that he had nothing more to do. He did not like to ask what this extraordinary arrangement might be for. His future son-in-law did not seem free to tell him. Wardley-Fish could not, standing there at the bottom of the stair, with twenty lumps of coal held in a silly little basket, explain it, not even to himself.

45

Hymns

On the following Tuesday, Wardley-Fish happened to be in Martindale's bookshop. His fiancée had a fondness for the romantic novels of Mrs Plumber, and it was whilst she was enquiring after the most recent (in a voice that seemed, in that environment, too loud and confident) that he came across a copy of the elder Hopkins's *Hennacombe Rambles*. And here, with his umbrella hooked over his arm, he found a younger Oscar described as "the little botanist in skirts." This made him smile, of course. But for the rest of it, the smile became less certain and soon completely disappeared.

It was as if he had netted Oscar in his home pond and could see him properly for the first time. And although he had visited the bare, wooden-floored cottage in Hennacombe and, indeed, listened at length to the elder Hopkins (who was *immune*, it seemed, to the freezing wind blowing through the open window) as the old man spoke of his wish that "Christ's Kingdom should come in our lifetime," he now realized—reading the book—that the pond was neither as he had seen it nor as Oscar had described it.

Wardley-Fish had an impression of a killjoy, love-nothing, a man you could not send a birthday present to in case he smelt the race-track on it, a man who would snatch a little Christmas pudding from a young boy's mouth. But where he might have expected to find a stern and life-denying spirit, he found such a trembling and tender appreciation of hedgerow, moss, robin, and the tiniest of sea creatures that even Wardley-Fish (it was he who thought the "even") was impressed and moved. Leaning against the counter at Martindale's with all the heavy physical awkwardness of a fellow waiting for his wife at the milliner's, he read this passage: "the pretty green *Ploycera ocellata* was numerous; but the most abundant, and at the same time most lovely species was the exquisite *Eolis coronata*, with tentacles surrounded by membranous coronets, and with crowded clusters of papillae, of crimson and blue that reflect the most gemlike radiance."

Now Wardley-Fish though himself a man's man, seeped in brandy and good cigars, and if—expediently—he had renounced the race-course, he had no intention of abandoning the hunt, which he still rode to at Amersham whenever it was possible. Further, he imagined himself stupid. He had been told so long enough, and had this not been his father's opinion also, he would never have been pushed into a life as a clergyman. His early wish had been to study law, but he was told he had not the brain for it. He had not questioned this assessment and had therefore decided, whilst still at Oriel, that he could only hope to advance himself through connections, the most effective of which would be made through marriage.

He claimed to have no ear for poetry or music and yet he was moved—it nearly winded him—by the elder Hopkins's prose. Where he had expected hellfire and mustard poultice, he found maidenhair and a ribbon of spawn. "I found the young were perfectly formed, each enclosed by a globular egg, perfectly transparent and colourless."

To be able to feel these things, to celebrate God's work in such a lovely hymn, Wardley-Fish would have given everything and anything. He felt, in these simple, naturalist's descriptions, what he had never felt—what he should have felt—in the psalm beginning "I will extol thee, my God, O King; and I will bless Thy name for ever and ever."

He stood at the counter, his head bowed, with that moist-eyed look one would expect to be produced by a sentimental story. His fiancée, returning to discover both the changed mood and the parcel which the saucy-eyed assistant was wrapping for him, saw immediately that the one had caused the other, and was therefore not sympathetically disposed towards the book. She knew him as bright and jolly. She liked him best in a red jacket fifteen hands high.

They found a hansom outside the shop and ordered it to Kensington. Riding through Hyde Park, with all the deep black trees shooting green, he continued to think, as he had thought, continually, since his secret visit with the coal, of his friend who had jailed himself in a room with only a birdless sky for company and only the prospect of a terrifying voyage to look forward to.

Once when he was young, so young he was not yet a boarder at Harrow, he had meddled with a stamp in his father's vast collection, a single blue stamp with a picture of a swan. He had been so careful, so reverent almost, and yet, somehow, the perforations had been damaged. His father, of course, had noticed, and it was not the birching which made him blubber into his nanny's white starched bosom afterwards, but that he had intended only admiration, and instead had caused harm, and this harm was irreversible.

It was his character to carry the burden of his mistakes with him, and so it would be with Oscar. He could not put it down. He could not clear his mind of it.

The carriage lurched on to the bridge across the Serpentine and Wardley-Fish, hearing his fiancée exclaim bad-temperedly, looked at her and knew he did not like her. Her little plump wrists seemed disgusting to him. He felt choked, claustrophobic, was made particularly so by the powder on her dimpled cheek.

He wished he had gone out to Africa. He had thought of it for a while. He had put the idea into the Odd Bod's head. They had talked of going to Africa together—this was well before the day at Cremorne Gardens—but there had been the problem of the water phobia. But now he knew he should have gone to Africa anyway and the ambition that had made him court the daughter of a bishop seemed contemptible.

He knew she would not like the elder Hopkins's book, and yet when he asked if he might read her a little, he did not do it provocatively, but rather in the hope that he might be wrong.

"Melody," he said, "I must share my secret with you." They had not spoken since they left the West End and, as this silence was unusual, he knew she would be uneasy. He did not normally read at all, and he knew his purchase of a book would seem strange. Still, he pulled the string on the green parcel, smiling queerly in her direction.

"We are almost there, dearest," she said, but took the paper and string from him and began to tidy it. Wardley-Fish did not see the reproof intended.

"A little only," he said. "Here. It is written by the Odd Bod's pater and not in the least what one would expect."

She nodded, severely, she hoped.

Wardley-Fish opened the book, not at the beginning, but at random. " 'The body is about one and a half inches thick.' " he said (this was not quite the sort of thing he sought) " 'and the same in height, of a purplish brown hue marked with longitudinal bands of a dull lilac, each band margined with a darker colour.' "

Melody Clutterbuck looked at her fiancée, perplexed. They passed a troop of guardsmen on horseback, a sight she normally loved. She did not even notice. She opened her mouth to speak, to object to the unsavoury scent—there was no other way to think of it—of this writing. It certainly did not seem appropriate for ladies. But her fiancée was ahead of her. He was already galloping on in search of better evidence. A paragraph here. A sentence there.

"You see, you see," he exclaimed, his eyes glistening wet. She had only seen him become this excited about horses. "The old boy is a marvel. The old boy is alarming. It is the 'Yea!,' Melody, isn't it? Your father's 'Yea!' Mr Carlyle's 'Eternal Yea!' The one your pater speaks of."

"Ian, please!"

"From this," he waved the book with great emotion, "to a room with no fire."

"Dearest, you make no sense."

" 'Within a day or two after this, the other two of the same species lay their spawn.' No, no dearest. It is botany, or zoology. The old fellow is a fearsome Evangelical so we need not worry ourselves about propriety."

But talk as he might, he knew he had gone too far. He surrendered the book when she held out her left hand for it and he watched it join its partner—she was, in spite of her firm chin, very agitated—as the pair of them, left and right, attempted to collaborate in rewrapping the parcel.

I am frightened of her, he thought, and it is far too young to know such a thing.

It was the Hon. Mary Braden-Loch's day At Home. The young clergyman performed expertly. Melody Clutterbuck was pleased to have him much admired and had soon forgiven him his outburst in the cab. She was alarmed therefore to notice, in a break in the conversation, the dead quality of his lovely eyes. She could not guess that they held the indefinite sky of a window three storeys above the streets of Notting Hill.

46

In a Trice

It was Mr Paxton—the same Mr Paxton who designed the Crystal Palace—who advised Lucinda Lealastrier to return to Sydney on the *Leviathan*. He spoke as an engineer, he said, and there is no doubt she would see nothing like it "so long as sanity is the general condition in my profession."

Lucinda expressed doubt that she should entrust her life to a vessel so described. He made it sound as if the ship were quite unsound.

"Its ability to float at sea is inversely proportional to the likelihood of it floating on the season of commerce. Go," he said, "it is as safe as an elephant. It will be a great experience, aye, and a rare one, too, because she will be bankrupt two years from now, and Mr Legare can go back to building bridges which is more his line of work."

She bought her ticket with her customary confusion about the price. It was fifty-five pounds for second class. It was too much money. It was seventy pounds for first class. She could afford it. She bought a first-class ticket, but in all her to-ing and fro-ing about the rights and wrongs of this, she never imagined that the largest ship ever built would be so empty. London had been lonely enough. This was worse. And it was because of this, because of the grand and supercilious spaces, that she had come down on to the wharf and she was, the minute her feet were on the ground, much happier.

It was like descending from a town hall to a market place—suddenly there was life all around her—steel rails along the wharf and cranes rolling to and fro, donkey engines thumping, white blossoms of steam, and even the rain, although it wet her boots, did not depress her. She was pleased to be down here, amongst practical people. There were practical smells—coal, coke, anthracite, mineral oil. It was the mineral oil that made her think about her glassworks with which, in her absence, she had developed a closer and more affectionate relationship. She forgot the anxieties and tensions her ownership produced and felt, now, on Southampton wharf, sympathetically drawn to the man who smelt of mineral oil—an engineer, she guessed, a freckle-faced Scot with a clenched-up face who would never be welcome in Marian Evans's drawing room. Her glassworks smelt like this. All glassworks did. At the glassworks she visited in Trent, in London itself, and even in Nottingham where they were making sheet glass for Mr Paxton, there was the same smell, the smell of her own works on Darling Harbour. The pear wood they used to turn the foot of a vase would be soaked, not just in water, but in mineral oil, and she was suddenly made impatient to return—as impatient as she had been to leave—to the aroma of burnt pear wood, mineral oil, and the acrid chemical smells of sulphates and chromates oxidizing to green and yellow.

She was twenty-two years old and fashionably dressed in grey moiré. Her back was curved; her backside, as was the fashion, pronounced but not to the degree suggested by George Eliot in a sharp letter written at that time. The pamphleteer's daughter, according to the famous novelist, could have sat a tea tray on the ledge of her backside, but George Eliot was fifty-eight years old and bad tempered with kidney stones and she had misunderstood the girl completely.

> She is such a "little" thing, it would appear that all conversation has been squeezed out of her. She sits with her hands pressed in her lap, totally silent, but with no consciousness of her social inadequacy and it is difficult, after the second hour, to maintain one's natural sympathy for her. George [Lewes] was kind and took her to the British Museum and then to tea where she seems to have attempted to seduce him into a game of chance. Apart from this outburst she seems to have said little, and it is so difficult, no matter what one's intentions, to hold a conversation with someone who will not talk.

Lucinda had expected her mother's friend to share her mother's enthusiasms. But while George Eliot had encouraged Elizabeth's essays and pamphlets, she had never shared "Elizabeth's fanatacism" for factories. And while she was interested to learn that the orphan had actually purchased a factory, she did not wish to discuss the manufacture of glass. If Lucinda had employed female glass blowers, perhaps it would have been different, but her single attempt in that direction had been a failure. George Eliot was not interested, and she had work to do.

Lucinda thought George Eliot was a snob. She preferred Mr Paxton who laughed at her outright but who had, just the same, explained his new project, presented her with a blueprint of the broad schemata, and written her letters of introduction to the glassworks he dealt with. To be patronized by Mr Paxton was an altogether more pleasant experience than being disapproved of by her mother's famous friend.

Lucinda had come to London thinking of it as "Home." It was soon clear that this great sooty machine was not home at all. She had left Sydney with thoughts of marriage and children. She had left—although it did not make her comfortable to remember this—in a temper with Dennis Hasset who, whilst remaining her close friend and confidante, obviously did not think her a suitable candidate for marriage. She had left him to stew in the juices of his own regret. She did not doubt she would have proposals in London, if only because of her wealth. She had steeled herself to fend off undesirables. Nothing like this had happened, although the stern Mr Paxton had behaved, twice, in an ungentlemanly way.

She stepped back to allow the steam crane to pass along its rails and, looking up to see what it might be carrying, saw a bellowing Poll Hereford with a canvas sling under its middle. The crane stopped and began to lower its burden on to the top of that mighty riveted cliff wall which was *Leviathan*.

The wharf resembled a sale yard and reminded the woman with the small bright eyes of the days she had gone into Parramatta with her father to buy a pig or sell the vealers. The air was redolent with fear and wet fur. The beasts were scouring, and thinking of this, she resolved to stand beneath no more airborne beasts.

She walked past the corralled animals, and did not mind the stares of the oilskin-wrapped shepherds who could not imagine why a woman, one of her class, would walk along a busy wharf in the rain. She was accustomed to this sort of stare and while she felt the implicit threat in it—the voodoo of a group of men—she was now a woman who employed such men, and her old fears in the face of their insulting confidence were allayed by the knowledge of her economic strength. It was wrong that she had this strength but she was, thank

God, pleased to have it. She did not make them lower their eyes, but she already had the power to do so. This power was primed by money, but it was not fuelled by it. And it was this, this turbulent, often angry sense of her own power, that was most responsible for her being lonely in London. Even George Eliot, no matter what her fiction might suggest, was used to young ladies who lowered their eyes in deference to her own. Lucinda did not do so. The two women locked eyes and George Eliot mentions (in the letter already quoted from) "a quite peculiar tendency to stare." It may well have been this, not her bits-and-pieces accent, her interest in trade, her lack of conversational skills, her sometimes blunt opinions or her unladylike way of blowing her nose—like a walrus, said George Eliot—that made her seem so alien. And when she did, at last, lower her eyes, her lids were heavy and sensuous. They produced an effect which was ungenerously described as "sly."

She walked past the long-nosed Derby hogs, all pushed into each other like pieces in a puzzle, and found a great collection of wet and rusty cages and two men arguing over one of them. A hansom clipped past them, bursting with clergymen, or so it seemed. She noticed the unusual red hair of one of them, but only in passing, being more taken by the argument which concerned one cage only, it being, apparently through error, filled with wet and shivering rabbits."

"Crikey Moses!" said the short one. He had an eager sort of face with heavy sandy eyebrows pressing down upon his blinking eyes. "The blessed colony is half eaten out by rabbits. Why would I want more?" He screwed up his face and sent his voice up into falsetto.

"Don't ask me, guv. It's all writ here."

"I'll take the rest, but not the rabbits."

"Sorry, guv, t'ain' either or. It's all or bleeding nothing."

Lucinda walked amongst the cages: rabbits, pigeons, pheasants, all addressed to a body known as the Acclimatization Society of New South Wales. There were also deer, half a dozen does and three bucks, all the males in separate cages, and one of them already bleeding badly around the head. And lastly, there were llamas, standing still and wet, each one in a separate cage, all marked with stern signs forbidding any contact. Lucinda tried to pat a doe, but it pulled its head away sharply and, when she persisted, tried to bite her.

She turned to walk back to the first-class gangway. The rain was beginning to ease back to its more usual drizzle. An officer, done up in braid like an Italian, saluted her. There were fifty-five days to Sydney. Fifty-five days before she would know if Dennis Hasset had—she bit her lower lip and scrunched up her eyes – married Harriet Borrodaile or Elizabeth Palmer. His letters had mentioned "the most appalling dances" but she did not trust the description. Dear God, let him still be a bachelor, not that I might marry him, but that he may be my friend. Dear God, please leave me someone with whom I can talk.

The rain started again, heavily, and the gangway ahead would not clear. She lifted her umbrella to see properly, peering up from the fourth step. It would appear that there were problems with an invalid. She recognized the red-haired clergyman as the one who had arrived in a handsom, or, rather, recognized the hair. It was he who was the invalid. She thought it strange they should carry a man backwards up a gangplank. But then, as she watched, she saw they were no longer going up, but coming down. And this was how she first saw Oscar, although there was not a lot to see because he had his hands pressed to his face.

The Reverend Oscar Hopkins was carried, moaning, backwards, off the *Leviathan*. The Reverend Ian Wardley-Fish carried the stretcher at the end where his feet were, and the Reverend Hugh Stratton, in spite of his bad back, carried the other. There were also, in this entourage, Mrs Stratton, Melody Clutterbuck, and Theophilus Hopkins, a bleak-faced old man whose eyebrows needed trimming; he carried a box full of soldering implements he had made especially for his son.

As Lucinda watched, the red-haired clergyman was blind-folded.

The handsome one with the blond beard clapped his hands together. The red-haired one was still moaning. The blond-bearded one said: "Speed. We need speed, Hopkins. That will do the trick." Then he clapped his hands together again, and gazed around like a man looking for a stick to kill a snake. He was quite drenched.

The old man with the grey-streaked beard held his gift like a sodden magus who has arrived at a disappointing destination. "Surely," he said, fiddling with the neck button of his oilskin, "surely, Oscar, you can *walk*?"

A large frowsy blonde woman with a loud Oxbridge voice and an enormous bosom now came forward and began to tug at the old man's coat. "Come," she said, "come, we shall go aboard."

Lucinda pushed past and got on to the gangway before they could cause any more trouble. She found the English tiresome in the extreme. She acknowledged one more ostentatious salute and hurried to her stateroom. She left her umbrella dripping by the door, took off her hat, unlaced her boots, and then, with nothing on her feet but stockings, sat at the little bureau and tried to write in her journal.

For all the things that had happened to her, all the people she had met, the miles of ocean she had covered, she could feel nothing worth writing except: "An exceedingly grand apartment which I spoil by the excess of irritation and agitation I carry with me everywhere. Would dearly love cribbage."

She heard the crane's donkey engine. She leaned forward, to see if she might catch a glimpse of one more cow, when a large cage swung past the porthole, so close she involuntarily flinched. In the cage were three clergymen, the blindfolded one, looking quite green, squatted in the middle. His mouth was open. She could not hear what noise he made. The older clergyman (he looked like an aged boy) held the blindfolded one's arms. He looked very still and very pale and his mouth was shut. But the blond one with the mole was all animation. His hands were raised. His eyes were dancing. He looked as though he would shortly spring into the air.

Lucinda could hear him quite distinctly.

"In a trice," he shouted, "I told you, Hopkins—in a trice."

47

Babylon

The saloons and cabins of the *Leviathan* were lofty and ornate. There was carving, scrollwork, plush. The grand saloon, in which Lucinda Leplastrier stood, quite alone, was almost three times her height, was sixty-two feet long and thirty-six feet wide. Two great funnels passed through this room but were covered with eight panels, four larger ones, which were mirrors, and four smaller ones, ornamented with paintings of children and emblems of the sea. There were couches upholstered in red plush, settees in Utrecht velvet, a carved mahogany organ, buffets and tables of elegantly carved walnut, arabesque panels filled with sentimental paintings. There were Brussels carpets on the floor and—those items Wardley-Fish had selected as somehow expressing the quintessential nature of the Leviathan's unseemly opulence–portiéres of carmine silk.

One could lean across the rail of the grand saloon as Lucinda did now, and gaze down into the second-class promenade. And whilst it is true that Mr Ishmael Kingdom Legare had not been quite so lavish there, he had, just the same, been generous with comfort and with space and if brutal iron girders crossed the ceiling of second class–they were also sympathetically decorated (after an oriental theme), being painted blue and red alternatively, the underside edged with gilt and the spaces between the beams divided into panels which were very lightly decorated in colour and gold.

Lucinda looked down at the second class and liked it better than the place she was in. She thought: I have done it again.

She had wasted money to be in a place whose privileges she somehow had imagined herself "entitled" to, but once she had been robbed of the extra fifteen pounds involved, the privilege would only serve to make her feel squeezed and constricted and her voice would sound coarse, not just to others, perhaps not to others at all, but to herself. She could not imagine how anyone with warm blood in their veins could feel at home amongst the cool and polished distances in first class. She had pretended to herself that she was one of them, but she was not. And so she imagined that she would be much more at home in second class. She liked the way the second-class cabins–they were in two tiers, like little terraces, one up, one down–all opened on to this central space, and she, conscious of her very public lack of well-wishers, was much attracted by the knot of people in second class; they were clustered around the men who had arrived by cage. It was not just curiosity made her wish to be amongst them, but something stronger, more physical, a need to push herself in amongst her kind, like a Derby hog or a rabbit in a cage.

The crowd milling around the clergymen had increased since she had seen it at the gangplank. There were schoolboys. There had been four, but now there were three. These three were making a presentation of a memorial scroll to the red-headed clergyman who made a small speech in return. He moved his hands much when he spoke. He blew his nose. There was applause. There was a broad-shouldered man with a heavy beard–not a clergyman, but obviously a pedagogue–who shepherded the boys into one corner and arranged for them to have tea and cake. The fourth boy returned at this time. She wondered who was travelling and who staying. She considered, once again, transferring her baggage down to a second-class cabin, but faced with the bored and supercilius expressions of the stewards, did not have the energy.

The red-headed clergyman was escorting the old man with the dark beard (his father, surely?), taking him from point to point around the second-class promenade, gesturing excitedly like a young artist at last admitted to the Royal Academy and the old man, excessively careful in his steps, was playing the part of the proud and newly frail. The younger woman of the party arranged herself (carefully, for she was fashionably dressed) on a velvet sofa, pressed her hands to her eyes, then looked up. Lucinda saw her smile, and returned it, not understanding that what she had thought was a smile was in reality a grimace.

Melody Clutterbuck – it was she who had grimaced – was almost sick with the embarrassment of being there. She was ill at ease and out of place. She was cowed by the ship, and yet it was not the ship that did it to her for she would not have felt like this in any other company. Had she been here alone with Ian it would have been quite different, or with her father, or almost anyone she knew. But she was, by blind and unjust circumstances, forced into company with those for whom this ship was not intended and she was, therefore, one of them. She did not know which of her companions was the worst. They were an ensemble; their performance was too grotesque to be contemplated. There were, for instance, the Strattons, a type all too familiar to Melody Clutterbuck. She had observed their fellows at the dinner table of her father, the Bishop, since her earliest childhood. They smelled of dust and sherry and had shiny patches on their garments; the male had slippery eyes which could not hold the gaze a second; the female had great opinions and was noisy with her cutlery; they had what could be most politely termed "hearty" manners. The Strattons displayed all the characteristics of their caste. They leaned forward over plates of buns which had been made with the intention of amusing children. When they had their mouths full, for that brief period when further biting was impossible, they cast eyes around like clerks from Sotheby's come to value furniture. They were grubby, of course, but it was not a grubbiness you could detect at a distance. It was there so deep within their fabrics that you might think it part of them, as indeed it was. They had cultured voices, and it was this last part, the contrast between how they sounded and how they looked, that made them so disturbing.

But these were the cream of her present society. They, at least, had precedents in her world. They were "types" and even if they were irritating, they also had a set place in the menagerie of life. But Oscar – Oscar made her flesh crawl and her hands dig into each other. Fingernail attacked flesh as if it might therefore create enough confusion in the brain, and with this smokescreen of pain block out of the other larger pain. She cound not bear the bony triangle of head. As a triangle it was far too long. The mouth occupied too small a space. The hair was quite beyond belief. He had a faint moustache now, but it was so feeble one wished to inform him there was no point persisting. She had a list. A long list. She could not, for instance, bear his fluting voice, his frightful flapping hands, his total insensitivity to how she felt about him which allowed him, in spite of everything, to bestow on her the most beneficent smiles. Even the way he ordered cocoa from the steward was, in the middle of this precise luxury, naïve to the point of idiocy. The stewards, it was easy to see, were the most frightful little snobs and Melody Clutterbuck sympathized with them (she also judged them – they were only stewards) when they saw the type of person they would be called upon to serve. In first class, she presumed, one would not be so embarrassed. She looked up at the lady in first class, made a little grimace, and was pleased to receive one in return.

The famous Theophilus Hopkins (he had made such a fool of himself with his letters to *The Times* attacking Mr Darwin) was, if it were possible, even worse than the son. He struck her as a somnambulis. His eyes had looked at her without giving any indication of knowing what they looked at. He carried his tin box as if it were the ashes of someone particularly dear to him. When he sat down he placed the tin box on his lap and rested his tea-cup on it. And yet it was not a lack of manners that Melody found disturbing. Indeed he could rest his cup and saucer on his box and make it appear almost respectable. It was the knowledge that he was batty. He was a handsome man in his way, and quite properly dressed. His hands, it is true, were large and horny, a tradesman's hands more than a gentleman's. But none of this mattered. What mattered was that he was likely to take it into his head that the ship was Babylon. It was this that Ian feared. She watched the old man warily, unsure what he was capable of. She had already endured two prayers, one at the foot of the gangway, and another as the colossal embarrassment of the crane got under way. Ian thought he might begin to lay about him with a whip, as Jesus had driven the money-changers from the temple. She wondered what was really in the tin box and had, indeed, offered to mind it for him. The offer had been courteously declined. She thought he was staring at the crimson portières. Ian claimed these would be the first to go.

Their party, however, was by no means the only one gathering in the promenade. There was a preponderance of males and if some of them appeared, beneath their new suits, to be colonials of the rougher type, then so much the better. The ranter would be stopped quickly.

He picked up his tin box. She steeled herself. The son took his arms. They walked a little way and stopped. The father's eyes were dark and casting all around.

48

Who Can Open the Doors of His Face?

The author of *Corallines of the Devon Coast* had an eye well trained to the nicest degree. And although we would recognize this to be the result of synapses made by his own passions, millions of connections made like the knots in the butterfly net he had left hanging on his study wall in Hennacombe, each knot occasioned by need and strengthened by use, Theophilus Hopkins, FRS, a proud man, was forever at war with any interpretation which gave him any credit at all. When he called his talent a "gift," he meant the word not as a simile for talent but an explanation of it. That the gift was considerable is attested to by those drawing of sea creatures, which were his life's work.

In the context of the *Leviathan*, this gift is worth insisting on, for we are discussing one of the great literal describers of his age, a man who could observe a butterfly, say, for ten seconds and accurately recall the form and coloration of body and wing parts.

This man saw nothing of the *Leviathan*. Afterwards he had almost no impression, except a (needless) concern that the huge paddle wheels on its side were it only means of locomotion. So if his eyes were, as Melody Clutterbuck thought, "all about," then what they were looking at was not to be found in the second-class promenade or saloon, not in the library, the games room, the dining room, or anywhere else he walked (one step at a time, no individual step in excess of twelve inches) as he tried to hide his arthritic pain from the beloved son the Lord had taken from him.

Oscar had left home in 1859. It was now 1865 and they had only met four times in the intervening years. These meetings had been more painful than either could bear, and not because the son had become a "sporting seat"—the father knew nothing of his source of income, imagining him supported by some Anglican mechanism—their disagreement had its roots in the most basic matters of theology. Yet every morning and every evening Theophilus had prayed for his son's soul, that he might yet sit beside God on the Last Day, that they, mother, father, babes and Oscar, would all be reunited and stand in Glory amongst the Saints. These were not prayers said by rote, but new ones, every time, and anyone who happened to be walking up the long red path to Morley might be privy to the extraordinarily detailed information they contained.

The most intimate details of Theophilus's sadness were discussed by everyone in Hennacombe, and yet there was no one with whom he could talk about it himself. The Strattons were kind to him. They were poor, far poorer than he was. They brought him broth and pudding with raisins in it. But he could not discuss the matter with them. They would not stand beside God in the Happy Day.

A second cousin of Mrs Stratton's held a post with the Church Missionary Society of London. That was how the Strattons knew that Oscar was to sail to New South Wales. It was they who brought Theophilus the news his anxious son had not yet summoned up the courage to deliver. Theophilus was miffed. It was worse than miffed. It was jealous. He bit the inside of his cheek and gnawed on his bottom lip until he broke the skin. He could not bear that they should invite him to accompany them on the train to farewell the boy.

God hath delivered me to the ungodly, and turned me over to the hands of the wicked.

Yet he must bear it. The Strattons were in error, but they were also kind. He must not be full of pride. He prayed to God to prevent him falling to "that sin which most often besets me."

He shared a second-class carriage with them to Southampton. He shared their too-sweet-too-milky tea and felt himself deceitful. He fully intended to save his son, not from Australia but from the Anglican heresy. To this end he worked at his Bible. He wrapped himself in his greatcoat—the carriage was unheated—and while the train rattled over the long low bridge at Teignmouth, he ignored the pleasures of the view, the bare-legged women collecting out on the mud flats, the lovely lustrous sheen upon the wet earth, the misty blue-white sky. He knew all of the Bible by heart and if you wished to quote a verse to him he could continue from there, reciting until you bade him stop. But on this day, as the train rolled through Exmouth and Lyme Regis, he tore little strips of paper and made diminutive notes upon them. He used these pieces of paper as markers in his Bible, all in readiness for the prayer he would say over his son.

The Anglicans insisted on talking. There was nothing in their conversation but money. He knew their situation was difficult. He felt a certain sympathy. But he had never heard such gross materialism. Mrs Stratton, so she told him, was engaged by a certain publisher to write a novel. Theophilus nodded politely. Inside he boiled. He did not doubt that Satan spoke through novels. Mrs Stratton wished to discuss the financial arrangements he made with publishers. He did not wish to speak of anything that might assist her plan. Mr Stratton wished to know how Oscar had obtained the money for his voyage. He did not press at this directly but came at it, like a mouse around a skirting board, all stops and starts and quick grey scurries. Theophilus thought this impertinent. He excused himself and went back to his work, but this did not stop the Strattons and they talked away, pennies and shillings, to each other. It was like sharing a carriage with a pair of grocers.

Theophilus became so out of temper with the Strattons—although he thought it unchristian to be so—that he was quite unprepared for the reunion with his son. He was hit before he got his muscles ready. He stood on grey, sooty Southampton station and was nearly washed away. He watched Mrs Stratton embrace his boy. Jealousy ripped him. He trembled. He did not embrace. He shook hands formally, but felt so light in the head he feared he would faint. He found a bench on the pretext of tying a bootlace, but when he got there, he dared not put his head down lest the blood rush to it. He placed his tin box beside him on the seat and his Bible on top of it. The Bible shed some markers. Mr Stratton picked them up for him. Theophilus stuffed them in his greatcoat pocket as if they were nothing but dead leaves.

He had felt faint ever since. He was like a man who arrives at Osaka when he had been expecting Edinburgh. Everything was odd, distant, trembling. His son was beautiful to him. His heart sang the Song of Solomon. He had his mother's fine, heart-shaped face, the face he had cupped in his hands at the wonderful moment when his seed spurted. *A bundle of myrrh is my well-beloved unto me; he shall lie all night between my breasts*. He had his mother's gorgeous hair and milk skin, his mother's animations and enthusiasm, her wide eyes and, most of all, her hope. This was not a dark face that would fall prey to pride of jealousy. It was a better face, a better face by far. He offered the gift. It was all he had.

The box, as you know, was a tin box containing implements for soldering, a technique Theophilus set great store by, but one never properly mastered by his son. He had made not just the box, but the wooden handles for the soldering irons themselves. He had given up his two best bottles (ones with ground-glass stoppers) for the acid and flux. He had made a smaller box to hold the resin. On the lid of the box he had riveted a little copper plaque on which he had etched: "O.J.P. Hopkins, a gift from his father."

But even when the son had accepted the box and thanked him for it, Theophilus could not contemplate him without agitation. He wished to kneel with him and pray. It was not shyness prevented him from doing it on Southampton railway station. (He was never ashamed publicly to bear witness.) It was the fear of being overcome with emotion. This was his flaw, the crack in his clay, and the more dreadful for being so unexpected: that one who preached so fearlessly in front of even the most hostile audience could also break down and lose control in public. He had disgraced himself at the boy's mother's funeral. He had tried to say a prayer for her. They had led him away. He had not been able to say the words. His voice had become a stranger in his throat.

When he heard the name *Leviathan* they were in a hansom, travelling across the slippery streets towards the docks. He did not think of a ship. He knew it was a ship. He had heard the Strattons lecture him with great authority on this subject. But when he heard the word *Leviathan* in Southampton, he thought of the giant whom God made to impress Job with his ignorance and powerlessness.

> I will not conceal his parts, nor his power, nor his comely proportions. Who can discover the face of his garment? Who can open the doors of his face? His teeth are terrible round about. His scales are his pride, shut up close together as with a close seal. Out of his mouth go burning lamps and sparks of fire leap out. The flakes of his flesh are joined together: they are firm in themselves; they cannot be moved.

This was the *Leviathan* Theophilus saw. He stood on the wharf and stared at it.

He saw his son tremble before the face of *Leviathan*.

Rain stood on the edges of his hair as on a holworth blossom.

"Surely, Oscar, surely," Theophilus said, "surely you can walk." But suddenly there was a stretcher, a blindfold, a cage. He wished to say his prayer but when he began no one noticed him. The pain from his arthritis was sewn through the fabric of his day, like a bright needle threaded with dull wire. The pain prevented proper concentration, but the name *Leviathan* stayed with him and gave him a curious and unexpected comfort, reminding him that he should not question the will of God, that he was ignorant in His sight, that his son might not be damned after all.

Theophilus Hopkins did not see the ship as the work of Satan. And what he did not like—satin, silk, plush—he did not look at. If the interior reminded him of anything, it was an Anglican cathedral, but he chose not to retain a single detail of it. He wished only to remember the face of his son.

He wished to go up on deck. He had a hunger for plain air. The sea was clean and uncorrupted.

Oscar could not go up on deck. They therefore stayed below, walking up and down, arm in arm, as Theophilus had seen men do in Italy.

Oscar praised the natural lighting and thorough ventilation. He had a firm grasp of the principles.

They went into Oscar's cabin where there was a sheet off celluloid, the new substance Theophilus had read about but never seen. The celluloid was marked with squares and was affixed to the porthole. He could get no proper explanation of its function, but did not persist. He thought they might say a prayer. He was wondering if the prayer he had devised on the train was the correct prayer after all, (It had been devised in jealousy and pride.)

Oscar showed how the bed folded up at day, and down at night. When the bed was down, Theophilus sat on it and was momentarily more comfortable in his joints. Oscar sat opposite him in a low chair with a carved back, but he could not be still and jigged his knee and played with his hands.

It was then that Theophilus gave Oscar the second present. It was tiny, wrapped in white tissue and wrapped with a black ribbon. It looked ominous, and the black (some leftover mourning ribbon from Theophilus's cabinet drawer) was perhaps in honour of the woman from whose womb the present had kept it, because it was said—superstitiously, of course—that such a thing would protect the child from drowning.

"Here," he said, holding it out with a hand that shook visibly. "It is your caul." And when Oscar did not understand: "From off your little head."

He drew his handkerchief from his pocket and unleashed the fragrance of Mrs Williams's ironing board. He blew his nose, not looking at his son. He was remembering a child and wife in a Devon lane—myrtles, perfumed hedges, luscious red mud, which caked so thickly on their boots that their feet became heavy and padded as creatures in a dream.

Oscar put the caul in the soldering box. It did not fit easily, but he crammed it in, jamming it around the bottle of acid, squashing it against the little box of resin, crushing the paper, kinking the mourning ribbon. He did not wish to harm it. He was much moved by the present. He clasped the lid shut and made a fuss of arranging the box on a long shelf behind his head. When he at last turned to face his father, his own expression was wary, hooded.

He was frightened of Theophilus's emotions. He could not name them. He could not guess their shapes and colours, and although he would spend the rest of his life wondering what these emotions were, now, when it appeared likely that they might be laid before him, as bare as knives and forks on a white tablecloth, he shrank from them.

He remembered his father's skin, that part of it where the black beard grew thin across the cheek, from there into the rippled mud-flat bay beneath the eyes. The skin looked like something that had been wrapped up too long. And there was a smell, a disturbing and familiar smell, which he recognized like the smell of a family home when it has not been lived in for a season. This combination of familiarity and distance was most disturbing. Also there were noises. They had been sounding for some time: electric megaphones. It would soon be time to go. Oscar felt the water stretching out endlessly behind his neck. The lines on the celluloid sliced through it, cut it into neat squares, which bled and joined again, were sliced, rejoined, sliced, rejoined.

Oscar did something jolly and scuttled out on to the promenade.

The air smelt of new paint and electricity. There was also something vaporous, like brandy, and leather, like a St James's shoemaker in the week before Ascot. Through all this there threaded, subtle but insistent, the smell of the sea. Oscar imagined he detected movement in *Leviathan*. He stood outside his cabin door.

His left hand grasped the wall rail. He grinned at Melody Clutterbuck.

Miss Clutterbuck barely saw the death's-head grimace. It was the father—he in the doorway behind the son—whom she was anxious about. She watched him creep from the top-tier cabin and thought he gazed around as from a pulpit. When he walked it was slowly; she did not think to attribute this to pain.

She stood and moved towards the other stair, like a customer in a bank who feels there are bank robbers in the queue in front of her but is not quite confident of her intuition.

Thus she did not escape the embarrassment. She stood still, pale in the face, blood mottling the plump hands, the hands clutching the gloves she had removed for tea. She saw the elder Hopkins drop to his knees. She thought she heard a groan. She thought: Evangelicals do not kneel!

She saw a steward begin to move towards the old man, and then he stopped. The praying mantis went down beside his father. Miss Clutterbuck imagined she heard the thump of bony knees on a carpet that should have been thick enough to muffle anything. She caught, just then, her fiancée's eyes, but only for a second because he—oh, you fool, you fool—was aping the fundamentalists. She looked to the Strattons but he was already on his shiny knees and she was lowering herself, resting her large hand on his shoulder. And now she saw strangers as well, those who had nothing to do with their pathetic party. A short man who smelt of wet animals came and knelt beside her. There was something horribly intimate in the sight of his balding crown. Others, some with crystal wine glasses in their hands, followed suit. The stewards remained standing, but even they folded their hands in front of them and bowed their heads like so many Baptists. Outside the megaphone continued blaring, but inside it was very quiet, and Melody Clutterbuck, not wishing to be thought a Dissenter herself, knelt.

There was a long silence, a minute, perhaps two, before Theophilus Hopkins, FRS began his prayer.

"Oh, Lord God," he began. His voice was tangled. He began again: "Oh, Lord God, this is my son."

The next pause was shorter, but felt more painful.

"These are his friends, and fellow voyagers."

You could hear Mrs Stratton's asthmatic breathing. She was swaying a little on her knees. Mr Stratton rubbed her back.

"Oh, Lord my God," said Oscar's father, the deep voice so broken that many did not hear the last words: "What can we do?"

Then he was on his feet. He touched his son, so briefly, a brush so light Oscar would always wonder if he had not invented it himself. He walked up the stairs quickly and in pain. He went out of sight with a peculiar hobble: fast, short steps and a tightly screwed up face. The congregation rose slowly, and were not keen to meet each other's eye.

Down on the wharf, Theophilus Hopkins prayed again. He stood before *Leviathan* and a crowd gathered around him. But the scales of the giant were fitted tight together and the sound of his voice did not reach the son who would not leave the promenade.

Oscar waited for his father to return. And while he waited, while it became clear, even to him, that his father had left forever, he could look nowhere but towards the busy bulkhead through which the old man had departed. A great pain took possession of his heart and clamped around his lungs so that although he stood, in the midst of his friends, with his red lips parted, no air came to rescue him.

He thought: I will never again look upon his wise old face.

He thought: I have been a poor son to leave him all alone. He embraced Mrs Stratton, shook hands with Wardley-Fish, Miss Clutterbuck, Mr Colville and the pupils from the school. There was a great fuss of sirens, bells, fireworks. Lucinda, watching from above, wondered why the clergyman sat by himself on the bright red *chaise-longue*.

Oscar was caught in the web of his phobia in the geometrical centre of the ship. He imagined everyone had gone.

49

The System

Mr Stratton gave Oscar a fright. He pushed his face close up. He did give not a warning. He came creeping over the carpet with one last glass of complimentary sherry in his hand. The boy did not look up, but Mr Stratton did not imagine himself invisible. Quite the contrary. He was the only visitor left on the promenade. He had been requested, twice already, to leave the ship. He felt his defiance bathed in limelight.

He imagined the young man waiting for him. It was only natural in his view, for there were matters too long postponed which must be spoken of between them. He had expected them to be spoken of earlier, but as they had not been, they must be spoken of now. He was a man with a nervous respect for clocks and timetables. Bells, alarms, sirens, all had a direct affect upon his physiology. But he would not be cowed by sirens today. They could row him ashore if necessary.

Mr Stratton sat on the settee three feet from Oscar. He placed his sherry on its back rail. He balanced it nicely there and really did not care that the alcohol might scar the varnish.

Oscar did not see him. All Oscar could see was the image cast on his retina by his departed papa's face, most particularly that penny-sized area of vulnerable skin beneath the eyes.

"You can no longer put me off," said Mr Stratton. He pushed his face up close to Oscar's.

Oscar leapt a good two inches from his seat.

"Hooo," he said.

Mr Stratton's face stayed complacently where it was, although the hand which served it went back, searching blindly along the edge of the settee for its master's sherry.

Oscar had remained very fond of both the Strattons and his pity for Mr Stratton had not diminished his feelings, quite the contrary, but today he was repulsed by the too-obvious signs of cunning he saw on the face which had once been—the past showed through the corruption of the present—so innocent and boyish.

Oscar was too preoccupied with the loss of his papa properly to grasp the clergyman's intention. He laid his hand on Mr Stratton's shoulder. "It's time," he said, "and a sad time too."

But Mr Stratton's face had become tight with suspicion. It was a face that knew the world was not as it is commonly presented. It knew there were tricks and larks played everywhere, by bishops, provosts, kings, even rural deans. It was a face ripe for some heresy, one that would make even the Lord God of Hosts nothing but a vain and boastful demiurge whose claims to omnipotence were based on ignorance and pride.

"There has been enough of cat and mouse," said Mr Stratton, pinning his eyes to Oscar's, "you must tell me now."

When Oscar looked at Mr Stratton's eyes, he felt that he must never have done so before this moment, that he must have, through politeness, even squeamishness, have slid around them, knowing he would see only unhappiness there. Today he was not permitted to avoid them. They were blue and watery; the whites were yellow, veined, stained, like the porcelain basin at the Swan in Morley.

Mr Stratton's hand brought the sherry glass to his mouth. The lower lip reached out to anticipate it. The foot of the glass came close to Oscar's nose.

"We have looked after your poor father," he said. "as best we could. We fed him when we could barely afford to feed ourselves and we could have no expectation of reward, at least not on this earth. Similarly, we looked after you. You could not imagine we had *profit* in mind," Mr Stratton laughed, a shallow noise made from old air at the back of the throat. "We educated you so you might bear witness. We did not think we were assisting a wealthy man."

Mr Stratton looked around the promenade, underlining the opulence of their surroundings in a manner which, had it occurred upon the stage, would have been pure ham but which here, driven before the rough current of his hurt, served only to fill Oscar's heart with shame.

"I thank you," Oscar said, "I have always.—"

"I have been thanked before," said Mr Stratton. "I cannot think that it has been beneficial to be taunted with fancy coffee or mysterious packets of currency."

For a moment Oscar was angry. The amounts he had sent the Strattons had not been insubstantial.

"Naturally you wish to speak to me," said Mr Stratton. "You do not wish to taunt me any longer." And he opened his mouth a little as was his habit when waiting for someone to speak. The tip of his pink tongue flicked quickly across his sherry-sticky lips.

The sirens were blaring. They had changed their tempo and were now short, sharp, insistent, like dagger thrusts into taut white canvas.

"Now you will tell me, God help me. You cannot leave without it." He took Oscar's wrist and squeezed it. He would not let it go. It hurt. "How does a Christian clergyman acquire the funds to travel in such luxury? I am not a cadger. I do not come to you with a begging letter. I am sunk low enough, but not so low. You must tell me how it is you have managed."

"You would not find the story pretty."

"You need not worry about my sensibilities, little lad." He gave the wrist a harder squeeze and his mouth, for that moment, was twisted by the spasm of his anger. "My poverty does not allow them."

"You would not be proud of me."

"Would not? Am not. Oh, I pray You, stop him *prattling*"

"If I were to tell you and my papa were to hear of it, it would be a torture beyond his toleration."

"You have my word he never shall," said Hugh Stratton and, seeing that Oscar still hesitated, "oh, dear Oscar, you must accept my *word*."

"I have gambled," said Oscar, "as you long ago suspected."

"So," said Mr Stratton, and let out some air, "gambled."

"I think the ship is moving."

"You have a system, then? Is that what it is called?"

"A system?"

"Yes, a system. Temple has explained them to me. You have a system and you will write it down for me."

And, indeed, he was selecting, from the over-full pocket of his shiny coat, a used envelope and a stubby pencil which he now managed to push at Oscar without ever once letting go his painful hold on the wrist.

"It is not so simple. It is not a thing you can just write down. We have left it too late."

Mr Stratton's hand relaxed its grip on the wrist and his jaw was slack and all the skin on his face seemed lifeless and crushed, a second-hand substance from the bottom shelf in the scullery.

Oscar wished to retrieve his wrist, but did not.

"Write it down, boy, please, I beg of you."

He did not know what it was he was asking. It was not possible. The charts and tables that made up the system were contained in sixteen black clothbound journals. They were at once as neat as the boxes of buttons he had classified in his father's house, all ruled with columns and divisions, and, at the same time, smudged and blotted. His hand was a poor servant to his mind—the first was a grub whilst the second was a fastidious fellow with white cuffs on his sleeves and a tyrant for having everything in its place.

These notebooks were in his trunk. They would be worth nothing to him in New South Wales. Surely there was time to run to his cabin and thrust them into Mr Stratton's hands. The clergyman would not understand them, of course, but the explanation could be conducted by mail and what was important was the gift. For the books did prove that a man could make a good living at the track if he should apply himself with Christian industry.

But no, he could not relinquish them.

He did not know why he could not. He had not expected to be asked, and when it happened he felt not generosity, but anger and confusion.

The books were so intimately involved with his life, were his life, his obsession, his diaries, his communion with his God, his tie to the monster who must be fed. They were private. They were secret. They were five years' work. He had travelled all over the south of England recording the coded information therein. He had assembled a history which, blots and smudges aside, was superior to any bookmaker at Tattersall's – the record of five hundred and twenty-five racehorses, positions, weights, whether rising in class or in weight, distances of race, conditions of track, etc, etc. And although he did not bet on mares or fillies, he had the information on them just the same.

"Please, I ask you to leave me, Mr Stratton," said Oscar gently. "You hold a very dangerous secret and can therefore be confident I will write to you from New South Wales. I will tell you how I have achieved it."

He was a miser. He was unchristian. He must give away the books. Even if he had owed the Strattons nothing, he should give away the books. But he was a weasel, cunning with excuses, with substitutes.

"I will send the letter to you by return post from Sydney. I give you my solemn word before God. And you are quite right that I have been thoughtless and unkind in not thinking of your situation. I feared only that you would inform my papa."

Hugh Stratton held the gaze of the young man's clear eyes, not quite daring to trust them.

"Write it down."

"It is not so simple. I cannot."

"You swear before God?"

"I do."

What did he swear? Simply that he could not transcribe the books in five minutes. This was true, quite true, but he had become too clever at this weaseling kind of "truth," which was not a truth at all.

"Is it horses?"

Give him the books. Give them.

"It is."

Mr Stratton let go the wrists. He nodded. He opened his mouth to say something, but the sirens triumphed. He nodded once more, then again. He was making a dangerous decision on how to fund his betting programme. He ran up the stairs, grimacing with the pain in his sciatic nerve. At the top of the stairs he called out something but Oscar did not hear. He was examining the bright red bracelet Mr Stratton had imprinted on his skin. He sat in the sumptuous cavern of the second-class promenade, alone with this new knowledge of his corruption.

50

Pachinko

In order that I exist, two gamblers, one Obsessive, the other Compulsive, must meet. A door must open at a certain time. Opposite the door, a red plush settee is necessary. The Obsessive, the one with six bound volumes of eight hundred and eighty pages, ten columns per page, must sit on this red settee, the Book of Common Prayer open on his rumpled lap. The Compulsive gambler must feel herself propelled forward from the open doorway. She must travel towards the Obsessive and say an untruth (although she can have no prior knowledge of her own speech): "I am in the habit of making my confession."

But even this, a conclusion which requires, of the active party, a journey as complex as that of a stainless steel Pachinko ball (rolling along grooved metal tunnels, sloping down, twisting sideways, down into the belly of *Leviathan*, up, sideways, up, up, and out of the door to face the red settee) may not have taken place if the ventilation system of *Leviathan* had not displayed a single eccentricity of which its designers had been totally unaware.

The eccentricity was this: it carried conversation from one stateroom to another, and that was how Lucinda was haunted by the sounds of bored stewards playing cards all night. They were not in the stateroom next to hers. That was empty, as were all the other first-class staterooms which she had imagined, when looking at the shipping company's brochures, would supply her with companionship for the voyage. (There were Bavarians in Imperial first class, but these were separated by a silken blue rope.) The stewards were several empty staterooms along, and such was the design of the ventilators that had they been closer, she may not have heard them at all.

Their conversations were perfectly transmitted, as if every one of them had a voice tube of his own.

She could not read because of it. It was not the noise. It was the subject matter. Now, she thought, it is Tuppenny they play, now Blind

Jack, now poker. The cockney with the high voice is the best player. She liked him. She imagined him with sandy, spiky hair and a habit of screwing up his eyes. He would grin a lot. Sometimes he would suck a match. He would give away no secrets. There was another one who always spoke more quickly when his hand was good. This one was from Liverpool. He was, of all of them, the most worried by his new job. He was previously chief steward of the *Sobraon* and Lucinda would have learned, if she had not known already, that the *Sobraon* was a well-regarded ship. This man's chief had been so outraged that he would depart his post for another ship that he had said that the chief steward would never be signed on again by him, "Not," he kept repeating, "under no circumstances whatever."

The stewards thought of themselves as the "crème de la crème." They were proud of their work. They were not the simple snobs that Melody Clutterbuck imagined. It was she who was the snob. These men were perfectionists. They were as proud as glass blowers. They had been tricked. They expected to serve people who would respect, or at least recognize, their finesse; but instead they found a preponderance of colonial bullies who wished to lord it. Down in second class there was a Mr Borrodaile, a rich and argumentative man who got drunk and threw biscuits down the ventilator.

Lucinda liked them all without seeing them. She would like to sit around a table with them. They could smoke and have a drop too much. She would not mind.

She did not belong in this stateroom with its vast curved empty space, its maroon carpets, its shiny icing of luxury. She did not even belong in the clothes, smart clothes from Marian Evans's dressmaker in the Burlington Arcade, and she recognized, the first night in her stateroom, with *Barchester Towers* resting in her lap, that it was only at Mr d'Abbs's house that she could be relaxed amongst ordinary people.

If these stewards had met her in the company of Mr d'Abbs, Mr Fig and Miss Malcolm (and it was by no means possible) they would play cards with her and not think about it. They would see that she could laugh, even drink and, if they were not careful, fleece them of their shore pay at three in the morning. It was a vulgar house, it was true, and in many ways, quite morally doubtful. It was a shock to realize that one "belonged" there—it was so second rate, colonial, even ignorant, but she could sit at the table there and not feel herself constrained by the corsets of convention. She did not have this dreadful tightness, in the throat, the arms, the chest.

In the dining room these stewards were actors in a play—they used different voices. She could not match the voice she heard at night with the voice that served her in the morning. When she sat at table she felt complicitous with them. She imagined that they, like her, felt restricted by their parts.

Meals, in any case, were an embarrassment. The dining room was all Grecian, with fluted columns, empty tables. There were four reluctant officers appointed to dine with her. She entered, blushing red. She ate as quickly as politeness would allow. She knew (or imagined) that her character, her passions, her occupation would all be unacceptable, even shocking, at this table. Her companions thought her a mouse. So she was. They made her one. She would rather have been playing Blind Jack or poker. There was, she thought, as she sliced her grey roast beef, *so* much to be said in favour of a game of cards. One was not compelled to pretend, could be silent without being thought dull, could frown without people being overly solicitous about one's happiness, could triumph over a man and not have to giggle and simper when one did it. One could kill time, obliterate loneliness, have a friendship with strangers one would never see again, and live on that sweet, oiled cycle of anticipation, the expectation that something delicious was about to happen. Which is not to say that the pleasures were all related to gain or greed. One could experience that lovely light-headed feeling of loss, the knowledge that one had abandoned one more brick from the foundation of one's fortune, that one's purse was quite, quite empty, had nothing in it but a safety pin, some dust, its own water silk lining, and no matter what panic and remorse all this would produce on the morrow, one had in those moments of loss such an immense feeling of relief—there was no responsibility, no choice. One could imagine oneself to be nothing but a cork drifting down a river in a romantic tale by Mr Kingsley.

In her first months as proprietor of the Prince Rupert's Glassworks she had played a hand of cribbage with the men during their breaks. She had seen this as a way whereby she could get to know them. But within a month they sent a message to her (back through Mr d'Abbs of all people) that they did not think it "proper" that this practice continue.

She would never be able to think of this message—delivered by an embarrassed Mr d'Abbs in the foyer of Petty's Hotel—without feeling the sting of their rejection. It hurt out of all proportion. It would not go away. She thought: All the time I have enjoyed the games, they have thought me a tart or something worse. She wished to weep for her stupidity, or slap them for theirs.

She had been proud of what the works produced. She was moved by the process as she always would be by the collaborative nature of human endeavour. She saw she had purchased a hell-hole that must always be a hell-hole and yet she was much affected by the way the men made themselves into a chain with chaos at one end and civilization at the other—the cockeyed little first gatherer, the sturdy, barrel-chested second gatherer, the handsome old third gatherer who would never be a master, the blower himself with his great grey beard and his arms as big as a boy's legs, the finicky stopper-offer who ran about, fast, bent over, like a mynah bird on a branch. She had felt it wrong to be the proprietor of such a hell-hole where the men must work in water-doused chaff bags, be awake at three a.m. (or ten p.m. or dawn) to meet the demands of the furnaces. But even though she could never become romantic about the hardness of their lives she also came to envy them their useful comradeship and it was through the doorway of a game of cards she hoped to enter it. She aspired only to play a useful part in manufacture, even though she was their "master."

Their rejection of her produced the most unchristian passions in her breast. "No gentleman," they told her, "would gamble with a lady." Her feelings were of the same order as those of a parent who wants to dash a howling baby to the floor.

She listened to the *Leviathan's* stewards and imagined being admitted to their game. She would knock on their door. She would introduce herself.

But she knew, of course, that they would immediately revert to their "steward" character. It would be an intrusion on their privacy too gross to contemplate. But surely, somewhere, there was a game got up. She imagined carpenters and engineers 'tween decks. She took her own deck of cards, the new ones purchased in Old Bond Street. They were Wetherby Supremes with the handsome black and gold filigree on their calendered backs which she always believed to be especially lucky. She snapped open the griffin seal which kept them in their place and shuffled them in her practical little hands, lengthening her top lip as she always did when excited—not a useful tic for a poker player to have—and cut them, splayed them, made a bridge and closed it. She had an ache. She felt it in the back of her knees, in her knuckles, a tension both pleasant and unbearable.

If she just walked, for instance, down to the regions known as 'tween decks, there would be an open door. There would be a game. She would stand and watch. They would not mind. She imagined it exactly. Four working men at a table. She would show them her own cards.

Silly. Too stupid for words.

She put her Wetherby Supremes in her velvet purse and walked out of her stateroom. She was going for a walk, that was all.

She was going—of course she was—to inspect her cargo in the hold. This was her right. She was a manufacturer. She might not look like one to you sir, but that only demonstrates your colonial nature. Not all manufacturers have side-whiskers and smoke cigars.

The equipment was from Chance Brothers. It would make the first window glass in New South Wales. She did not expect a town named after her for this. But neither, sir, did she expect to be patronized.

She opened the door to C deck and descended the stairs. She did not think about what she was doing.

Lucinda was looking for a game.

She moved along steel intestines of empty corridors from which she viewed, not four men around a table, but empty cabins whose new mattresses were still wrapped in brown paper; in some there were wood shavings and sawdust, even on D deck—a carpenter's tool box with a set of chisels so sharp that the sticky-beaking passenger cut her finger and had nothing but sawdust with which to staunch the flow.

I was not like being inside a ship at all, but like the innards of a reveted bridge, a great mechanical beast, the organs of an empire whose chimneys rose high into the Atlantic sky.

E deck contained animals, stall after stall of sheep, cattle, llamas. There was a sort of terror here. The air was not pleasant. It was rich and thick enough to make her—she who still thought herself a countrywoman, at home with dung, mud, beasts—rich and thick enough to make her gag. There were caged birds, too, and a young lad who said it was his job to feed them and wanted, most of all, to know what it was like atop. He was a strong, well-made boy, but his face was pale, and his face thrust at her from the fetid gloom—one yellow electric light every ten yards—and she did not feel easy with his belligerent curiosity. He was not what she was looking for.

He asked if she was a nurse. She was not a nurse. Then he wanted to know if it was true, what he had been told, that there are ladies and gentlemen atop who played racquets and hoops and would she please, when they were in Sydney, employ him, for he was good around animals and practical, and would not, not for his life, ma'am, go back to cruel England again. She barely heard him.

She asked him where the hold was. He did not know, but pretended he did. She knew he was lying with his directions, and yet she had the compassion to see him as innocent and herself not so—a beast in heat looking for a beastly game.

She found her way, by mistake, to the engine-room. She did not actually enter, but opened a great riveted door where the fragrance of oil was strongest and, looking down into the giddy steel pit, saw the two giant connecting rods churning round and round, a nightmare from Gargantua, and men, so far below they seemed like smudged ivory dolls, stripped to the waist, with tiny shovels. No one here was playing cards. They stopped and looked up at the intruder. She stepped back and closed the door.

If she had felt this bad in Sydney, she would have cooled her passion by visiting the Chinese. There were no Chinese here.

She did not like the feeling of this ship. It had tossed like a cork in the Bay of Biscay and all those long steel corridors seemed to be painted with the smear of sweat. There was no life in the ship. There had been races for ladies scheduled by a games committee but now it seemed they would not be held, for there were so few ladies on board and most of them not of a racing age. She climbed steel stairs, heading upwards. She passed an officer who blushed to see a woman where he had not expected one. She did not ask him where the hold was. She continued up. She passed a door on the other side of which something improper seemed to be occurring.

She came finally to a small kitchen of the tea-and-toast type. there were two doors. She chose the right-hand one. Ahead of her was a red-headed clergyman sitting on a plush red settee. It was the second-class promenade. She felt herself "nabbed," "caught in he act." She thought it undignified to turn back. She held up her head and straightened her shoulders. She came forward. She walked directly towards him. She introduced herself to him, and when he said his name, she did not hold it.

"I am in the habit," she said, "of making a confession."

"Quite," he said.

"Perhaps this is not a practice you approve of."

"No, no," he said, "of course not."

"I wonder, then," she blurted, "if you might oblige me at a time convenient to you." And then, not quite knowing what she had done, and certainly not why, she fled to those regions of the ship where Oscar dare not follow.

The sea looked like a dreary waste of waters. To the east she could see the smudged ambivalence which was Cape Finisterre. The great smokestacks above her head poured forth the contents of the stomach of the ship, black effluent into the chamber of the sky.

51

Mr Borrodaile and Mr Smith

Mr Borrodaile of Ultimo and Mr Smith of the Acclimatization Society often watched the young clergyman. He had sat at the same place every day for fourteen days, and even now when it was warm enough for Mr Borrodaile to set himself up with a hammock on the deck, the Gluepot did not move. He would not come up on deck to see Tenerife although—he admitted it freely—he had never been away from England before. In Tenerife Harbour he sat exactly as he had in the middle of the Bay of Biscay, with his Bible on his lap and his lips—Mr Borrodaile noted it first—moving. Mr Borrodaile imagined the parson moved his lips because he read his Bible, but Percy Smith, although he thought it best to not contest the big fellow's opinion, knew the parson must be praying—he was too well educated to read in such a way. (Mr Borrodaile, who was worth ten thousand pounds, moved his lips when reading. Mr Smith had seen him do it.)

"He's a queer one, no doubt," said the tweed-jacketed, mutton-chopped, cleft-chinned Mr Borrodaile, the same one who had thrown ship's biscuits down the ventilators.

"He is and all," said Percy Smith, but not unkindly. Mr Smith was a shortish man (the top of his head did not reach Mr Borrodaile's shoulder) but broad, with strong arms showing under his rolled-up sleeves and a sense about him that his thighs and calves would be the same. He had a slight roll to his walk, a farmer's gait, and this rather rural air was somehow endorsed by the profusion of colourless hairs around his ears—they gave him a sandy warthoggish quality, quite cosy really. Yet he was, for all his rural appearance (the animal hairs forever on his jacket, the odour of his charges about him), a cultured man, and if the culture had been acquired piecemeal, by the light of tallow candles, he was no less cultured for all that.

Percy Smith had talked a lot to the clergyman, but he had not yet asked him why he always sat in the same spot or why he would not come to view the windmills of Santa Cruz. They had discussed Darwin. Mr Smith had been surprised to find a clergyman unruffled by the subject. He was still delighted with Oscar's observation—he had made a note of it in his diary—that if Darwin was in error, then God must have placed dinosaur fossils on earth to puzzle *homo sapiens*. It was not just what he said, but the way he said it. There was a lightness, a transparency in his manner which seemed to Mr Smith—who was, for all his fervour for things Australian, sentimental about "Home"—representative of all that was sweet and cultured and cultivated in "Dear Old England." Mr Smith could not reproduce Oscar's manner, and when he repeated the clergyman's observation to Mr Borrodaile, he did not seem to strike the right note. He looked up at Mr Borrodaile and waited for a response. Mr Smith blinked, he could not help it—no matter how intently he held a gaze he always gave the impression of timidity.

Mr Borrodaile grunted and began to talk about a beast he had shot at Cowpastures. It had been, the wet-lipped Mr Borrodaile insisted, a devil. Mr Smith did not quite grasp what position this devil would support in the argument. This embarrassed him, so although he nodded and held the big man's eye, he blinked more furiously than ever.

"Upon my word," said Percy Smith and then began, assiduously, to dust his knees.

Mr Borrodaile thought: A dog with fleas.

At the other end of the promenade, Oscar sat in his seat. He had his Tacitus with him. He had his Bible and his Book of Common Prayer. He had a bottle of Florida water, a tea-cup and a saucer and a copy of *Punch* and these he placed on the velvet plush seat which, with no proper table having been provided, was, due to such prolonged and unbroken habitation, looking as soiled and sweaty as the incumbent whose carrot-coloured hair had become wildly screwed and tightly curled in the steamy atmosphere.

There were passengers who, like people recently fallen in love, must matchmake for everyone around them. The parson did not know what sunsets he was missing. They brought them to him, also their zephyrs, their balmy breezes, their enthusiasm for a hammock beneath the night sky. The Northern Star was still visible but soon it would disappear from their lives, perhaps for ever. The young man with the fine-boned, china-white face smiled and nodded and his green eyes rested carefully, not intrusively, but respectfully, upon their burnt and passionate faces. He smiled and nodded, but was inexplicably resigned to sweating inside his suit. This stubbornness made some people quite cross, but Oscar had other side-effects of his phobia to contend with, and the most pressing was this: what size were the windows in Miss Leplastrier's stateroom?

He had promised to hear her confession, but then a steward had informed him that the windows in the first-class staterooms were so big "you can see all the way to Japan." This was exactly the type of view he must not have. He felt giddy even imagining it.

And yet he had promised. Two days had passed, and the unresolved obligation rested heavily upon him.

There were many Anglicans, the majority, who had held confession to be a very Puseyite idea, by which they meant it was popish and therefore wrong. But the sacrament was in the Book of Common Prayer and although he had never offered it to a stranger, he had often undertaken the service for poor Wardley-Fish who would periodically become so beset by his own sins that he would fall into a debilitating depression from which trough he could contemplate nothing but the damnation of his soul. Oscar had therefore come to see the sacrament of confession as an act of love, like nursing a sick friend, and although it often involved what was bad-smelling (the soul's secretions could be no less disturbing the body's wastes) there was a profound satisfaction to be obtained from the service thus offered.

He did not, in the case of Miss Leplastrier, expect to have his charity so tested. He could not imagine her sins amounting to more than a little pride or covetousness. He would be pleased to offer her God's peace, but he could not do it if the windows were as large and giddy as he now feared.

His cowardice so tortured his mind that he was relieved when Mr Borrodaile came and offered him diversion by speaking of the tariffs between the colonies. He could more easily ignore the peripheral vision of Miss Leplastrier promenading above him on the first-class deck—he imagined her looking down on him, waiting for him to bring her that peace that passeth all understanding.

Mr Borrodaile said it was an outrage that the people who lived in Wodonga should have to pay duty to get an item up from Melbourne. Oscar did not understand either the politics or the geography. This was not apparent to Mr Borrodaile who was not the sort to ask a lot of questions. He had no questions at all; although much to tell.

He told Oscar he had shot a devil at Cowpastures. He described its coat and the contents of its stomach. He said that clergy were needed in New South Wales, that there were whole areas, dubbed "parishes" on the government maps, where the people grew up godless, the children never saw a school, and the blasphemies and curses were shocking even to a man of the world like himself.

If Oscar had a thought to convert the blacks, he would be better off not to waste his time. The most remarkable fact about these "chaps" was their total absence of religious belief. Every other nation, Mr Borrodaile asserted, rubbing the odd little plateau at the bridge of his aquiline nose—like the arm of a leather chair, this part of his nose appeared shiny from wear—every other nation, no matter how savage, had some deities or idols of wood or stone, but the Australian blacks believed in nothing but a devil-devil which they thought would eat them. He had all this, not as hearsay, but from a black he had named "Bullock" on account of his demeanour.

Oscar could not help casting covert glances at Mr Borrodaile's large black shoes. He had never seen a pair so big. Mr Borrodaile also had large and violent hands protruding from his stripe starched cuffs. He chewed his nails, right to the quick. Oscar watched the hands fold and rearrange themselves. Mr Borrodaile said there was opium and gambling in Sydney. He held Oscar's eyes when he said this, insisting on something Oscar could not fathom. His eyes were hooded; the whites had a damaged, bloodshot appearance. There were bars, Mr Borrodaile said dolefully, with "gay girlies." He said, also, that it was a practical place and that Oscar would soon have his face burnt red unless he took care to keep a hat on. He said it would do no harm to have some grace said at dinner and it was high time "Your Reverence" stopped sitting by himself; and then he announced he was soon to take a stroll on deck, that two circuits made the mile, that it was no good asking "Your Reverence" who gave new meaning to the term Glue-pot for it looked as if he were not only a Glue-pot himself but that he had also ("Ho ho") sat on one.

Mr Borrodaile collected Mr Smith (who had been dozing in a club chair), relieved him of his *London Illustrated News* (which had lain like a nursery blanket across his wide chest) and set off up the stairs to see if they might spot a flying fish.

Oscar imagined himself watched by the pretty lady in first class. He arranged himself in a certain way which he hoped conveyed authority. He crossed a leg, straightened his back, and turned the pages of his book at regular intervals. He would ask Mr Smith to investigate the size of the first-class windows on his behalf. Oscar stared at his Tacitus and waited. He stared at the page for perhaps twenty minutes until he heard Mr Smith's soft colonial vowels.

"Hello, Parson, still at your studies?"

He threw himself down beside Oscar who retrieved his Florida water just in time.

"By Jove, Borrodaile sets a pace," Percy Smith wiped his sweat-red brow with a handkerchief. "He is still up there. I would say he has a five-foot stride. He left me by the bow."

"And when you pace," Oscar asked, putting his book away, "do you pace past the first-class cabins?"

"Oh, I dare say we do, but it's such a cracking pace," Percy Smith laughed, "it is all pretty much of a blur and I would not know what I was passing with those great long legs of his. I am not criticizing. It is admirable. But I'm afraid I'm a disappointment to him in this heat. Now you," he said, tapping Oscar's shin, "have got the right configuration. He has his eye on you. He will get you on the deck with him, I guarantee you."

"Oh, no."

"He has mentioned it," teased Mr Smith

"Good grief."

"He has compared my legs unfavourably with yours."

"In length perhaps, not strength."

"In strength, too."

"He is mistook."

"In strength, in every respect," smiled Percy Smith. "No, I am afraid you have been chosen. I have been retired. If I were a horse I fear I would be shot."

"But I cannot go on deck, Mr Smith. It is quite impossible."

"When you refused him cards, he understood you. He told me he had a great respect for you. But he is a man of strong feelings, and he's just as likely to take your refusal as a slur of some sort. But perhaps I am wrong. I have only just made his acquaintance. But he is an emotional chap. I can vouch for that. He told me his grandmother was a beauty from Spain, so that perhaps explains it."

"Yes," said Oscar, "but the fact that it is impossible for me to walk on deck has nothing, nothing whatever, to do with Mr Borrodaile."

"Mr Borrodaile would not see it that way," said Percy Smith and may—it was hard to tell—have suggested something critical of Mr Borrodaile in his censored smile.

There was a dogged quality in Oscar which, in the midst of all his nervous excitements, plodded stubbornly onwards in the face of difficulties. This left him no time to see Mr Smith's treasonous smile. "But," he said, "I have an ailment."

When Percy Smith heard that the parson had an ailment he tucked his chin down into his neck; his sandy brows pressed down heavily on his gentle blue eyes; he folded his big scratched arms across his chest.

"And it is because of this ailment," said Oscar, beginning to open and shut his hands as if they were hinged lids, "that I would ask you to describe for me the size of the first-class windows."

"Portholes," corrected Percy Smith. "But what is this condition?" Even while he asked this, he was leaping to a conclusion–there was only one reason for looking through a first-class window. There was only one passenger in first-class and she had–Mr Borrodaile had remarked on the feature with disturbing enthusiasm–a very pretty sweep from her back to her backside.

"Portholes seems the wrong term. I have heard they are quite large, but my condition has prevented me discovering the truth for myself."

"You tease me like a girl. Is it meant to be a guessing game we play now?"

"I am sorry, but I find it quite embarrassing."

"It does not concern a young lady by any chance?" Percy Smith was not smiling. But he bit his lower lip and his sandy eyebrows no longer pressed upon his eyes so heavily.

Oscar felt the rush of blood to his ears; he felt it gather in great hot pools, one in each lobe. "Oh, no," he said. He really looked quite prudish. "It is nothing ungentlemanly. I really only wish to know the dimensions of the windows. It is the seascape, you see, that actually concerns me. It is the quantity of sea . . ."

"The quantity of sea?"

"The quantity, yes, of sea, of water, that would be on view from a first-class cabin."

He looked quite cross. He picked a fleck of spilt gravy from his rumpled thigh. "It is a professional matter, Mr Smith, please do not laugh at me. It is not an *amour*."

"Now, now, friend Parson," said Mr Smith and stroked Oscar on the shoulder as if he were a nervous beast who must be quieted. "I do not give a tinker's curse. I am a quiet enough man, I know, but just as I know you are not a wowser, you must see that I am not one either."

Oscar had never heard the term before, but he had other more important misunderstandings on his mind.

"But first," said Percy Smith, now picking the animal hairs off his own jacket, "you must unclench your teeth a little and listen to me. Are you listening?"

"Of course, but your smile suggests you know something you could not know."

"I tell you, young man, *relax yourself*. There will be nothing done on your behalf today. But tomorrow, perhaps, and then you will no longer need to moon like a certain Montague beneath the window of a Capulet."

Their conversation was cut short by Mr Borrodaile who returned to fetch Mr Smith for a game of quoits up on deck. As it was to be played "penny a poke" Mr Borrodaile assumed, quite loudly, that the Gluepot would not be interested.

52

Montaigne

Mr Borrodaile did not like a woman at his table. It constrained and restricted the natural flow of conversation. It meant that almost every door was temporarily locked before you. You were shackled, chained to your place, with nothing to talk about. Nothing? Well, what? Flowers? The children's health? The problem of one more maid got above herself or ofi to marry the footman? But a man could not, if he were a gentleman, discuss politics (because they knew nothing of it) or question God (because this frightened them). Business was not suitable, nor were sporting matters, and the bottle, which might otherwise move back and forth so gaily, stayed in its place upon the sideboard and could not be sent upon its proper business.

So when Mr Borrodaile strolled into the second-class dining room, two snorts under his belt, as light and pearly as the southern evening light, he was put out of countenance to see at his table, not only the young parson (whom he had invited himself) but the young woman from first class whom Mr Smith had taken upon himself to introduce into their company. He had known, of course; Mr Smith had informed him of his presumption. But he had forgotten. He had forgotten totally.

Now, of course, he remembered, and all that well-being he had so carefully nurtured in his measured stride around the deck, the long deep breaths of ozone, the equally satisfying inhalation of good cognac, all of it just went.

He sat down in silence. He was a large man and knew his silence to be heavy. He put on his "cut-downs" and examined the menu. He affected not to hear their good evening. He looked around to find the wine steward, looking also for the perpetrator of this blunder, who was, the nervous nelly, checking his charges 'tween decks. The purser—a hearty chap, too—had been placed amongst the teetotal Cornish farmers.

He heard the clergyman—wrists like a girl, voice all reedy like a flute—enquire of the woman about the book she had been reading.

"Montaigne," she said.

Mr Borrodaile felt his neck go prickly, as though two or three grass ticks had settled home at once. As with grass ticks, he did not scratch, but took his large fingers to the source of irritation—and found nothing there but skin.

"Ah, yes," the parson said, folding his white fingers and nodding his head in a parody of prayer, "ah, yes, Montaigne."

Mr Borrodaile did not like this sort of talk at all. He was a practical man. His father had been a wheelwright and he had, himself, been apprenticed to the same trade, but when he thought of "practical" he did not mean the kind that leaves wood shavings on the floor and precious little in the bank. He imagined the clergyman well above him and did not like it. And yet—in the case of Montaigne at least—this was not so, or if it was, the advantage was no more than one might have from standing on a brick, *that* much above, or, if there were no brick available, then the volume itself laid on its side. Oscar, having said "Montaigne" had nothing more to add. He had no knowledge of Montaigne, no more than is obtainable from dozing off three nights in a row with a musty volume cradled in your lap. He had not even reached the second chapter (the one on idleness) before his pointed chin was digging into his chest and his reading glasses had fallen into his lap. So he did not reach—and this is a great shame—Montaigne's easy on smells. It is a shame because Oscar's olfactory sense was as highly developed as his father's sense of sight, and he would have particularly enjoyed that first line: "It is recorded of some men, among them Alexander the Great, that their sweat exuded a sweet odour, owing to some rare and extraordinary property."

Mr Percy Smith, alas, was not one of these men. And when he

arrived, all bumpy with apology, he brought with him the smell of the fretting llamas which had detained him. Lucinda, for one, did not find this smell unpleasant and was, in contrast to Mr Borrodaile's cigar and brandy, to name it "honest."

Mr Smith bent his head low to attack his consommé which Mr Borrodaile remarked was nothing more than beef tea in a flat plate. Mr Smith nodded, but looked up, blinking from under his sandy eyebrows, to ask about the conversation. He had enjoyed his bit of Darwin with the parson, and when he heard "Montaigne" he judged the couple would be well matched. He was about to confess he knew little of Montaigne but would be pleased to hear. He liked the look of the table far better now that the red-veined purser had removed himself. It looked a friendlier place altogether.

It was Lucinda who had answered Mr Smith. It was she who said Montaigne. Mr Borrodaile did not like the sound of it at all. It produced another three phantom grass ticks, these last just below his collar where he could not touch them. He imagined the young woman was being pretentious, using a foreign word for "mountain" where an English one would have done. He was not entirely confident of this, and yet he wished it known, in a relatively safe sort of way.

"Montaigne," he said, affecting a reasonable chuckle, putting his cut-down spectacles back in his jacket. "Montaigne, hill mound and tussock."

This produced a puzzled silence, but before it had extended more than a second or two, Percy Smith—he would have been faster, but he had been engaged with his consommé—produced an appreciative chuckle. He was well aware of Mr Borrodaile's sensitivities.

"Britt-ayne," said Mr Borrodaile, pushing on like a man slashing at dense undergrowth in country he does not know. Hack, hack. God knows what vines will trip him, thorns snag him. Slash. "Bourgogne. Bretagne. Montana, quite right." He was laughing uproariously now, a high laugh for such a big man, like a string of firecrackers. Tears ran down his cheeks and lost themselves in his moustache. "Oh, dear," he blew his great big nose, "my wounded aunt."

The two men felt they had missed something important, but Lucinda Leplastrier, although she did not understand the sense of the words, saw and tasted the prickliness beneath Mr Borrodaile's laughter and it made her remember things about Sydney she had forgotten. This man was rich and powerful in Sydney. She did not know him, but she could be confident he would dine at Government House. He was a barbarian.

"But speaking seriously," said Mr Borrodaile, as the corned beef was placed in front of him (he prodded it with his knife, separated the slices, but said nothing of its quality). "Speaking seriously," sharing his gaze between Mr Smith and Oscar, "I would like to hear the parson's opinion of tallow."

"I have none," Oscar smiled, and fiddled with something in his pocket. Lucinda, glancing at him sideways, approved of his answer just as much as—having suddenly placed Mr Borrodaile—she disapproved of this fellow who had made his great fortune out of buying land and chopping it up. This was a calling which moved her to great anger, and not only because she had had experience of it at so young an age.

So this was Borrodaile. He named streets after himself.

"You cannot travel," said Mr Borrodaile, swallowing too much at once. "Excuse me," He paused to clear his pipes with burgundy. He wiped the shiny piece of dimpled chin between the hedges of his drooping moustache. "You cannot travel out to New South Wales without an opinion on this subject. Upon my word, Parson, it's like going to Ireland without your umbrella. If it is llamas, then I think it matters not a pickle whether your head is empty or not. Even Mr Smith will tell you this. But tallow, your young Reverence, this is a thing you must know about. The price of town tallow when we sailed was two pounds a hundred-weight and if I were a young man with any capital, this is what I would invest in."

"But the price may change," said Lucinda.

Mr Borrodaile looked at her and blinked.

This was not a subject he would allow disagreement on, not even if the dissenter were protected by crinoline and stays. He had no time for anyone who wished to raise sheep for mutton. There had been too much mutton in the colony already. He was a tallow man, a chop-them-up-and-boil-them-down man, and he liked to have a chance to say so.

"Change!" said Mr Borrodaile, holding up his knife and fork and looking down at her along his shiny-bridged nose. "By God, girlie, of course it will change. It will go up."

Oscar found this bellow quite upsetting. He did not like the blasphemy. It was even more shocking when it came from so large and powerful an instrument. He saw that the diminutive Miss Leplastrier had done nothing to deserve such vitriol. It offended his sense of what was fair, and he was moved to take up a public position in her defence.

And yet he did not really think of "sides," only of trying to adjudicate, to assume the responsibility for the harmony of the table. This, really, was his great talent. It had made him a good schoolmaster. It was born of his hatred of discord, his fear of loudness. The weakness, therefore, ended up a virtue, and he brought his sense of fairness to every social situation so that he would divide curiosity and attention like a good socialist, dividing them fairly according to the needs of the participants. As for himself, if you left aside the subject of horse-racing—which he imagined he had now abandoned—and the construction of the *Leviathan*—on which everybody at the table was well versed—he thought he had nothing worth saying on matters secular. He had found his pupils at Mr Colville's school to be more worldly than he was.

"And what would you invest in, Miss Leplastrier?" The question was quite innocent. He did not imagine she was in a position to invest in anything.

Lucinda Leplastrier put her knife and fork together on her plate, the fork with its tines upwards. She knew her hair was a fright. She could feel it slipping from its clips. Her cheeks were burning but she forced herself to look slowly around the table, to take in every face before she spoke. She had taught herself this trick in Sydney. It was a sea anchor thrown out to slow her before the gale of her emotions, and although she did not actually feel it herself, it gave her an appearance of almost queenly dignity.

"I would invest," she said. She counted to three. She lost her place. "I would put my capital into something that I loved very much."

"Very pretty," said Mr Borrodaile, and made a show of applauding.

"Perhaps not 'loved' then, Mr Borrodaile. Let us say that I would invest in something from which I would derive innate pleasure. And if it were land, for instance, I would first find some land which would produce what I wished, and then I would prepare myself for good seasons and bad seasons, but I would cherish my land."

"Dear girl . . ."

Lucinda made a little face which was born in that painful territory between a wince and a smile.

"But mostly, Mr Hopkins," she said, to Oscar (who leaned forward and thus, although he wished no rudeness, was complicitous in excluding Mr Borrodaile), "I would advise someone with capital in accordance with what I understand the parable of the talents instructs us to. I would advise that they make something that was not there before. I do not like your tallow works, I must admit it, Mr Borrodaile." She returned her attention to him as she spoke. Her voice was soft, even regretful. "And this is not merely because they produce a most unpleasant odour, but because I have lived and worked at farming and I cannot bear to see a beast used for so base a thing, and now I am sure I have allowed you to call me silly and feminine."

"Dear girl, I have thought no such thing." But his hooded bloodshot eyes thought worse things and brought them out, one after the other, and displayed them. It was a private showing and Percy Smith was not aware of it—he smiled at Lucinda and shook his head in such an idiotic and patronizing way that she revised her good opinion of him immediately.

"The principle," said Oscar, inviting them all to join hands in some communion which they were—even Lucinda—now reluctant to approach, "the principle, Mr Borrodaile, is surely a good one."

"Oh, for God's sake," spluttered Mr Borrodaile, then tried to catch his blasphemy before it landed. His mouth, for a second, lay open like someone who has eaten food too hot and wishes to spit it out, expel it, anyway, but cannot do it from politeness. He could not take it back. He could only push on, hack his way forward, and not worry that he could not see where his next step would lead him. "I knew you were a clergyman when I saw you from behind. You see, it's in your walk." He swilled his burgundy.

"By criminee, I'll show you."

Lucinda sucked in her breath. Even Mr Smith accustomed by now to the erratic and energetic movements of his friend, his erupting passions, his hurts, slights, revenges, even Percy Smith, lining up his spoon and fork beside a most unseasonal plum pudding, looked alarmed. Mr Borrodaile was not deterred.

Oscar and Lucinda were both burning red, as if they were parties to an adultery.

Mr Borrodaile stood with his back to the mirrored pillar, grinning idiotically. He gave the ends of his moustache a little tweak. He adjusted his shirt cuffs like a baritone about to sing. He was drunk, of course. He composed his face, but his face was not the point. The point was this: Mr Borrodaile would 'do' a walk.

He clasped his big hands together on his breast. He inclined his upper body backwards from the vertical. He sucked in his ruddy cheeks and raised his eyes like a choirboy in procession. He walked. He was a wooden doll with tangled strings. His legs jerked sideways then up. The upper body swung from side to side like the mainmast of a brig at anchor in a swell. The hands unclasped and clasped and then flew apart to grasp at—at what? A butterfly? A hope? A prayer?

Mr Borrodaile perambulated, undulated, swayed and smiled for the entire length of the dining room, weaving daintily where architecture dictated.

The purser scraped back his chair and those in second class who had previously complained of Borrodaile's "shenanigans," now looked towards the officer expectantly, but he was not moving back his chair to arrest him, but rather to applaud. Mr Borrodaile was walking exactly like the red-haired clergyman, no, not "exactly." He was not like the chap at all, and yet he had its essence. His walk was to the original as a jiggling skeleton is to a dancing boy.

Mr Borrodaile's big dimple-chinned face was red with pleasure. He strode along. He put his head back. He swung his arms. The applause was quickly general.

Oh, what a bully he must have been as a boy, thought Lucinda, seeing this most accurate performance, a performance which, in spite of her resolve to the contrary, made her smile. But she would not applaud it. Its intention was too cruel—to make all that was good and kind in the young man appear to be weak and somehow contemptible. She was ashamed of her smile and was therefore surprised, when she at last allowed herself to look at the subject of this mockery, to see that he was not only smiling broadly, but applauding as enthusiastically as the bullies at the purser's table.

He took her breath away. How confident he must be with himself. She resolved there and then that she would like to know him better.

"Well, well," said Oscar who was not as confident as Lucinda imagined but was, rather, protected by a curious blindness about himself. He could not avoid seeing what was comic and grotesque in Mr Borrodaile's walk, and yet it did not occur to him, not even for an instant, that these might be elements of his own physical self. He would never perceive himself as odd and could only see Mr Borrodaile's mannerisms as theatrical devices intended to convey an inner reality. Thus he saw the clasped hands merely as symbols to represent him as unworldly, the jerky legs as enthusiastic, the idiotic smile as kindly. And he was not displeased. Indeed he was touched that Mr Borrodaile should so readily perceive those qualities in his clay that he had so laboured to strengthen.

"Well, well," he said, leaning back in his chair and cracking his knuckles. "It would seem we cannot keep our hearts secret from those who observe us keenly." He looked up at Mr Borrodaile who had come to stand, smirking, above is shoulder. "My congratulations, Mr Borrodaile, it is a great gift."

Mr Borrodaile could not help but feel irritated. He leaned forward and "borrowed" the parson's glass of wine and stood there smiling and sipping it without apology.

"A great gift," said Oscar, twisting his long neck so he might speak directly to Mr Borrodaile while, at the same time, avoid the portholes which ran along the wall behind him. "And I do not mean your performance—I am pretty well uneducated in theatrics and cannot judge it."

Mr Borrodaile was discomforted. He replaced the parson's wine glass and moved to take up his proper seat and it was then that Oscar caught sight of what he had hirtherto succeeded in avoiding.

The sickening silk sheet of sea made a gagging ball in his throat.

He stopped speaking.

"Not the performance," prompted Mr Smith while Mr Borrodaile, realizing that he was at least being spoken to in a respectful and complimentary style, now took his seat politely and leaned forward attentively to hear what his victim had to say.

"I cannot judge it," said Oscar, calming the panic in his gagging throat with a little dry bread. "But your sensitivity to the inner man, to those parts which we do not readily show the world, indeed which we often take great care to hide—this perspicacity, Mr Borrodaile, it is really admirable."

Mr Borrodaile looked very pleased.

Lucinda hid her delight in her water glass.

"This is a gift," said Oscar, leaning forward, gesturing as if to hold a casket of some weight. "It is something which should not be used merely to amuse passengers on a long voyage. It is something a Christian should use in life."

As he spoke, Oscar became bigger and more eccentric than even Mr Borrodaile's impersonation might have allowed. He was, with excitement, embarrassment, a little wine, more of the character that Wardley-Fish loved, more like the schoolmaster sixty boys from Mr Colville's school would still remember in their dotage. He was animated. His long arms waved across the table, missing burgundy glasses and hock bottles, but only because his fellow diners removed them from the radius of his arms. His voice beame higher and took on the famous fluting tone. He looked from one face to the next, drawing them into the bubbling pot of his enthusiasm until they, too, felt that what they had witnessed was not a cruel mockery but an affirmation, an insight, a thing of much greater moment than they had at first realized. They polished it in retrospect, buffed, varnished it until it shone in their imaginations as a precious thing and its perpetrator—the rude and contemptuous Mr Borrodaile—was made, at least temporarily, into something fine.

Lucinda, who had begun by thinking Mr Hopkins merely clever, was, when she saw there was no guile in this enthusiasm, so moved by his goodness that her eyes watered.

Mr Borrodaile was also moved, but in a different way, and for a little while—half an hour or so—he was a different person. He showed an interest in the feelings and opinions of his fellow passengers. And his eyes, when they looked at Lucinda Leplastrier, no longer showed those cold instruments, like surgeons' tools, that he had displayed so nastily (snapping open the case: There! See!) so short a time before.

There was phosphorescence beside the ship. It was announced by the head steward, and there was a scramble for the deck where the spectacle could be properly enjoyed and that was how Oscar, not wishing the party to break up, turned the full blaze of this enthusiasm to the subject of phosphorescence without ever once looking over his shoulder at the glowing vision which filled the portholes of the dining room.

53

Phosphorescence (1)

He could see which way his conversation would lead his dinner companions: surely, inevitably up the stairs and into the warm night to which his phobia denied him access. The more he held them with his descriptions, his explanations, the more he was ensuring that they would finally leave him so they might witness this miracle he was so brilliantly evoking.

To Miss Leplastrier (she spoke with the delectable top lip and bright and curious eyes) he spoke most of all and when, at last, the push of his enthusiasms joined with the pull of his phenomenon, and they rose in a body from the table, he also rose. And although he did not promise he would accompany them up on to the deck, neither did he indicate that he could not, and whilst a court of law would declare he had not misled the party as to his intention, the courts of heaven would not be so easily deceived.

At the bottom of the grand slippery staircase which led to the upper deck, he quietly left the noisy company and felt himself like a sad and ugly creature in a fairytale, one for ever exiled from the light and compelled to skulk, pale, big-eyed, sweat-shiny in the dark steel nether regions.

54

Phosphorescence (2)

The sea rolled around *Leviathan's* bows as white as milk, studded with bright sparkles of blue light. The milk curdled. The sea was marble with clear black water in between. A bucket was lowered. It banged and swayed and then was lost in darkness. The white clouds dispersed, but the sparkles remained. Then one of the points suddenly exploded. It was a flare beneath the water. The great ship floated in liquid light. The bucket had not yet reached the sea. Lucinda could see, in the luminescent sea, the most splendid globes of fire wheeling and careening like things from a prophecy.

But she had no interest in spectacles. If spectacles had contented her she would have stayed alone in first class. She was thirsty for intelligence and kindness, and the phosphorescence had been merely an agent, a conduit for these emotions. Mr Hopkins had brought them both together, the spectacular and the personal, and she had liked, far more than any phenomenon, the way he had moved his hands, not like an Englishman at all. He seemed full of life, bursting out of himself. His collar stud was popped loose and Lucinda liked him for this almost as much as anything else.

"Then let us go," she had said, standing at the dining-room table.

"Let us be Witness to the Miracle." She had made herself sound ironic, but she had not felt in the least ironic.

Then they were all up from the table at once, and out of the door and up the stairs, and she kept herself just ahead of Mr Borrodaile's shepherding hand which felt it necessary to *guide* her through a doorway as if it might be a dangerous reef she would not otherwise have the wit to navigate. She did not look back. She had imagined Mr Hopkins still in the party.

There were not sufficient passengers to crowd the deck, but the phosphorescence had exerted a pull, like a tide, and the inhabitants, against all the rules of rank and conduct, had been sucked up, or had swarmed into the warm night air, clustering beside the great water condensers amidships. There were stewards and cabin boys, engineers, the young lad who tended the animals, third-class passengers with voices born in Limehouse and Holborn, Liverpool and Manchester. It was only then, when she was wedged into this mass, that she discovered that Mr Hopkins was no longer of their party. She imagined this to be somehow her fault. She had been too forward again. She had frightened him away with her imperiousness. Her ironic manner had been offensive. She had not held herself in sufficiently, but why must she always hold herself back? They would have her tie a silk rope between her ankles so she would move in a fettered way. Even Dennis Hasset had tried to persuade her to shorten her stride. His excuse was the cut of her crinoline, but it was not, she suspected, his reason.

She would obviously be wise to take his advice, to leash herself in. But she was everywhere leashed in, in any case. It was the condition of her adult life to feel it. She refused the conventions of whalebone and elastic, but still she was squeezed and blistered, pinched and hobbled.

Lucinda was angry with the phosphorescence. She had jettisoned something much more valuable on its account. As she looked at the sea her upper lip diminished itself as if what she was was nothing but a fairground—whizzing lights, sickly sweetmeats, tawdry barkers. Mr Borrodaile was unpleasantly attentive. He said the globes of light were sea blubbers. She did not like to feel him bow his bulk when he wished to talk so closely into her ear. He had forgotten that he had heard this information from Mr Hopkins at the same time she had. She could not fathom the workings of his mind. For now he continued to regurgitate more of what he had ingested at the dinner table: he told her that the sea blubbers were called medusae, and that what appeared to be sparks were in reality *entomastraca,* although he did not say it quite correctly.

"Entromysteriosa," said Mr Borrodaile, not quietly either.

But Mr Hopkins had not even bidden her good night. She could not think what she had done to deserve so gross an insult.

The phosphorescence was wonderful, of course. How could it not be wonderful? But wonder, even wonder at one of God's great miracles, cannot be sustained when one feels foolish and unhappy. Lucinda made herself stay on deck for a slow and dragging fifteen minutes before she declared herself satisfied with the phosphorescence.

But Mr Smith would have her stay. He put his thumb and forefinger on the sleeve of her jacket, but did it in such a blinky, owl-like sort of way, that she could not be angry with his familiarity, indeed, was pleased to see that he at least thought of her kindly.

"But the bucket is not here, Miss Leplastrier. You must not leave until you have seen the bucket demonstrated."

"Do stay," said Mr Borrodaile, but she could feel that she had, by moving away from his whispering mouth, exhausted his good will towards her.

"But what is in the bucket is only what is in the sea, surely?" Lucinda said. "There is no extra ingredient."

"Wait," said Mr Smith. "Look, here it comes."

"Make way," said Mr Borrodaile.

He stood on Lucinda's foot. The pain was quite excruciating, but she said nothing. She could not bear the possibility of fuss, the likelihood that he would, when apologizing, put his big hand on her arm or shoulder.

There was much jostling as the bucket was brought on to the deck. She was smaller than everyone. They pressed around her, and Lucinda, who had come to second class wishing to feel and smell her kind around her, was oppressed and choked by all these bodies. She squeezed her way to the front, more to escape the rich odours of humanity than to view the bucket's contents. It contained a great number of flashing bodies.

"Go on, Smith," said the harsh voice of Mr Borrodaile.

"In a minute, Borrodaile," said Percy Smith. His tone betrayed more independence than was his want. "I am waiting for the engineer."

"I am the engineer," said a man beside Lucinda who smelt strongly, not of oil but whisky.

The engineer held out the bottle with a ground-glass stopper. Mr Smith leaned across Lucinda's shoulder and took it. He moved into the small clear space next to the dull zinc-colored bucket and, having unstoppered the glass vessel, sought Lucinda amongst the audience. "H_2SO_4," he declared. "Sulphuric acid." He knelt, and dropped a little acid into the bucket. "Quick," he said, stepping back. "Quick and lively now."

Lucinda was pushed so hard she could not have avoided the "demonstration" if she had wished to. The bright points in the bucket grew bright, some white, some yellow, but all intense, like tiny stars suddenly blooming in the heavens. They then flickered, faded, died. The bucket became dark.

"You see, Borradaile," called Mr Smith, "that proves it."

Lucinda thought: You dull man. You would murder God through the dullness of your imagination.

She squeezed herself backwards and—with Mr Borrodaile's loud voice asserting that nothing was proven—walked along the empty part of the deck towards her even emptier cabin. She looked up to find the North Star but the *Leviathan* had drawn a belching black blanket across the sky and the heavens were as dead as the inside of a bucket. She thought: I do not like factories. Am I still living my life to please my mama? She entered the first-class promenade and, without realizing what she would see there, looked down into the second-class promenade.

She saw Oscar Hopkins sitting—ostentatiously she imagined—by himself. When he waved at her, she pretended not to have seen him.

55

Jealousy

What Wardley-Fish said in Cremorne Gardens was true: he did not fit. His very position, alone in the second-class promenade, advertised the fact. He was a queer bird, a stork, a mantis, a gawk, an Odd Bod. He was afraid of water. He was separated from life itself. He sat on his settee like a fellow in a bath-chair and had the wonders of the oceans reduced so they might be brought to him in an ugly fire bucket.

Mr Smith came down the stairs quite drunk and tried to put a single medusa in a glass of gin. He claimed it was a famous drink in America. The creature flashed bright yellow—a shriek of light—and died.

Mr Smith told Oscar he was "poor company" and went off to play poker with Mr Borrodaile and the engineer. The stewards took the bucket away and sponged the carpet.

Oscar was, in many respects, a humble man. But he also had the mental habits of a Dissenter who knows himself saved when the rest of his neighbours are damned. So no matter what ascendancy Mr Borrodaile, for instance, might have over him at the dinner table, Oscar felt himself, in his secret heart, to be "above" him. And it offended him, offended him beyond toleration, that such a man might walk up the stairs to witness the phosphorescence when he, who knew more about the phenomenon than anyone else aboard the ship, could not.

He had watched the dinner party ascend the stairs as he had once watched pagan singing and dancing at the summer solstice in Hennacombe. He had been jealous then, seeing old women with big bonnets twirl and laugh while he must sit hidden behind a tree. He had felt the same emotions watching his father in the sea. Even when he was afraid of the water, even at the moment he was most in terror of it, he was slashed and whipped by jealousy.

He had seen Miss Leplastrier on the promenade. He had waved, but being short-sighted, could not be sure of her response. He could not bear the thought that he had driven her from him. He told himself he was honour bound to hear her confession and it was this, not the vision of her large eyes or her pretty upper lip, which he admitted to himself as he rose at last from his plush velvet seat and made his way unsteadily towards his cabin.

He took out his set of brushes and his hand mirror from the little cedar drawer. He brushed hard at his wiry red hair and tried to make it appear more civilized, but the more he brushed, the more it stuck out sideways. When he had finished his toilet, the top of his head resembled the foliage of a windblown tree. He located the lost collar stud and remedied it. He noticed the beginnings of a small pimple on his nose. He found a porcelain pot of ponatum (intended to subdue hair), opened it, sniffed it, and closed it up again.

He opened the soldering box and took out the wrapped caul. He crammed this in the side pocket of his jacket. It did not do anything to diminish his phobia. He then set out to ascend the stairs to the first-class promenade. Once he was up there he enquired of Miss Leplastrier's stateroom so dolefully that the steward who escorted him there imagined not a phobia but a serious spiritual crisis.

56

Lure

Lucinda took her pack of cards and shuffled them. Their waxing was bright and new and the inks shone bright beneath, like coloured stones in an aquarium. She stood in front of the pretty walnut table and dealt herself a hand for poker. She stood hard against the table, its edge pressing her thigh. She splayed the five cards, face down, then turned one over with her fingernail. King of spades. She turned it back. Her hands were actually aching. She pressed them hard together. She walked around the table and stood opposite the five splayed cards. She dealt five more. She cut the pack. She turned up a three of diamonds. She stood looking at the table. If she had been seated at the place the cards suggested she might have looked across her opponent's shoulder at the moonlit millpond of the sea. But had she actually played those cards, the sea would not exist. Nothing would exist but that small spherical world of which the cut pack was the exact geometrical centre.

She walked to her bureau. It was a definite walk with nothing dreamy about it. She took her purse from the bureau drawer. She carried it to the table. She spilled its contents on to the table—big pennies, chunky sovereigns, pound notes, a single "fiver."

She walked around the room then, circling the table in her stockinged feet.

There were men playing cards in earshot. Let them see they were not alone in their passion. She tugged a cord, a red rope with a gold tassel on its end. This was to summon a steward. But when the steward came, his eyes refused to see the lovely lure she had constructed for him. He left the stateroom and returned with tea things on a silver tray. He did not avoid her gaze, nor did he meet it especially. He wished the young lady a pleasant good night.

She had made a fool of herself twice in one day.

57

Confession

When she found Mr Hopkins standing in her doorway, the first thing she thought, when thought came, was—the cards. She had laid them as a bait, but not for him, for anyone but him. But there was a moment, before this, when she did not think at all. Her mouth echoed the open door.

And then she thought: The cards. He must not see the cards, or money either. There were coins and notes, a fiver as purple as a bishop's vest—it was such a luminous colour, like flowering lasiandra, signalling invitations to stumble-footed insects which would help it mate without knowing what they did. All this was calculated to catch the eye, but not this eye, another one.

She thought: What a dear face. The extreme delicacy and refinement of the face impressed itself on her. She did not, not yet, question the propriety of this visit, unchaperoned to her room; that would come in a moment, and with it anxiety, like a draught of hot whisky. She had completely forgotten her request for confession. She saw only the very pleasant man she had feared driven away by her forwardness.

"Do come in." These were the only words that either of them spoke. She tried to lead him into the curved corner of the stateroom, further from the game of poker. She thought to point out the luminescent sea. She knew herself favoured with "landscape windows" and thought to make a conversation of the fact. But he literally turned his back upon them, and moved like a crab in the opposite direction, finding his way into a chair like a blind man, at the very table she did not wish him to sit.

She was aghast, too much in terror about having her vice discovered to think his behaviour peculiar. She noticed perspiration on his brow, but it did not come to her mind until much later, when the incident was over.

She thought it odd he did not excuse himself for sitting while she stayed standing. "You must excuse me," he said instead, "for not coming earlier."

She smiled and bowed her head. She remained standing so that his eyes, in looking up at her, would not fall upon what was on the table in front of him. He had seen already. He must have seen already. And yet, it seemed, he had not. What was he talking about? Coming earlier? On deck? She wondered if she might find a cloth to throw across the table.

"You see," he said, "I have a phobia about the ocean. It is something I have suffered from since very young. My father is a naturalist, you know, and was in the ocean all the time, and I with him, too, when I was a little chap."

"I see." She did not see. He was agitated and sweating, but she did not notice. She was like someone hearing Spanish when she expected Greek. He had picked up a card from the table and was toying with it.

"In any event I developed a nervousness about it, like the nervousness some get with heights. So to accompany you on deck this evening, or to come up here, with all this glass—to hear your confession—well, I feared it was more than I could manage."

But she could not confess to *him*. She wished only his good opinion.

"This is not known to Mr Smith or Mr Borrodaile," he said.

"Frankly, I would prefer they did not hear it. But I owe you an apology for not answering your call to confession when, as you see, I was capable of coming all the time."

But she must not confess. She wished he would put down the card. (Surely he knew what it was.) She repeated what she had heard from George Lewes, although she did it at ten times his lumbering speed—that the Queen had been praying with Presbyterians at Crathie and was becoming passionate about the dangers of genuflexion and confessions. So confession was, she argued, unwise.

"Ah, yes," he said, "the Queen. And yet, you see," (and here he bounced his leg beneath the little table so you might actually hear the coins jingling) "it is not enough she does not like it, because the Church of England has it written into the prayer book and it will take more than the Queen, more than our Lord—it will take an Act of Parliament—to get it out again. I do not support this way of running things, Miss Leplastrier, but you may confess as you wish and know yourself completely free from heresy."

Oscar had a tiny prayer book, just three inches high and two inches across. He was flipping this open in a practiced way, as though he heard confessions every day.

Lucinda was now in a panic. She could not confess to this young man. She could see his wrists—long white bridges to beautifully shaped hands—and a little bruised shin showing between rumpled sock and trouser turn-up. He had a heart-shaped face, like an angel by Dante Gabriel Rossetti. She could not confess to him, and yet the ceremony had already started. He had a soft burr of West Country in his vowels. She thought she had no voice at all.

It was time for her to speak. She heard a voice out on the deck. It was the Belgians crying for their Pomeranian. She clasped the back of the chair in her hands. She felt her voice very small. She watched his shoe and shin protruding like a branch from beneath the table. The shoe bounced up and down. The shoe did not match the sacrament, but when she looked up and saw his hair like the hair of angels and very still, limpid grey-green eyes, she confessed. She talked so quietly he had to lean forward to hear her.

It was a little silver voice you could fit in a thimble. It did not match the things it said. The shoe stopped bouncing. The penitent had closed her heavy lids across her eyes. She spoke swiftly but quietly, in a silvery sort of rush.

She confessed that she had attended rooms in Drury Lane for the purposes of playing fan-tan (although she had fled when stared at).

She confessed to playing a common dice game on a train full of "racing types," and although she had not gone to the races, she had boarded this train, having read that such things occurred in such trains, for the express purpose of playing dice. She had been asked to leave the game because her sex was apparently repulsive to the patrons.

She had tried to persuade Mr Paxton to take her to a cock fight.

She had eavesdropped on stewards. She had set up a table in her room like a trap for them. She had wished to play poker.

There were other matters but her confessor hardly heard them. He sat with his head bowed, trying to still his wildly beating heart. He clenched his hands and pressed them down between his legs. He groaned.

Lucinda heard this noise. She sat with her head bowed, not daring to look at him. She waited for absolution. She heard another noise, muffled, its meaning not clear. She thought, He will not be my friend now. She clenched her eyes shut to drive out such temporal thought, clenched them so tight that luminous bodies floated through the black sea of her retina.

When Oscar tried to think good thoughts he always thought of his father. He did this now: it was this that made him groan—the loneliness he had caused this stern and loving man.

The voices of the stewards came through the ventilation, but neither of them listened.

Still, the priest withheld absolution.

"This dice you played on the train," he asked, "was it Dutch Hazards?"

Lucinda looked up quite sharply, but the priest's head was bowed and twisted sideways towards his right shoulder. "Yes," she said. "It was. We also played another game."

"Old British, perhaps."

Lucinda felt her bowed neck assume a mottled pattern. "In New South Wales," she said, "it is known as 'Seventh Man.' "

Her feelings were not focused, were as diffused as a blush, a business of heat and blood.

Oscar could not keep the picture of his father clear. A certain reckless joy—a thing without a definite form, a fog, a cloud of electricity—replaced the homely holy thoughts.

"And who was it," he asked, unclenching his hands and bringing them up on to the table, "who provided the Peter?"

Lucinda Leplastrier put her head on one side. She opened her eyes. Her confessor had a blank face, what was *almost* a blank face, but was prevented from being completely blank by the very slight compression of the lips.

Lucinda narrowed her green eyes. "The Peter?"

"Is the term unknown to you?"

She was looking at the mouth. She could not quite believe what she saw there. "No," she said, very carefully. "No, I think it is quite familiar."

"I thought so," said Oscar Hopkins. He closed the little prayer book and stuffed it in the pocket which contained the caul. When his hand touched the caul, he remembered the ocean behind his book. It caused no more than a prickling in his spine.

"And these terms, Mr Hopkins, are they also familiar to you?"

" 'Fraid so." He smiled, a clear and brilliant smile.

Lucinda also smiled, but less certainly. "Mr Hopkins, this is most improper."

Oscar took a handkerchief from his jacket pocket and wiped first his clammy hands and then his perspiring brow. "Oh?" he said. "I really do not think so." He looked so pleased with himself.

"But you have not absolved me."

"Where is the sin?"

She was shocked, less by what he said, but by the sudden change of mood that took possession of him. He spoke these words in an angry sort of passion quite foreign to his personality. His eyes went hard. He made a jerky gesture towards the cards—ha! he had seen them after all—in front of him. "Our whole faith is a a wager, Miss Leplastrier. We bet—it is all in Pascal and very wise it is too, although the Queen of England might find him not nearly Presbyterian enough—we bet that there is a God. We bet our life on it. We calculate the odds, the return, that we shall sit with the saints in paradise. Our anxiety about our bet will wake us before dawn in a cold sweat. We are out of bed and on our knees, even in the midst of winter. And God sees us, and sees us suffer. And how can this God, a God who sees us at prayer beside our bed . . ." His hands were quite jerky in their movements. There was a wild sort of passion about him, and the eyes within that sharp-chinned face held the reflections of electric lamps. Lucinda felt the hair on the back of her neck stand up. Her eyelids came down. If she had been a cat she would have purred.

"I cannot see," he said, "that such a God, whose fundamental requirement of us is that we gamble our mortal souls, every second of our temporal existence . . . It is true! We must gamble every *instant* of our allotted span. We must stake *everything* on the unprovable fact of His existence."

Lucinda shivered, a not unpleasant shiver and one not caused by cold. There were so many reasons for this involuntary ripple, not least the realization that her vice would not lose her his friendship. But it was also caused by recognition: she saw herself mirrored in him, the sudden coldness of the gambler's passion—something steely, angry even, which will not be denied. She was disturbed, too, to find her confessor belittling the worth of her confession and this—the pulling out of the tablecloth beneath the meal—gave a salt of anger to her own emotions even while she delighted—celebrated, even—the vital defence my great-grandfather was assembling, like a wild-haired angel clockmaker gesturing with little cogs, dangerous springs, holding out each part for verification, approbation, before he inserted it in the gleaming structure of his belief.

"Every instant," said Oscar, and held up a finger as he said it, calling attention to a low roly-poly laugh issuing from the ventilator.

"There," he said triumphantly, as if he had caught the laugh, as if the laugh was the point of it all, and he was like a man who has trapped a grasshopper in mid-air, smiling as if the miracle were tickling his palm.

"There. We will never hear that man laugh that laugh again. The instant is gone."

It would not be apparent to anyone watching Oscar Hopkins that this was a young man who had sworn off gambling now he had no further "use" for it. His views seemed not only passionate but firmly held. So even if you had not agreed with him, you would not have doubted his conviction.

Lucinda had no idea that she had witnessed a guilty defense. She thought all sorts of things, but not this. She thought what a rare and wonderful man he was. She thought she should not be alone with him in her cabin. She thought they might play cards. She thought: I could marry, not him, of course not him, but I could marry someone like him. There was a great lightness in her soul.

"Every *instant*," he said.

She felt she knew him. She imagined not only his passion for salvation, but his fear of damnation. She saw the fear that would take him "before dawn." It was a mirror she looked at, a mirror and window both.

"That such a God," said Oscar, "knowing the anguish and the trembling hope with which we wager . . ." He stopped then, looking with wonder at his shaking hands. This shaking was caused by the fervour of his beliefs as he revealed them, but there was another excitement at work—that produced by the open, admiring face of Miss Leplastrier. "That such a God can look unkindly on a chap wagering a few quid on the likelihood of a dumb animal crossing a line first, unless," (and here it seemed he would split his lips with the pleasure of his smile, which was, surely, caused more by Lucinda's admiring face than by the new thought which had just, at that moment, taken possession of him) "unless—and no one has ever suggested such a thing to me—it might be considered blasphemy to apply to common pleasure that which is by its very nature divine."

"Mr Hopkins," Lucinda said, coming at last to sit down, "we must not place our souls at risk with fancies."

She meant this sincerely. She also did not mean it at all—there was nothing she liked better than to construct a fancy. She put great weight on fancies and was not in the habit of using the word in a dismissive way. The Crystal Palace, that building she admired more than any other, was nothing but a fancy of a kind, and there were ideas like this, the philosophical equivalent of great cathedrals of steel and glass, which were her passion, and she held these to her tightly, secretly.

"Not a fancy," said Oscar.

He picked up the cards and put them together. It was not his intention that they play. It was Lucinda who suggested the game of cards. But later, when she knew Oscar better, she confessed that she had only done it because she thought it was what he had intended.

58

Reputation

It was already a scandal. It was known about by Mr Smith and Mr Borrodaile, by Mr Carraway, Mrs Menzies, Mr and Mrs Johnston. The stewards, of course, all knew—for they were not only judges but also conduits and they wound their way from class to class and even down into the rivet-studded steel innards of the ship, not quite as far as young Master Smiggins (whose task it was to ready the live-stock for the approaching storm). He knew a lady had "lost her reputation" but he had this from long-nosed Clemence, the apprentice engineer. He did not know it was "his" lady for whom he had planned to work.

"She gone and bleeding done it now. She lost it now," said Clemence who was frightened by the animals.

"What?" asked Master Smiggins.

"Er *reputation*. I told you, didn' I? *Compreyvous*?"

"Course I bloody *compreyvous*. I got a sister, ain't ? Now nick off. I got me animals and the sea's coming up."

"Coming up your back passage more like," said Clemence, but stepped back, ready to run.

Master Smiggins kicked the llama doe in the backside and forced it into its crush. He strapped the crush shut.

"There," he said, "all tucked in now. Can't roll out of bed no matter what." He went to deal with the buck. "Now, don't you fuss," he said. He looked around. Clemence had gone. "Lost *her* reputation," he said. He had a stick to prod the buck with.

"Course," he said. "*Course* I bloody *compreyvous*."

59

Thou Rulest the Raging of the Sea

Lucinda liked to play poker on a table covered with a grey wool blanket. This, of course, is how she first played cribbage in the house of Mr d'Abbs, and on windy nights, alone in her rented cottage at Longnose Point, she sometimes laid a blanket across the oilskin on her kitchen table and dealt herself a hand of patience. It was a comfort to her: to drink tea, to riddle the grate on the stove, to feel the soft blanket beneath the slippery cards. She did not feel the same affection for the tables in gaming houses. She liked the games, my word she did, but it was a different sort of "like" to the one she had for the grey blanket-covered tables of her home and Mr d'Abbs's. The tables of gaming houses were cold and slippery. It was an icier pleasure, a showy dancer's thrill, like a tight, stretched smile or a pair of shiny patent-leather shoes.

In her stateroom, alone with the priest, Lucinda took a blanket from her bed and draped it across the little table. She knew this action lacked propriety but she did not let herself address the matter. She must have it right. She would be blinkered. If he was shocked, she would not look at him. She would have everything in its proper place. She took a little amber lamp and set it to one side.

She thought: Alone in my bedroom with a priest.

"There," she said, but could not bring her eyes up to look at him. She laid her hand flat on the blanket. She had been biting her nails. She hid the evidence beneath her palm.

"So," she said, and looked him boldly in the eye.

His face was not how she had imagined it. She had rebuilt it in her imagination, had made it long and censorious when it was, in reality, doe-like, almost pretty, with soft eyes regarding her from beneath long lashes.

"Shall we play?" he asked.

Lucinda blushed.

They played with penny bets.

It was such a *still* game. She may not have remarked on this quality were it not for the fact that he had previously been so agitated, such a kicker and scuffer, a squirmer in his seat—she had felt him next to her at dinner, had felt the vital life in his body through the table, through the legs of her own chair. But now she felt only this concentrated stillness. It was not a lifeless stillness—it was not that dead-eyed mask most men adopted when playing poker, their eyes gone blind like statues. He was a cello, a violin, he was all strapped down like Ulysses at the mast.

She lost. She felt so light, an airy, dragon-fly wing of feeling. It was always like this when she lost. She felt such guilt and fear after she had lost that she did not imagine she liked losing, and yet this sensation always came with it, and once, seeing the carcass of a grasshopper all eaten out by ants, only its delicate and papery form remaining, she had recognized, in that light and lovely shell, the physical expression of this feeling she had when losing.

She shed her money, sloughed it off. A penny, a penny, a three penny piece. Mr Hopkins played the most exquisite poker. She complimented him, as another woman might have complimented her partner at a waltz. She sat up straight. She fanned her cards neatly. She had lost a sovereign but she did not wish to stop. She knew she would have the perfect voyage now. She knew herself happy.

At half past one the ship began to bluster in the wind and she felt the beginning of a long, deep swell. The ship made noises which made Lucinda think of a pianist cracking knuckles. She accommodated the motion of the ship to her idea of happiness.

She smiled at Oscar. He smiled back. He rested his left ankle across his knee. He jiggled it, but he did not knock the table and she did not notice.

At two-thirty the game turned again. He pushed through, bluffing to victory three hands in a row. He was breathing through his mouth. There was perspiration of his forehead but she took this to be produced by the excitement of the game.

He observed that the ship, although large, seemed to move as one would imagine a small ship to move. He remarked on the size of the sea. It was such a large thing, he said. " 'Who hath measured the waters in the hollow of his hand, and meted out heaven with the span, and comprehended the dust of the earth in a measure, and weighed the mountains in scales, and the hills in a balance?' " He smiled, showing the neat, ordered set of his lower teeth.

She smiled. She had no appreciation of his phobia.

He raised his betting. A crown to see her. There was a tremor in his voice it would have taken Mrs Williams to explain.

The game had changed. It was no longer still and calm. Lucinda no longer played leaning back. She bent forward. She rubbed her neck. She was making small red spot, just from friction.

Oscar was pale. He played with a sort of clipped breathlessness. His foot tapped against the table leg. She minded this not at all. He took her for two pounds and five shillings. She raised the betting again. She was so light, almost giddy. She confessed her happiness out loud. She hardly noticed the pitching of the ship. Her hat case tumbled off its rack and a vase of paper flowers—left carelessly on a side table, slipped and rolled—not breaking—across the floor.

It was three twenty-three. The first wave washed across the deck. They turned ("Hoo," said Oscar) to see the next wave—its white head towering over them like a ghost in the night.

It was frightening. Lucinda found it frightening. She made some silly comment and turned to see her partner, white-faced with terror, his mouth open, crouched over the table trying to pick up cards without looking at them. He was not handling these cards as a card-player might, but like a savage. He was cramming them into his pocket. He made a repetitive noise—"Uh-uh-uh-uh"—that came from the back of his throat, the top of his stomach.

The wave smashed across the deck. You could feel the weight of it in your vital organs.

"Uh-uh-uh." He crumpled up more cards. She was angry with him. They were her Wetherby Supremes, from Hare's in Old Bond Street.

"I have led you astray," he said. He was standing now, gripping the edge of the table. He was not looking at her. He was pulling a paper parcel from his pocket. As he pulled it out he produced a shower of the crumpled playing cards.

The parcel, of course, was his caul.

The ship reared and crashed down so far you could feel your stomach falling after it had landed. You would not think so large a thing could be tossed so far.

On the bridge it took ten men to steer the rearing beast.

Through the din (creaking, groaning, a slamming door) she could hear bells ringing.

He said: "You must forgive me."

The vase rolled past her feet. She had time to wonder that such an ugly thing should not break, would probably survive a shipwreck when everything beautiful and useful was sunk to the bottom. She picked up the vase. She held it in her lap. The clergyman was banging his thigh with his clenched fist.

"Yes," she shouted, "yes, of course, I forgive you."

But she did not understand him. She did not put the two together, the cards and the storm. It did not occur to her that one might be the cause and the other the effect. It did not occur to her to think in so primitive a manner. She could not guess that a man who knew that phosphorescence was produced by sea blubbers could also believe that this storm was a sign from God.

But Oscar knew he should not have gambled just for pleasure. He knew his defence of gambling had been displeasing to God. He knew he had led the young woman into sin. Waves slapped the face of the ship. Water surged across its high deck. The mighty *Leviathan* reared and rolled sideways across the cliff face of the storm.

"Oh, dear" said Oscar, "I am afraid."

The portholes could be opened with a little winding handle. He clutched his caul to his chest and lurched uphill to get there. Then he stood, facing down into the dark pit of the sea while he forced himself to do the thing he dreaded most—unwind the handle.

Lucinda thought he wished to be ill. She stumbled down the sloping floor to help him. Then she saw what he was doing—putting her Wetherby Supremes out the window, posting jacks and queens like letters.

"No," she yelled into his ear. She scrabbled at his hands and tried to pull away from the porthole. His lips were moving. His eyes were shut. She scratched the back of his hands but could not stop him. She saved a two of clubs and a five of diamonds. Her emotions were confused—anger, sympathy, alarm. He turned to look at her and she saw his eyes wandering in their gaze. He clutched at her. She was frightened and stepped back, and he fell into a swoon at her feet.

She did not know how ill he was. She was not even sure what had happened. She felt his pulse and would have loosened his collar except she did not know how. She tried to find the stud, but his neck felt warm, unduly intimate. It was wrong to be angry, but she was angry, about her cards, about the blanket which he had dragged off the card table. The room looked as if a scandal had been committed there. She picked up the money and the blanket. She was thrown against the wall twice. She got the blanket back on to her bed and smoothed it as well as she was able.

She should call the ship's doctor, but it was four o'clock in the morning. Surely he would wake in a moment? She sat and waited.

Oscar did wake, but he was not able to leave her stateroom unassisted. She had had to call two stewards, just before dawn, and it had been their unenviable job—the ship was now pitching and rolling to a disappointing degree, and walking was therefore difficult—to carry the rigid man from the spinster's stateroom, down the stairs and put him to bed in his own quarters.

60

Cape Town to Pinchgut

The scene was witnessed by Mr Borrodaile, or so he claimed, for he was able, at breakfast the next morning, to paint a very detailed picture of the scandal for the rather queasy and waxy-skinned Mr Smith.

The Captain also visited Lucinda, and perhaps his manner was contaminated by the knowledge that his great ship was a failure in bad weather—he had one helmsman in sick bay with a broken arm—but he behaved in a censorious and snobbish way, Lucinda thought, just like a glove salesman in Harrod's who feels he should not be called to wait upon colonials.

Lucinda was hurt by all of this, but she could tolerate it. She hardened her heart against all the ship except Mr Hopkins and set herself to wait for his recovery. She expected, as a matter of course, that he would apologize, and she looked forward to the moment when she could say, and sincerely too, that there was nothing to apologize for. It was the Captain who should apologize, and if she had had the power she would have made him. She had a vindictive part to her character, which she recognized and was not proud of. It had started as a tiny thing, but grown larger with the nourishment provided by men like the Captain, and the sniggering Borrodaile whom she met, clad in sou'wester, his grinning lackey at his side, on the rolling. slippery poop deck.

After this she would not go on deck again. Neither, or course, was she free to seek out Mr Hopkins herself, and although his visit to her would not save her reputation, at least he could offer his support and friendship.

It stayed rough down the coast of Africa, and although she understood why this might keep Mr Hopkins in his cabin, by the time she had been five days a prisoner in her stateroom, she felt herself deserving a proper apology.

He did not come.

She took her meals in her room which, for all the grey skies and green cat's-eye-coloured sea, was most unpleasantly hot.

She escaped ashore in Cape Town, and endured the self-righteous "tsk-tsk" of a Mrs Penhaligon (the wife of a Cornish farmer) but she still did not sight Mr Hopkins.

Out of Cape Town the weather was rough again and Oscar stayed out of sight, cooped up, green and moaning. He was attended by a steward with the comic name of Sidebottom. He had his caul between his fingers so persistently that it soon became, through the twin agencies of perspiration and agitation, a most unpleasant piece of matter. His stomach could hold no more than beef tea and dry toast. He read his Bible when his eyes could bear the dancing print. He prayed. He promised God that he would never bet again.

My great-grandfather did not manage to emerge from his cabin until the Pinchgut cannons saluted the great ship's entrance into Sydney Harbour, and Lucinda Leplastrier, released at last from the most unpleasant voyage of her life, saw him sitting in the geometrical centre of the ship, on a red plush settee, in the second-class promenade.

He looked up and smiled, but Lucinda had waited so long for that smile that it became, when it arrived, like something which has preoccupied one during a fever—it produced an unpleasant effect, evoking all the twisting tyrannies of an illness which one has, at last, escaped from.

61

A Business Principle

Owning a business is like having chooks. You cannot go away and leave them, indefinitely, in the care of neighbours. You can buy an automatic feeder, and there are many good ones on the market—you will see them advertised in the back pages of the *Weekly Times*. You can arrange for your friend or your neighbour to "keep an eye on them" for a night or two, and no harm done. But do not expect to be away six months or a year and then return to find your hens in good condition. You will have mite and pullorum rampant, the water run out, your best layer dead from a dog, your rooster wounded by goannas—the list is not intended to be exact, merely an indication, but the point is, you cannot do it. And if you want to see Venice, Florence and the Old World, then first eat your chooks, or sell them, and then you will know you will have nothing worse to come back to than a chookyard full of rank weed.

Lucinda did not know this. Or if she did, she managed to pretend that she did not. She was off to London to be married (although she fully intended that she would—God knows how—return. She imagined a certain type of husband who would make this possible). She thought she could leave the country for a year and entrust the Prince Rupert's Glassworks to the care of others. Note the plural. This compounded the error, for if there is anything worse than leaving your business in the care of one person, it is leaving it in the care of two and if there is anything worse than two people, it is to do what Lucinda Leplastrier did—she left her business in the care of three people, and only one of them with any practical experience of glass.

It is true that the vicar of Woollahra had some knowledge of the chemical composition of glass, but he was at last one to claim himself a manufacturer, and he shared with Wardley-Fish a dislike of dirt. He could not bear to have it on his hands. He did not like to be in places—even the ragged school he preached at every third Monday morning—where other people had it on their hands. When he was in the glassworks he could not concentrate.

If Dennis Hasset had imagined himself actually responsible for the well-being of the glassworks he would—for he was a conscientious man—have declared himself unfit. But he knew that Lucinda had also asked her accountant, Mr d'Abbs of d'Abbs and Fig, to keep an eye on the business. He was to bank the incomings, pay the billings and the wages. For all this he was to receive a fee. The Reverend Mr Hasset was to receive no fee. He was a friend. He was there to "keep an eye on things."

Lucinda had asked both of these parties to trust the opinions of her senior blower, Arthur Phelps, who not only knew something about the manufacture of glass, but, being the senior blower, was therefore the natural leader of the men in the works. There is a deeply ingrained hierarchy amongst glass workers, and the senior blowers are its aristocrats. You would only need to watch Arthur Phelps to know that this was true, to see him, with the blowing tube in his mouth, his cheeks distended like a trumpet player, move his cigarette from his left-hand side of his mouth and—with no manual help at all—"walk" it around the tube and thence to the right corner.

Mr d'Abbs was a natty little chap whose dress (a blue corduroy suit, a woollen tie, a curly walking stick, perhaps) suggested more of the aesthete than the accountant. He painted a little, and had tried his hand at verse, but he was not sensitive to Arthur Phelps's displays of skill. He did not "see" the set-up at the works at all. Neither, no matter what his other good qualities were, did the vicar of Woollhara.

Arthur Phelps was a broad man with a plastic face, a big chest and a large belly which he liked to refer to as his bellows. He took his responsibility seriously and he felt himself abandoned by Lucinda and mucked about by the other two. He was forever being given contrary instructions and his sleep was ruined as a result. (Mr d'Abbs would not have credited that an ignorant working man, a grog-artist at that, would behave in such a way.) Arthur Phelps tossed and turned in his bed at night until his wife went to sleep with the children in the kitchen. He worried that they were making too many poison blues and insufficient beers, that their sand would run out before Mr d'Abbs's clerks paid the carter for the last load and thereby ensured the next, that the vase footings were of a style gone out of fashion, that Mr d'Abbs wanted a greater production, whilst the vicar of Woollhara, the very next day, would come poking about with his umbrella, opening a door at the wrong moment, letting in a draught that wrecked a jug handle, and holding up production while he worried at Arthur about the "seeds," those tiny air bubbles, which had lately been appearing in their products.

This seediness was offensive to Arthur, too. He was ashamed of it. But it was produced by nothing other than the taste induced by Mr d'Abbs. No one appreciated how hard the lads were working, or with what will. It was not for the Natty Gent or the Bible-basher that they did it, but for Miss Lucinda. They talked about her fondly. And if they were as patronizing as fathers and brothers, they were also as protective. They tried to satisfy the demands of her advisers. They tried to work quickly, even though the commands were given in an ignorant manner, with no respect for craft or the status of the craftsmen. As a result of this haste a young gob-gatherer had his lungs burnt and this, whilst always a possibility, never happens in a well-run works. He was not a silly lad, but helpful. They took up a subscription but Mr d'Abb's contribution was insufficient. It was all wrong. It was because of this that Arthur began to weep. It was from imagining what would happen to the lad, worrying when the clay would arrive for the new crucible, how the twenty gross of seedy "poisons" would be sold. He was sitting on his stool. The second gatherer was collecting from the glory-hole. Arthur had a draught from his beer in readiness for the next blow. The gatherer handed him the rod, and it was then that he began to weep. The fireman, who had just come on, ran down to Sussex Street to fetch Mr d'Abbs, but the men thought so little of Mr d'Abbs that this did nothing but confirm their already low opinion of the fireman. Arthur said nothing to Mr d'Abbs. He blew his nose and drank his last pint of glassworks beer. He took a bottle for a souvenir, and Mr d'Abbs had the good sense not to attempt to stop him.

They kept the furnaces going another week, but the works had lost their heart. Dennis Hasset saw what was happening, but did not even try to arrest the process. His mind was occupied with other matters. He was arraigned before the Bishop of Sydney to explain his sermons.

62

Home

Dennis Hasset held the Virgin birth to be unproved and inconsistent with the perfect humanity of Christ. He rejected the miracles of the Old Testament. He doubted many of the miracles of the New. He rejected the doctrine of verbal inspiration. He did not think there was sufficient evidence to prove the physical resurrection of Christ. He accepted Darwin's theory of evolution, not merely as it applied to insects and animals (at which point Bishop Dancer drew the line) but also as it applied to humankind. He described his position as Broad Church.

Bishop Dancer knew this position by the earlier label of heresy. He was a churchman of the old Tory school and had no time for Evangelicals (on the Low side) or Puseyites (on what was known as the High). He could not tolerate genuflexion or vestments, and the sight of candles—other than for the purpose of illumination—had him doing little manoeuvres with his dental plate. He was of the roast-beef-and-Yorkshire-pudding school of theology, and thought the vicar of Woollahra's polite and reasonable sermons to be the beginning of the rot. He would like—to use plain language—to "do him over" for heresy. But if this new Clerical Subscription Act would now prevent this, he would take him away from his fireplace and lamps at Woollahra, and send him up to the Bellinger River, to Boat Harbour in the Parish of Never-Never, where he would find his parishioners about as sympathetic as those at Home during the Reform Bill (at time the Bishop remembered all too well—he had been pelted with turnips and had his windows broken). Boat Harbour was filled with foul-mouthed sawyers, ex-convicts to a man, and was, as far as Bishop Dancer could gather, a little hell on earth. In the face of these difficulties the Reverend Mr Hasset's faith might yet be reborn, or so, in any case, the Bishop managed to persuade himself.

When Lucinda arrived at the Woollahra vicarage on the Tuesday before Palm Sunday, she knew none of this. She was in an emotional state for reasons of her own. She did not know if she had come to censure Dennis Hasset for what she had just found at her glassworks or if she was here to seek comfort in the face of this same catastrophe. All the way across the town—and what a tiny town it now appeared to be—she had thought of sarcastic and bitter things to say to him. But as she dismounted outside the vicarage (which was also meaner than her memory had allowed) she was suddenly fearful—perhaps it was the dullness of the red brick, the hollow shadow of the front veranda—that the state in which she had found her works was the result of some personal tragedy that had befallen her friend.

She had found the St Rupert's Glassworks deserted, its crucible gone grey and lifeless, the metal set hard inside them. Under the glass blower's wooden throne she found a miaowing kitten with pus-filled eyes and paralysed back legs, a creature in so parlous a state that Lucinda, dressed in an ostrich-feathered hat and expensive black gloves, must take a heavy poker and, with her face twisted, her eyes closed, kill it. She felt the crunch travel up her arm.

When the kitten was a soiled and lifeless rag, she leaned the murdering bar against the throne. She thought: I had the strength.

And although she was mostly shaken by what she had done, there was a small part of her that was proud.

So when she was reunited with her old friend, it had already been a most disturbing day. She did not meet him in quite the place she had imagined, not in the gentle book-lined study she had so often recalled, but in a room filled with wooden crates in which Dennis Hasset was permitted to camp while the new incumbent and his family made themselves at home in the remainder.

Without a fire, the room proved both cold and damp. Lucinda shrank inside her rabbitskin coat. She had not even been shown into the room politely. She had been greeted at the front door by a too-pretty child with a hoop. She had found her friend sitting on a rough wooden crate and the floor around him slippery with old letters. He was smaller than he had been, hunched over, and although there was no invalid's rug across his knees, his posture suggested one. Even when he stood he did not appear to straigten properly. She thought his hand very cold and bloodless. They looked at each other and although she sought much from the dear and familiar face she imagined she saw nothing there but exhaustion and defeat.

"What a miserable day," she said.

Dennis Hasset thought her eyes "pouchy" and her skin pallid. He had looked forward to this reunion, but now he was irritated by her tone. She made it seem as if the condition of the weather was his responsibility. He peered out of the window, shrugged, and then sat down again. He reflected how quickly women age.

"I am afraid," he said, "that I must offer you a crate. The chairs are taken, but not for the purpose of sitting, just taken. I am so very sorry about your works. It came at a bad time."

"Your study is in ruins," she said.

He shrugged.

"I find it quite disturbing," she said.

"We grow too attached to things."

"Yes, but it is a shock." The shock was not so much to do with what the room had become, but in the realization that this place–which she had all but eliminated from her memory–was the seat of all those feelings which make us call one city "home" above all others. It had been more of a home than her cottage at Longnose Point. It was certainly far more of a home than Mr d'Abbs's house although it was the latter she had so romanticized in her absence, making it into a place of "comradeship" and "jolly good times," which labels involved forgetting all that was tawdry and corrupted about the house and its occupants.

But this room, Dennis Hasset's room, had contained all that was true and good in her life. She had forgotten this because he had not proposed to her as she had thought he might, and she had been angry with him. But now she was back, she saw that Sydney would be unbearable without this friendship, this room. Everything in her wished to cry out like a child at the injustice of her homecoming. But she was not a child, and she would no longer demand her hot cocoa and her seat to sleep in by the fire. She was a grown woman with a damaged friend and she forced herself to shown concern for him, teasing his story from him like a bandage from a congealed wound.

And yet there was a part of her, a substantial part too, that did not give a damn about Dennis Hasset's story. This part was angry. It thought Dennis Hasset a weak fool and a poor friend. It judged him for not valuing her sufficiently, for slumping over in his seat, for not lighting a fire. It coexisted with this other part that loved him. And these two factions fought within her all the while she listened to his story. She thought he had a kind and intelligent face and it was not wise to speak so indulgently about his enemies.

"But surely," she said at last, "Boat Harbour can be appealed against?"

He shook his head.

"But it is unfair. You still see yourself a Christian?" She wished he would sit up straight.

"Of course."

"Then *damn* him," said Lucinda, not softly either, "then *damn him in hell*." And tears were coursing down her cheeks and he leaned over and enfolded her hand with his. But she did not wish her hand held. It was too late for that now. And, anyway, her tears were selfish tears, not really shed for him at all, but for herself. He had a big hand and it did not comfort her, merely reminded her of how small her own was. "He behaves like a *cad*," she said, removing her hand on the pretext of finding her handkerchief. "Oh, Mr Hasset, please, and where is Boat Harbour?"

He smiled and shrugged. She saw that he did not realize that her life would also be affected.

"Is it far away?" She had come to have war with him about his neglect of her works. She had despised the way he sat so hunched on the crate, but she would not be without him. He was a good man, but too soft.

She felt herself to be red and blotchy in her cheeks. The tiny veins on her eyelids would be showing.

"Far enough," he said. "It is the territory of the Kumbaingiri Tribe. What does 'far' mean in this country? I don't know, Miss Leplastrier. I am so awfully sorry about your glassworks. The two crises arrived coincidentally."

"They were all I had."

"You have them still," he said reprovingly, feeling she cared too much for her own predicament.

"Yes, but not my partner."

The softness of her voice made him catch his breath. He checked himself. He had been, generally, too emotional of late.

"I think I will never forget how you came into my study and I thought you a Mr Leplastrier. Do you remember the to-do we caused?"

"We were most improper."

"Oh, we were a degree or two hotter than improper."

"And we were noted," said Lucinda who, although she was smiling, was feeling her neck and shoulders set upon by a swarm of hot prickles.

"They could not help themselves," said Dennis Hasset, grinning broadly.

"Then it is I who am responsible for your exile."

"Oh, no."

"Oh, yes, and you have tried to hide it from me. I was such a child. I never thought the harm I did you."

"Hush."

"I never thought."

"Hush. Do you hear me? You're wrong. You are quite wrong. Now, please. It is wholly theological, I promise you." This was not exactly true. His situation had not been helped by the association.

"Do you give your word?"

"I do," he said. She did not catch the small grimace he made at the sound of his own falsehood.

"Then do not go," she said. "If that is truly the case, then you do not have to go."

"I do not follow your logic."

"There is no more logic in my argument than there is truth in yours," she said softly.

He did not know whether to smile or frown at her. He remembered the afternoons he had found her, unannounced, asleep in his armchair. "How sad life is," he said.

Lucinda stood and went to the window. She was surprised to find the view the same. She turned up the collar of her rabbit fur. She pulled on her gloves, as if she intended to leave, and then took them off again and arranged them on a crate, laying out the fingers, flattening the thumb. "You do not *have* to go. You have a choice."

Dennis Hasset stretched himself and no one, seeing the languid confidence of this action, would guess that he had felt himself charged with weakness and found guilty. "I need a living," he said. "Only a bishop can provide one. There is no choice."

"Oh, you must not."

"Must not what?" he said crossly. "What *must* not?"

"Must not nothing," she sighed. She sat on the crate. She could feel the splintery roughness of the wood catch on the fur. She thought of her father's whiskers on her child's face.

He raised his hands (tense, hard, splay-fingered) and then let them fall (soft as rag toys). The rag hand rubbed the whiskered face. "Oh, Miss Leplastrier, he smiled, "we owe each other more charity than this."

Lucinda picked up her glove and examined it closely. "Dear Mr Hasset," she said, "I am fond of you." She frowned as if the stitching were unsatisfactory. She had a red patch the size of a florin on each cheek. "I am so very, very sorry to be the one responsible for your removal from my company. And I admit—even now I am thinking only of myself and how lonely it will be, and what pleasure I have had buying the works with you, and I always hoped we could plan more together. I have purchased the cylinder process from Chance and Sons."

From the corridor, too close, a woman's voice: "Arthur, *do not do that*!"

Lucinda leaned forward, frowning, speaking more quietly. "It is delivered, already, and tomorrow I will engage engineers to install it. The furnaces will be alight within the week. And it seems to me, though I have no profound knowledge of the Thirty-nine Articles, or how many miracles it is you dispute, I do not see why you must go."

There were brisk footsteps in the passage. It seemed they would have a visitor, but no. The footsteps stopped, and then went back the way they had come.

"It is like being locked inside the Tower."

Dennis Hasset smiled. "I must go where I am sent."

"By God?"

"Of course."

"Or a man, a bishop?"

He passed his hands over his eyes.

She said: "You do not agree with this Bishop?"

"Oh, please, Miss Leplastrier, please, do leave it alone."

"I shall not."

"Then," he looked up, his face red, his eyes flashing, "you are impertinent."

She stood. She felt humiliated, as if her face had been slapped, her backside paddled with a leather slipper. She began fiddling with her gloves again. "So it is impertinent to feel anger when your friends are mistreated and abused. It is impertinence to think injustice should *not* be accepted with a bowed head. You do not accept the Virgin birth, Mr Hasset. *I* do not accept the wisdom of turning the other cheek."

He could not be angry for long. It was his handicap, a corollary of his general lack of passion. His tempers were like sparks from flint, but not tinder to catch on. When he spoke he was ironic, self-mocking and the seemingly simple words he spoke were cross-referenced to other self-critical thoughts that he imagined she would see but which were, of course, clear to one but himself. "Your opinions," he said, "are strongly put."

Lucinda's gloves would not come right. Here was a thumb inside out. She had to blow to make it come out right. "Yes, and I am generally most unsuitable. I am loud and opinionated. I am silent and stupid. I am an embarrassment in proper society. My mother's friends, those who wrote most passionately and invited me to come Home, discovered, when they had me in their parlours, that their passion had been mistaken. They thanked the Lord – the ones not playing atheist – that they had not lost a daughter to the Colonies. They would agree with you. I should not speak so bluntly to you. I should not address you like this, even if I do hurt on your behalf, on both of your behalfs. What will happen to you, Mr Hasset? You are too fine to be in a place where there can be nothing but mud and taverns. There is no church?"

"There is no church *building*."

"Stay." She had her gloves on, as if ready to depart. He did not rise. She sat. "We can have the works together."

So, she thought, I beg.

She saw him consider it. She saw a little life come into his eyes. (Say yes, say yes.) He straightened his back. He crossed his legs.

"I know nothing of business."

"We neither of us do."

He looked at her: her cheeks flushed, her eyes bright, her lips parted, leaning forward and clasping her small, gloved hands together. He smiled, and shook his head. "You put the negative as a powerful argument for the positive."

She knew she could keep him. In one minute, two minutes, everything would be resolved. "It does not *matter* what we know. You said to me, when I was Mr Leplastrier, just walked into your study (this study here), you said I had a passion for things."

"And so do you."

"You said it is a passion that matters."

"I think so still."

"Then it does not matter that we are ignorant of business. Our ignorance is temporary. Oh, Mr Hasset, dear Mr Hasset, we will make good things, things of worth, things we are proud to make. We will not be like these tallow-boilers and subdividers. We could be the most splendid Manufacturers of Glass."

"And neither of us lonely."

She looked at him with her mouth quite open, not knowing that her lower lip was almost indecently plump. She could not hold his eyes. They were soft and grey but she could not look at them. She shut her mouth. She felt herself go red around her neck and shoulders. She began to take her gloves off again. It was very quiet. A bullock team was pulling up the hill outside, but the driver made no noise. There was just the squeaky wheel of the dray and, twice, the flick of the whip, which cut through the air like a bird-cry in the forest of their talk which had become, with this single comment, all stumps and hedgerows and not a tree to hide behind.

"I must go," he said, when the silence had become unendurable.

"So you may preach what you do not believe to men who do not care what anyone believes."

"That is not kind."

"But accurate."

"No, not accurate either. I will preach what I believe."

"That there is no Virgin birth."

"That Christ died for our sins that we might be redeemed through His blood, that we might sit at the side of God in heaven."

She was surprised by the passion in his voice. She was too used to hearing him say he had none, and too ready to accept it without complication. They had discussed church politics, but never once religion. They had talked on her subjects: glass, factories, the benefits of industry. He had catered to her needs and enthusiasms and she had been conceited and self-centred, and yet today, at this moment, she would rather not be an industrialist at all, would rather, if she could be persuaded it was Christian, have a little farm somewhere up-country.

"So," she said, nodding her head, mentally listing her discoveries, "so there is a part of you that wishes to be sent away?"

"Quite a large part," he admitted.

"And all this," she gestured at the shattered room, the crates, the papers spilled across the floor, "in a sense it pleases you."

He nodded, suddenly self-conscious. He rubbed his hands together, looked down, then out of the window. He was hiding his pleasure from her. She told him so. He admitted it. And these words, the accusation and the admission, were uttered, on each side, so calmly, so matter-of-factly, that they were like the slash of a razor which, being so sharp, causes no pain when it first cuts.

But when Lucinda saw that the great weight she had placed on their friendship was far greater than the one he did, she felt more than simply foolish.

"Will you take all your books?"

"They say there is a problem, generally, with mould."

"So you will leave them here?"

"Oh, no, I will take them."

Looking at his handsome, smiling, apologetic face, she hated him.

It was a spasm, coming and going in a moment. "Oh, don't you care?" she exclaimed. "Must you *wait* for mould to happen to you?"

And Dennis Hasset watched her, alarmed, unhappy, nervous of what might happen next. It occurred to him that he might propose to her and she would accept him. This was an odd idea, perfectly new – she had been a child when she went away, and he had been her protector – and the novelty was not unattractive. He glimpsed a passionate life, freedom from the tyrannies of bishops, something quite original. He had always imagined marriage to a tall and handsome woman. He did not think Lucinda handsome. It was no impediment.

The impediments were elsewhere. The first concerned the salvation of his soul and, peculiar though it might seem, he agreed with Bishop Dancer about the benefits of Boat Harbour. He did not *feel* his faith sufficiently. It was too much the creature of his intellect and he yearned for something simpler, rougher, more true to Christ.

The other impediment was no more than a rock under a wheel. (He hardly knew it was there, but it was enough to stop the wheel turning.) Dennis Hasset was a snob when it came to commerce. And as much as he would love to be free of the tyranny of bishops, he could not bear to walk down the street and be thought a merchant or a manufacturer. He thought glass a substance of great beauty, but the very originality of the life that Lucinda Leplastrier suggested to him, the very thing that made it so attractive, was what made it absolutely unacceptable.

He did not dwell on any of this. The ideas and feelings were too much a part of him. He gave Lucinda no clue as to why he should now, ever so subtly, withdraw himself from her. She had one glove on, one glove off. She was barely aware of herself, turning over books in an open crate. She did not understand the reason for her rejection and humiliation.

At the time she most wished to flee, she willed herself to stay. She forced herself to enquire about his journey and even made an appointment to drink tea with him before he sailed. But when she at last left the Woollahra vicarage, it was with the bleak understanding that there was no one in Sydney left to see.

She had to send a boy to call her coachman from a nearby tavern. He was not steady on his feet. She did not care. She could not remove the picture of Dennis Hasset's sad and smiling face from her mind's eye. It was to stay there a long while yet, no matter what instruments she used to scratch at it.

63

Longnose Point

To know you will be lonely is not the same as being lonely. When Lucinda came down the Parramatta River in Sol Myer's boat, she imagined her life would be a lonely one, and she felt strength through recognizing it. And yet what she imagined was not loneliness, which is boggy and sour, but something else which is bright and hard. The difference between what she imagined and what she finally experienced is the difference between a blade of a knife —an object of chilly beauty—and the chronic pain of an open wound.

She imagined she had been lonely in Sydney and London, alone in her icing-sugar cabin aboard the *Leviathan* but until Dennis Hasset sailed for Boat Harbour, she had kept ahead of it. She had been a dancer racing a burning fuse. She had been busy, had plans, been on the way to London, on the way back. Her life had been a series of expectations, and even in her first years in Sydney, when she had spent many nights alone with nothing but the company of her cats, she had always the prospect of company if she wanted it. She had thought herself lonely, but she had enjoyed her solitude.

She had moved out to the edge of Balmain and rented the falling-down cottage on Whitfield's Farm, down along that rocky promontory which ends in Longnose Point. It was two storeys, stone, with a big old kitchen overlooking the Parramatta River. Joubert and Borrodaile (yes, the same) had not yet begun to subdivide this land. It was a bankrupt estate, with just a caretaker at the farm and the orchard heavy with the sweet, drunk smell of rotting windfalls. The grass grew waist high in summer and the road to her door was a silvery green—the grass rolled flat beneath the jinker she drove herself. She repaired the leaking stable. She planted some snapdragons and pansies. She had her crates of books delivered and carried up the loud, uncarpeted stairs. It was a romantic place to be, and it did not cease to be so the instant the vicar disappeared from Sydney Heads on the *Susanna Cuthbert*.

She had plans. She had equipment to install. She met with Mr d'Abbs, but rarely socially. Rushcutters Bay now seemed too far away and she imagined the urge to gamble had quite left her. Her work was so demanding she would be asleep an hour after she had eaten. She woke early. She was alone, but not yet lonely. Her head was burning with dreams of glass, shapes she saw in the very edges of her vision, structures whose function she had not even begun to guess.

She would build a little pyramid of glass.

A tower.

An arcade to cover all of George Street.

She did not think of farms or marriage.

She ate her porridge left-handed with a pen in her right. There was a peak of anger in her passion, a little of the I'll-show-you-Mr-Hasset-what-it-is-you-could-have-had.

She could not draw. She put her visions on paper and made them seem gross and malformed. She found a Frenchman, a Monsieur Huille, an artist, a friend of Mr d'Abbs. The lessons were not a success. Monsieur Huille, while very free with his own criticisms, would not put pencil to paper himself until, finally, as a result of his pupil's blunt insistence, he executed the most dismal oak tree. Pigs (or possibly dogs) grazed beneath its wispy limbs. The drawing was so very bad that Monsieur Huille, pretending to be posthumously affronted by her insistence on this "proof," resigned. He took the evidence of his incompetence with him. He said it was worth twenty pounds, but later she found it, leached by rain, blown in amongst the hay in the stable.

At Easter she attended service in Balmain by herself, although that evening she rode across to Rushcutters Bay. Mrs Burrows was there, so there was no cards. She found the conversation dismal. She was separate, but not lonely.

After Easter she advertised for a woman to learn the art of glass blowing. She had imagined she might thereby create a partner for herself. She found a woman who played the trumpet at Her Majesty's. The woman was strong. Her lungs were good and she had large and powerful hands, but the men would not work with her. The furnaces went cold again, and Arthur Phelps, having come back to work for her, went back to the timber mill.

She wrote angry letters to Boat Harbour. But even these letters, once one is above the undergrowth of irritation, are celebratory. She described, with obvious pleasure, the scene in her own crate-filled study on the Easter holiday of 1866. And if she could not draw, she could execute a still life with words. She showed the exiled Dennis Hasset the deep burnt shadows, the splash of eggshell-white from the open heart of a book, the drape of a Delft-blue scarf on a chair, the sleeping marmalade cat, the long slice of sunshine cutting through the curtained windows on the northern wall and stretching itself, thin and silver, across the cedar floor. She made him, intentionally, homesick for Sydney, although he had never before thought of it as "home." He felt the warmth and the clean cut of the air. He imagined a gentle nor'easterly blowing, a sweet moist wind which brings rain, but later, slowly.

In a letter dated 22nd of August she reflected that an intelligent reader need never be alone when she could spend her evenings in Barchester or with Mr Nickleby, for instance.

August is the first month of the westerly—rude, bullying winds that cut across from Drummoyne or scream down the river from Bedlam Point and Hen and Chicken Bay. By August the upstairs rooms in Lucinda's cottage had become cold and dark. There were no slices of silver sunshine on the cedar floor. The cat had retreated downstairs where it had inflicted one more wound on the already scratched pine door, miaowing bad-temperedly until its mistress had let it in by the fire.

So what might we expect to find downstairs? The young manufacturer with drafting board and ruler? Or, with the day's work over, deep in the spell of Mr Dickens or Sir Walter Scott. Both *Waverley* and *Bleak House* lie on the floor beside her chair. But she cannot read them. Every word leads her, by one course or another, to Dennis Hasset, to her own situation, her lack of industrial education, practical skills, to the publicly pitied condition of spinsterhood and isolation.

Lucinda is asleep, her head collapsed on her shoulder, her book lying where it has fallen on the Turkish rug. The lower lip which looked so shockingly sensuous to Dennis Hasset not two months before, now, in sleep, seems sulky and disconsolate. Her cheeks seem quite flat. The eyes quiver behind the heavy blue-veined curtains of her lids. Her jaw is heavy, lifeless. The wind rattles the windows in their sashes. The fire hisses. There is no gas light but a smoky parraffin one whose blackened mantle needs attention. The cat, alert, stares at the rattling window.

This is not the sleep of exhaustion. It is produced by two glasses of brandy, by the lack of oxygen in the room, but most of all by the viscous, sour, treacly chemicals of loneliness.

You may suggest that she should have a maid. But she has a maid. All right, then—a maid to live with her. She has had. But she no longer wants a maid to live with her. Maids are young and alive. They have young men. They sit in the kitchen giggling. They only serve to make her feel more lonely.

Well, then—she should go out. To where? To Mr d'Abbs, of course, where she had so many pleasant times before. But it was not just the mediocrity of Mr d'Abbs's *ménage* she found depressing, not that peculiar Sydney combination of ignorance and bull-like confidence, it was Mr d'Abbs's determination that she not live a lonely life. There was always now some "philosopher" or "poet" (feeling old and finally in need of marriage) placed at her left-hand side.

Then she should have accepted other invitations. And, indeed, she would have liked to drink tea and talk about the most ordinary things. She would be interested in dancing the quadrille and discussing the adventures of babes in arms. Were not these things of interest in novels? Then why would they not be of interest in life?

But Lucinda had alienated all the people she might now wish to cultivate. It was not merely that her stride was wrong or her hair inadequately coiffured, her fashions, generally, inconsiderate of other feelings. She had held herself aloof. She had indicated she felt no sympathy for that loose congregation which one might call "her class." Even her house, the house she chose herself, placed her apart from people. Her display of arrogance would not be forgiven. Society would not invite her in a second time.

Fortunately, she did not yet realize that she was not welcome in her own works. She imagined this dry, brick-floored factory to be her home. It was her only connection with life. She liked the smell of working men, and I do not mean that in any vulgar sense, but rather that she valued the smell of common humanity. The smells suggested labour, warmth, usefulness.

In winter her own house was cold. It smelt of floor polish. She could no longer bear to be there.

64

The Multitude of Thy Sorceries

She had been happy once, properly happy, deeply happy. Now, as she hung her lantern on the nail in the stables and fussed with her stubborn gelding, she could not believe what she had become.

It was nine o'clock at night. And she was going for a trot.

She did not think where this trot would end. She did not even think very much about the place in which it began. It was frightening out here on Longnose Point.

There were so many things she could not think of. Her mind was dashing along corridors while she kept just ahead of it, slamming doors.

She was going for a trot. She tightened the harness. She walked the horse along the mud-heavy track past Birchgrove House. The caretaker was singing. He was alone and singing, drunk, too. Last week he had burned down the cow bails in the night. Lucinda kept two pistols wrapped in a blanket underneath her seat.

Rain came in long rips and ripples. She sought out the time when she had been happy. She shut out the drunken singing. She withdrew from the westerly wind. She was in Parramatta with her father. They were going home. Their big four-wheeler crossed the cobblestones and set off, their old waler biting at his familiar enemy, the percheron, beside him. They got up a nice trot, a little too fast, through the High Street (look out there!) past the doctor's phaeton, the farmers' buckboards, the swarms of drays and sulkies. There were big-skirted women, frock-coated shopkeepers, farmers with bow-yangs tied to their trousers so their thick legs looked like sausages with their ends tied off with string. When the waler tried to bite the percheron, her father hit it with a long stick. She laughed to see the little jump it gave, and did not know a horse could kill you.

They carried scents behind them. She could still list them, the smell of bran, of pollard, oats, the soft, dusty, yellow smell of seed wheat. The smells joined to other smells, a necklace of smells, with some in Parramatta, others along the way home where, for instance, you might find the air suddenly rich with honey, and beside the road the privet hedges not yet called a noxious weed and shaking their luxuriant white blossoms at you, or appearing to, for it was not the privet itself but rather—see, Lucy, lookee see, quick—a splendid parrot, no, three, four parrots—brilliant red, blue, such jewellery shaking the white clouds of honeyed privet.

Past Grass Corner they thundered over a wooden bridge and through a little cutting. Once her father stopped there. He gave her the reins to hold and jumped down. He was short and wide, strong in his arms and shoulders. He did exercises to strengthen his legs but they always stayed the same. He smelled of apples and sometimes—on the trip to Parramatta—of eau-de-Cologne. He carried paper bags with him at all times. Any bag that came his way was carefully folded and he would not hesitate to beg or borrow from anyone who possessed a bag but did not seem to value it. Lucinda was never embarrassed by this. She never knew that stage of life where everything her parents did—the way they spoke or combed their hair—was an embarrassment. She was not critical of paper-bag collecting. She knew the bags were there to hold her papa's soil samples and that he might at any moment (like this one now, as he jumps down from the buckboard and unfolds the handle of his neat little spade) might use the bag that had hitherto held jelly crystals to contain a scoop of astringent sand, or a pungent, black, heavy soil, heavy with humus, or a clay so perfumed it seemed, to her senses, anyway, to be as luxuriant as privet. The clay in this cutting was a wonder. You might pass through it like a lesser person, a neighbour called Houlihan, Molloy or Rourke, a person who thought no more about this clay than he thought about Livy or Montaigne, but once you stopped you could contemplate a crimson bright enough for all the robes of paradise, a nankeen yellow that might—her papa joked—be mustard off your plate. This joke led to her eating the soil when they were off again (labouring up Dyer's Hill from which broad plateau they would descend into their own little valley) expecting she would taste, at last, that hot forbidden substance; she found it only gritty mud which her laughing father wiped off her solemn face with a handkerchief.

It was this very clay her father used to make the kitchen pots. Her mother made fun of these pots and it is true that they were lumpy and there was always trouble with getting a good seal with the lid, so much so that precious paper bags were used to fill the gaps, like the papier-mâcé which served to plug the gaps between the slabs of their hut, and in neither case did the paper succeed as a seal against ants (red and small black) who came to contaminate the food with the scent of formic acid.

Her mother put down a plank of timber and showed her how to roll the clay to make a snake, and with the snake to make a pot. She remembered the way it began, always, so pleasantly, her fingers dry, the clay malleable, but somewhere, she did not know why, it would go wrong. Her mother, beside her, could make the clay obey her, and even if she made a mistake, she could nip it in, smooth it over, while the clay in Lucinda's hands was soon wet with slip and worked and reworked until, slimy, slippery, without form, it would break in her hands. And it did not matter that Mama had words for it (she always had words for things) and showed her how the coil could contain itself no more, had changed its structure from one state to another, from butterfly back to grub; nor did it matter that she understood perfectly how this was. It did not help. It could not stop the feeling—her hands first slippery, then desperate dry, the skin puckered, all life gone—the awful feeling of despair when a lovely pot she had begun to make was nothing but a twisted mess, like something you might stand in by mistake.

The melted-mustard roads of her memory led her, tonight, to this spot. It was not the escape she had intended. It brought her full circle, from despair to despair. She was up on the ridge that they had named after Governor Darling. There were houses now, all pushed close together for comfort. Through soft yellow windows she imagined she heard women's voices, women with round stomachs stirring pots, wiping children's faces. It was nine o'clock at night and squally and wet, but inside the houses she imagined children, zinc baths, steam, red, cooked little bodies. The manufacturer of glass once more felt pointless. It collapsed inwards, like overworked clay. She would have liked, she thought, to sit at a table and polish cutlery. She would not recoil from the sweet milk-sick smell of children.

And yet she did not stop. Of course she did not stop. She knew no one in these cottages. She drew her big oilskin coat around her and pulled her sou'wester down to the edges of her eyebrows.

There was a fire over at The Rocks. She made a Christian symbol of it, and then drove the symbol from her mind by thinking of why there might be, in real life, a fire at The Rocks. There were plague rats. They piled them up and burnt them in the streets.

She came down the rutted track of the ridge. She was frightened again, to be out by herself. These fears came and went, like the cold pockets of air by creeks. She did not believe in ghosts, but now she was easily frightened and jumped three inches in her hard seat when someone in a long coat rushed across her path. She wished she were back home, and then she reminded herself what it was like to be home. She used her whip unsentimentally, drawing a deft flick along the gelding's flank. The flick produced a skip of rhythm, a toss of the head, and they set off at a brisker pace, following the slippery clay-white lines of the track round the shores of White Bay.

There were racing fools with no lanterns. A drunk wagoner with half his load tumbling off behind him. How cowardly Mr Hasset had been! To abandon her, here, when he did not even wish to go away.

She was angry, with Dennis Hasset, with the hallooing gallopers who rushed out of the dark, with the rutted track and the mud-churned soak where the drunker wagoner dropped a plank which almost jammed between her wheels.

Anger made her reckless. She drove fast. She was going for a trot. She went all the way into George Street although she did not like it at this time of night. She dared herself. She did not care. She brought her jinker up past the theatres. Her Majesty's. The Rappallo. Lyceum. The weather had not kept the crowds at home. The street was a river of wheels and horses, the banks awash with the flotsam and jetsam of men's hats.

There were gangs of larrikins afoot, up from The Rock with their hands boasting against their braces. She was afraid. Inside her big coat, she was small and white, soft-breasted, weak-armed, all soaked with sweat in the wind-cold night. A man spoke to her from a carriage. She put the tired gelding into a canter. There were shouts of, "Gee-up, Nelly." Laughter. She came in under the shadows of St Andrew's. The loathed St Andrew's. It stood grim and dark, the castle of Bishop Dancer. A crowd by the nave door announced not late service but a fight. Two policemen ran towards it, momentarily brilliant and livid-faced in the gaslight. She swung into Bathurst Street at the last moment, nearly colliding with one more unlit sulky. The sulky gave up a wail of silk-and-feathered screams. Lucinda felt contempt. It curdled in her jealousy. She struck her horse and followed the line of wide verandas as if she were going to see her dear friend at Woollahra. But there was nothing at Woollahra. There was a too-pretty child with a hoop who said the house was hers.

"I am going mad," she said. She said it out loud. "I am unlaced and not connected." It was a frightful city in which to contemplate madness, all hard with eucalyptus, snapping sticks, sandstone rocks with fractured faces and cutting edges. You could not, not in Sydney, dear God, allow yourself to fall nto such a weakened state.

"A mad woman," she whispered. "Trrrot up."

She was going for a trot. The horse knew this. He knew the destination. "Not a mad woman," she said, as they went down into the smoky dark of The Rocks. You could not see the fire so close. It was on the other side. The drains reeked. They reeked everywhere, but it was worse here towards the quay. Her nerves were on edge. "Dear God, forgive me."

She intended nothing more than a little Pak-Ah-Pu. This was a lottery run by the Chinese down at that end of George Street. It was dark down there, and dangerous. The front of the establishment had a candle burning—no gas—inside a glass lantern. There were men standing around in twos and threes. She could smell putrid meat but also liquor. These two smells were carried on the salty air of the harbour. The wind played on the rigging of the tall-masted ships. She tied the rein to the railing. Even before she betrayed her sex by the sound of her walk, the men around her were unnaturally silent. The big wet coat was an inadequate disguise. She affected a stiff-spined *haut froid.* she told herself this: "You're the boss."

The front room pretended to be a shop. Everyone knew this was not the case, even the policemen on the beat (who wore gold rings and heavy watches). Lucinda did not look at whatever dusty goods were displayed, but walked—she heard her boots echo on the wooden boards—towards the curtained doorway at the back. She could *hear* how small her feet were. She felt their unmaleness.

The truth is that she no longer wished merely for a Pak-Ah-Pu ticket. She was having a trot. There is nothing to Pak-Ah-Pu except a lottery. There is none of the sting (her term) you get in a good game. But she began, once she reached the table, as she had originally pretended.

It was nearly half past nine, time for the last draw of the day, and there was therefore quite a crowd standing around the table. Several of them were drunk, but they did not sway. They had that rather sullen stillness which is the mark of a betting shop late in the day. The floor was littered with crumpled paper, cigarette ends, matches broken nervously in three. The men had a look at once scuffed and glazed. She felt—or imagined—an anger, barely contained, but the anger may well have been her own.

She gave the Chinaman at the table her sixpence. She was given her ticket and she marked, quickly, urgently even, ten of the Chinese characters on the paper. There were eighty all told. She did not know what they meant. They were printed on coarse grey paper. Twice she pushed the unpleasant little chewed pencil stub (property of the house) through the paper. She wrote her name (not her real name) on the paper and gave it to the Chinaman who put it into a bowl, which appeared to be black but was probably a dark Chinese blue. The light was bad. She could see the squashed stub of a fat cigar near her foot. She tried to look at nothing while she waited for half past nine.

It took three and a half minutes. All this time she stood immobile. The air around her was still. Occasionally a man said something in a low voice. This would be followed by laughter. Once she heard a word she knew referred to copulation. She was quite drenched inside her oilskin coat. All this fear she felt, this hostility and danger, was but the aura surrounding something else, a larger body of feeling which was dense, compacted, a centre of pure will—Lucinda was willing herself to win. Her anger became as inconsequential as blue-flies, then less, like summer thrip.

Six correct marks would bring her ten shillings. Seven would deliver four pounds, eight shillings and eight pence. Eight good marks was twenty-three pounds, six shillings and eightpence. This was all written on the blackboard above the back wall. She was not silly enough to waste her will on ten. She decided on eight, imagining that this was within her limit. There was a smell of incense, another like wet dog, and that other smell—the bodies of men who work hard sweaty work and only bathe once a week. You can produce a similar smell by leaving damp cleaning rags in a bucket. Not an attractive smell, but Lucinda liked it. The cigar smoker had lit another cheroot and made the air slightly blue and streaky. Through all this there came the soft crying of a baby in another room. Many of the Chinese, she had been told, had European wives. It was said the Chinese men were kind to their women. These were fallen women, beyond the pale. It was said—

the reverend friend had said so—that they were loved and found happiness. She tried to block out the sound. She shut a large and heavy door on it and pressed it—for it did not wish to go—firmly shut.

There was movement now. A shoulder, blind of feeling, pressed against her. The men pushed, like fish feeding, or piglets rushing the teat—all feeling contentrated in the mouth, the rest of the body quite numb. There were eighty characters. They would put twenty in a bowl. Of these twenty, they would select ten. They were doing it now. She was crushed all about. The Celestial, one eye half-shut against his own cigarette smoke, drew out ten yellowed ivory ocunters and placed them on a little wooden tray.

She had been told that these characters represented virtues. She had trouble recognizing them in this light. There was the one with the roof, the one with the two Fs standing huffily back to back, the one with eyes like a cat staring from the grass, the one like a river, Jesus Christ Almighty, dear Lord forgive her, she had eight correct.

She felt light, high as a kite. The Chinaman gave her money but did not approve of her. She could not imagine him being kind to his wife. She did not give a damn what he thought. She was going for a trot. She was going to hell.

Don't think that!

She clenched all her muscles to resist the idea. Then, almost at once, she did not care. The punters saw the small woman in the big oilskin coat walk towards the door. She walked briskly and bossily towards it—not the door to the street, but the door in the back wall.

She was going for a trot.

The second room was where fan-tan was played. It was dark all round its edges, much darker than in the Pak-Ah-Pu room. But the light above the zinc-covered table was brighter and the zinc itself threw back a dull glow into the faces of the noisy players, making them look sickly, tinged with green. No one looked up when she entered. She stayed back for a moment in the cover of dark. She felt, suddenly, quite wonderful. She could not explain why this change should come, that she should move from blotchy-faced hell-fear to this odd electric ecstasy merely in the moving from one room to the next. She felt herself to be beyond salvation and did not care. She would not be loved, not be wife, not be mother.

She felt the perfect coldness known to climbers.

The croupier was thin, with gold in his mouth. She could smell the rancid oil from his pigtailed hair. All sorts of smells here. Sailor's oilskin, someone's newly polished shoes. The croupier made a small cry—probably English, although it sounded alien, mechanical, as if he were an extraordinary construction from the Paris exhibition. The dark enveloped her, warmed her like brandy. The croupier threw—such a *svelte* motion—the brass coins. They sounded, as they hit the zinc, both dull and sharp; light, of no substance, but also dead and heavy. It was lovely to watch, just as lovely as a good butcher cutting a carcass, the quick movements of knife, the softness and yielding of fat from around kidneys, the clean separation of flesh from bone. The croupier's tin cup covered some of the coins while his right hand swept the others away. She was a Christian. Her mind found the parallel—Judgement Day, saved coins, cast-out coins—without her seeking it. Sheep on the right. Goats on the left. She drew the curtains on the picture, turned her back, and concentrated all her attention on the heather as he lifted the cup and set the coins—see how sweetly this is done, the suppleness of long fingers (three of them ringed, one of them with emerald)—and slid the coins into sets of four.

There was much barracking now. Cries of yes, it is, no, it's not, groans, and then an odd cheer, squeaky as a schoolboy's which attracted comments, not all of them good-natured.

"It's two."

"Toe," said the Celestial. "Numma toe."

He had placed all the coins in sets of four. There were two remaining. Anyone who had placed their stake on the side of the zinc designated "2" had trebled their money.

The Chinaman gave out the winnings. He slid out six coins across the zinc. Someone expressed a wish to pass water in an eccentric style. Another wind. There was laughter and crudity. Lucinda was not lonely. She pressed forward now, to make her bet, but also to reveal herself. They must know she was there. It was to prevent their embarrassment. She would rather she did not reveal herself, but she must not delay it. She did not look at the faces of the men as she pressed between them to reach the bright square of pitted zinc.

She said: "Excuse me."

It took longer to register than you might expect, partly because of the alcohol, which gave the air in the room its volatility, but also because of the intense focus created by the zinc square which, at the moment she chose, contained nothing of any significance except the numerals (1, 2, 3, 4) which red forms had become almost ghostly with the heavy traffic of coins across their painted surfaces.

At last they felt her otherness, her womanness. She felt the bodies move aside. Where there had been a hot press, she now experienced a distinct and definite cooling.

But she was not lonely, and she was not frightened or shy. She looked at the Chinaman—*he* was lonely, she saw, and very young—but she observed this in a way that did not involve her capacity for compassion or sympathy. What moved her were his ringed hands, the black metal cup, the brass coins, the red scratched numbers, and these things, being merely instruments, provided the anticipation of an intense, but none the less mechanical, pleasure.

She placed a florin against the four. This was soon joined by the more customary coppers. The "4" won. She felt herself liked. She felt the hot pulse of their approbation. They went from cold to hot. It was done as quickly as the cutting of a cockerel's throat. She did not acknowledge it, but she welcomed it. She was not lonely. She looked at no one. She played with inspired recklessness. She felt she could control the game with no other tool than her will.

4, 3, 2, 4, 4, 4, 4, 1, 4, 3, 3, 3, 4, 1.

She won until she touched the quicksand of the final "1." Then she could not get the run of it again. She was out of step. There was a hidden beat she could not catch. The men stopped following her then. They no longer announced their bets as "the same as the missus'. But they did not withdraw from her either. And when, at three o'clock in the morning, she snapped her purse shut, she had no more money than the poorest of them. The purse was empty, freed from all weight, contained nothing but clean, watered silk. She felt as light and clean as rice paper. She allowed herself to notice her companions. She felt limp as a rag doll, and perfectly safe.

She saw that the boot-polish smell belonged to a would-be gentleman in a suit with too-short sleeves, the rancid smell not to the Chinaman at all, but to an ageing man with fierce ginger flyaway eyebrows and a strong Scottish burr. There was an odd-looking chap dressed in the style of the Regency and two young sailors who could not have been more than sixteen. She also noted the engraving of Queen Victoria in the deep shadow of the wall and, immediately beneath it, a living face in three dimensions which was disconcertingly familiar, although she could not, immediately, place it.

She opened her purse again. She pretended to look for something in it. There was, as I said already, nothing in it. She opened her purse to cover her confusion. She knew the face well, almost imtimately. She managed to conjure, from the hitherto empty purse, a ticket from a London omnibus. She looked up and found the fellow winking at her. She tore up the ticket and dropped it on the floor. She snapped her purse shut. She tucked her purse in her bag. She was already imagining withdrawing her hatpin from its felt scabbard, when she remembered where she had last seen that heart-shaped face and flaming angel's hair.

"Oh, dear," she turned, smiling, holding out her hand, quite forgetting that these manners were unexpected in this part of George Street. "Why," said the mystery woman, abandoning her stern countenance as easily as a painter's drop sheet. "Why," she said, advancing on my suddenly terrified great-grandfather. "Why, Reverend Mr Crab."

She swore later that Oscar's mouth dropped open. She described it for him. He was like a ventriloquist's doll from which the ruling hand has been rudely withdrawn, leaving the subject slumped, without a spine, unable to lift so much as an arm.

The silence that now fell on the little room was not complete—the Chinaman began to clear away his brass cup and coins. There can be no doubt what the misunderstanding was—he feared another Royal Commission into gambling. He imagined the slack-jawed, red-headed youth to be one more Reverend commissioner intent on proving his father an opium addict and his wife a prostitute. He slipped the coins into the pocket of his floppy coat, the cup into his back pocket and arranged to have himself dissolved into the shadow of the wall.

The room did not empty immediately. There were those more curious than fearful who waited a nosy minute or two while they considered the association of clergyman and oilskinned woman. In all likelihood they too came down in favour of a Royal Commission. In any case they soon departed.

"Oh, dear," Lucinda said. "I am so sorry."

"It is not Crab."

"No, no. I am so sorry. I don't know where the name came from."

This was an untruth. She knew exactly where it came from—the image of a crab scuttling from red settee, to cabin, to red settee.

"It is Hopkins, not Crab," he persisted.

She thought his response too hurt and humourless. "It is the reverend," she said, "that I should first apologize for."

He smiled then, and she remembered how much she had liked him.

"Well," he said, flipping a coin into the air and catching it (slap) against the back of his wrist, "I suppose I must face up to facts—my disguise is done for. But in London, as I suppose you know, they would not be half as particular. In Drury Lane they *expect* to see a little cloth."

"You could try Ah Moy's."

"That's true. But it is such an awful trek."

"I am so sorry."

"Oh," he said, yawning and stretching—she could see his tonsils, a clean pink cave and quite surprisingly uncorrupted—"I am better off because of it. I should thank you, Miss Leplastrier, for saving me from my weakness."

They were walking now, proceeding awkwardly, embarrassed, indecisive, through the Pak-Ah-Pu room. The customers had all departed but two Chinese with a ladder were hanging a large Union Jack on the wall. They bowed politely, although this was not an easy thing to accomplish from the top of an unsteady ladder. One of them lost his balance, or perhaps he jumped intentionally. He was a nimble old man who landed with ony the slightest "oof;" he escorted them to the door on George Street with many polite Good evenings.

"This is dangerous work you do, Miss Leplastrier," said Oscar when the door had been bolted behind them and they were left alone in the dark and rain-shiny street. "You know we are not a minute from the Crooked Billet Inn where whatshisname obtained the pistol which he used to trick poor Kinder into shooting himself? Do you have a carriage? For me, alas, it is shanks's pony."

"Then you do not have a living?"

"I do not wish one. But the Bishop would not hear of mission work. He gave me Randwick (it is far too grand for me) and there was a lovely carriage and a gelding by the name of Prince. But unfortunately I took some bad advice."

Lucinda was cold and wanted to be home with her cocoa but she could not leave him to walk four miles in this weather. She must drive him to his vicarage which lay in exactly the opposite direction to the one she wished to go in. She watched him warily, more detached than was her custom, as he stood before her, flapping his long arms around in the damp waterfront air, explaining, in such innocent, educated English, how it was that he had lost his horse and carriage (the one provided by the Randwick vestry) to a common racecourse tout who was also, he discovered the next Sunday, a member of his congregation. She was both enchanted and appalled by his innocence and it was this quality she was confused by, not knowing if it were genuine, or if it were a cloak for a mad or even criminal personality.

She drove him out to Randwick and on the way they managed to leave alone the tender scar which was their voyage aboard the *Leviathan.* When he proposed a game of cards she found herself, against her better judgement, asking if he could accept her IOU.

65

Bishop Dancer's Ferret

Bishop Dancer is a man you would most quickly understand if you saw him on a Saturday in Camden, dressed in his red hunting jacket and high black boots, leaning forward to accept some hot toddy from the stirrup cup. He had a handsome ruddy face which these days extended to his crown. What hair remained clung to the sides and back of his head; it was fine and white, cut very short, as was his beard. With no mitre to assist you, you might be inclined to think him a gentleman farmer. He had big thighs, strong shoulders, and although you could see the man had a belly, it was not one of your featherown bellies, but a firm one. He sat well on his horse and it was a good specimen, too—sixteen hands and no stockhorse in its breeding.

Dancer could not, of course he could not, have clergy who were notorious around the track, who lost their horses or their carriages because they heard a horse was "going to try." Sydney— a venal city—was too puritanical to allow such a thing. But had you informed Dancer of this story after dinner, he would have found it funny. He could find nothing in his heart against the races and he left that sort of raging to the Baptists or Methodists. The true Church of England, he would have felt (but never said) was the Church of gentlemen. Sometimes gentlemen incur debts.

He had interviewed Oscar closely on his arrival. He put him through his paces, questioning the fidgety fellow as closely as a candidate from Cambridge. He was looking for signs of this Broad Church heresy. He could find none. He accepted Virgin birth, the physical Resurrection, the loaves and fishes. The Bishop allowed him his view on Genesis with a little uneasiness, but it was no longer politic to make a fuss about this matter. He soon sniffed out, however, Oscar's Low Church background. In normal circumstances he would not have cared for it at all. He loathed Evangelicals with all their foot-thumping "enthusiasm."

He did not like their "bare boards" approach to ritual, and there was plenty of this in Oscar's attitude. Bishop Dancer was delighted to find it so. "This fellah," he told himself, "will be my ferret out at Randwick." And when he thought it, he imagined Oscar quite literally as a ferret, his long white neck disappearing down a hole.

He asked the untidy applicant about candles on the altar. Oscar throught they should be lit only for illumination. He asked about vestments. Oscar thought a simple surplice quite acceptable, but preferred a plain black cassock. He asked about genuflexion. Oscar confessed himself uncomfortable with the practice.

Bishop Dancer became quite hearty. He had the young man stay to luncheon. He had him fed beef, although the beef was cold, and was not even mildly disconcerted when the young man refused his claret. There was going to be fun out at Randwick, that bed of Puseyites with all their popish ritual. There would be a first-class row out there, but he would win. He must win. For he had, by one of those anomalies which made the diocese so interesting, the right to appoint the incumbent himself. If the Randwick vestry did not like it, they could go over to the Church of Rome. They would not get their new parson dressing up in white silk and red satin. This one was a nervous little fellow, the Bishop judged, but he would not budge on this issue. He would not be susceptible to Tractarians, only to missionaries. Even at luncheon he persisted with a request that he be sent "up-country" (wherever that might be—when asked he could not say). Bishop Dancer told him bluntly that mission work was a waste of time. The blacks were dying off like flies, and if he doubted this he should look at the streets of Sydney, man, and note the condition of the specimens he saw there. The field was over-supplied with missionaries and Methodists fighting Baptists to see who could give the "poor wretches" the greater number of blankets. Leave the blacks to the Dissenters, Dancer advised. God had work for him to do at Randwick.

It did not occur to Oscar that a bishop might lie to him. He accepted Dancer's story and, indeed, relayed it to Theophilus who disseminated it further through the columns of *The Times*. It was because of this gullibility that Oscar allowed himself to be placed almost next door to the notorious Randwick racecourse. He was Bishop Dancer's ferret, but it was not Kebble, Pusey and Newman who were to cause him the greatest stress in his new parish, but Volunteer, Rioter, Atlanta, Mnemon, and Kildare.

66

St John's

Sydney was a blinding place. It made him squint. The stories of the gospel lay across the harsh landscape like sheets of newspaper on a polished floor. They slid, slipped, did not connect to anything beneath them. It was a place without moss or lichen, and the people scrabbling to make a place like troops caught under fire on hard soil. St John's at Randwick was built from red brick with very white mortar. The fine clay dust that overlay everything, even the cypress hedge beside the vicarage, could not soften the feeling of the place. It was all harsh edges like facets of convict-broken rock.

He had been ready to minister to his flock, but found them to be creatures of their landscape. They did not embrace him, but rather stood their distance. He found their conversation as direct as nails. They found his to be tangled, its point as elusive as the end of a mis-handled skein.

They warned him about snakes, spiders and the advisability of locking his windows at night. He thought the fault was with himself. He had his housekeeper bake scones and invited the vestry to tea. They sat stiffly on their chairs and conversation could not be got under way. He felt young, inadequate, inexperienced. He asked them about the parishioners, but it seemed they knew almost nothing. Only when he asked if there were natives in the congregation did they show themselves capable of smiling.

They knew he was Dancer's man. They waited and watched. They found his form of service as unappetizing as unbuttered bread.

He prayed to God to give him the key to their hearts. He had nothing else to do but pray and write his sermons. In the long winter afternoons he listened to the drum of horses' hooves. He sent his sixteen volumes of track records to Mr Stratton and swore never to gamble again. He had promised God in the midst of that dreadful storm. There was reason enough for Mr Stratton to gamble, but not for him. He was clothed and provided for. He had shelter enough for a family of eight. He had three hundred pounds a year, and a housekeeper to feed him mutton every night. He did not require wealth. He coveted nothing.

The horses drummed through the afternoon. The track was hard in April but softened with the rains in May. He preached sermons against gambling.

It was Mrs Judd, his housekeeper, who warned him off his gambling sermons and told him about the "generous gents" who not only contributed to the church's coffers but kept book at the nearby racecourse. This information gave him the excuse his cunning gambler's mind required. He must go to the course and see for himself.

Because he could not bet with men he had preached against, he got himself involved with a series of messengers, runners, touts and spivs who carried his money away and brought precious little of it back. He followed no system. He was just having "some fun" just like a smoker might have "just one" borrowed cigarette. The touts and runners led him, in due course, to the floating two-up games at the five hotels which lay, strung like beads on the deuce's necklace, between Randwick and St Andrew's. There was fan-tan down in George Street. There was swy and poker and every card game to be imagined among the taverns down in Paddington. Oscar had never seen such a passion for gambling. It was not confined to certain types or classes. It seemed to be the chief industry of the colony.

He was homesick, disorientated. He had enemies all around him and he could, you might imagine, if he had his heart set on playing rummy with Miss Leplastrier, at least have the brains to close the curtains. He was not so gormless that he didn't know he had these enemies, and yet he thought it wrong for him to know such a thing. So although he was not innocent of this knowledge, he felt it somehow, magically important to act as if he were. He left the curtains open.

"Oh," he chimed, all knees and elbows, from the sofa, "this is *nice*."

Lucinda Leplastrier did not think herself a snob, but she had inherited, from her mother, a strong objection to the word "nice" being used in this way. It struck an odd note. It did not match his educated vowels. She compared him, she could not help it, with Dennis Hasset and this had the effect of making everything Oscar did seem to be immature and frivolous.

And yet when you saw the way he dealt the cards you could not help but feel the whole thing might be a pose. Nothing fitted.

He was not vulgar, but the furnishings in his vicarage were vulgar in the extreme and she could not believe he could move amongst all this and be insensitive to it. The carpet had a stiff set pattern large enough to feel you might be tripped on it. It was a rich and gaudy green. The marble mantelpiece had the appearance of being carved by craftsmen more accustomed to sarcophagi, and the mirror above it was covered with a green gauze netting, placed there to stop flies spotting the glass. There was an excess of chairs, nine of them without counting the sofa on which she sat and the gent's armchair in which he seemed to squat, leaning forward so eagerly she felt herself pushed back. The thing with the chairs was colour. The brightest hues were in evidence: a blue not unworthy of a kingfisher, and whilst handsome, no doubt, on the bird, not something that sat comfortably with the carpet. No one had thought, whilst they spent so extravagantly, that the brilliant settee might have to sit upon the brilliant carpet.

She could not marry him.

Of course he had not asked her to, but she had sometimes, in remembering their meeting, been regretful that she had not acknowledged his final smile. She need only look at the ugly and ill-matched assortment of little tables—oak, maple, cedar—to know that she need have no misgivings.

There were paintings on the wall, though they were not paintings at all, but "chromos." The only thing she had in common with him was a serious weakness of which she was not proud. And, lonely or no, had it not been for the following incident, it is unlikely she would have sought out his company again.

67

The Messiah

The housekeeper at Randwick was a certain Mrs Judd who, had she not had reasons of her own for wishing to scrub the floors and black the stove and swat the flies that trapped themselves behind the orange and lilac panes of glass in the big sitting room, could have stayed at home and eaten chocolates. The Judds were wealthy members of the congregation. Mr Judd's father may or may not have been transported, but Mr Judd was the successful proprietor of a hauling business, had teams of all sorts travelling throughout the colony, owned a ship which plied the coastal trade, and a splendid mansion in Randwick itself. He was a burly man and although his hip was injured—a defect which served to tip his broad body a little to the starboard and give him the appearance of someone with an invisible chaff bag on his broad back—he still worked as hard as the men he employed. He had only had his wife in control of the vicarage of St John's, but he liked to inspect it himself from time to time. He had a possessive feeling about the building, as well he might—his donation had paid for the greater part of it and it was his taste (or his upholsterer's) which dominated its interior. If there was a slate loose or missing from the roof, it was Mr Judd who would repair it, not by calling a tradesman, but by getting up on the roof and attending to the matter personally. He was a rough man, but a great one for the Church. And at the very centre of the maze of his tender feelings towards this institution there lay this single thing—he had a fine baritone voice, and he was proud of it.

Each year at Randwick there were all sorts of services in which great works of sacred music, the *Messiah* for instance, would be performed and then this rough and brawling man would feel himself transmuted into something very fine—spun gold from Mr Handel's pen. For this reason he loved the Church and habitually made himself humble around that being who provided these great moments in his life—the vicar.

No one had, as yet, discussed the *Messiah* with Oscar. There had been a *St Matthew's Passion* just before he had arrived. There had been a fuss in settling in this new man and no one had mentioned the *Messiah*. Mr Judd could not bring this up himself. It would appear vain. And yet he sensed the performance was in doubt. He had heard that Bishop Dancer did not care for Handel, but then again he had heard the opposite. He was a direct man in most matters. He did not go in for this tangential shilly-shallying which was the hallmark of the ruling classes. But in this particular matter his emotions were too much involved. He could not ask the vicar the simple question that so occupied his mind. Instead he made himself humble. He chopped wood and brought it to the wood-box personally. Likewise he scraped clean the wooden shutters and stripped them back to the bare wood and then repainted them. While the rest of his fellow vestrymen held themselves aloof, and tight-lipped, Mr Judd was forward and friendly, attempting to engage the stork-legged new chum in talk of music.

But Oscar happily confessed he was tone deaf and could no more talk about music than he could about the breeding possibilities of merino sheep, if that was a subject at all. He wanted to talk about the blacks. Mr Judd did not; he sandpapered the louvres in silence. He soon became so anxious on the subject that he had–vanity or no–to sound out the more musical members of the congregation on their opinion of the new chap's attitude. The betting, he discovered with dismay, was against Handel. This was Bishop Dancer's man. Look at his vestments. There would be no Handel this year, Matty, good heavens no.

Mr Judd came and clipped the hedge and he returned, with his wife, at six o'clock on a Friday morning, in order to sweep up the clippings. He was deeply unhappy. He was also–it came in fits and starts, was sent away and invited back again–angry.

He was surprised to see the lights on and the window unshuttered. He bade his wife stay on the path while he climbed–very quietly–on to the veranda, and peered in.

Well, you know what he saw.

There was also money on the table. He saw this, too. He saw a woman, cards moving, money. It was then that he started hammering on the pane.

68

Serious Damage

Unless you have the most particular reading habits it is unlikely you will be acquainted with the so-called "Wednesday Murders." People of my grandmother's generation still spoke of them, but they are forgotten nowadays. The most distinctive feature of these murders was not suggested by their name, which merely celebrated a coincidence–

that the first two murders occurred on Wednesday nights of successive weeks. But the murderer would not let himself be so easily pigeonholed and thereafter took lives on a Tuesday (the third victim) and Sunday (the fourth). In spite of this—and let this be a lesson to anyone dealing with the press—the name stuck.

The murders were so ghastly you might think it peculiar that Lucinda, no matter how lonely she might be, would leave her house at all, or, accepting the peculiarity, you may wrongly attribute great courage to her when you hear she had driven, unaccompanied, through streets that were still, for the most part, unlighted. Further, she was by no means insensible to this murderer. She was informed that he was, in all likelihood, a butcher or, the press suggested, an unsuccessful apprentice. This was not melodrama or gutter-press imaginings. It was clearly suggested by the manner of the murdering, the nature of the cuts, the chops, the bonings.

You could not live alone and not think of the Wednesday Murderer, and Lucinda, once her maid had gone at nightfall, was not only alone, but alone on an island promontory in a wind-buffeted cottage in which the floorboards sometimes groaned out loud, in which timbers—or was it the nails in the timber?—made inexplicable noises. Lucinda, alone with her nervous cat, sometimes thought about these matters to such a degree that she could not leave her chair beside the fire, not even when the coal scuttle was empty and it was three a.m. and cold enough for her breath to show. So the very excursions which may seem to us so brave, seemed to her most cowardly—she was not only fleeing loneliness, but also fear. She thought herself more vulnerable in a house than on the highway, in her bed than in a fan-tan parlour. And even though her good opinion of Oscar had been seriously damaged by his selfish behaviour aboard the *Leviathan* (a damage that showed in her unreasonable annoyance at the angle of his elbow, or the way his trousers rucked up to show a bony white shin with red garter marks left, like a high-water mark, above the fallen socks) she was not displeased to spend these hours with him, or not as displeased as she might have allowed herself to be if the Wednesday Murderer had not been at large. She was waiting for daylight.

He told her that his mantelpiece clock—a huge contraption with its brassy innards showing—was ten minutes fast. She did not doubt its gaudy unreliability and felt herself more reliably informed by the sky outside. She judged it almost six a.m. She had enjoyed herself, although not in that personal way she had enjoyed herself at Mr Borrodaile's table. On that occasion she had enjoyed *him*, and had allowed her mind to construct all sorts of pleasant fancies. She had thought him an angel painted by Mr Rossetti. This was before he showed himself so thoughtless. But rummy was a game you could play with perfect strangers, with a man in a mask, or even (she imagined) a clever machine. She had arrived with nothing and now she had nearly five pounds—it was all there in notes and coins in front of her. She had taken the money slowly, and she had found the process as satisfying as drawing bent nails from old timber. She had enjoyed it as much as she had enjoyed the dizzy lightness of losing at fan-tan. It did not once occur to her that she might be punishing him.

She was not tired. She could not afford to be tired. She had time to go home and bathe before taking tea with Mr Rolls, a builder lately arrived from Melbourne. She began to gather in her winnings. The notes were larger in those days. You had something more substantial for your efforts. If you pulled out a pound no one would mistake it for your cigarette papers or—if you were not of that class—your calling card. It was at this moment, as Lucinda began to gather these triumphantly proportioned notes together, that Mr Judd pushed his ruddy face against the window. He had been a boxer in his youth and this had left his face a little out of balance, the nose a fraction to one side, the ears of independent character. When you knew him you found him strangely soft and, though his hands were likely scabbed on the back and horny on the palm, you would find him gentle around gentle subjects—I am thinking of music when I mention this. But it is easy enough to imagine that such a face, without introduction, might appear—I will not say murderous—frightening.

Lucinda should have made allowances for the glass. It was not plate, but crown, of uneven thickness and marred by a yellow tinge produced by chrome salts in the sand. You can say she should have reacted more scientifically. She did not. She saw a butcher's face with hairy eyebrows. She saw a pig snout of unnatural yellow. That the face was partly veiled by a patch of condensation did not make it seem less terrifying.

She could not scream.

She made a noise which may be crudely signified: "Erg."

Oscar smiled uncertainly.

"Erg."

She made him nervous, anyway. She knew better Greek. She seemed well schooled in theology. She did not smile readily. She played cards with a cool elegance and skill which shocked him. He liked her smell. He did not know how to treat her, and when she stared at him and said "Erg," he became embarrassed.

"Well," he said, shuffling the cards. "Well, well, well." He did his fancy shuffle. He had taught himself this, although he had seen it done in a "hell" in Jermyn Street. There it had been done by a very frail and very drunk old actor who could, in shuffling cards, make a moving bridge one yard long. Oscar had taught himself this. It was, he supposed, a conversation piece.

Mr Judd saw the bridge and could contain himself no more.

He banged.

Oscar's face then behaved as it had when Lucinda had called him "Crab." It lost its bones and colour. The muscles on his scalp contracted and pulled each hair to smart attention. He opened his mouth and Lucinda was treated this time, not to a clean pink tunnel and a little peak of epiglottis, but to some half-munched coconut macaroon suspended, mid-mastication.

But then, of course, he turned and discovered Mr and Mrs Judd.

Lucinda could not credit what she saw him do. The unfriendly attitude of the intruders was perfectly clear, but the gangling vicar stood, wiped his mouth with his handkerchief, went to the window, unlocked it, and let them in. Well, they did not enter, not immediately, but the man's voice entered and she did not have time to separate it from her nightmare, could not decipher all the moral outrage, felt herself to be swamped by an alien wave of tobacco-smelling rage.

"Mr Judd," she heard her host say. "Mrs Judd. Please do come in."

Come in? Lucinda was incredulous. Come *in*? Her hand was at her hat, feeling for the silver pea-sized knob that marked its end. She thought about the properties of glass, not its wont to go yellow when there were chrome salts in the sand, but its tendency to shatter, to make shards which lie upon a carpet in the shape of crescent moons, scimitars, stilettos, daggers, pig stickers, a jigsaw armoury waiting to be released from its captive sheet and nothing more needed by way of a key than a pebble, a coin, a lump of coal.

"Please," said Oscar, clapping his hands and rubbing them. "Please do come in."

Lucinda removed her hat and held the pin behind her back. Oscar stepped back and both Judds, the second one with great difficulty—she was not only portly but impeded by skirts—stepped from the veranda, across the sill, and into the sitting room.

Oscar watched all this with almost as much astonishment as Lucinda. He had hardly been aware, so nervous was he, of what he had been saying. And although it is true that he invited the Judds in and that, when he made the invitation, he was standing on one side of an open window and they on the other, he had not intended that they treat his window as their door. And yet—and he admitted this to himself later when he sat, groaning and punching his left hand with his right, in judgement on himself—it was he who had stepped backwards, and the stepping back was, in a sense, like moving a magnet back from a nail in that you must, if you know anything about the natural sciences, expect the nail to follow and it is no good—his father would have told him as much—protesting your innocence when you know it is a law, a law without a name, but a law of physics none the less: when you have such a concentration of energy with all its vectors angled at you, and if you say "come in" and step back at the same time, the object of your attention will—it is like water on an inclined plane—follow the line of least resistance and come right in.

Now Mr Judd was unaware that he was obeying a law of physics. He knew nothing about physics at all. He knew about jute and hessian, about chaff and oats, about yokes, bows, bullock chains, the length of grass on the roadside between Sydney and Yass, but he was ignorant of the forces that propelled him. When he found himself standing on the vicar's Quality Bradford First Wool carpet, he was mortified. He looked down at his boots and saw the right one not properly laced and the left one with leaf-mould clinging to it and then he looked and saw his wife—God help me—trying to follow him. That was so like her. It was so exactly like her. Why could she not be aware of the picture she made? She was all backside and bosom and her poor little legs were too plump and short to get up to the sill, but there was no retreating now—he had to help her in.

Mr Judd was angry with his wife, but he would not show it in public and he offered her extreme solicitude and did his best to help effect a dignified crossing. When she was, at last, standing inside he made sure her dress was properly rearranged before he thought about anything else.

Thus he found himself, a manly man, fussing at her skirts like a dressmaker. For a moment he was at a loss, to see the figure he cut. Then the habits of a lifetime reasserted themselves and he did what he always did when caught at a disadvantage—he attacked.

"I'd not be the sort of fellow comes climbing through a window," he said. "And you should know that of me by now. But I'll tell you this, sir—we will not have it! We will not. All we want is our Handel. It is nothing but the glory of God, you don't see that. But 'Be not drunk with wine,' " he had not meant to quote, but the words came to him.

He could see no wine. It was not wine he was quoting. " 'Be not drunk with wine,' " he looked at the cards. They were in full view, and money too. " 'Wherein is excess; *but be filled with the Spirit*; speaking to yourselves in psalms and hymns and spiritual songs, singing and making melody in your heart to the Lord.' "

This produced a silence. They all stood with red faces and tried to understand their situation. Oscar thought "handle." There was a cold draught from the open window.

"You gambled," Mr Judd said, and he shook a surprisingly dainty finger at the clergyman.

"It is true, Mr Judd," said Oscar. He hugged his thin chest and then rubbed his hands. "I have gambled. I am sorry if it has caused offence."

"It's no good denying it."

"I'm not denying it."

"Don't you think the Almighty has an ear? Don't you imagine he'd like our hymns of praise?"

"Oh yes, indeed, Mr Judd. Indeed."

"Then you should not be gambling, sir. It is a folly and a sin."

Lucinda was unsure of what was happening. She no longer thought these people murderers, but she thought the situation to be most unstable. The man looked violent, and the woman seemed to think it her wifely duty to transmit, silently, an equal level of anger towards her. She glowered and moved her feet beneath her skirts, just like a cow bailed up for milking. Lucinda stood up.

"It does seem to me," Oscar was saying, "that we have the threads of quite different concerns involved in this upset."

Lucinda said nothing. She thought his conciliatory tone quite inappropriate.

"Upset?" said Mr Judd. "I am not upset."

"She is slipping out," said Mrs Judd.

"On the one hand, you have the issue of my gambling. On the other you have, it would seem, a love of music."

"Of sacred music. *Sacred* music."

"She is putting on her hat."

"She is my guest, Mrs Judd."

"A pretty name for it."

"Mrs Judd," warned Mr Judd.

"I'll not be stopped," said Mrs Judd. "I have never heard of such a hypocrite. Yes, a hypocrite. We made him lovely vestments. You will not wear them, isn't that true? You think God would rather see you looking like a crow."

"I wear–" said Oscar, but was stopped from saying more.

"You dress like a scarecrow," said Mr Judd.

"I will *not* be stopped. He dresses like a scarecrow," she agreed, "and throws out our *Messiah,* and here he is with cards and women in the temple, and–" she looked backwards to the open window, and stopped a moment. "And here we are," she said at last.

These last three words seemed to signify that she had, against the current of her natural good manners, been induced–it was witchcraft, perhaps–to climb through her employer's window and stand on expensive carpet in muddy shoes.

Lucinda had retreated from the draught and was warming herself against the fire. It is true that she had put on her hat, but not because she wished to leave, but because she was returning her hatpin to its proper place. She would not need that type of weapon.

"You are a rude woman," she said, "and you are a rude man."

Mrs Judd opened her mouth. Mr Judd stood on his wife's foot. Mrs Judd's mouth stayed open and her head jerked shraply sideways as she tried to read her husband's face.

"You imagine," Lucinda pulled her skirt tight against her legs until she felt them burning, "that you are civilized, but you are like savages with toppers and tails. You are not civilized at all, and if gambling is a sin it is less of a sin than the one you have just committed. You should pray to God to forgive you for your rudeness."

Oscar was aghast to hear such patrician arrogance from a women he had seen, half an hour before, light a cigarette and draw the blue smoke up into her flaring nostrils (an action he found sensual in the extreme). He would have apologized to the Judds but he did not have the opportunity.

"You may leave," said Lucinda.

And the Judds, indeed, made uncertainly towards the door.

"Through the window," said Lucinda.

And the Judds left through the window. Lucinda had them shut it after them. She watched them–it was not quite light–walk down the long mustard-yellow driveway. She could see them both talking at once.

She began laughing then. It was not a simple laugh, and was occasioned as much by her surprise at herself (how angry she must be at Sydney) as by delight in her own mischievousness. And her face, laughing, was lovely. For the first time inside the vicarage she was herself, unguarded, open-faced, and you could see the young girl and imagine her in the days on the farm near Parramatta. She looked pretty, but Oscar did not see this for he was sitting back on an ugly green chair with his hands plunged into his unruly rusty hair.

"Oh dear," he said. "I'm done for."

And then Lucinda was like an athlete who, with her body warm, has ripped a muscle and not felt it. As she cooled, she stiffened, and felt—it hurt more than you would think possible—the damage.

69

The Tablecloth

Bishop Dancer's office—his entire house—was being redecorated. He could not bear to be around the place. He did not like to hear his wife hallooing for some tradesman, the sudden draughts from unavoidably open windows, the equally unavoidable sawing and hammering. It was an irritation to be there and he could not effect his business courteously. Particularly *this* business.

This was how it came about that Bishop Dancer lunched with the Dean of St Andrew's and his wife. He did not much care for the dean, but he needed to borrow an office and the dean's office was the only one available which would bring with it the proper tone. "Tone," you might correctly guess, was not a thing that a man like Dancer would normally concern himself with. He had the strength to carry his own "tone" without borrowing it from the dean's heavy desk and velvet drapery. But in this case he had been defeated. The office he required was one in which—there was no avoiding it—he might effect his own surrender to the Randwick vestry.

He did not like to lose at all, but he particularly disliked losing to people like this—jumped-up shopkeepers and stable hands, rag and bone men who would once have acknowledged their calling with three hats worn on top of each other but now dressed up in clothing of the classes they used to serve. Sometimes he thought of Sydney as an orphan's party with a dressing-up box. What a grotesque sight he found it—piemen affecting the dress of gentlemen, ladies' maids with glass tiaras. They were out there now, in the anteroom of the dean's office. Mr Allcock with his top hat and shiny breeches, Mr Judd, Mr Henry, and their leader, Mr Graham, MP, the well-known Puseyite.

The bishop stayed at table, although the table was by now for the most part empty. He wished to make a demonstration to the dean, but the dean was apprehensive. He had invited the bishop to lunch from courtesy. He had watched him drink an entire bottle of his best claret and now he was nervous of the consequences.

"Let me show you," said the bishop.

"My Lord," the dean began. He could see that Dancer was in a dangerous sort of mood and he knew what had caused it. The press had got hold of this matter of the Randwick vicarage where, it was said, there had been behaviour of a most immoral type. It had involved women and cards. This had been Dancer's appointment. He had boasted of it. He had called the incumbent "my Reverend Mr Ferret."

"Do not 'My Lord' me," said Dancer. "Let me show you this thing and then you will see I was not boasting."

The bishop appraised the table. It was modestly set for such a demonstration. Almost all the luncheon service had been removed from the white tablecloth. There was a little silver tray of condiments, a showy gravy boat, a claret bottle with half an inch of sediment in it, two wine glasses, three of water. It was a bright day. The westerly had stopped momentarily and sunshine broke through the peach blossom outside the window and fell prettily across the table.

"I did not imagine it a boast," the dean said, pushing back his chair a little, but lacking the courage to stand. "But the wait will not improve the mood of your visitors. I imagine them quite high and mighty in their tone."

"Do you know?" said Dancer. He also pushed back his chair. He held the tablecloth as he had once seen his sister hold the train of the Duchess of York's wedding dress. He looked at the dean. The dean was a neat man. He kept a little brush and pan beside him at table and was not embarrassed to whisk away a fallen breadcrumb. His hair was, to Dancer's taste, overly neat. It was of a coarse material, steely grey, and looked as if it had been trimmed, one hair at a time, by razor. "I have aways thought, Dean, that men in our position should value the importance of relaxation."

The dean tried to look nonchalant. He could not. He folded his arms across his chest. It was a broad chest, and he was a young man and well built, and yet, Dancer thought, he behaves like a fussy barnyard fowl. It was easy to imagine him pecking at the crumbs on the white tablecloth.

"I am quite relaxed, Bishop, I assure you. In fact I was rather wondering," and here the dean pushed his spectacles back on his nose and his mouth folded in a manner both prim and smug, "If Your Lordship was not feeling the pressure of this Randwick scandal"

"Scandal?" said the bishop, testing the tension on the tablecloth. "There is no scandal."

"To bring your man before the ecclesiastical court."

"My man? Ha, ha, Dean, really. The silly little fellow was an *Evangelical.* Hardly my man. Now, concentrate. Watch. You will not see this done in many other deaneries." Dancer felt the cords of his muscles stretched with a not unpleasant tension—they were tight like a baited line with a flat head pulling insistently on one end.

"Allow me then to remove the gravy boat."

"Sit *down,*" ordered Bishop Dancer. The dean sat down. He buttoned up his coat.

The bishop took the pressure on the tablecloth. He felt it nice and tight. He narrowed his eyes and concentrated and he could feel, with the pressure on, the position of wine bottle (which, being both light and tall, was a tricky one) and the gravy boat, the set of condiments. He took the tension up another notch until he had it at the point just before movement.

Then he pulled the cloth right off the table.

The bottles rose, teetered again, but settled nicely on the polished cedar. It made a long, low, ringing noise as it came to rest.

The condiments were never in doubt. It was only the gravy boat, an eccentric three-legged affair, which caught. This was partly the fault of the legs, and partly the fault of the dean who had insisted that the tablecloth always be starched crisply. A starched fold had caught the leg, the bishop guessed, and it would have done no real damage at all if the dean had only trusted him. But the dean, being as nervous as a rabbit, had started out of his chair the instant the cloth was pulled. He broke cover, so to speak, and placed himself directly in the line of fire.

There was very little gravy left, hardly a spoonful. It made a small mark on the dean's thigh, but even this would not show—sponged or not—once it was dry.

"There," said Bishop Dancer. "You didn't believe I could do it."

That night the dean would beg God's forgiveness for the thoughts he had thought at that moment. But as he picked up the broken pieces of the gravy boat, his anger was not even mollified by the thought that it had been of a pattern he had never liked.

"I will replace it," said Dancer, folding the tablecloth with a surprising (to the dean) precision.

"You will *not*," said the dean, his face pale, his hands full of sharp shards. "You will kindly go to your vestry and leave this matter to me."

The bishop had to stop himself from ruffling his hair and it was not until his evening prayers that he, too, found room in his heart for remorse, but even then, praying on his bare knees in his nightshirt, as smile insinuated itself on to his face. He could not help it. Surely God would allow this contradiction?

70

The Good Samaritan

The cloth was, likewise, pulled out from under Oscar's life. But do not imagine that the bishop's party trick was metaphorical, for were it so it would not be equal to the devastation. If we wish a metaphor we must load the dean's table with Doulton saucers, candlesticks, boats for gravy, bowls for custard, vases full of flag flowers, and even then we will not have anything to equal the damage Bishop Dancer did to Oscar. To provide an equivalent we would have to take to the table with a saw or axe.

Once Oscar's indiscretion came to the attention of the press, he was finished. It did not matter that Dancer was a card-player himself, or that he was not beyond a "something on the gee-gees." His private sympathies were of no account. He must cut himself free. He must rebuke, dissociate, etc. And Oscar Hopkins, whose whole character had been built around the certainty that he was one of the chosen, now found himself to be very publicly cast out. His name was made notorious in Sydney generally. He was not considered a suitable person to employ.

That he was not a match for his scandalous story, neither in terms of personality nor appearance, did not make people question the slanders that were now told about him. Indeed, his innocent manner made his guilt appear more shocking.

He took rooms in a common lodging house in Bathurst Street. He learned how much we are the creatures of our station, one minute all snug and warm, worthy of affection and the esteem of total strangers, granted respect without a question, credit without a pause, and the next, the most despicable creature on whom it is quite permissible to spit; someone whom the slovenly owner of a run-down boarding house—unshaven, with a collar missing and a tattoo visible on his hairy wrist—admits only on condition of a large deposit.

September and October were reckoned the perfect months for new settlers to arrive in Sydney. September was no longer cold and windy. October was not yet hot. The blow-flies, bush-flies and house-flies were not the offence they would be when the York hams were in the ovens and muslin-wrapped puddings were boiling and bumping against the walls of cast-iron pots.

September and October were bleak months for Oscar Hopkins. He was cut adrift from those who loved him. No mail could reach him, and he, for his part, was too ashamed to let anyone at Home know the disgrace that had befallen him.

His mail waited for him at the diocesan offices. His letters were locked up in a clerk's drawer together with the egg sandwiches which the occupant of the desk brought for lunch each day. The envelopes gained fatty butter spots. They smelled of egg. They lay there unopened and Oscar had no idea that Wardley-Fish was calling him in a passion, that he did not love Melody Clutterbuck, that the engagement was broken, that he, Fish, had been a self-deceiving wretch, an opportunist, a poseur. Wardley-Fish was booked to sail on the *Sobraon* to Sydney.

Had Oscar read this locked-up letter he would have seen himself described as "good." This goodness was contrasted with the writer's "worldliness" and "falsehood," which he was now, in the act of buying this ticket on a clipper, casting from him, "like swine, dear Odd Bod, which I hereby drive across the cliffs of Dover, so they might break their nasty bristly backs and drown, for ever, their hoarse and brutish swine-ish souls."

Had Oscar read this letter he would have held himself responsible for the broken engagement. But if blame was a commodity like eggs or butter, he already had more than he could safely carry. And even while he prayed to God to ease his burden, he cast around for more to pick up and carry. He prated as if he were greedy for punishment. He prayed as a man of forty, suddenly aware of his neglected gums, might brush them, not three times a day as the dentist recommends, but nine times, until they are red and raw and puffy, aching, in quivering shock from all this zeal.

He prayed he might be spared the hellfire.

His neighbours in the boarding house complained about his behaviour. They heard him groaning. They did not see the backs of his hands and if they had it is unlikely that they would have recognized the cause of the wounds thereon. You would need to have lived in a contemplative order to understand that these deep wounds are made by the nails of one hand attacking the back of the other. Not stigmata, but the stab wounds of prayer.

And yet he also, at the same time, on the same day, went to the racetrack. He bet on Falcon and Presto and Maid of the Lake and believed all the time it was (it must be) an offence against God who had smitten him on account of it. He felt the surge of those exhilarating chemicals which his body knew were manufactured at the racecourse, but he did not bet because he sought pleasure – on the contrary, he feared it – but because he was desperate and had no other way to support himself.

You cannot bet effectively by day if you are to fear hellfire in the night. Any anxiety of this order prevents the proper functioning of those analytic skills which are a punter's only asset. So of course he lost more than he won, and it did not matter that he hung around the stableboys and jockeys, paid them a shilling for their friendship, that he studied the form as if he were cramming for Bigs at Oriel – he spent the two months of the racing carnival in very poor condition and was swooped by magpies at the start of the Drapers' Purse.

He lost weight although he did not have a lot to lose. His collar hung like a harness around his neck, and he walked in the way of men who would wish to be invisible, close to the walls of buildings, with hands deep in pockets and eyes forever caught at that point where the foundation stones of the buildings rise from the edge of the pavement. And it was in this condition that Lucinda found him, although he did not have the comfort of a wall to walk beside, was quite exposed on all sides as he hurried across the yard at the back of the post office. The *Bombay*, two weeks late with the English mail, had arrived the day before and so everyone was crowded round in George Street where the mail was collected. The yard was quite deserted. There was no throng to give him shelter from inquisitive eyes which might recognize the cut of his grimy broadcloth as belonging to a higher calling. The nervous and defeated demeanour of its wearer was at once perfectly in keeping with the letter he had come to post and, also, completely out of keeping. An observer would never have suspected the educated tone, i.e.:

> Dear Papa, I am so sorry to have caused you, by the extended silence which this epistle will now serve to end, so much anguish. You will think, when you put these pages down, that I am destined for that eternal fire of which we have been forewarned. I must confess that I feel myself to be an inhabitant of a purgatory through which I journey, the one hour in deep despair, even terror, the next in a state of (perhaps unhealthy) exaltation that he who has vouched safe my soul shall see fit, for all my sins, to redeem me yet.
>
> But, my most dear pa, I have a request to make of you, and it is to write to me, but to forebear doing so in that manner which your fond heart will first incline you toward, for I know that your most loving inclination will be to instruct me on the steps I must take to save my immortal soul. This advice I will most surely cherish, and I do not ask you to neglect your stern duty, but also, in a postscript if you like, to write to me about the little lanes of Hennacombe wherein we three once walked so happily.
>
> I am homesick for hedges and birds with pretty melody, for the lovely chalky blue sky of England. This colony seems so hard and new, all newly broken ground, much clay and sandstone, but nothing yet to make the soil friable. The birds are bright but raucous. Everything is lacking in gentility and care, and society as a whole (although better dressed than anyone in England could imagine) seems little concerned with the common good, only individual benefit. This view is perhaps unnecessarily bleak and I pray it is a distortion caused by the unhappy predicament I now find myself in. However it does seem that there is nothing for a man to do once he has gained the reputation that has been so unjustly given to me.

Such was the weight of the detailed confession that followed that it was no wonder he walked in such a leaden way that Lucinda, who had been thinking of him constantly ever since she had found the "scandal" in the *Sydney Mail,* did not recognize him.

She had not immediately recognized him in the *Mail* for that matter. She saw the name, of course—Hopkins, but she did not think of him as Hopkins but as Crab, the creature who had scuttled sideways towards the porthole he was so in terror of. She read of Judd, the Reverend Mr Hopkkins, and unknown "lady," and it was a full minute before she saw who and what it referred to.

"Oh, dear God, forgive me," she said. She was sitting in her kitchen at Longnose Point. She did not bother to think where the maid might be but went, straight away, on her knees and pushed her hands into her eyes and rubbed at them as if she might, in making all this lightning in the blackness, undo what she had so carelessly done.

She thought: I should not be allowed abroad. This is the second man I have ruined. She sat up and folded the *Mail* in her lap. She would go, this instant, to Randwick and apologize, or to the Bishop or whoever was important in the matter. Her next thought was that she must stay away and not compromise the poor man any more. Her third thought—and this was the one that she finally acted upon—was that she must present herself and see what aid she might render. She dressed herself in her most drab and proper clothing, an unpleasant brown wool and a severe black bonnet which only served, against her best intentions, to accentuate her lovely complexion so it was, like a Ribstone pippin, a soft underwash of crimson overlaid with murrey brown. She drove herself out to Randwick. There she encountered not the Reverend Mr Hopkins but Mrs Judd who stood her ground high on the veranda and would communicate nothing except the pleasure of finding herself in so obviously powerful a position.

Lucinda drew her whip along her gelding's flank and sped out of the vicarage, rattling the cattle-grid and leaving a cloud of talcum-fine clay dust for Mrs Judd to sweep off her veranda.

She thought: I have made it worse. She thought: I will leave it alone.

She made towards the ridge road through Darlinghurst, intending to visit the glassworks. She did not articulate this to herself, but her face, which had, through the agency of her tense upper lip, grown long, now softened and regained its more usual contours. The idea of this visit to the glassworks was a formless, nameless, anticipated pleasure, such as a tobacco addict has when coming out of church. It was the next thing. The next nice thing. But it was only a habit, and when she saw what it was she had been thinking she saw that the packet was empty.

It was three weeks since she had promised Arthur Phelps—he who called his gut his bellows—that she would not visit the works. How had she promised such a thing? Was she not the owner, after all?

Arthur had kept his broad hands busy with his tobacco and papers. His eyes had been absorbed by the business of licking and lighting. he had not looked at her, but she had looked at him, at the great sweating girth encased in wet hessian bagging, at the male, foreign otherness of his white-haired skin. He had spoken to her—all the time fussing with a dainty cigarette he could have attended to blindfold—with great politeness and discomfort. He had taken her out into the yard where the window glass was being packed into wooden crates. The wood was newly sawn and sweet and sappy in the spring air. Yellow straw was lifted by the nor'easter and hung like scratches in the sky. Arthur kicked at the dry rutted clay with his big blunt boots.

Lucinda waited for him. She saw he had a great sense of his own authority, a "natural" sense, far greater than that which would lead her to book a first-class cabin.

When he had finished fussing with his little cigarette he lit it within the sheltered cup of his hand. "Mum," he said, "It is better if I am sent for and come to see you at your office."

The timber mill next door screeched, a long shrill line of pain up the heart of a new cedar log. Arthur had gone to work there before. If he did not like it at the works he could, doubtless, find work at the mill again.

"You mean no harm, mum, I grant you. But it makes my boys be edgewise and standing on politeness, and then we see the gob-gatherer get the gob wrong and the second blower have his walls uneven and the item not worth taking further, mum. They are poor ignorant lads, and easily distracted by a lady."

This simple speech made her feel a despair too deep for tears, or even anger. Her mouth opened.

"If by chance you wish to visit," Arthur said, "then perhaps, mum, you let it be known aforehand."

"How long aforehand, Arthur?" She watched the glasspacker. He was using insufficient straw.

"Oh, just one day, mum, no more. You let it be known, and we will be ready for you, mum, and a proper inspection it would be, mum, like in Her Majesty's Navy, and not all rags and bags and odd socks either—all lined up and shipshape."

"But this is my business, Arthur." There was no edge to her voice—a voice that was often thought to be too easily icy or sarcastic. There was no will. Her eyes were dry and scratched like the straw-littered sky. "I am the proprietor."

And Arthur Phelps said: "I know, mum, but it be our craft, mum, you see. It be our *craft*."

And she had accepted this. She had accepted because she could never forget the emptiness, the hollowness which had occupied the very centre of her being when she had returned from London and found the works empty, the furnaces cold, and that kitten—the murdering crunch of its skull was part of the same feeling–that loneliness, sickness, with nothing bright or soft or sympathetic. She knew she should not have accepted Arthur Phelp's demands. She was angry that she had. She now went to the works at night when the firemen were working, stoking the furnaces or, sometimes, putting in a new clay crucible. She made the firemen uneasy, too, but they had not the conceit or the craft, and dared not ask her to leave the wooden throne on which Arthur drank his pints and practised his trade. It was warm and dry in the works. She was there almost every night. She brooded. And now she would brood about Oscar Hopkins as well. The furnace doors would swing open silently and clang shut abruptly. The firemen's shovels would scrape along the floor. She would sit on Arthur's throne and drink brandy from a flask. She would think of homes, homes she did not have, homes she had lost.

She day-dreamed of letters to the bishop which she did not send, advertisements in the personal columns of the Sydney Morning Herald which she did not place. She went to Ah Moy's but did not see him. She attended Homebush and Randwick. She gambled as if there were a horse that might, by the churning force of its hooves amongst the mud, blot out the pain she felt. She bet fiercely. She did not see him anywhere; and when at last she did, in the post-office yard, she did not recognize him, not at first. The gap between her memory of him and the figure he had become produced a most unsettling feeling.

"Mr Hopkins?"

The man spun. He had a pimple on his top lip, although pimple is perhaps too polite a term for such a swollen infection whose surround was of a deep and angry red. He had a cut on his cheek and this also had the appearance of infection. When he saw who it was, he buttoned up his coat as if by doing this he would hide the way his gaunt neck poked out of his oversized secular collar.

"Miss Leplastrier," he said. He had no hat to lift. He produced a letter from his pocket and waved it in the air instead.

She also had a letter. It was to Mr Paxton asking details of some channelling he had designed to prevent condensation dripping from glass ceilings. She waved it.

They posted their letters. She tried not to watch Oscar count out his farthings to make up the price of the stamps. She saw the back of his hands marked with their praying stab wounds. She had never before in all her life been aware of causing so much harm. All the qualities which had before so irritated her, the nervous frailties, the boyishness, the innocence which she had found so disturbing, now seemed to her to be very fine things indeed.

Her carriage was in the yard at Druitt Street. She hailed a hansom and did not need to cajole him into it. Her manner was what Arthur Phelps would label "bossy." She had the cab drive to the boarding house in Bathurst Street.

Lucinda was appalled by this boarding house. She was so affronted by the condition of life, by the filth on the floor, the lampblack streaking up the walls, by the slovenly appearance of the owner that – when the propriety of her visiting Mr Hopkin's room was raised by this "creature" – she struck his desk top with her umbrella.

She did not look closely at what she found in Mr Hopkin's room, although a half-empty bottle of colonial hock stayed in her memory. He had a trunk. She had the cabby bring it down and they drove to Druitt Street and, having transferred both passenger and luggage to her own vehicle, drove out to Longnose Point.

She left Scandal behind her. She drove Scandal in front of her. She did not care. She drove all her emotions through a tight funnel. She had the maid bring her hot water and bandages. She laid towels on her dining-room table and laid his injured hands on top of them. She imagined him wounded from fighting with his fists. The wounds were red, surrounded by purple; they opened yellow, like lips of skin. They were, she thought, like flowers of flesh, like banksias.

She cleaned the pus from his wounds. He made high hooting noises like a nightbird.

71

The Stratton's Wager

If the Reverend Mr Stratton had been a horse you would not have bet on him. He would have had sweat foaming on his flank where it was obvious, not hidden in the secret folds of his woollen combinations. But horse or no, the signs were there for anyone with an eye to see them: a certain wildness in the eye, an inclination to bolt out of the gate before his wife had closed the door. He stamped around beside the gate while she came along the path.

"There is plenty of time, dear Hugh," she said, hurrying, just the same, along the path, arranging a scarf around her face—for although it was only September there was a cold wind blowing off the sea.

"By what clock?"

"We only have one clock, Hugh. We have not had two clocks for eight years."

"Nine years," said Hugh Stratton, holding out his arm. "that was my point."

"Then I do not understand the basis of your question. Please explain it to me," she said in that humble, neutral tone of which she was, secretly, so proud. She knew this was perhaps a risky tone to take with Hugh in such a fractious and nervous state, but she could not, even if she had wished to, respond in any other way.

"The basis of my question," said Hugh Stratton, who would see that Theophilus Hopkins lay in wait for them a little further up the hill, "is that we have one clock, while Tommy Parsons has quite another."

It was Tommy Parsons who drove a pony trap along the high road each day sometime between eight o'clock and nine o'clock. It was Tommy Parsons Mr Stratton was reliant on if he were to get to the races today at Newton Abbot.

"Tommy Parsons," said Mrs Stratton, "has, in all likelihood, no clock at all. I would be most surprised, Hugh, wouldn't you, to see Tommy Parsons with a clock."

Hugh Stratton sighed bad-temperedly. "My point," he said, "my point, dear Betty, is that the little Methodist will not have a clock. He will have no idea of time at all. He could be cantering along the high road at this moment while we are here arguing about the time and, lookee, the Evangelical awaits us. He will make us later."

And indeed, Theophilus was now walking down his short path with his notebook in his hand. He pretended that he had not seen the Strattons at all and, so set was he on this deception, that he let them walk right through his gaze before he "saw" them.

"Ho," he said.

"Ho," said Mr Stratton, but in a way that made Mrs Stratton give his arm a cautionary squeeze.

"Do you have news?"

"The mails have been bad," said Mrs Stratton. "It has taken two weeks for us to get our papers up from Oxford. I can't think what is causing it."

"Ah, yes," said Theophilus and, without attempting more conversation, stood there, looking at them both, nodding his head. He had a little lump of porridge in the corner of his mouth. It made him look neglected.

"And how is your health, Mr Hopkins?" asked Mrs Stratton.

"You must excuse us," said Mr Stratton.

It is not yet eight," said Mrs Stratton who was always embarrassed by these meetings with Theophilus and, just because she would like to rush away, felt she must prolong them.

"Then go," said Theophilus in a loud voice which brought Mrs Williams's wild grey head to the window. "I do not seek to detain you."

"That is true," said Betty Stratton. "It is I who seek to detain you, whilst my husband takes the opposite position."

"Oh, help me," said Hugh Stratton.

Theophilus looked at Hugh Stratton as he always looked at him, as if he were a variety of beetle that God, in his infinite ineffable wisdom, had placed upon the earth. He saw the yellowed eyes, the livid skin, the deep creases like knife cuts beside his mouth. He saw the fury in his eyes and imagined it was because he had lost one more member of his congregation to the Plymouth Brethren. The Great Wolf himself must show just such a yellow-eyed rage when a lamb is placed safe inside the fold.

"You must excuse me," said Hugh Stratton, doffing his hat, "but my contrary position in the argument must place me on the highway." And, with a twisted smile which was not intended to be unfriendly but, given the turbulent state of his emotions, ws all he could manage, he set off up the path and left his wife and Theophilus Hopkins in the tangled skeins of their mutual embarrassment.

Hugh Stratton carried one hundred and twenty-one pounds and sixteen shillings. The six shillings jingled in his trouser pocket. The soft leafy currency lay fat and soft and silent next to his heart. This was the sum of his wife's capital, the interest from which had hitherto allowed them some softening of their harsh position. It had paid for Mrs Stratton's periodicals, Mr Stratton's trips to Oxford, and a bottle of sherry once a week. Today he would apply this sum to the system supplied to him by young Master Hopkins.

Hugh Stratton was much impressed by what the system could provide, and never more so than when he had seen his protégé ensconced in luxury aboard the *Leviathan.* The image of those gold-leafed ornate columns had stayed a long time in his mind. And yet he was the wrong person to be setting off up the hill on his way to deal with bookmakers. He did not have the personality to control the system. His wife was thorough, dogged, calm, all those qualities she made clear to the world by her style of walking. Hugh Stratton on the other hand—everyone at Oxford had said so—had brilliant insights but never the patience to be a distinguished scholar, was always in too much of a hurry for a result, an effect, the reassurance that all his work was not being wasted on a fallacy.

Having decided that they would wager the whole of their financial foundation, Betty Stratton was quite capable of going round the racetracks in the proper manner, taking her time, slowly observing and collecting the information they would need to make Oscar's system work effectively, but Hugh—who felt he must control it—was too fearful to work properly. He made scrawling notes and could not read his writing. He watched a race and somehow saw nothing. He talked to a jockey but, so keen was he to appear expert, he would not ask an explanation of terms he did not understand.

And yet here he was on the way to the racecourse where he would throw their fortune into the maws of the bookmakers' bags. He believed the evening would see them wealthy, and yet he did not believe it sufficiently, and while the front of his expectations was bright and freshly painted, with red plush and fluted columns, there lurked, far beneath all this, like the memory of a dream involving rotting teeth, the knowledge that his preparation was inadequate. He could not bring himself to look at what was wrong. He must rush forward. He must not miss the pony trap. And if you saw his sweating lip, the angry stare in his eye, you would know that this was a man who had already decided to ruin himself and that only his wife, hurrying behind, with her body severely inclined from the vertical, still imagined that they might at last improve the financial conditions of their lives.

72

Mrs Smith

Lucinda had a maid, a Mrs Smith, a childless widow just turned thirty. She was not lively or talkative, but these qualities which Lucinda had once thought essential now seemed—after ten maids had come and gone inside twelve months—no longer so.

Mrs Smith was good at her job. She was small and thin, but you would not call her slight, for her limbs were strong like an athlete's and she liked to scrub, and beat, and sweep. She did this work silently, as if holding her breath. When she spoke, her eyes remained quite unengaged and the only thing that seemed to put them into gear was church. She was a Baptist. She did not find the house too lonely, although this had been a common complaint with her predecessors. She did not wish to go dancing at Manly or walking in the Domain. She wished only to have every sabbath to do what she described as her "Christian Duty" and she declared this so fiercely and belligerently that Lucinda imagined that Mrs Smith's religion was a jewel-bright and private room where an Anglican's presence would not be welcome.

The normal terms were fifteen shillings a week and every other Sunday afternoon and evening off, and one free night a week. But Lucinda did not try to bargain. She offered Mrs Smith sixteen shillings a week and agreed to her terms. Mrs Smith said she would give the extra shilling to the Lord.

The arrangement was not cheerful but it was practical. The silver was properly cleaned and there was none of that bitter tasting crust on the fork tines that had so distinguished the tenure of the ninth maid.

The bathroom smelt of bright and pungent patent formulae. Waves of ammonia seemed to emanate from the waterside windows which were always, no matter what the weather, sparkling clean. And if the house became slightly hostile and chemical by day, this was conquered in the night by the rich aromas of the stews which were Mrs Smith's great skill. The stews were a surprise. There is something wild and generous abut the better stews. They are best put together on the winds of impulse, guided by the compass of intuition. These were all qualities that Mrs Smith would have appeared to lack. You would expect something thin and watery from her pot. There was no indication that this was a woman who threw her herbs in by the stalkful, cut her meat big and would know whether the fungus she found on the borders of Whitefield's paddocks could be eaten even if it were a poisonous-looking yellow and shaped like a lady's fan.

When Oscar Hopkins was brought into the house, Mrs Smith, similarly, showed herself to be not mean as her mouth suggested but both compassionate and practical. It did not occur to her to question the propriety of introducing a man into a house occupied by single women. She saw nothing untoward with him being attended to on the dining-room table. She fetched towels from the linen press and she got good thick ones lest the heat from the water she had been asked to boil should damage the french polishing.

Of course, she did not know who Oscar Hopkins was. She did not know he was a scandal.

She saw his hands and, having more experience of the agonies of prayer than her mistress, recognized those half-moon-shaped infections. She tore up a cotton chemise – really still too good to throw away, but of the right softness and texture for cleaning wounds – and then she stood back, her arms folded, her head on one side, her eyes apparently as neutral of expression as a bird's and watched her mistress tend to the man.

She did not say anything in front of the man, but her face softened a fraction as she fitted her big-fingered hands together, rocking one hand back and forth on the tines of the other.

In the kitchen she whispered to Lucinda: "Them cuts was made by praying," And she demonstrated how this might be done, shutting her eyes while doing so.

Lucinda was repulsed and excited by this fervent prayerfulness. It seemed alien, popish, like Italian paintings of the torture of saints. She felt judged by it. She respected it, perhaps excessively, she who thought the kneelers at Balmain not soft enough. She found the iodine behind the cochineal where Prucilla Twopenny had hidden it.

The iodine hurt him, and when Lucinda would not bear to be the agent of more torture, it was Mrs Smith who took over the medication. She bound the young man's hands and asked him did he think he could manage to hold a mug of cocoa.

It was also Mrs Smith who made up the bed for Oscar. It would seem the question of it being sinful had not entered her mind at that stage. Indeed it did not enter until she had been to church on Sunday.

On the Saturday she waited on them both, bringing toast and porridge to the little room upstairs, which looked through the thin grey veil of gum trees to the cobalt blue of the Parramatta River. Mrs Smith was in no way censorious. Indeed Lucinda was touched to see how bright and excited she was. You could imagine how she might be as a wife with a husband, or a mother with a son. She bullied him gently into taking golden syrup on his porridge and, with her luscious spoon held above the young man's plate, smiled conspiratorially at her mistress across the table.

In this nectar drop of time, Lucinda was moved. She thought: I am happy.

There were cockatoos on Cockatoo Island in those days, and they brought their shrieks and tearing beaks to breakfast on the Monday. They gathered in the Morton Bay fig on the south side of the house and made Lucinda laugh when they raised their yellow crests or waddled self-importantly along its smooth-skinned, wrinkly-elbowed branches.

It was then that Mrs Smith requested a word and Lucinda, having no indication from the face, went with her innocently, imagining that they were to confer on some domestic matter or that she was being asked to declare a holiday for Pentecost or Ash Wednesday. She went, still holding her napkin.

Mrs Smith could not carry her emotions as far as the front parlour. She got as far as the bottom of the stairs when she turned abruptly and said: "I cannot stay, mum. Not while you comport youself in such a way, mum."

"In what way?" Lucinda felt nothing but confusion as though she had been riding a trap which has, quite silently, lost a wheel, and there she was tipped over in the rock-studded roadside when the minute before she had been reclining on a cushion and thinking dreamy thoughts about the shape of clouds.

"The *'gentleman,'* said Mrs Smith. It was all she could manage. It was as if the word itself would choke her.

"But, Mrs Smith, it was you who made up his bed. And as you are in the house yourself, it seems to be perfectly proper."

"Your morals are your own aflair, mum. As are my own."

"Have your friends at church been speaking to you?"

But Mrs Smith would not answer so direct a question and her eyes took on a dark and hard and glittering righteousness. She lifted her chin and clasped her hands in front of her pinafore. The passage where they stood was a dank place. Neither of them moved for a good two minutes.

When Lucinda returned to sit opposite Oscar at the table, he did not immediately notice the distress in her face. He noticed, rather, that she had tied her napkin in a large hard knot which she could not, no matter how she plucked at it, untangle.

73

Judge Not

If you saw Mrs Smith with her dun-coloured shawl around her shoulders, her cane basket in the crook of her wiry arm, saw her come up the hill past the butcher's in Mort Street, Balmain, you might remark, if you remarked anything at all, that here was a woman that kept the shutters of her life screwed shut, who kept herself close to the wall as she walked, and thus occupied that thin strip of dry shadow when all the rest of the street was wet with sunshine. A private women, you would think, until you found something livelier to interest you (there—a tinker sitting in the gutter mending a tiny saucepan with a burnt black handle) and then you could forget her.

And yet, three days after Mrs Smith had left Lucinda's employ, there was not a maid in Sydney who did not know of the unorthodox situation out at Whitfield's Farm. This did not mean that there were no further maids or cooks available, but rather than the ones who put themselves foward were opportunists who imagined that they could, given the impropriety in the house, request a premium for their services. There was not one who asked for less than a guinea a week. This was offensive enough. But there were other things, not easily graspable, about their attitude—for while they swindled, or attempted swindling, they adopted an expression (all in the eyes and mouth) of moral superiority.

These interviews left Lucinda feeling soiled and angry, and she would have had no help at all had not Mrs Froud stepped forward.

Mrs Froud was the wife of Lucinda's second gatherer. She came to "do" two afternoons a week. Mrs Froud was jolly and friendly, but you could see—or so it seemed to Lucinda— that she had made an assumption. This assumption was quite incorrect. There was nothing to make an assumption about.

Oscar lay in his room and sucked his sheet. He wrote to Mr Stratton about the dangers of gambling life.

> My dear Patron, [he wrote] I cannot help but have the greatest reservations about the serpent I have placed in your trusting at a time when I knew too well the effects of its poison. I sent my journals to you because I promised you, and now I beg you to make a promise: burn them. I regret the day I first set foot upon the track. Opium, surely, would not be so great a curse. This will all seem far-fetched to you, but let me tell you that at this moment I am kindly lodged by a fellow sufferer, and although we inhabit a small house, no bigger than my father's cottage, we hardly speak to one another for fear that something that we say or do will lead to a horse, a game of cards and we shall, without intending to, find ourselves once more in that state of mad intoxication.

There were pages of it, all pretty much the same. They reflected Oscar's idea of what was happening in the house, but what was so obvious to him was not obvious to Lucinda at all. While he shrank from conversation, wary of where it might lead, she had hoped for it. While he tried to diminish himself, to make himself small and inoffensive, she sat at table and waited for him to join her. She did not like to go running to his room continually, and yet she could not leave him there alone. She imagined he was gripped by loneliness. She saw he did not hate her, and yet she felt him pulling back. The reason for this presented itself to her one night while she was preparing for bed.

He thinks I have him in mind for a husband.

It was only to set his mind at rest that she invented the romantic story of her passion for a clergyman whom Bishop Dancer had so cruelly exiled to Boat Harbour. She wished to make him imagine that her heart was already spoken for, that all she required from him was company and conversation. She wished him calm, steady, and to quit all this nervous scuttling about the house.

But she told her story to a man whose emotions were in such a state that he could barely hold the load they carried, let alone the unhappy story she asked him to lash on atop. He was much moved, too moved. It was ridiculous, he knew—he hardly knew her—but it took everything in him to stop bursting into tears. He chewed his lip, he grimaced, he excused himself while there was still sultana cake uneaten on the plate. She heard him creaking up the stairs. The door shut to his room. She picked up her tea-cup and threw it at the wall.

74

A Degree from Oxford

"This chap, Miss Leplastrier, is he any good?"

Mr d'Abbs held her eye quite fiercely for a minute, but he could not sustain. He had a small smile, quite ironic, and it twisted his thin moustache and made him look not quite respectable. And while he enjoyed being thought of in this way—it was no commercial liability in Sydney—it was not the truth at all. He might let her glassworks go cold through timidity or cautiousness, but he would not break the law.

"He has a degree from Oxford."

"Oxford," said Mr d'Abbs. He was pleased, but did not wish to appear impressionable. His hands—large hands for such a small man—played briefly with his blue silk tie, then held the edge of the desk, then slid until they found the drawer, and in the drawer a cigar. The cigar was such a big one that Lucinda, when she saw it, thought it made him look like a caricature in *Punch*.

"Oriel," she offered.

Mr d-Abbs blinked. He leaned forward a little as if he expected her to say more. When there was obviously no more to say, he frowned. "It is not just a question of clever men," he said. He fussed with some grey ash which had landed on his green corduroy jacket. "Really, there is no cleverness required. The work itself would drive him mad with boredom. All it requires is neatness. So why do you come to me with a man from Oxford?"

Mr d'Abbs really wanted to be flattered. He prided himself on his employees as he prided himself on the paintings and lithographs that crowded his walls at home. He was an artist himself. He liked artists. He was a philosopher. He liked philosophers. He provided them, in the midst of commerce, with a refuge.

He could not tell anyone, not even his wife, what pleasure it gave himn to know that now, at this instant, in the clerk's room next door, he had Mr Jeffris the poet and surveyor, Mr Trevis-Dawes the pianist, Mr Coyle the water-colourist whose views of Pittwater and the Hawkesbury adorned the cedar panels of his office. He did not wish to talk to them, and he certainly did not socialize with them. But he was very pleased, more pleased about this than anything, that they were there.

"So why come to me?"

"Oh, Mr d'Abbs," said Lucinda, "do not tease me."

"Tease?" said Mr d'Abbs, looking pleased. He relit his cigar and sent clouds of smoke into the air.

"You told me yourself about your Mr Cloverdale."

"Speaks Hindi, that's correct. It is absolutely no use to him in Sydney. But he is an honest man, Miss Leplastrier, and neat."

Lucinda assured him of Oscar's character. She said nothing of gambling. (She should say. She would not.) Mr d'Abbs was now explaining that money was kept in the office. He stood, took out a big bunch of noisy keys from his pocket, and opened the safe with one of them. He showed her money. There was ten thousand pounds in his safe. He showed her the money to stress the importance of honesty, but the other reason, the real reason, was that he could not believe it was him, little Jimmy Dabbs, Ditcher Dabbs's boy, who was standing in his own office in the colony of New South Wales, a cigar in one hand, ten thousand pounds in the other.

"Fancy that," he said.

The things that moved Mr d'Abbs were clear to Lucinda. Sh was embarrassed for him, not that he should be so pleased about himself, but that he should reveal his pleasure so clearly, that he should stand naked at his bathroom window, not knowing he had an audience for all his imperfections.

"He knows Latin," she said, "and Greek."

Mr d'Abbs looked up at her and blinked. He smiled and tapped a wad of banknotes against the back of his wrist.

"He has excellent references from his London employer. He was a schoolteacher." She spoke quickly, leaning forward, listing his achievements until she had said Greek three times and Latin twice. She spoke on and on, not because she wished to exaggerate Oscar Hopkins's attainments, but in order that she be too busy to notice the private reverence Mr d'Abbs showed the wad of currency—the one bright colour in this room of sombre water-colours.

Lucinda held her hands together. It gave her the appearance of "imploring." Her little shoulders were uncharacteristically rounded and Mr d'Abbs, without knowing quite what had triggered it, felt a stirring of the loins.

Others found Miss Leplastrier attractive. Absalom had taken a fancy to her. Old Gerald MacKay had dubbed her the "Pocket Venus" and sworn he would have her for wife. But Mr d'Abbs, if you discount that unfortunate occasion when he had placed his hand on her knee, had forgotten how to see her in this light. Their friendship at the card table had continued, but in business he found her the complete shrew. When she had returned from England she had thumped his desk with her little fist.

But today he found her very "girlish." He could imagine this young Hopkins being smitten with her. She had a soft white neck.

He tossed the banknotes into the safe—thwack, ding, money's nothing to me—and locked its door with a heavy brass key. He returned to his new squeaky leather chair to hear how she would manage to tell the story of her involvement with this defrocked priest who she now sought to recommend to him.

Well, she could not tell it, of course. She might slam her fist on his desk or drink Scotch whisky from a crystal tumbler, but she could not tell him about this one face to face.

Jimmy d'Abbs knew the story. Of course he did. He was not a member of Tattersall's, the Masons and the Sydney Club for nothing. He smiled and nodded encouragement, but she told him nothing, and there was no hint, no rumpling of her white starched collar to suggest the amours he imagined her conducting with the priest in the tangled privacy of her bed.

Lucinda found it hard to look Mr d'Abbs in the eye. She felt her cheeks colouring but could not stop them. She told Oscar's story without mentioning cards or horses. Mr d'Abbs noted the omission but was unconcerned. One could gamble and be honest. He gambled. He played most games a gentleman would play.

He asked her would she be so kind as to have Mr Hopkins supply a sample of his handwriting.

"What shall I have him write?"

"Some Latin," he said, "a little arithmetic." He placed the

cigar in the ashtray so it might go out. "Some Greek."

"Greek?"

Don't frown at me, young lady. "Greek," he said. He would like the Greek as he had once liked Mr Jeffris's trigonometry. What other accountant would demand a sample of your trigonometry?

The thought of Mr Jeffris—who was his head clerk these days—made him uneasy. Mr Jeffris did not like him to employ new clerks without consultation. This was fair. They had agreed on it. But was it not Mr d'Abbs's own practice? Was not that his own name on the door? Did he not have the right to employ whomever he liked without there being doors slammed and ultimatums issued?

"There is no hurry," he told Lucinda.

But when she arrived at Longnose Point that night, she brought a present with her. It was wrapped in maroon tissue paper from a Pitt Street stationer's—ink, a new nib, and three loose sheets of ledger paper.

75

Heads or Tails

Lucinda had painted a picture of Mr d'Abbs. She had made him a shy creature, a dormouse with a waistcoat and a gold chain. Oscar had imagined a small pink nose all aquiver, seen his hands go to his face as he attended to his nervous toilet. He had gone to the meeting full of tenderness for Mr d'Abbs, not merely for his timidity, but for his Christian charity, that he should risk his own business name by employing a man in such public disgrace. But when he came, at last, to sit in Mr d'Abbs's office, he found that Mr d'Abbs was not a shy man at all, or if he was, his shyness was of a highly selective quality, was sensitive to distinctions of sex, perhaps, and rank, certainly, just as the Chinese are so attuned to the pitch of the human voice that one can ask directions to

Li-Po, for instance, and not be understood until one's pitch is perfect.

It was the eleventh day of October and early in the afternoon. Rain drove against Mr d'Abbs's window and although the venetian blinds were fully hoisted the sky was so dark and bruised that it was necessary to light a lamp. The office looked across at the windows of other offices in which there were also lamps lit. Oscar listened to the thunder and imagined he would soon have his shirt sodden and clinging to his skin.

"You have no hand," said Mr d'Abbs. "You have no hand that would be worth a damn to anyone."

Oscar sat on the edge of his chair. He was aware of the spots on his trousers. His attempts at cleaning them had made them worse. They were dark spots ringed with watermarks. He felt them to be visible badges of his disgrace. And although he had warned himself about the dangers of fidgeting, when Mr d'Abbs peered bad-temperedly across the desk, Oscar could not stop himself from rubbing at his trousers with the back of his thumbnail.

He put his head on one side and looked at Mr d'Abbs.

Mr d'Abbs was accustomed to unconventional men. Indeed he collected them—artists, poets, philosophers—it was the great pride of his life that he could provide them, in the midst of commerce, with a refuge.

But this was not an artist. This was a clergyman. He had expected someone at once broader and tidier. He had not expected "artistic" qualities in a sacked clergyman. This was a very queer chap, and Mr d'Abbs gazed at him quite openly, astonished to think that it was this uncombed stick-limbed fellow, this grasshopper, who had finally cracked the defences of she whom Havey Fig had dubbed "our pocket Venus."

White hailstones danced on the window ledge. There was a wild whinny from a panicked horse in the laneway below. Mr d'Abbs stretched his legs under the desk, crossed his thin white ankles, and wished he had never been so rash as to promise anything to Miss Lucinda Leplastrier.

The priest's sample penmanship was still uncrumpling—he could hear it now—in the wastepaper basket beside his chair.

"I have seen some bad hands," said Mr d'Abbs.

"Indeed," said Oscar, crossing his ankle over his knee, then realizing that it showed his stocking and that, in any case, it was not the correct pose for an employee, he put his foot squarely on the floor. "Indeed, I would imagine you had."

"Well, before all this," said Mr d'Abbs, waving his hand grandly although there was not a great deal in the office to wave grandly at. "My own brother, now there's a fellow." And Mr d'Abbs saw, with his mind's eye, what Oscar could not even guess, a boy with his arms all itchy from those tiny red mites that were known as "harvesters"—they came at harvest time and dug deep into the skin. They were a great discomfort. They were worse than thistles bound up in the oat sheaves.

"He was left-handed, like yourself," said Mr d'Abbs, recreating his brother contorted around his pen. "But they changed him over, you see. He was perhaps a little old when they tried, for although my mater was a determined woman, it never really took. It mattered not so greatly to my brother, but for you, sir, in your previous profession . . ."

Oscar blushed bright and painful red at the memory of his "profession." He had thought it a secret in this context. Now he bowed his head under the weight of the shame. "Yes," he said, making himself look Mr d'Abbs in the eye, "it is a great inconvenience."

Mr d'Abbs named this look a "glare." He thought it quite alarming.

Oscar smiled.

Mr d'Abbs found a cigar in his drawer. It was crumbly, decidedly crumbly. He brought it out anyway and placed it on the blotter. "An inconvenience, sir. Indeed, a great inconvenience. I knew a parson in Basingstoke who was left-handed and could never hold a living, for once they saw him hold the sacrament in his left hand, they would not have him, and they would be off to the bishop, clipclop, and back again with a new chap."

Oscar saw Mr Judd riding off down the road, Mrs Judd behind on a big-bellied sway-back. Clip-clop.

"Ah, now you smile, you see, but I warrant you never had a living in the English countryside."

"I never did."

"I know you never did, sir. You would not have smiled had you done so. I met a witch in Mousehole, in Cornwall. She shook hands with me as though she were a man. You could not be a left-handed parson in those parts. You know your Latin? *Sinister?*"

"*Sinistur, sinistu, sinistu, sinistrum, sinistris.*"

"*Sinistartorium,* said Mr D'Abbs. He got his left hand into his drawer. He found the cigar clipper.

"The ablative?"

Mr d'Abbs did not answer, but he looked up he appeared most

pleased. "Well," he said, "there is no Latin here, although my head clerk, Mr Jeffris, has a fondness for the classics. But what will we do with you? You smudge. I may possibly tolerate you, but Jeffris is a fiend. He will box your ears. No, sir, I am not assuming the poetic. I describe the action. It is prehistoric. It is proof of the ape in us if ever I saw it. One moment a civilized man and the next an animal. And yet he is such a genius at this work that I must permit him, for a good clerk is the secret of any successful practice. Don't let anyone tell you otherwise. It is the poor clerks with their celluloid cuffs who allow us gentlemen time for our club or leisure to dine at Government House. It is the clerks, sir, and I am not a radical. My observation is scientific. My task is to stand at the wheel, to tip the rudder a smidgin this way, a fraction that, and yet what will I do? Are you up to the job? It is different work from praying."

Oscar could think of no wwy to answer such a question. He rubbed his hair. He found a piece of twig in it, caught there from his morning walk on Longnose Point. He pulled it out and looked at it—a gum twig three inches long.

"I hope you are up to it," said Mr d'Abbs, gazing at the twig and cocking his head.

There was a little silence. Oscar put the twig in his pocket.

"I hope you are up to it, because if there is one thing more unpleasant than employing a man—and you probably won't see that, in your position, eh, that the act of employment is itself unpleasant?—if there is one thing more unpleasant than employing a man, it is telling him that he can be employed no more."

Mr d'Abbs's leather chair was new and slippery and he had, whilst talking, slipped down in it, but now he sat up, fussed with his lapels, tugged at his silk tie and placed his corduroy elbows on the desk.

"You would not believe the scenes this little room has witnessed, Mr Hopkins. Men you would imagine civilized, men from Merton and Oriel, astronomers, masters of poetics—they have sat there, exactly where you sit and have threatened attacks on me, my chldren, my property. Gentlemen, too, or so they pretended, and next thing you know they are threatening me with litigation and saying they have friends in Government House and so on. And it does not matter that I have long before, well before, had a calm chat with just as I am having one with you, that I have explained the unpleasantness and worry. It all makes no difference in the end. But, please, write this down when you leave here today. Make a note of what I say to you, and when

Mr Jeffris finds that you do not meet his standards and you feel the inclination to throw a brick through my bedroom window, refer to your notes."

It was only when Mr d'Abbs stood up and held out his hand that Oscar realized he had been employed as a clerk. He should have been happy, but he was not. He felt no elation, only anxiety as to what would befall him.

"Well," said Mr d'Abbs and picked up the bell from his desk. He swung it, and he hoped the impression was that he swung it gaily. He did not, however, feel at all gay. For now he would have to endure Mr Jeffris's revenge for employing the chap. There would be days, perhaps months, of doors slammed, papers thrown, compressed lips, monosyllabic answers, a series of jarring chords and drumbeats, which would lead, in the end, to the scarecrow's dismissal. He put the bell back on his desk and looked at his new clerk. The fellow was tapping his left foot and jiggling the coins in his right pocket—a combination of activities which gave him an unusual stance, the pelvis forward, the right shoulder dropped down, and the whole of this topped by a gruesome smile, the intention of which was not at all clear.

Oscar had very few coins in his pocket. There were two pennies, great big coins—six would make an ounce—and three threepences—coins so light you would never feel their weight in an empty pocket. Now he pulled out a penny and looked at it. He did this so innocuously that Mr d'Abbs, who was staring at him, imagined that the simpleton was merely curious to see what had been making the din in his pocket. Mr d'Abbs hardly throught about it. But when the lopsided clerk jerked the penny in the air and caught it—snap—Mr d'Abbs thought about it then, by Jove he did. But as the only thing the action resembled was a person tossing heads or tails and, even though this might fit the character of a gambler, it did not match his demeanour, nor did it sit with the situation, the office, the interview, the money in the safe, the cigar in the drawer, the clerks next door, and so even when Oscar examined the coin on the back of his hand, Mr d'Abbs concluded that it was simply a nervous habit, like jiggling a leg or pulling sticks out of your head, unfortunate, but no more than the sort of eccentricity Miss Leplastrier would find—who could doubt it?—a positive recommendation of character. He sighed.

Oscar heard the sigh. He let it stand for the one he would like to make. The penny was a sign from God.

Heads.

He had to take the job.

76

Mr Smudge

Mr Jeffris did not biff him. He had expected to be biffed and yet he was not, not all the time he worked there. Neither did he see any of the other clerks – there were twenty of them in that long thin room – receive anything more than – and this was in one case only – a sharp tug to the nose and as this assault was inflicted on the very youngest of the clerks and occasioned great laughter, even from the victim, it might not seem, in the telling, so bad a thing.

And yet there was about that room an almost unbearable tension, and if there was no actual biffing, one lived with the *possibility* of a biffing and it was this, Oscar thought when the whole nightmare was ended, that made working under Mr Jeffris such a tiring business that no sooner had he eaten his evening meal than he wished to sleep and would, if circumstances permitted, go a full ten hours without stirring.

His muscles were kept tense and tight all day, and yet no one threatened, and there was not a word to say on the subject of biffing. There were, in fact, very few words said on any subject at all, and although Mr Jeffris did not declare a policy to him, it was obvious after the first hour that he did not wish one clerk to talk to another and Oscar had the feeling, on entering the office, that it was not unlike an omnibus in which people travel every day and the passengers, having become familiar with each other, may exchange a nod (or perhaps not) but will not really acknowledge their community until there is a tragedy or a humorous mishap. When this arrives they will express their solidarity through laughter. Oscar provided an opportunity almost immediately.

Mr d'Abbs had rung the bell, not gaily at all, but sharply, nervously. He had introduced Mr Jeffris who did not, on first impression, seem in the least prehistoric. As for being proof of the ape in man, Oscar could not see it. Mr Jeffris was a young man, no older than Oscar, with the moustache and bearing of a Guards officer although, being just a fraction shorter than Mr d'Abbs, he was too small to have met the physical requirements. He had jet-black hair and apart from the moustache – a thicker, deeper one than Mr d'Abbs – was cleanshaven. He had a dimpled chin and a blue cast to his very white skin. Mr Jeffris did not smile, but he did not scowl. He hardly moved his face at all, and yet he communicated the most colossal and even dangerous passion. It was all in there, expressed in the gap between the angry intensity in the eyes and the very still, leashed-in quality of the muscled body.

Mr Jeffris was very civil to Mr Hopkins. He led him into the clerk's room. This was a long office with a big stove in the middle. The black chimney traced an unexpectedly long route on its way to the wall, a long dog-leg, and you could see by the way the desks were arranged along its route, that it gave off a much-desired heat in winter and that, in its journey from hot to cold, it also indicated the rank of the clerk, Mr Jeffris being close to the stove and the youngest clerks well away.

Oscar noticed the eccentricity of the flue, but did not understand it. He was more surprised by the expensive mauve and brown wallpaper (on the one hand) and the bare paint-speckled floor (on the other). It did not quite fit, and although no one bothered to tell him, it was because the previous tenants, very successful lawyers, had taken their carpet with them. The thing that made the greatest impression on Oscar was the depth of the room which only had five windows, all of them at the Sussex Street end, and so he was surprised to be led towards the light and to be given a desk next to the window from where he had a view, not only of the interesting iron-wheeled, cobblestoned goings-on in Sussex Street itself, but the muddled little jigsaw pieces of Darling Harbour which were visible at the end of two alleyways across the way. He could see the smokestack of Prince Rupert's Glassworks, too.

When he was shown this desk Oscar feared that he was being unduly favoured. He did not wish to make enemies so easily.

"But this, surely, he said to Mr Jeffris, "is far too fine a desk for me?" He said this in a whisper, for the room was very quiet, but just the same it produced a nasty roar of laughter. There was scraping of chairs, coughing, snorts, wheezes, a barnyard. Oscar's cheeks went flat like potters' clay slapped hard with a paddle. He looked at Mr Jeffris who was biting his moustache. Then he looked at the other clerks who had already stopped. No one looked his way.

He thought: I will not put up with this rudeness.

Then he thought: I must.

The fine spider-web capillaries in his cheeks were awash with blood.

He sat at his desk, finding something in its sticky wax surface that was repellent to his fingers. He clasped his hands in his lap. The urge to stand up and walk away was still very strong. It came on him in waves like stomach-ache. Mr Jeffris gave him three musty-smelling journals with moth-eaten leather spines. These were the debtors journals for John Hill & Co., John Bell (Homoeopathic Chemists) and Senior's, also chemists but making no claim to homoeopathy. Oscar was not a snob about commerce, but it was completely alien to him. When he saw the books he felt that he would never understand them. Mr Jeffris gave him the business's receipt books and asked that these receipts be transcribed into the journals. And although you might not think this so foreign an activity for a young man with a passion for racehorse journals, he did not see the similarity. He felt only despair that life could be passed in so low and slow and meaningless a manner. Mr Jeffris gave him a pen with a new nib, a pot of ink, and a sheet of pink blotting-paper which seemed, perhaps due to its colour, but then again perhaps not, to produce a fit of coughing and scraping amongst his fellow workers.

And that was how Oscar was employed. He tried to feel grateful. He sat on a hard wooden chair with no cushion, at a table with a wobbly leg which sometimes contributed to his smudges and blots. He found the work trying and the hours too long. Nothing in Hennacombe, in Oxford, in Notting Hill, at Randwick, had been so stultifying. As a clergyman he had enjoyed his mornings at the desk. He had drunk a little jasmine tea while he thought about the most demanding duty of his week—his sermon. Nothing had prepared him for the flavour of something so dull and mean.

He wrote down the names of items he could not imagine and, in columns next to them, prices he could not afford to pay.

He transcribed Shower Baths.

Slipper Baths.

Hip Baths.

Foot Baths.

He entered Bagatelle Boards.

Chiffoniers.

Superfine.

Millefleurs Powder.

And he sweated in the harsh afternoon sunshine which blazed across his desk and every day became hotter and hotter. He did not ask for a curtain. He knew what rude laughter would accompany the request. He would end his days with no feeling of release, but with a dull headache and his shirt sticking unpleasantly to his skin. His dreams shrank until they could accommodate no larger idea than a curtain, or a crisply folded poplin shirt. He only had two shirts. The white one he wore for two days, the blue one he wore for three. And although he bathed three times a week and changed his collar daily, his shirts smelt like the old rags Mrs Williams kept in a bucket in the scullery in Hennacombe. The smell was remarked on by his fellow workers without anything ever being said. It happened, somehow, in the silence, although "silence" is perhaps the wrong term. It was more that there was a pressure of silence, a lid of silence beneath which there were odd and secret stirrings of sound.

The Reverend Oscar Hopkins sat in his own stink above a dung-fowled Sydney street suffering alternate waves of anger and depression which could b e triggered by a blow-fly trapped behind sun-bright glass or the bells of St John's at Pyrmont, or St Andrew's in the city.

He had told the Ecclesiastical Commission that his gambling had not been covetous, but he had not acquitted himself well. He had been nervous, overpowered by their confidence and authority. He had felt himself to be as venal as they imagined him to be. His voice had shaken as he stood before them, bishops in purple drinking tea from floral cups. He had said that he had never gambled for personal gain, and they simply did not believe him. And so he was cast out, spat upon, become anathema.

Mr Jeffris called him Mr Smudge. This was thought to be a great joke. He was appointed as clerk responsible for mixing ink, a messy job which ruined his shirt cuffs and had him going home each Monday night with ink soaked so deeply into his skin it took a pumice stone to remove it, or remove most of it, for even after a long and painful rubbing, a shadow still remained, a blue cast lay on his skin and he named it, joking to Lucinda, as his Monday Shadow.

Elizabeth Leplastrier's daughter was not tolerant of his messy style—his blue ink, the unpleasant smell of the shirts. And yet she thought it her Christian duty to assist him and so she laboured with him (not altogether graciously) on Saturday morning, stirring his clothes in the copper. Her face was wet with steam. Her eyes stung with smoke. He dripped boiling water all around him, splashing her, splashing himself, ooh-ing and ouch-ing as he thwacked the blue shirt and the white shirt down into the trough.

He was not manually dextrous, that much was obvious. He went at things in too much of a rush to do them neatly. He was ungainly, made bony angles, would hurt himself badly should he have ever needed to work in a glassworks.

Lucinda was interested in the way men made things, how they organized themselves. She sat her guest down in her kitchen and questioned him about the way in which the ink was manufactured. He surprized her with the fastidious nature of his answer—it did not fit in with all the shirt thwacking and dripping water.

To make the ink he must first take a brown paper bag of ink powder, a little metal cup, and a large bottle. He must carry these utensils to the alleyway which ran through the heart of the building. In the alleyway was a tap. There were other taps in the building, of course, but it was forbidden—there were signs above the taps expressly forbidding it—to make ink at these basins. No, he must go into the laneway which served as a thoroughfare, not only for snot-nosed message boys cutting through from Kent to Sussex Street, but also for the wagons and drays from the wheelwright who occupied the tangled courtyard in the centre of the building. Wind blew along this alley way even in the most clement weather and the tap was one of those wide-mouthed types with a lot of air in its gurgle, "all wind and no water" as a passing rag-and-bone man observed to him. Here, crouching against the urine-sour brick wall, Theophilus Hopkins's son, now twenty-one years old, an age at which his father had already published two distinguished monographs, must measure out the ink powder from its paper bag with a flat steel spatula and transfer it, guessing the quantity, into a metal cup. This was not only menial, it *was not easy*. Ink powder blew in the wind. Specks of stinging pigment lodged in his already baleful bloodshot eyes. He must mix the powder into paste in the cup. The tap gurgled, spluttered, splashed. The spatula handle became wet, then blue. The blue was now on his hands, his face, and still he must dilute the sludge so it would pour, and then transfer it to the ink bottle and then, if there was time, and they had not sent young Summers down to tell him to hurry up, that the ink was needed as quickly as you like now, Mr Smudge, he would wash.

He made Lucinda laugh, but when the froth had subsided she was left with a black and slightly bitter taste, and this scene did not fit with her idea of Mr d'Abbs, who, no matter what his frailties and vanities, she had always through of as a kindly man, not one to subject another human being to comic indignity.

She had many things to worry about at that time, things she would, herself, have imagined to be more important to her than her nervous, ink-stained lodger.

But she could not bear that he be called Mr Smudge. It was wrong of him to tolerate it, and worse that he should joke about it. The gurling tap stayed with her. She saw it clearly: its wide grey mouth, its verdigrised brass cock. It produced a feeling well out of proportion to its weight. It was she who was the author of this situation and she accepted more blame than she thought she should. She took it on herself while judging herself foolish for doing so. And when she had far more weighty matters to occupy herself with, she left her own office (just a little down Sussex, before Druitt) and walked—her back straight, her steps brisk and businesslike—down the alley way towards the wheelwright's.

The tap was on the south wall. She had imagined the north. There was a smell—men's urine—which would normally have made her quicken her step, certainly not stand still. There was no brass in the tap at all. It was a dull grey thing, a fat and ugly machine, dull grey, streaked with ink, the source, it seemed, of the drunk-man smell.

She turned it on, then off. Her lower lip was tucked in tight. She splashed her shoes. If Mr d'Abbs used his poets and his astronomers thus, he was not even a shadow of the man he posed as, but a barbarian like the rest of them.

Lucinda was suddenly very angry. She did not like her shoes wet. She would see the room wherein her friend, the "aesthete," the Medici, housed his poets. It was, perchance, a stable, a cupboard, a chookhouse, the bottom of a well.

She went up the cedar-panelled stairs towards the offices and found Mr d'Abbs (he must have passed her whilst she fiddled with the tap) on the stairs ahead of her. He looked at her wet shoes, but said nothing about the cause of it. Indeed, they travelled together all the way to Mr d'Abbs's anteroom without having said so much as a "Good morning." Mr d'Abbs was flustered. Lucinda imagined this related, somehow, to the tap. But he had not seen her at the tap. He was flustered because he did not like the routine of his arrival interfered with. He was not expecting Miss Leplastrier. He did not like what he did not expect. He was, in effect, receiving her. Yet it was not his job to receive. It was Mr Jeffris's entitlement, and this had been settled long ago. Now he was unsure of whether to go into his office and leave Miss Leplastrier in the anteroom or to usher her in irrespective of the rules; but then it seemed she did not wish to see his office, anyway.

She would inspect the clerks' room.

Oh no, she would not, not on your nelly.

The anteroom was very small, and although its couch was

comfortable enough and it had an ashtray, a brass spittoon and a copy of the *London Illustrated News,* it was hardly bigger than the carriage in which Mr d'Abbs had been driven to the city. They stood, therefore, very close together, both made uncomfortable by such intimate confinement with a member of the opposite sex.

"There can be no question," he said, making a fuss of placing his unbrella on the stand intended solely for the use of visits, checking his cuffs, and smiling in the direction of his client's shoulder (not in calm sequence either, but as if he were a machine with some part not securely connected and he wished, against the rules of his own manufacture, to do all three things at once). "There can be no question of you disturbing the clerks."

Lucinda nearly invented some excuse. Then she thought, No, I shall not demean myself by lying. She drew her shoulders back and tried to find his eye. She explained she wished to see the conditions under which the clerks laboured.

Mr d'Abbs thought: Ha!

He judged the woman smitten. And whilst this explanation made him smirk (she wished to see lover-boy, that was all) it afforded no relief.

She put her busybody little hand on the door of the clerks' room. This door had a small enamelled sign. It said "Private." There was a small chip out of the "e," but the meaning was clear. Mr d'Abbs stared at the sign as if the sheer intensity of his staring could force Miss Leplastrier to obey it. But she turned the rattly little knob in spite of him.

Dash it. He would tell her the truth. He would, in effect, throw himself on her mercy. You could do this with a woman. She would understand his agreement with Mr Jeffris. It was not an agreement at all. It was never spoken of, but it was understood that this, on the other side of the door, was Mr Jeffris's territory. Not even Mr d'Abbs, the captain of the ship, entered this room. If he wished ledgers brought into his office, he rang.

"Come, Miss Leplastrier," he said good-humouredly, and opened the door leading to his own office. "Come. We will have tea brought to us."

But behind his back he heard a little "snick."

Lucinda stepped into the clerks' room. There were so many men in there, and rows of desks. It was not such a bad office, better than her own. She noted the big stove, the wallpaper. It seemed ordered and businesslike, although a little dim. She saw a little man–no taller than herself–come walking towards her. She wondered where Oscar sat.

The little man, she guessed, was Jeffris. He was broader in the shoulder, more handsome and athletic than she had imagined. He was attractive, but in a dark, unsettling way she knew better than to dwell on. He seemed to prance. He had little metal caps on the soles of his shoes. She heard him come towards her. Tap, tap, tap. She was, without having any reason, suddenly, frightened. She had opened a gate and found a black dog bristling at her, growling in the dangerous part of its throat.

In her ear she could hear (but not understand) Mr d'Abbs: "I have let him have this office, you see. A head clerk is everything. It is what it is all built on. You see, you understand. A head clerk is basalt, granite, you see, although it may not have occurred to you before." The words were dead leaves rustling. She felt him plucking at her with fingers like a begging gypsy, sharp little fingers plucking at the crêpe shoulder of her dress, the flouncing on her sleeve.

Lucinda did not care for the look of this Mr Jeffris. He had dark and hostile eyes. She had earned his hate just by opening his door. It was too late to retreat and she walked beyond the reach of Mr d'Abbs's plucking invocations and out into the office, between the desks of clerks who, although they were grown men, and some of them quite stern and military in appearance, shuffled their feet and hid amongst their books like schoolchildren.

She saw Oscar at last. The light was bright outside the window so he appeared to her in silhouette—the tangled shape of his hair was what marked him out. It was only when she was very close that she could see the expression on his face. He would not deny her. She saw that. He looked up and smiled but it was a pitiable expression. Oh, Lord, she thought, the poor man will have to stand. She swung on her heel. She felt the eyes of all the clerks. She smelt the alleyway, the sour smell of urine. She felt their scorn for her small body, her womanliness, for the sound of her tread on their boards. She nodded to Mr Jeffris, and to Mr d'Abbs who had returned to the open door like a dog forbidden the parlour. When she reached him, she turned.

"Thank you," she said. "I wished to see the conditions."

She did not stay to talk to Mr d'Abbs. She felt a fool. She hurried back to her office, thinking how little she knew about how the world of men was organized.

That night she heard the puzzling postscript to her visit. Everything in the office had been thrown out of kilter. Mr Jeffris had stormed into Mr d'Abbs's office. There had been shouting. The clerks had stayed at their desks, not looking at each other.

77

Happiness

She did not *expect* to be happy whilst parcelled up in a grubby apron, clogs on her feet, scrubbing her own floors, or being snubbed at the greengrocer's, kept out of her own works, denied the company of Dennis Hasset, becoming so cut off from life that her only companion was a homeless stray, a defrocked priest with blue-stained hands and a sweat-weary smell. These unpromising circumstances served to distract her attention whilst happiness snuck up on her like a poacher in the night.

She had not known she was happy, but it had been silently remarked on by others, by the glass blowers, by Mr d'Abbs, by Mr Chas Ahearn who had paid her a visit and brought her a gift of bantam eggs. They noticed, because her manner was gentler, because they were spared those ironies and sarcasms which Mr Ahearn, for one, had thought much too pronounced of late. She kissed his cheek and called him "uncle" and the old chap blushed to the lobes of his big fleshy ears.

Yet she had not recognized the moment when her scales had tipped from "down" to "up." She had been too busy to notice, until this morning, the Sunday before Advent. She was walking with her lodger down past her piebald cottage (half of it whitewashed, half red brick). It was an hour or so before early service and the Balmain bells were still silent. Sleek Herefords (the property of the bankrupt estate of Whitefield's Fram) gorged themselves on the new spring pasture. Lucinda wore a long white cotton voile with tiny roses worked into it. She carried her gloves and prayer book in one hand and her bonnet in the other. She walked along the thin cattle track along the spine of the point. There was still dew, not a lot, but she felt it soak into the hem of her dress. She did not mind. Oscar strode through the calf-high grass beside her. Nothing happened. Nothing was said. But she thought –I am happy.

She looked at Oscar. He did not notice her. He was busy looking out for snakes, surveying the harbour–a sea of rough hills poured full of silver glass. H had his head up, his head down, his eyes everywhere at once. He had stuck a tiny blue wild flower into the band of his tall black hat. She thought what a pleasant companion he had turned out to be, and if they were in such disgrace that the barely educated vicar of Balmain should think it best not to "see" them as they filed past him out of church, it was a most superior kind of disgrace.

She had judged him too hastily. This was a bad habit. It had caused her trouble before. She had compared him to Dennis Hasset and had pursed her lips when he picked up his tea-cup in a certain way, or placed the pot back on the table a little too heavily. She had felt slighted when he had scurried back into his room and shut the door on her. And yet–how quickly it happened–she had come to be proud of the propriety with which they now shared the house, the sense of measured discipline (a virtue she much admired) that they brought to their conduct so that there was a great closeness, the closeness of initmates, but also a considerable distance, the distance not of strangers, but of neighbours. They occupied a positon well above those Philistines who snubbed and slighted them. God, who saw all things, would not find their conduct unbecoming.

They did not gamble or take hazards of any type.

Oscar had no experience of female friendship. At first he was shy with her, stammered, tripped over himself, tried to make himself invisible around her. Only in his unholy dreams did he ever imagine anything even slightly more intimate. And if there had been a maid, this is how it may have stayed. But Mrs Froud had retired due to being in a certain condition, and there was no maid at all. There was a cottage that must be looked after, a fireplace that must be red-leaded, soap to be made, carpets beaten, the brass doorknobs taken to with halves of lemon. Seeing how the young mistress worked–quick, small steps, slap of brush, flick of duster, smack of mop, clatter of bucket, an energy quite in excess of what was promised by her physical size–the lodger took off his shiny jacket, rolled up his sleeves to reveal thin milk-white arms, and worked beside her. Lucinda was embarrassed at first. She did not think it manly.

And yet this is how they became friends, by scrubbing the pitted, checkered tiles of the kitchen floor, working side by side, creeping backwards. They did their jobs inexpertly. They drank tea by the potful and kept the leaves to use in rug-cleaning. And when they had at last finished, usually around midnight, Lucinda would kick off her shoes and let them drop on the damp floor and Oscar would put his feet up on a chair. He would be smudged with red-lead, or W. G. Nixey's black-lead, and have sticky wax on his elbows. She thought him an "old woman," a "kind soul," "odd fellow." Sometimes she looked at him and saw him as if she had never seen him before—a "vision," humming, stirring his tea with the blunt end of his knife, hooting with high laughter, talking Latin which he expected her to understand. He was, in his conversation, so elliptical, so tangential. He made her feel plain, uncultured, inelegant. She did not guess her cast-off shoes were "dainty," the object of his admiration.

She saw what she had seen aboard the *Leviathan*—that he was not a man to be so easily patronized, that he was a passionate man, an enthusiastic man, who would plunge into the jungle of ideas, not fearfully, but impatiently (thwack, slap, wet clothes from the copper), but also a pleasure.

He was very homesick and liked to talk about England. It was a different England from the one which had so disappointed her. It was a dear, green place, and she could not know that the Strattons' house was damp and cold or that the Baptist boys had made him eat a stone. He talked fondly of the Strattons whom he called "my patrons" and did not tell her that Hugh Stratton, having as much success with horse-races as he had had with farming, had used Oscar's system to lose all his capital and was into debt so deep he was now begging money from men he had not known since Oriel.

There was a bright white pack of cards in the cedar sideboard by Oscar's elbow. He saw it there, sitting askew beside a ball of grey wool and a tangled tape measure, saw it frequently, each evening when he reached out for the sherry decanter (engraved with the image of an emu) and poured out the two thimblefuls which was their "nightcap." He said nothing about the cards. He imagined his hostess—so disciplined in her running of the household—untroubled by them. He wished he had the strength of character to fling them away, but having made himself ridiculous aboard the *Leviathan* he dared not.

They did not discuss cards, but what they did not talk about gave their evenings a tense and tingling edge and left them both happy, yes, but wakeful in their beds.

Lucinda might sneak from her own house at midnight to place a wager somewhere else, but she dared not touch the pack that lay in her own sideboad. She knew how passionate he had become about his "weakness." She dared not even ask him how it was he had reversed his opinions on the matter. But, oh, how she yearned to discuss it with him, how much she wished to deal a hand on a grey wool blanket. There would be no headaches then, only this sweet consummation of their comradeship.

But she said not a word. And although she might have her "dainty" shoes tossed to the floor, have her bare toes quite visible through her stockings, have a draught of sherry in her hand, in short appear quite radical, she was too timid, she thought, too much a mouse, to reveal her gambler's heart to him. She did not like this mouselike quality. As usual, she found herself too careful, too held in.

Once she said: "I wish I had ten sisters and a big kitchen to laugh in."

Her lodger frowned and dusted his knees.

She thought: He is as near to a sister as I am likely to get, but he does not understand.

She would have had a woman friend so they could brush each other's hair, and just, please God, put aside this great clanking suit of ugly armour.

She kept her glass dreams from him, even whilst she appeared to talk about them. He was an admiring listener, but she only showed him the opaque skin of her dreams—window glass, the price of transporting it, the difficulties with builders who would not pay their bills inside six months. He imagined this was her business, and of course it was, but all the things she spoke of were a fog across its landscape which was filled with such soaring mountains she would be embarrassed to lay claim to them. Her true ambition, the one she would not confess to him, was to build something Extraordinary and Fine from glass and cast-iron. A Crystal Palace, but not a Crystal Palace. A conservatory, but not a conservatory. Glass laced with steel, spun like a spider web—the idea danced around the periphery of her vision, never long enough to be clear. When she attempted to make a sketch, it became diminished, wooden, inelegant. Sometimes, in her dreams, she felt she had discovered its form, but if she had, it was like an improperly fixed photograph which fades when exposed to daylight. She was wise enough, or foolish enough, to believe this did not matter, that the form would present itself to her in the end.

Before she reached this point there were many essential matters she must attend to. The most important was to find a foundryman who would listen to her long enough to understand what it was she wanted made. She had travelled all round the shores of Darling Harbour and up the smoky lanes of Leichhardy, and on the Sunday morning when she finally knew herself happy, part of the happiness, surely, was produced by the knowledge that she had, in that sour old misogynist Mr Flood, found the man who—even if he had no God, no taste, no sense of humour—could cast the parts she required and work out how they could all be made to fit together. Indeed, he would deliver her a "proty-type" on Tuesday.

She pointed out an ibis to Oscar as it rose from the mangroves of Snails Bay. She named it for him, but she could not bring herself to say anything of her secret. All this she would share only with the vicar of Boat Harbour.

Oscar had seen her letters to Boat Harbour. They sat on the mantel, swollen, tumescent; he imagined them love letters. She knew he thought this. It had been her intention that he think this. The misunderstanding allowed them to share the house, to be friends. But she teetered, all the time, on the brink of sharing this thing, this single most important thing with him.

On the morning she knew herself happy she looked across at her companion and saw his fine heart-shaped face, the fast birdlike movements, the blazing crop of hair; she saw the way he hit out at the grass with his walking stick; she saw the right hand plunged deeply into his jacket pocket; she saw a dear friend and companion, but she also saw a slightly dangerous, excitable, even self-absorbed young man. She might give him her secret (frail, as vague as a cloud) and see him destroy it because he did not know what it was he was handling. Or he might see it perfectly, more clearly than she did, and he might wrestle it from her, usurp it with his enthusiasm.

So she did not show him the bat-boned glass castle and if there were a cloud then it was a cumulus with towering columns, canyons, spiralling heights, vertiginous depths. When she thought about it, all the tendons in her hands went tight. She played her fingers now, on Longnose Point. She closed her eyes, screwed up her face. It was a delicious feeling—tense, unbearable, an itch, an ache. Sydney Harbour had a silver skin. A cormorant broke the surface, like an improbable idea tearing the membrane between dreams and life.

78

Ceremony

On the Sunday following the Balmain Regatta, Arthur Phelps walked two miles to Whitfield's Farm. He brought his youngest boy with him. The pair of them were in their best, the little fellow in a sailor suit and Arthur in a three-piece tweed. They had carried their boots with them to save the leather and had stopped up at Brichgrove House to lace up, accept a draught of water and a fresh-pulled carrot from the garden.

Arthur had washed his beard and combed it. It was snowy white and soft like the hair of a new-washed dog. Lucinda almost did not recognize him. He looked so grand, like Mr Henry Parkes. He smelt of soap and mothballs.

She invited him in, but he would not come in. She held the door open and noticed mosquitoes entering whilst her guest wiped his boots on the treadmill of the front-door mat. She had had this "respect" before. It always made her most uneasy.

Arthur had a speech to say. He stood up straight and tucked his "bellows" in. His boy was being bitten by mosquitoes, but Arthur was making his speech and would not let go the lad's hand. When she heard his speech, Lucinda felt her ears burst into hot flowers. Arthur not only knew Oscar's name, he was linking it with hers. He was making an assumption. This was the first thing to shock her. The second was that Arthur was inviting them both to visit the works. They were invited together, as a couple.

Of all the ways this shocked her, this is how it shocked her the most: that this man, this glass blower who would presume to order her not to attend her own works without prior notice would now, the minute he assumed her to be connected with a man – and do not mind that the connection was thought to be scandalous – would walk two miles, on the sabbath, to make sure the lord and master should inspect his new territory.

And yet she accepted. How weak she was! Because she was touched that he should walk two miles, and ashamed of the great wall of anger which threatened to swamp her. She did not even permit hersalf a sarcasm. She accepted. She said: "Very well," (you fool, you fool) and closed the door while Arthur was still saying good night. She would send a message, later, and find a prior engagement, but she put it off, and put it off, and the following Saturday saw her walking down the hill of Druitt Street towards the works. It was obvious to Oscar who walked, stick-thin and tangle-toed, beside his compact and tightly ordered friend, that she was not pleased. He thought: She is over-laced. But she was not laced at all, merely angry. The "lacing" was in her face, which had compressed lips, diminished mouth, which could not be hidden by her wide-brimmed hat.

The hat was too wide for someone of her height. It threw her out of proportion and made her smaller still. She knew this. Twice she stopped, in a public street, to fiddle with it, but all she succeeded in doing was making herself untidy.

Oscar did not understand the emotional weather. He was just released from Mr d'Abbs's office and was not keen to donate his Saturday afternoon, his first leisure of the week, to an inspection of such an ugly-looking enterprise. He had become accustomed to picnics at Manly and Watson's Bay. Here, the air was fetid, although from what manufacture was not clear. A sawmill screamed. They crossed the shit-littered cobblestones of Druitt and entered a yard. In the yard were open-sided sheds. They stepped across puddles. There were crates of bottles in piles (one blue, one brown) of broken glass.

Australia was a loathsome place. He wished he had never come. Now he had drawn poor Wardley-Fish to follow him, or so he had been informed by a stale, fat-spotted letter recently released from diocesan custody. Wardley-Fish's ship was on the sea and could not be prevented. What would Fish say to find himself confronted with all this?

A suited man with ragged cuffs ran across the yard and disappeared into the round brick building with the rusty tin roof. Lucinda pointed towards him, at him, his cuffs, the door he entered by. She pointed with her Japanese umbrella—a sharp, short-tempered sort of polk.

Oscar took all this bad temper on himself. He felt the umbrella pierce his rib cage. He knew he was not wanted here. Well, he did not wish to be here! He looked at Lucinda's bad-tempered face and did not like her. He smiled and raised his eyebrows and it was with this peculiar mask, no longer shaded by his tall hat, that he entered the works.

Nothing was as he had expected. Where outside it had been untidy and damp, inside it was very neat and pleasantly dry, like the palm of a pastrycook's hand. There were no windows in the walls; they were high up, under the roof. There were six furnaces in the middle of the room, and another five along the side. There was a long bed of trolleys and machines at present not in use. He assumed this was for making window glass, and he was right.

But what he expected least was to find the works garlanded with flowers: cornflowers, lachenalias, poppies, white and yellow daisies, freesias, flag flowers, daffodils, jonquils. They were tied in bunches to the big piers that held up the roof. They stood in great green-glass jars around the wall. They were embedded in a fishing net that hung between the furnaces and the doorway and beneath this banner of flowers the men all stood, their strong bow-legged forms pressing hard against the confinement of their suits. As Oscar and Lucinda entered, they burst into song.

"Oh, Lord, who filled our souls with love unbounded."

Lucinda looked straight ahead. She was moved, of course she was moved. The fools had worked so hard to please her. But she was angry, too, and the tears that ran down her cheek were caused by quite different forces than those which were producing the identical phenomenon in her lodger. Both lots of tears were salt, I am sure, and were probably within the normal range of salinity, i.e. between one per cent and two per cent salt, but this is merely to show you the limits of chemistry, for while Lucinda's tears were produced by diametrically opposed emotions, Oscar's were all in one direction and had their source in such grand territories as joy, wonder, humility, and love for these suit-trussed workers who had publicly enacted love for him, a stranger and an outcast.

79

Pot and Kettle

They were strangers to each other, two vessels on the one stove, the kettle whistling out great clouds of joy, the stew pot quietly burning, and each blind to the condition of the other.

There was a glass-blowing demonstration. Lucinda imagined Oscar to be bored and polite. He drank a pint of beer with the men; they offered her none. She put a smile on her face and despised them all as fools.

She was belligerently unchristian.

Mr Hopkins's tongue was quickly swollen with drink. It was bloated, as fat as an ox's inside his fine, small-toothed mouth. They had him sing a hymn for them. He had no voice. And whilst she knew her audience did not mind, she minded.

She was frump and dullard. He was as loose and floppy as a puppet. He watched them demonstrate how a tankard is made, six times. No one seemed to worry about the cost of keeping the furnaces going. She could not mention it and still keep herself controlled. They spilt their ale on the brick floor and put their arm about him and called him (Michael Casey did) "Father."

She was in the centre of a great cold space. She smiled until her face hurt. She enquired of squash-eared Billy about his wife and children and noted he could not tell her the age of his children. She did not care that he was poor. She smiled at him. He was drunk. He tapped her on the shoulder as he spoke to her. She left him as he tried to calculate the age of his middle child.

Mr Hopkins was out in the yard. He had taken it upon himself to inspect her sand and coal. He was with Arthur Phelps.

She could howl. Could run round and round the yard like a dog hurt by a wagon wheel. And the sun was now so bright.

She thought herself a child. "I think, Mr Hopkins," she said. "that we have another appointment."

He saw then, or so she thought. It was to his credit. He shook hands with Arthur and refused the invitation to come back inside to say farewell to "the boys." Arthur hung on his one hand with two of his.

"It is a great pleasure," he said, still holding the fine-boned hand with a clasp that felt, to Oscar, to be made from padded calico gloves, "it is a great pleasure, sir, to see our missus take up with such a gentleman as you, sir. And any time you wish to know anything at all, sir, when we have the window-making in full tilt, you just come along and we will be pleased to explain it to you."

Oscar turned, his hand still held in the straightjacket of the blower's hand, and saw Lucinda, who had been by his side when this speech began, walking away. Her shoulders were round. Her neck was forward. He did not know what had gone wrong. Had he not been manly amongst her men?

"Thank you, Arthur, I will."

He heard cheering. He turned and saw the men had spilled out of the works and had lined up against the wall with their tankards. They were cheering their employer who was walking past, her head bowed. When the cheering began she put up her umbrella to shield her face from them.

"Goodbye, Arthur."

"Goodbye, sir, and it is a privilege, sir and I myself was never married and that is a fact, sir, and it is not that I am not a Christian. My mother was a Baptist and my old dad a Unitarian, and we attend a chapel now and then but I will tell you this, sir, for it is a comfort to me and may be one to you . . ."

"Thank you, Arthur."

"An old chap, a Mr Hollis, a what-you-call-them Christian Socialist, informed me that the institution of marriage—I'll walk with you, sir—don't worry about the lads. Give them a wave, sir, that's right. This old fellow, oh, what a beard he had, silver-white and down to his belt. He could tuck it in his trousers, and sometimes did when he was shickered. He told me that the institution was nothing our Lord said, but was introduced at a later date, and by one of the popes no doubt, and it was all to do with property, and not our Lord Jesus, but was related to the Church taking over the recording of things. Well, my memory is a leaky vessel. Give them a wave, sir, they're pleased to have you. They are happy for the missus, that she has a man at last. It has been hard for her. There are some of us that will regard you as a real relief, sir. Well, goodbye, and it has been a privilege."

Oscar hurried after the black, umbrella-humped figure. He waved back. And he made such a comic figure, his hat pushed back on his head, as he leaped across a puddle, waved an umbrella, jumped to avoid some oxen droppings, that the men all laughed, but not maliciously. They walked back to their barrel smiling and shaking their heads. Their new master was an odd bird, but not a knave.

What appointment? Oscar knew of no appointment. An appointment for her, perhaps, but not for him. He was disappointed for he wished to do nothing so much as talk to her. He felt he had opened a door into her life. He would like to sit somewhere, a place with marble tables. If it had been London they would go to the

Café Lux in Regent Street. A glass of port wine for the lady. Or merely China tea, and then they could talk about this glass business of hers.

It had never occurred to him that a process of manufacture could be beautiful. Had you, an hour before, asked him to tell you what he would call beautiful he would have drawn on the natural world, and named the species along the lanes of Devon, or brought up for you, plunging his hands into the rock pools of memory, the anemone his father had drawn and named, these fine soulless creatures which had, just the same, been made by God. He would haved shown you the Stratton's harvest stocks (and forgotten they had scratched his arms and made them itch all night) or the rolling, dangerous sea seen through a familiar window with a two-foot-thick sill. He would never have led you into a building with a rusting, corrugated roof, or taken you between lanes made from bottle crates, or littered with glittering shards. In these places you expected foulness, stink, refuse, and not, certainly not, wonder.

But it was wonder that he had found, and he had felt it in his water, before he saw anything to wonder at, that this dry, swept place—he knew this the minute he was inside the door—contained something exceptional.

They led him to a glory-hole, had him look in, into the protean world where you could not distinguish between the white of pure heat, the white of the crucible, and the white of the molten glass which they named "metal." When Arthur had said "metal," Oscar had understood "tin" or "silver" or "gold." And when the gatherer drew out the substance it could have been all of these things. The red-hot orb at the end of the long rod which he watched, passing from man to man, from glory-hole to glory-hole, acquiring more metal, being blown a little, swung, handed on, until it came to that largest, most slovenly of all of them. And then he who dubbed himself (privately, whispered it in Oscar's ear) to be none other than the famous knight Sir Piss-and-Wind, took the long rod and was, at once, drum major, bagpipe master, trumpeter, transmuter, as he transformed the metal into a tankard. He sat himself at last on his wooden throne and rolled the long rod back and forth across its arms whilst he smoothed a base with wet pear wood which hissed and steamed in clouds around his tea-and-ale-stained whiskers. He took a snake of red elastic glass from the third gatherer and, lifting it high—where it looked as angry as a snake in an eagle's claws—made it, with a flourish, into a question mark, and thence, a handle. It was all so fine, so precise, and it was a wonder that this miracle was wrought by a whiskered Falstaff with a fat belly and a grubby singlet showing through the layers of wet, sour hessian.

"I am a human bellows, sir," Arthur claimed, waving his hand for someone to come and take his creation from him. "That is what I have made of myself."

But it was not this that thrilled Oscar about glass, that a man had made his body to comply with the needs of manufacturing, but that a man so obviously gross and imperfect could produce something so fine.

Glass, Binding white. Glowing red. Elastic. Protean. Liquid. Vessel for light.

He hurried after the proprietor. He was a tangle-legged usurper, a shiny-suited thief. He was a butterfly collector, an art buyer, walking fast after the thing that had produced such wonder. He would be a part of this, any way at all.

She fled him, walking quickly, like an honest citizen who feels a pick-pocket on his tail. She headed up York Street and then turned in towards the crowds at the markets. He pushed his way through narrow alleys between the stalls. It was a sunny spring day, but in here there were lanterns hung between the sausages, and he followed her large black hat as she turned, bumping into people between bolts of calico, piles of moleskins, racks of blue metal shovels lines up like weapons in an armoury, and out into the blinding light of George Street. She walked at such a pace that even Oscar, with his legs a good foot longer, his stride another two feet in advantage, had trouble keeping her in sight.

But he would not let her go. He justled and skipped, pushed and pardoned. He tracked her back down Sussex Street. They passed the alleyway above which the majority of his colleagues still worked over their ledgers. Only six buildings down, but on the other side of the street, she went into a tall brick building with bright yellow sandstone ledges to its windows. Prince Rupert's Glassworks (Office) 5th Floor.

Printing presses occupied the first three floors and the building thumped with their rhythms. The staircase was filled with the harsh and volatile odours of inks. Through an open door he saw men in aprons filling their formes from fonts of type. He was sweating as heavily as if he had sat in his normal place in Mr d'Abbs's establishment.

The firms on the fourth floor were, either through lack of custom or because of progressive management, closed for the Saturday afternoon. The landing was quite deserted, apart from a charlady on her knees, clicking her tongue about this second vandal come marching across her work. She was not mollified by tiptoeing.

Three firms had their names displayed on dark wooden doors on the fifth floor, all done in different scripts in careful gold leaf with jet-black gold shadows. The first one he looked at was St Rupert's Glassworks.

He knocked, but only lightly, and entered after the very briefest pause. It was no more than a single room, a desk, three chairs, all crushed beneath a sloping ceiling. There was no rug on the floor, but the wall behind the desk held a framed etching of the Crystal Palace, and on the wall opposite the windows (at which Lucinda now stood, her graceless hat held in her hand) there was a great bank of glass shelves displaying a dustless collection of bottles (green, bright yellow, poison blue) and square book-sized sheets of glass in various finishes and colours. As the sun now played upon these shelves they glowed and bled and washed across each other like the contents of a casket in a children's story.

Smiling Oscar thought: A bower-bird.

Her desk was cedar and also topped with glass. It held a single pot of ink, a pen, no blotter. A tall blue vase held a flag flower, which was now decidedly past its best. A single petal and a fine dust of pollen lay upon the glass-topped desk.

The smokestack of Miss Leplastrier's factory grew from her left shoulder. She did not turn. He could see the soft whirl of hair at the base of her neck. When he stood behind her—he was very close, no more than a foot away—he could see that the men had set up a tug of war in the yard. It was obvious that several of them were very drunk indeed.

It was only then, so close, that he saw her shoulders shaking. This emotion frightened him. He had not expected it. Now he did not know what he should do. He joined his hands together. He was aware of how sticky and sweaty he was. He thought: This is a private place. He thought: I must smell. He spoke her name. He touched her shoulder. She turned. Her proud face was all collapsed, like a crushed letter thrown into a basket. Her clear skin was suddenly marked with little channels—creases, cuts, in a delta down her chin, on her nose, and her big green eyes were glasses held by a drunk, brimful, splashing, not gay, of course, but caught in the pull of the outward tide of anger and the inward one of hurt.

He had no idea what caused it all but, stooping a little, he opened his arms to her and held her against him. She was so tiny.

80

The Private Softness of Her Skin

He was tender with her. He wiped her eyelids with his handkerchief, not noticing how soiled it was. It was stained with ink, crumpled, stuck together. Her lids were large and tender and the handkerchief was stiff, not nearly soft enough. He moistened a corner in his mouth. He was painfully aware of the private softness of her skin, of how the eyes trembled beneath their coverings. He dried the tears with an affection, a particularity, that had never been exercised before. It was a demonstration of "nature." He was a birth-wet foal rising to his feet.

He fetched the chair from behind the desk. When he lifted it, the back separated from the seat and clattered to the floor.

"Oh dear." Lucinda sat, sniffing, on the window ledge. "Everything is in collapse." And, indeed, this was how the office seemed to her, not merely today, but today more than before. It had never been what it appeared to be—the physical monument to her success, her solidity. There was a heavy desk, various bureaux, cabinets, samples of manufacture, but she could never see them as solid, but as theatrics. This office was her place of exile, and never more than when the window framed a picture of drunken men playing tug of war. She felt humiliated and powerless, like a child dragged down the street by a large dog on a leash.

There was a claw hammer in the desk drawer. Oscar—although he was at first too energetic and it seemed that he would fail—succeeded in hammering the chair back together. She obliged him by sitting in it. Her back was bathed in afternoon sunshine.

She said: "You must think me really quite ridiculous."

He said: "Oh, no, not at all."

She held out her hand, received the handkerchief he offered, and blew her nose. She was anointed with a blue ink smudge. It sat right on the tip of her nose. "Am I right to say you guessed the reason for my tears?"

But he had guessed nothing. He felt himself to be too big, too tall, too awkward. She was so condensed and gathered. There was nothing superfluous about her. He squatted with his back against the opposite wall. His legs too long and thin, untidy as a heap of unsawn firewood.

"No," he said, "no, really, I have no idea."

Her face changed subtly. You could not say what had happened—a diminution of the lower lip, a flattening of the cheek, a narrowing of the eye. But there was no ambiguity in her intention. She had withdrawn her trust from him abruptly. "If you have no idea," she said, "how can you not think me ridiculous?"

"Because you do not have a 'ridiculous' character."

They looked at each other and saw each other change from combative stranger to familiar friend and back again, not staying one thing long enough for certainty. She had velvety green irises of extraordinary beauty. Her eye-whites were laced with tangled filaments of red.

"And are you curious?" she asked, pulling and pushing, challenging him even while she promised to confide. "About the reason for my tears? Are you curious a little bit?"

He was curious, of course he was, but he had a lover's curiosity and he feared what she might say. He imagined the tears were somehow connected to the fat letters she left lying on her marble mantelpiece. He imagined they were produced by Dennis Hasset. He was curious. He was not curious at all. He had a lover's selfishness, was grateful for the intimacy the tears had made possible, was resentful of what they seemed to threaten.

They looked at each other until the look became a stare and both of them lost their nerve at once.

"Yes," he said, "of course I am curious."

He wet the corner of the handkerchief again and tenderly removed the smudge from her nose. She tilted her head a little and closed her eyes.

She told him how the men, her employees, had offered him a fellowship they had denied to her. Her mouth changed while she told it. It became small. He was aware of the cutting edges of her lower teeth.

He was sorry for her. He was a fool, and had been party to a great unkindness. He was sorry, so very sorry, and he said so. He was also privately elated that the tears were not to do with Dennis Hasset at all, and although he tried not to grin, he could not help it.

"Well," he said, "you should know why I came bounding after you."

"Not to dry my tears."

"Are you curious?"

"Oh," she smiled. "I am curious, of course."

He acknowledged her irony with a bow of his head. "I chased after you to tell you I had never seen anything, in all my life, quite as splendid as your works." He frowned.

Lucinda coloured, but it was not clear what she felt.

He pressed his clenched hands beneath his knees.

She said: "Oh dear."

He sighed and said: "Yes."

"Yes what?"

But he had only said "yes" in response to what he hoped "Oh dear" might mean, and he was not brave enough to be explicit. "Perhaps," he said, picking up his battered hat from the floor, "we should take tea." He was thinking of the Café Françasi, a place with marble tables.

"I will show you," she said, standing and smoothing down her velvet skirts. What this meant was most uncertain.

He did not ask her "what" or "where" but followed her as she left her office. His mind was out of focus at the edges, sharp at the centre of its lens. Her walk was unexpectedly jaunty, crisp, clear, echoing. On the landing she opened a door marked "Acclimatization Society of New South Wales."

Oscar thought: Mr Smith.

"Gone," she said, tapping the sign. "Vamoosed. Mine now."

She unlocked the door and swung it open. He waited for her to enter, but she would not. She stepped to one side and made a gesture like a theatre usher. They collided and tangled in their own politeness. "Look," she said impatiently, "just look."

What she asked him to look at was Mr Flood's "proty-type,'; that construction which, only a second before, had occupied the crystal centre of her life. But when she stood beside Mr Hopkins in the doorway she no longer saw the cleverness of Mr Flood with his singed, hairy arms and his dividers and tables predicting "actual shrinkage." She saw only a dumpy little structure with a pitched roof like a common outhouse.

"You may approach," she said drily. "It is not sacred. It is merely," she said, imitating Mr Flood's pinched nasal tones, "a 'proty-type.' "

But Oscar did not see as Lucinda imagined. As the dust danced in the luminous tunnel of the western sun, he saw not a dumpy little structure, not a common outhouse either, but light, ice, spectra. He saw glass as those who love it perceive it. He understood that it was the gross material most nearly like the soul, or spirit (or how he would wish the soul or spirit to be), that it was free of imperfection, of dust, rust, that it was an avenue for glory.

He did not see an outhouse. He saw a tiny church with dust dancing around it like microscopic angels. It was as clean and pure and free from vanity. It was at once so beautiful and yet so . . . decent. The light shone through its transparent, unadorned skin and cast colours on the distempered office walls as glorious as the stained glass windows of a cathedral.

"Oh dear," he said, "oh dearie me."

When he turned towards her, Lucinda saw his face had gone pink. His mouth had become quite small, as if the thing which made him smile was a sherbet sweetmeat that must be sucked in secret.

He said: "I am most extraordinarily happy."

This statement made him appear straighter, taller. His hair was on fire around the edges.

She felt a pleasant prickling along the back of her neck. She thought: This is dangerous territory you are in.

He was light, not substantial. He stood before her scratching his head and grinning and she was grinning back.

"You have made a kennel for God's angels."

Whoa, she thought.

She thought: This is how the devil looks, with a sweet heart-shaped face and violinist's hands.

"I know God's angels do not inhabit kennels." He stepped into the room (she followed him) and crouched beside the tiny glass-house. It was six foot long with all its walls and roof of glass, the floor alone in timber. "But if they did, this surely is the kennel they would demand."

"Please," she said.

"But there is nothing irreligious," he said. "How could we have a sense of humour if our Lord did not?"

She smiled. She thought: Oh dear.

"Do you not imagine," he said, "that our Lord laughs together with his angels?"

She thought: I am in love. How extraordinary.

"How could God, who is all-knowing, not understand the foundation the joke is built on? I mean, that here is something the size of a wolfhound's kennel which, thanks to your industry, is a structure of such beauty and joy as to be a habitation fit for His angels."

He stood still now, having, while he spoke, danced like a brolga around the little glass building. He held out his arms as if he might embrace her and then brought them back across his chest and hugged himself and hunched his back a little.

She thought: He will ask me, not now, but later.

"And haven't you done something?" he said. "Haven't you *done* something with your life? I must confess to envy."

The setting sun bounced off the red-brick wall of the next-door warehouse. It was this that made the little room so pink. The light refracted through the glass construction on the floor and produced a spectroscopic comet which they stood, neatly, on each side of. Lucinda duplicated his stance without meaning to; that is, she hugged herself, kept her arms locked firmly around her own body while she felt the space between them as if it were a living thing.

81

Promenade

All this, Lucinda thought, I have inherited from my mama: that I am too critical, that I ride my hobby horse into the ground, that I have a bad temper, that I will not relax and be quiet and because of this I push away those who mean me well. I will not allow anyone to be a simple "good chap" as my papa always could. How can I be in love with him and be so lacking in the most simple trust?

These thoughts were occasioned by her response to Oscar who, whilst walking up Druitt Street towards Castlereagh, had attempted to take her arm. She had snatched it back on reflex. She was immediately cross at herself for doing so. Tears smeared the gas lights as if they were water-colour. Do not cry. I will not. Take his arm. I cannot. Take it. I *cannot.* You must.

She took his arm, looking straight ahead, her heart pounding.

It was that time of the evening when there is blue in the sky and yellow in the shop lamps. They promenaded, arm in arm, up the hill, towards Castlereagh. He had, he declared, "an idea" he would not tell her. The idea gave his mouth its rosebud smile. He would tell her his idea at dinner—she would be his guest. He teased her nicely with his silence on the subject. He was tall and stretched, with a long, twisting neck and a high black hat against the constraints of which one could see his hair protesting. She was short—the brim of her enormous hat was barely level with his shoulder. His gestures were jerky, hers controlled.

She had no criticism of his dress, which was bagged at the knees, dropping at the lapels, rucked around the buttons, while she – although she wore a flowing white cotton – appeared (she knew it and wished it was not so) as starched and pressed as a Baptist in a riding habit.

They were different, and yet not ill matched.

They had both grown used to the attentions that are the eccentric's lot – the covert glances, smiles, whispers, worse. Lucinda was accustomed to looking at no one in the street. It was an out-of-focus town of men with seas of bobbing hats.

But on this night she felt the streets accept them. She thought: When we are two, they do not notice us. They think us a match. What wisdom does a mob have? It is a hydra, an organism, stupid or dangerous in much of its behaviour, but could it have, in spite of this, a proper judgement about which of its component parts fit best together?

They pushed past bold-eyed young women with too many ribbons and jewels, past tight-laced maidens and complacent merchants with their bellies pushing so forcefully against their waistcoats that their shirts showed above their trousers. Lucinda was happy. Her arm rested on Oscar's arm.

She thought: Anyone can see I have been crying. She thought: I have pink eyes like a dormouse. But she did not really care.

82

Oscar in Love

My great-grandfather was in love, and although he managed to hide all the signs of his despair from Lucinda, he was miserable. He made little jokes about the natty gents in checked waistcoats, laughed, patted her arm, but whatever happiness he felt he saw only as a sign of all that would be denied to him.

This was because he had an idea in his head, and I do not mean the idea that he had promised to reveal to Lucinda at the dinner table. This was another idea, quite separate. The idea that caused the real trouble was the one that Lucinda herself had lodged in his head – that she was in love with Dennis Hasset. She had done everything possible to make the idea stick. She had left the swollen envelopes on her mantel for days at a time. She had told him she was in love. She had spent hours of her Sunday at her secretaire. The letters grew so fat that they required excessive amounts of red wax to seal them properly.

The idea had taken hold, and such was the stubborn set of Oscar's mind that it would not easily be knocked loose. So it did not matter that she took his arm. It was the prior action, the snatching away, that stayed in his mind. It was here the truth seemed contained, and in the second act, the taking of the arm, he saw only pity.

Oscar did not like Dennis Hasset. He had not met him, but he did not like him. Not that he imagined the man had bad qualities. Quite the reverse. He imagined him good, clever, handsome, generous, as a manly man who would be attractive to a lady. He could think of nothing to do to press his claim in competition, nothing except to display an excess of goodness, of selflessness, as if this behaviour, this loving self-denial, would provide him with the rewards that selfishness could not.

It was this that lay behind the dangerous wager he now planned to undertake in the dining room of the Oriental Hotel.

There were only two other tables occupied in the cavernous black-and-white-tiled dining room. A farming family occupied a table pushed gracelessly against a fluted pillar. A single gentleman in a frock coat sat beside a window; he read from a chapbook while he ate.

Lucinda was not hungry. She ordered as Oscar did. Her mind was occupied with the problem of how to undo delicately the clever knitting of her lies concerning Dennis Hasset. She could not concentrate on anything as ordinary as food.

She thought: This is what it is like when you love a man. She watched him as he buttered his bread and cut it into nine small squares. Should not this hitherto alien act now feel dear to her?

"Do you know what I envy you?" she said. "It is that you are not constrained."

She meant: The way you walk, walk in here, your clothes like that, and do not give a hoot what opinion the waiters or the diners may have of you.

He smiled, his piece of bread held between thumb and forefinger.

"You do not mind who ses you or who hears you or what they think of you. You know your own value, I think, and this puts you in a strong position."

"And you?"

"Oh," she rearranged a small pin in her hair. "I am too careful." He thought about this for a moment or two while he chewed his bread, and as he had the habit of chewing thirty-two times, this gave him the appearance of great sagacity whereas he was merely wondering, whilst he counted, whether he should disagree with her own assessment of herself and cite her Pak-Ah-Pu and wonder if this was, really Miss Leplastrier, the habit of a careful woman.

But he said instead: "It does no harm to be careful."

They sat in silence. He seemed not to be discomforted by it. She was. The silence made her so-called love for Dennis Hasset seem too heavy and insurmountable an obstruction. It made her feel dull. It made her too aware of the waiters watching them. She did not like the Oriental Hotel with its crawling adoration of wealth. She began to resent the dining room and think how she would never have come here on her own initiative.

"What a lovely place it is," he said, gazing around.

She thought: Do not be irritated and do not judge. He is not Them and he is not You. He is himself, uniquely so. When he admires, he admires as someone who cannot afford this luxury, not as someone who takes it as their right. Be like your papa who would want to know how the fluted pillars were made and what sort of fish that man is eating, and where it was caught and whether it is sweet to taste.

"Shall I tell you my idea?" he asked her.

"Oh, yes, do please."

"It involves glass."

"A subject close to my heart."

"We sometimes guard the things close to our hearts."

She did not look at him. She said: "You do not need to tread so carefully with me."

"Yes," he said unhappily. He saw no invitation to intimacy in this. His preconceptions made such an interpretation impossible and so he understood her back to front.

Lucinda heard his tone. She thought: I have been too bold. I am always in too much of a rush.

"And," she said, working against the current of a depression which now rose up and seemed destined to take possession of her mood, "of glass, tell me, what was your idea?"

The waiter brought their consommé, not in a soup plate, in a deep bowl. Did he always have consommé? She had always thought it food for invalids.

"You could manufacture convervatories."

"Is this your idea?" she asked, her heart now truly leaden"

"Oh, no," he grinned.

"I would *loathe*," she smiled, "to manufacture conservatories."

They both looked at each other, their soup spoons raised above their bowls. In that moment she felt ridiculously happy. She felt he loved her after all. She could not stop smiling. "So what," she said, laughing, "is *your* idea?"

He sipped his soup. He had a nice sipping mouth. She liked the way it came to meet the spoon. She desired the mouth. She breathed out very quietly.

"You must tell me," she said.

"Indeed."

But he did not tell her. Instead he bent over his soup bowl and went at it with speed. Once, half-way through, he looked up and raised an eyebrow. Lucinda felt that mixture of irritation and affection so well known to Wardley-Fish.

"There," he said, wiping his mouth with a fastidiousness perhaps induced by the quality of the napkin, "now I can speak without my soup going cold."

"You are a practical man," she laughed. She felt a little unreal—a thrumming sensation behind her eyes.

"In some respects, yes, I am," he said. "How does your correspondent enjoy his living in Boat Harbour?"

She shut her eyes against the question's slap. She was shocked to feel its cold hostility. And even though hostility was not intended, she was not mistaken in detecting it.

She straightened her cutlery. She said: "Well enough."

"And does he have a church built yet?"

She thought: Fool, fool, do you think I care for Hasset?

She said: "They hold service in a room above a cobbler's. They threw his predecessor into the river."

"Oh dear."

"Perhaps," she said, "they will do the same with him."

Oscar looked up sharply, but Lucinda was finishing her soup. When he at last saw her face it was like a room swept clean of meaning.

A waiter took away their bowls.

Oscar said: "Mr Hasset should have a church."

She did not wish to discuss Hasset. She said nothing.

Oscar did not like to think of Hasset either. It was the first time he had spoken the name out loud. When he said it he saw a hoe or a mattock, neither of them implements he had any fondness for. and yet he must say the name for he had an idea involving it, an idea that involved such a dreadful laceration of his own feelings that it is really hard to credit. And yet it was all born out of habits of mind produced by Christianity: that if you sacrificed yourself you would somehow attain the object of your desires. It was a knife of an idea, a cruel instrument of sacrifice, but also one of great beauty, silvery, curved, dancing with light. The odds were surely stacked against him, and had it been a horse rather than a women's heart he would never have bet on it, not even for a place.

"And what would his feelings be, do you imagine," he said, "if, when Mr Hasset awoke one morning, he looked out of his window and saw a church?"

Lucinda opened her mouth to reply.

"Made of glass," said my great-grandfather. (See! This is the sort of man I am!)

It was at this point that the waiter brought the flounder. They said yes or no to tartare sauce, watched vegetables being spooned on to their plates, accepted spinach, rejected squash, and hardly knew what they were doing. All their emotions were fused together in this glass vision in which they saw that which cannot be seen–wonder, joy, the transparent traceries of angels dancing. They were smiling at each other in such a way as to be almost indecent and the chef poked his head around the door to see what he had heard reported by the waiter.

The fish's flesh was white and moist. She lifted it carefully from its skeleton, and then replaced it.

"But what would one intend?" she asked, her voice very level and cautious. "What would one intend with such a gift?"

He hardly knew what he intended. That he be a perfect friend to her, that he show himself above jealousy, that she employ him, that he help her assemble this flawless thing, that he possess it in some way, that he be permitted to be a party to the manufacture of a prism, a prayer to God, that the prayer be made from glass and she would, therefore, because of it, love him. He could not see this glass church in his mind's eye without smiling. It had a force of its own. He looked at it as I once saw my own father, standing in a shiny-floored corridor in the Sydney Museum of Arts and Science, staring at a china cup inside a case.

"It would be a lovely thing," he said.

"Yes, I see that."

He would not look her in the eye.

"Such a gift," she said, "would not be personal?" she meant personal as having to do with her and Hasset. So preoccupied was she with this problem that she did not even imagine the possibility of ambiguity.

"Oh, no," he said, "not personal." He thought she meant personal as between him and her; he was embarrassed to have his scheme so clearly apprehended. "Oh, no, most definitely not."

"Do we understand each other?"

"Yes." He looked her straight in the eye and she saw, then, the strength in him. He was so light and frail, so soft in his manner, that it was always a surprise to see this, the steel armature of his soul. She thought about kissing and then she pushed the matter firmly from her mind. She would not frighten him away.

"Yes," she said, "it would be a lovely thing." She had never dared to imagine anything so commercially senseless. She would be laughed at by all the whiskered sages of church and business. She thought: He is mad; I am mad. But when she objected, what she said was not in tune with her spirit which skipped impatiently ahead like a reckless little stone sent dancing across a river.

"But it is hardly practical, Mr Hopkins."

"It is a dangerous word," he said, smiling, entranced by her upper lip.

"Which word is that?"

"Practical. It is the word they use in Sydney when they wish to do something damaging to the spirit. Excuse me, you must think me rude."

"No, no, although you must not hold *me* responsible for Sydney."

"I never struck the term so much at Home. But here, you know, it is a word dull men use when they wish to hide the poverty of their imagination. But would you say it was 'practical' to sing hymns, to give glory to God, to pray, to fast? And what is the practical purpose of a church? For if it is only to provide shelter for Christians – and my dear papa would take this view – then it is better to have your congregation gather in cobblers' rooms. But if your church, no matter how small, is also a celebration of God, then I would say I was the most practical man you have spoken to all year."

"And there would be nothing *personal* in its intention?"

"Do I appear a rogue?"

"No," she smiled, "you do not," and because he made her smile she did not think it a puzzling answer to her question. "Your fish . . ." She meant that his fish was cold, uneaten, although he still held a knife and fork as he had from the beginning.

"My fish does not matter. My fish is dead, but we are alive. We are gamblers in the noble sense. We believe all eternity awaits us. And am I wrong in supposing that you could pack a church in crates and transport it by cart? It is like the stairs at the library. It is what they call prefabricated. It comes in pieces. It has nuts and bolts and so on."

"Or by ship?"

"You could transport an entire cathedral and assemble it across the mountains. Can you imagine a glass cathedral?"

She could. She saw its steeples, domes, its flying buttresses, motes of dust, shafts of light. "Mr Hopkins, we are mad to think of it."

"Not mad, I pray not mad. but the sheer joy of contemplating it is hard to contain."

She thought: I cannot separate love from glass; I must be just a little mad.

He said: "I think it is this *feeling* that you are tempted to call madness, but there is a more accurate description . . . but I will embarrass you . . ."

"You need not protect me."

"I embarrass myself. However . . . it is ecstasy we are feeling."

She nodded, smiling, her eyes swimming. "But also mad."

"No, no, no." he banged his fist on the table. The cutlery jumped. The gentleman with the chapbook stood up and left. He said something, more than three words, less then twenty, but it does not matter what it was and did not matter at the time.

"And you," Lucinda said, "would it be amusing for you to assist me in this endeavour?"

"I am a practical man," said Oscar, giggling.

She paused, not knowing if he meant it ironically or literally. "But perhaps you might assist me none the less."

"With pleasure," said Oscar, who, now he had part of what he had coveted, was guilty and uneasy, as if he had stolen something from her.

"Can you imagine Hasset's face?"

The face she meant to conjure up was astonished, gawp-mouthed, sad to have been excluded from the manufacture of such a miracle. But the face Oscar saw was a man whose love has been rekindled. That was the risk inherent in the venture.

"But it is you, dear lady," Oscar said, "who must see his face. For it is you, surely, who must deliver it to him."

"Oh, no."

"But surely . . ." he protested, his heart already lightening.

"Oh, no, I cannot leave the works."

"You would not . . ."

"It is quite impossible," she said sternly. "They are only just recovering from my last absence."

"Then I shall," cried Oscar, "on your behalf."

Lucinda did not understand the source of his jubilation. She frowned, wondering if the balloon of their dream was not about to be pricked.

"It is approached by sea," she said. She remembered, although she had no wish to, his behaviour in the storm aboard the *Leviathan*.

"Then I shall go by land," he grinned, and clasped his hands contentedly and dropped "But, Mr Hopkins, I do not think you understand."

He thought: It is difficult, yes, and dangerous. It is a bet against the odds, but if I am the adventurer then the odds, surely, must be swinging in my favour.

His smiling face made Lucinda fear for him. He was so frail, and white. He brought his fingers together and flexed them underneath his pointed chin. He could not imagine – she knew he could not – what this countryside was like. He used soft words like brook and lane and copse. He could not imagine its saw-toothed savagery.

"I will be your messenger."

"Mr Hopkins, please, no."

"You think it outside my scope?" asked Oscar. He was not offended, and the reason he was not offended was that there was no room in his soul for such a thing. His body was awash with all those chemicals he had hitherto found only at the racetrack.

"Say it," he said. "You think it beyond my scope."

"There is no shame in that," she said, and reached across to pat his sleeve.

"There is no truth in it either," he said jubilantly, feeling a caress in the pat. "I wager you I can do it. You may nominate the date."

His face was very pale yet also very bright. The skin was taut, the eyes were glistening and fixed on hers. She thought it best to take her hand away.

"Mr Hopkins, I like you too much to encourage you to injury."

"But I *must*."

"Come, please, this is madness now.,"

"I must," he said quietly. "It would mean a great deal to me."

It was then she knew that he loved her.

"You are doing this for me?"

It was not a question he wished to be asked. He felt his own silence humming in his ears. He would not look at her.

"Yes," he said.

"Do you think I wish you dead?"

"I am too happy to wish for death," he said. "I have no intention of becoming dead. Mr Judd, for instance—and I know you do not care for him . . ."

"*Care* for him?"

"But I take him as an example. Mr Judd makes journeys like this all the time. I am prepared to wager you I can have the glass church in Boat Harbour by, say, Good Friday."

He had no basis for this date. He plucked it from the air. It felt appropriate. He had no idea how long the church might take to manufacture. This aspect of his wager, the financial part, was of no interest to him.

"And what can you bet?" she asked.

He saw her face change as she spoke. Her eyes became sleepy-lidded, and her lower lip pouted.

"Ten guineas."

"It is not enough."

"What is enough?"

She opened her mouth and closed it. It was so quiet in the dining room Oscar heard the noise of the skin of her lips as they separated.

He placed his hands palm down on the table. "What is enough?" he repeated.

"Your inheritance," said Lucinda quietly. She had not bet in two weeks but she had never, in all her life, made a bet like the one she was about to make with Oscar Hopkins.

"My father may live until he's one hundred. He is not a rich man, anyway."

"It makes no difference."

"And you would bet?"

"The same."

"The same amount?"

"The same. My inheritance."

"You already have it."

"Yes."

"Your works."

"Yes. Everything."

"You wager all that?"

"Yes."

"Then you are mad," said Oscar. "You are mad, not I. For heaven's sake." He scratched his head and looked around the dining room, surprised to find it empty. He felt himself the subject of her passion and yet (she loves Hasset) did not understand it.

"Five weeks," he said, "without even a game of penny poker, and now this."

Lucinda smiled at him. She felt light. She would have him taken care of. She would employ the best tracker, an explorer, a surveyor. They would carry him safely, and they would bring him back. He would win. She would lose. She would give him all the armour she had hitherto used to keep herself safe. She *was* mad. She was pleased to be mad. She loved him. She would be locked after.

"Sleep on it," she said. "there is no requirement that you accept."

"But I *must* go."

"Sleep on it."

"I am not sleepy," he said. He was awed by her. He loved her.

"Then come home with me," she smiled, "and we will play penny poker until you are."

She could marry this man, she knew, and still be captain of her soul.

83

Orphans

Our history is a history of orphans, or so my mother liked to say. She used the word in a sense both literal and sentimental. She did not mean it in the sense that it is true for the nation as a whole, but only as it applied to the three corners of the family history, to Oscar, to Lucinda, to Miriam Chadwick, who lost her mother when the *Grafton* was wrecked crossing the bar at Bellingen heads.

Miriam Chadwick would never forget how the black dye came and took her lovely peach silk dress. The dress fell like a rose, "Prince's Pride," into a copper of Indian ink. It sat there a second, its colour all the more precious and intense because of the glistening emony framing of the dye, sat there as if it might have the will to resist the insinuations of death itself, and then—like the withering of a flower, but much accelerated—the dress sucked in the black and first it ran in blurry lines along the fine pleats and then it spread, a rush of grey, a blanket of black, and Mrs Trevis took the laundry stick and poked it, shoved it down into the dye, like a stake to the heart, and stirred.

Miriam never forgave her employer that stab. Everything else, but not the way she drowned the dress. There was a slight grunt, and then a strong-armed stir. She saw it, in the year that followed, over and over again, saw the mole on the wrist, the black hairs on the pale arm.

Mrs Trevis had not expected a governess so young or one so beautiful. She was not sorry – you could not blame her if you knew her husband – to have her wrapped in mourning, and yet she did not mean the dyeing viciously. It was impatience and nothing more. She felt Miriam's upset about the dress and was inclined to judge her harshly for it, that she seemed as much grieved about finery as she was over the human being whose demise occasioned it.

And if you are inclined to think the same, that she makes too much of the loss of a dress and not sufficient of her dear mama – whose body was delivered by the tide on to the flat at Bellingen Heads, found by crows before people – then you must consider her position, which was not only to be marooned, an orphan in a hard and hostile environment amongst people whom she would, at Home, have regarded as her inferiors, not only to be quite impoverished, but to have been plunged back into mourning when she had, at twenty years of age, spent almost all her adult life in black.

First there had been her maternal grandmother, then the paternal grandfather. Her mother, a dressmaker, had been most particular as to the correct etiquette for mourning and had followed, as far as her intense curiosity could reveal it to her, the Royal Precedent. Thus there would be three months of deep mourning, an entombment so complete that neither hands nor face should be shown without their covering of black. The process back to life was taken in gradual stages, like a diver ascending from the deep, until, at six months, one could eat in a public place, in nine months be seen at the theatre, and at the end of a year one might cast off one's black and, with luck, be asked to dance the Grenadier Waltz.

She was eighteen, and still in mourning for her paternal grandfather when her father, also in mourning himself, went down with pneumonia. It was winter. She sat in the coal-sleepy room, and even while she nursed him, while she sat beside his bedside, lifted his heavy body to a sitting position so he might more easily breathe, and saw his face all blotched, lost, suddenly old, his eyes shut, his lips dry and swollen so they were the size of the black boy on the Church Missionary Society money box, even while she waited and wept and heard him gurgle and choke himself to death, she felt another grief, another despair, an anger, selfish perhaps but intensely felt none the less—that she would end up an old maid because she must now spend another year in mourning.

But in the end it had not been a year, for her mother—although strict on matters of etiquette—was also a practical woman. She did not wish to waste precious space in their trunk with clothes they would never use once they were in New South Wales.

The mother was a strong-willed woman. The emigration had been her idea. She had announced it without consultation. It was she who found the daughter a position as a governess at Boat Harbour. In her ignorance she had imagined a town like Bournemouth. It would be a healthy place, she said, and gay. She made their new clothes, scandalously bright, it seemed to her daughter, to suit this new location. She chose taffeta and "Peking" silks. They had boarded the *Sounion* in a style that elicited much admiration (from strangers—the family had been farewelled in Hammersmith). They wore, mother and daughter, dresses of the palest and prettiest colours, the daughter in peach, the mother in a moiré grey, but both of them in bright petticoats and Miriam's crinoline cage producing an effect like a trumpet flower you might imagine growing in exotic latitudes: once on board, of course, this finery was packed away, for they could afford no better than steerage, and it was in that very trunk, the same big wooden trunk, all bound around with black iron bands, that the dress had travelled in the little brig from Sydney, transferred to the whaler outside Boat Harbour, and which had floated to the shore when all those souls had drowned.

This was on Christmas Day in 1858. Miriam had been the only one of thirty passengers saved from drowning. Her left arm was broken, and never quite set right, but she was alive.

Her whole trunk was delivered to the Trevis house, for it was there she was to be employed as a governess. And on her first morning Mrs Trevis filled her copper with black dye and put her lovely new clothes into the copper, one by one. Miriam felt sick in her heart, as sick about this blackness as anything else. She would never forget that moment. The peach dress, a fallen bloom in a copper of ink.

When the clothes were dyed and dried and ironed, she put them on. The black got into her skin. It was the humidity. There was nothing to be done about it any more than there was to be done about the sandflies, the mosquitoes, the tropical rains that flooded the river and took the stock floating away. She taught the children as best she could. There were few books to help her.

There was dancing, of course, quite a lot of it, too. But it would not be possible for her to go. She wrote long letters to Mrs Carson, who ran the governess agency in London. They pretended to take a cheerful or optimistic line while exactly communicating her despair. She begged to be sent to a place where learning might be appreciated. She complained she was asked to set the fire, to sweep the house, to "muck in." She put this term in sarcastic inverted commas. Nowhere did she make a comment on the Trevises' class or education and yet, somehow, it was made clear that they were below her.

Miriam could not have known it, but all of Mrs Carson's life was dotted with letters like this. They irritated her, and although she would permit two or three of them, the fourth was likely to attract a strong rebuke.

In January 1862, a year of floods so great they would not be repeated until 1955 (floods George White and his cohorts on the council like to forget when they issue development permits) Miriam Mason was married to Johnny Chadwick by Dennis Hasset's predecessor, the one who was thrown into the Bellinger River. There is no parish register showing this marriage, but there is a photograph of Johnny Chadwick in the local museum. He is standing in front of a log hut which the Historical Society has decided was his schoolroom. In fact it was his house. He is surrounded by his pupils, and you will read, on the little typewritten note George White had Sellotaped on to the bottom of the photograph that he died as a result of snakebite in 1863. It does not say that the snake was enraged by being thrown around the school ground by the pupils. They had long sticks which they used to flick it through the air towards each other. Johnny Chadwick, it seems, had tried to kill the snake.

In any case, Miriam had to dye her clothes again and she went back to work for Mrs Trevis who, of course, did not remind her that she, Mrs Trevis, had cautioned her against ripping up her old mourning clothes for dusters.

But with, oh, what zest, she had, in her optimism, torn up her black and did not care it was a waste. And she had got herself again her lovely fabrics, silks and taffetas sent up from Sydney, and made the long dresses which were cool and light, and she began to see the beauty of the place, the long slow sweep of the river, its wide green banks, the green ever widening, pressing in against the khaki of the bush, and Johnny Chadwick was very quiet, but handsome and gentle, and they would sit in front of their hut and he would read her Walter Scott by the light of a lantern while white ants hatched, swarmed, and died and she had been foolish enough not to see this as a poignant symbol of mortality.

She wrote again to Mrs Carson. Mrs Carson replied with what can only be described as a stiff note.

Thus when Dennis Hasset arrived in Boat harbour she observed him from her cage of deep mourning. She stood high on the veranda at the Trevis house at Fernmount. From the veranda you could see the river as it swept around the promontory below. Into this view came the Reverend Dennis Hasset, correctly dressed, a book in his lap, sitting on a barge surrounded by his personal effects.

And if I say that she began—there and then, without having said a word to him, or heard one from him either—to lay plans for him, it would be unfair to judge her harsh and scheming. It is important to look instead at her options.

The first was to continue as a governess, a poor governess for the Trevis family who, having no education themselves and no great respect for it, were inclined to view a governess as a labourer and, should she be found with anything as useless as a book, would be requested to do something more practical around the place. Thus she was not only depressed and unstimulated, but she was also continually weary.

The second possibility was marriage. Having had experience of the two states she was much disposed towards the latter. She therefore took the eyeglass from Mr Trevis's bedside and while her pupils pulled each other's hair, she spied the clergyman on the barge. This happened two weeks before Oscar played his famous game of cards at Randwick vicarage.

84

The Weeks before Christmas

The bet had a life. They contained it. It was a bee in a box, an itch in a place that could not be scratched; it was this—not their now continual games of penny poker, crib, solo, those shifting diversions which could not satisfy any of their locked-up passions but left the house scattered with whole (one penny) or half (ha'penny) matches–it was this bee in the box, the Big Bet, the glass bet, which gave the days their excruciating tension, their lovely current, the nights their lightness, expectation. They did not kiss or hold hands. The bet gave them a future which they stretched towards.

There was a drought all through the state of New South Wales, but the first week of December was balmy with teasing nor'easterlies lifting and falling like clean muslin pudding cloths on a clothes line. The nights were clear and bright-starred. Lucinda and Oscar took tea at the zinc table above the black water. The frangipani was at last sprouting leaves from its nubbly fingers. The jacaranda was in blossom. They watched the flying foxes wheel above them, like shadows of thoughts, things so indistinct they would not exist without two witnesses.

They were joined together in their conspiracy. They ached–like lovers do–to share their secret, but they had no one to share it with. Lucinda could not tell Hasset any part of it. She could not bear to have a sensible objection. She felt guilty, just the same, about keeping the secret from him. Soon he would hear she shared a house with a defrocked priest and that she accompanied the same peculiar gentleman everywhere, even as far as the New Steyne Hotel in Manly where she had clumsily danced for the first time in her life. Lucinda wrote Dennis Hasset long, dull, detailed letters as if this steady drone would block out the secret whispers of her heart. These letters, of course, made Oscar anxious and jealous. He had no one to share his agony with except Wardley-Fish and Wardley-Fish was the subject of a scandal of his own and was incommunicado, passing through the Suez Canal, sunburnt, drunk, telling outrageous stories until he went too far and became IT, the passenger the others try to avoid sitting next to on the promenade.

Oscar was like a man in a fairy story who is granted his wishes. He was employed by Prince Rupert's Glassworks. He was a party to the manufacture of glass. He walked with Lucinda into the works on a Monday morning and saw the glass-rolling machine from Chance Brothers turn the great red rubbery sheets of glass, like pastry, off its shiny metal rollers. Lucinda was at his side, seized by fury and jubilation in equal parts. She thought: I must not come here with him again; all my passion is as cold as ice. She meant, of course, that he was accepted so easily where she could not be, that he walked in a way that he would be probably shocked to learn appeared proprietorial.

Oscar was not insensitive to Lucinda's feelings. And when she sought to involve Mr d'Abbs in the project he did little more than murmur around the edges of his doubt. It was then that he saw what fierce loyalty Lucinda had towards those she thought her allies. And it did not matter that Mr d'Abbs had proved himself incompetent in caring for the works or in other vital matters, she would consult him about the design of the glass church.

"He is artistic," she said, "as, of course, you know."

Oscar thought he detected a little belligerence in this sentence, and so did not remind her of the story she had told him not two nights before, of how Mr d'Abbs recommended Monsieur Huille, the drawing tutor whose cows had looked like pigs.

This was how Oscar came to return to Mr d'Abbs's office not two weeks after he had left his employ. He saw then, as he would see many more times before the glass church was loaded into its wooden crates, that it was an idea that had a strong attraction. There was hardly a soul who would not want to clasp it to their bosom, and even if they began, as Mr d'Abbs did, by making a mess with their cigar or their snuff, telling you sternly what an impractical idea it was, they always ended up in the same place, the place Mr d'Abbs came to on this sweltering December day, with a slightly silly smile on their face, a "by the deuce" on their lips, and, in Mr d'Abbs's case anyway, a plea (an assumption, Oscar thought) that he be permitted to draw up the plans for it himself.

"I could make the time available," said Mr d'Abbs. He opened his drawer and took out a single sheet of best white bond. He placed this sheet of paper in the middle of his desk. He opened another drawer and took out his French pen and then, on the paper, he made two or three fast strokes. He looked at those strokes appraisingly, his head on one side, and then looked up as if to say, "Not bad, not bad at all." Then, having satisfied himself as to his aptitude, he folded the paper into three, slid it into the breast pocket of his unseasonably hairy suit, and placed the pen carefully back inside the drawer.

Oscar bit his lip to hide his smile. He glanced sideways and saw Lucinda, sitting upright in her uncomfortable chair, looking as solemn as she did at morning prayer. She had decided to trust Mr d'Abbs a long time ago and did not seem likely to change her mind. This observation produced a razor-sharp corollary: her heart would remain similarly loyal to Hasset. So thought Oscar, squirming in his chair. He made a grotesque face, a caricature of agony. No one saw him. Lucinda was looking at Mr d'Abbs. Mr d'Abbs was now engaged with another piece of paper. This was a yellow sheet with green lines, of the type on which he was accustomed to make his notes (he called them "briefs"). He took out the pen again, unscrewed it, examined the nib against the glaring window light, pursed his lips so that his thin moustache buckled and let the tip of his pink tongue—like a tiny creature in a hairy shell—come out to sense the air.

"Now," he said to Lucinda, having ignored his ex-clerk from the beginning. "Now, what would be your intended congregation? That is the place to start with a church. It is one of the great mistakes made with churches. Too large and you have everyone feeling that the service is a failure. Too small and there is never enough in the plate to feed the vicar's family and then you are forever wasting your time with fêtes and benefits and all sorts of amateur theatricals, which are, in country towns, believe me, a chore to sit through. So this is the place to start, but it is a difficult thing to assess. It is more dependent on the quality of the sermon than the size of the parish."

"He speaks very well," Lucinda said, "and sometimes a little contentiously."

"Four hundred," said Mr d'Abbs, and wrote it down.

"It is only a little town," said Oscar whose own sermons had always been such an agony to him.

"One hundred, then," said Mr d'Abbs.

No one argued with him.

"And as to Doric and Corinthian, do you have a preference?"

"But, Mr d'Abbs," said Lucinda, leaning forward in her chair, "there is no Doric and Corinthian. It is to be constructed from glass and cast-iron rods, as I told you. We will not require this sort of support. The principle is the same, the same exactly as a glasshouse."

"Yes, yes, of course." Mr d'Abbs screwed the cap on his handsome tortoise shell pen and laid it down beside his sheet of paper. "It's still a thing, ma'am, that you must decide. You look at it from the outside, as an amateur. Quite naturally, quite understandably, you do not imagine that it matters. It does not *need* to matter to you." (Oscar was offended on Lucinda's behalf. He found the tone quite patronizing.) "But it must matter to me. It must matter a great deal. It is all a question of aesthetic laws. You may not *see* them, but they are there, just as the Ten Commandments are themselves not visible in this room."

"I'm afraid," Oscar said, "that I am quite bamboozled."

Mr d'Abbs looked at him with great displeasure. It was an embarrassment to have an ex-clerk in this position. He was about to ignore the question when he saw that Miss Leplastrier expected him to answer it.

"It is a question of integrity," he said.

"In which way?" she asked.

"In which way, what?"

"In which way can it affect the integrity?"

Mr d'Abbs took out his watch and looked at it. Then he uncapped his pen and drew a little diagram on his yellow paper. He was not an architect. Of course he wasn't. He had never claimed to be. But he had drawn things up. It was in his line. One begins with some conveyancing, and then a little financing is necessary, and a client, owning the land, then needs a building. This would be a dandy little church. A lovely thing. He would have an artist do perspectives, of course. He had never mastered the perspective, but it had not prevented him from designing the new portico for the Sydney Club, but that, by Jove, that was Corinthian, and wasn't it admired. Bishop Dancer had paid him a great compliment—"d'Wren" he had called him, phonetically a difficult joke to understand, and a little high-flown, but he had been flattered. There was no reason why this little church should not have a dome. By golly!

"It affects the aesthetics," said Mr d'Abbs. "I would recommend the Corinthian, and if you doubt my advice—and why shouldn't you?—I am only your accountant—go up to Castlereagh Street to the new Sydney Club and tell me what you think."

Oscar looked at Lucinda. She did not seem troubled that a pagan style should be used to celebrate Christ's death and resurrection. She seemed to have accepted Mr d'Abbs's proposition. She said: "The whole will be framed around glass sheets three feet long and eighteen inches in breadth. The main columns should be five inches in diameter, no more. Each individual column would weigh about three hundredweight, or so I am informed."

Mr d'Abbs smiled and nodded, but—unlike Mr Flood, the foundryman who was always making calculations with his callipers and adding and subtracting figures in his grimy notebook—he wrote nothing down.

Indeed he screwed his cap back on his pen.

Lucinda and Oscar sat side by side, like passengers in that contentious vehicle—the Pitt Street tram. They faced Mr d'Abbs who picked up the bell on his desk and swung it. He put it down again and smiled at them for all the time it took Mr Jeffris to answer his employer's call.

"Mr Jeffris," said Mr d'Abbs, when the head clerk had, at last, arrived. "You are, are you not, a licensed surveyor?" He said this just as he had, on other occasions, wished an employee to assure him that he was (or not) a Greek scholar, a published poet, a concert pianist, the cousin of a duke.

"I am," said Mr Jeffris. He stood in the formal at-ease position and nothing in his demeanour gave any clue to what he felt about Mr Smudge's elevation. He did not look at him. He stood beside him, facing his employer.

"And have you surveyed the road to Boat Harbour?"

Mr Jeffris said nothing. He sighed, a rather bad-tempered sigh, and Mr d'Abbs, as if this sigh was the most sagacious answer imaginable, smiled proudly at Lucinda. Then, lifting a finger, as though he were the conductor of an orchestra calling for a certain grace-note from a flute: "Is there a road to Boat Harbour?"

"No, there ain't," said Mr Jeffris, and Oscar, who had no fondness for Mr Jeffris, still felt sorry that he had made this slip. He was a man who had worked hard to eliminate his ain'ts.

"But surely," coaxed Mr d'Abbs, "one could muddle one's way through?"

Mr Jeffris did not answer.

"You surveyed the road up into New England, is that no so?"

"I was employed thereon," said Mr Jeffris who was beside himself with rage at being required to act this part for the benefit of Mr Smudge. "I was under the direction of a Mr Cruikshank."

"But this road will not do?"

"It is a fool's way to travel," said Mr Jeffris, no longer able totally to disguise his feelings. "And the question is hypocritical because no one would choose to do it. You do not approach Boat Harbour by road but by the sea. There is a tricky bar, as everybody knows, but anyone would prefer the bar to the other."

"And what would you say to Mr Hopkins here, if he were to tell you his intention to go by land?"

"Beg yours?" said Mr Jeffris who was genuinely perplexed.

"Mr Hopkins intends to travel to Boat harbour by land."

"No," said Mr Jeffris, too surprised to be bad-tempered any longer. He turned to look at Oscar who had the feeling that he was being seen by Mr Jeffris for the first time. "Is this so, Mr Hopkins?"

"I am afraid it is."

"And why not water?" said Mr Jeffris. His tone had changed. It was gentler. You could see the echo of it in his eyes.

"And why not water?" he repeated.

"I have my own reasons."

Mr Jeffris normal mood was that of a man whose temper was a large rock balanced precariously on a rusty nail. His clerks were inclined to walk around him on tiptoe. But now, as he regarded Oscar, he somehow made himself go soft and calm. The rock lowered itself on to the sand.

"These reasons," he said gently, "would all be categorized under the label 'exploration'?"

"Oh, no," said Oscar, and giggled.

Mr Jeffris's forehead made a complicated frown.

"He refuses the steamer," said Mr d'Abbs.

Mr Jeffris did not even look at Mr d'Abbs. "And you must go?" he asked Oscar softly, so softly that Lucinda could not believe this was the same man she had thought a "dangerous dog" when he had come clicking across the clerk's office in his metal-tipped shoes.

"For your own reasons," suggested Mr Jeffris, "you are compelled to make this journey?"

Oscar smiled at Mr Jeffris. He did not smile because he was happy. He smiled because Mr Jeffris's manner had made him frightened of what he had taken on himself. He smiled because he wished to lighten the grave solicitousness of Mr Jeffris's expression. But Mr Jeffris would not comply. He looked at Oscar sadly, up and down, as if he were a beast at Homebush saleyards who must be called to shoulder a burden in excess of its strength.

"I would not be you," said Mr Jeffris, "for anything."

Oscar felt his windpipe knotting. He stroked his long neck and turned his "smile" to Mr d'Abbs.

Mr d'Abbs was pleased. He was pleased with the resources of his office. He was pleased to offer these services to his clients and give them free, gratis.

"Thank you, Jeffris," he said. "Back to the troops now."

Lucinda thought how arrogant and dismissive this was, but it was not arrogance, only the impersonation of arrogance, something Mr Jeffris permitted him in public.

Mr d'Abbs undid his pen and drew—no one could see what he rendered—a lovely little barque with a seagull overhead.

"And so," he said.

He added some waves.

"And so," he screwed back the pen top, "you will obviously be transporting your prefabricaton on the sea."

"Perhaps we should discuss it further," Lucinda said to Oscar.

"Good lady," said Mr d'Abbs, "what is there to discuss?"

Oscar stood. He saw the childish drawings on Mr d'Abbs's pad. His face was triangular, chalky—bone, skin, locked-up eyes. Lucinda's heart was filled with pity. Oscar sat down again. He could not have been more terrified if he had sat, once again, inside a cage on Southampton Pier.

85

A Prayer

It was half past six in the evening and very hot. A feeble light entered the staricase from a high window, but not sufficient to show the decrepit state of the wallpaper or the condition of the runner. Mr Jeffris walked up the stairs with his gloved hands clasped together as if he might inadvertently touch something he would find repulsive. When he reached the first landing he plunged off into a dark passage, walking briskly where a stranger to these lodgings would have been compelled to pause and strike a match or feel the way along the wall. He rose two steps, turned to the left, and stopped at a doorway which was not only locked but padlocked.

He did not fuss with his keys. The door lock made a dull "thuck," the padlock a sharp brass "snick." The knob rattled. Mr Jeffris was home.

It was a small room with a window looking out at other windows and down into a small cobbled yard where three large black cats, the pets of the lodging-house cook, lay on top of a pile of lumber and grey rags.

The room was hot. Mr Jeffris threw open the window, pulled a face at what he smelt, and half-closed it again. Two or three blow-flies entered the room and began, once they were there, to buzz and crash heavily against the glass. Mr Jeffris ignored them.

He removed his frock coat. It had wide shoulders and a narrow waist, and although the style was almost thirty years out of date, the condition of the nap was such that one could only conclude that it had been recently tailored. Mr Jeffris placed this coat on a wooden hanger, brushed it, and hung it on the long rail he had himself suspended from the picture rail and then—it was a complicated system involving a triangulation of forces—held out from the wall by a length of twine which dissected the air above his bed and was secured to a picture rail above its head.

When Mr Jeffris sat on his bed (which he now did as he removed his boots) his knees almost touched the heavy bookcases which he had constructed himself in the same neat and handy style with which he had made all the other improvements in the room. Everything was at once temporary and sturdy. It would serve for a decade. It could be packed in a moment. It was, in short, a "camp."

At the foot of the bed there was a clear area marked by a sun-faded rug. Two dumb-bells, placed to one side of this rug, announced the purpose of this extravagance of space in so small and cramped a room.

As he sat on the side of his bed, his hands placed flat on his knees, he exhibited such a perfect stillness that he might have been at prayer.

In fact, he was beside himself. He sat still as you might sit still on the edge of an abyss, or at the top of a pole, or on a tightrope strung between your lodgings and the country of your dreams.

There was a silver-backed mirror and a comb in a carved chest on his bookshelf. He could reach them without moving from his seat. And when he leaned across and removed them it was easy to see that the chest was placed in this position for this reason. And when he combed his moustache, which he did now, slowly, very slowly, the action had the quality of a prayer or a meditation practised daily. He had a long lip and the hair was thick and luxurious. When he had had enough of combing he reached for the barber's scissors. he held up the silver-backed mirror and then snipped a little here and there. Only the movement of his broad chest betrayed his agitation.

All of his adult life had been spent in preparation for the day when he should survey unmapped country, have a journal, publish a map. Three times he had been employed on journeys of exploration and three times he had resigned before the party had its animals purchased. He had standards, those of his hero, Major Mitchell, and he had no intention of lurching around the country with incompetents, idiots blindly putting one foot after the next and – no matter what names they named or maps they drew – having no idea, in a proper trigonometrical sense, where on earth they were. Hume, Hovell, Burke, Eyre had all drawn their maps badly. They were useless for both settlement and exploration, but their authors were heroes and Mr Jeffris was a clerk in an office in Sydney.

Mr Jeffris, against hope, against all good sense, had prepared himself as Major Thomas Mitchell would have him do. He had copied from Mitchell's *Memoirs* his self-depreciating advice to those who would follow him. Mr Jeffris had him. Mr Jeffris had executed the Major's prose in his admirable copperplate; he had made a frame for it; he had hung it above his bed.

> A little mathematical knowledge will strengthen your style, and give it perspicuity. Study the writings of great men. I would place Caesar's *Gallic Wars* at the top of any list, but would advise you not neglect Pliny, Plutarch, Sallus and Seneca. Study these writings both for the subject and the manner in which they are treated. Arrangement is a material point in voyage writing as well as in history: I feel gread diffidence here. Sufficient matter I can always furnish, and fear not to prevent anything unseamanlike from entering into the composition: but to round a period well, and arrange sentences so as to place what is meant in the most perspicacious view, is too much for me. Seamanship and authorship make too great an angle with one another.

He would have copied more had the sheet of paper he had begun with been sufficient, for there was something of the actor in Mr Jeffris, and when he wrote the words of his hero on this piece of paper he felt himself become their author whose own frock coat (in an engraving dated 1835) bore a striking similarity to the one that Mr Jeffris had had made in 1864.

Following the advice of Major Mitchell had led Mr Jeffris into areas a coster's son might not normally expect to enter. He had taught himself Latin so he might read what he must know. He had studied water-colour technique in order that he might record the landscapes of the New World. He had spent five years of his life as a brown-nose, arse-licking apprentice, assistant, dogsbody to the incompetent, asthmatic Mr Cruikshank in order that he might master that science which Mitchell placed above all others: surveying. He had come to Sydney that he might study under Mr Martin (the oil painter) and in so doing he had ended up employed by Mr Martin's friend, Mr d'Abbs.

Mr Jeffris could not tolerate incompetence. He could quote scripture to support his view. He could not differentiate it from sloth. It was an offence to God who made us in His image. And yet he found it everywhere. It was as common as dust. There was not a man he had served who had been free from Mr Jeffris's censure.

Mr d'Abbs was incompetent. It was a wonder he had any business at all, and would not have had if he had not set up his kitchen and his cellar in the service of the fuddled complacent friendship of his dinner table. It was all social. That was obvious. He sat down with them at dinner. They drank too much wine and put their arms around each other. They imagined they discussed Philosophy and Great Issues when they could barely pronounce the names of the men they misquoted. He was "good old Jimmy d'Abbs," but he was a tosspot and incompetent. He could not add up. He could not bother to add up, and yet such was the condition of life that Mr Jeffris was called upon to serve him. It made Mr Jeffris angry, angry every minute he was in the office. He spent his days leashed in, trussed up; he could hardly bear to be there, except he must. But one day he would go. One day he would not be there to make sure the work was done correctly, and then all the second-rate firms who had grown to trust the idiot would find themselves in fearful trouble. d'Abbs would never have a head clerk as good, not because there were not others to be had, but because he would not know how to recognize one.

Jeffris had dreams about d'Abbs. He dreamed he slapped him and stabbed him in his sparrow's chest.

But now, like an ass which God has given frankincense to carry, d'Abbs had brought him this gift—an incompetent cleak who had it in his head he would go to Boat Harbour, by land, across unmapped territory. He was a frail little thing, a skippy girl with milk-white skin and a weakness for poker.

With a patron, wrapped and sealed, in tandem.

Mr Jeffris sat very, very still. He must be careful. He must approach the matter as if it were a timid animal, a little birdie to be trapped—no, not trapped, he was not strong enough to think himself a predator—but to be coaxed, persuaded, wooed.

Mr Jeffris stood and then kneeled. There was barely room for him to squash in between the bookcase and the bed. It was a week before Christmas. He asked God that he might be granted this Great Journey.

86

Christmas Day

That Lucinda should greet Mr Jeffris so enthusiastically when he arrived uninvited at her back door late on Christmas night, his arms full of presents, a bottle of warm colonial hock under his arm, should shake his square short-fingered hand and bring him into the parlour and thus ignore all her intuitions about the man she had privately likened to both a spider and a vicious dog, was merely one more product of the devastating sermon the Reverend Mr Dight had preached that morning, Christmas Day.

The reverend gentleman had not planned this controversial sermon, although Mr Chalmers, the warden of the vestry, was always at him with his "Do not be afraid to make a ruckus." But Mr Chalmers was in trade (three butchers' shops with prices writ in whitewash on their window panes) and was too often inclined, the Reverend Mr Dight thought, to regard the building of a Christian congregation as being no different from establishing good will in the High Street.

Mr Dight knew his warden to be delighted with his sermon for, in the midst of his passionate address, he had looked down into his congregation and seen, in the midst of two hundred grave and attentive faces, Mr Chalmers's round and polished countenance wreathed in smiles. Mr Chalmers imagined that his nagging for a ruckus had at last produced results, but the Reverend Mr Dight had not planned the sermon. It is possible that he had it in his mind, that he carried it, like black flies on a sweat-damp back, without knowing it was there. But it was only when he stood in his pulpit—in that moment before he would begin to fiddle with his bookmarks—that he saw that *They* (the fornicators, gamblers) had dared to show their impudent faces on this holiest of days, and then the black flies rose in a fury, and he took for this text, not the Good News he had marked, but rather Matthew 5: 27–30. "Ye have heard it said by them of old time, thou shalt not commit adultery."

He then had the pleasure of seeing his impromptu sermon take effect as his most carefully prepared addresses never had. There was a ripple, a shiver that moved across the congregation like wind across the face of a pond. He froze them. He had them so quiet they hardly dared unfold their arms or cross their legs the other way. They formed a human lock around the two fornicators who sat rigid in their pew, their red necks advertising guilt.

On Christmas Day the sky was a rich cobalt blue. The grass at Whitfield's Farm (being understocked) was long and golden and crackling underfoot.

The day had seemed perfect to Lucinda in every detail. She and Oscar had set a table in the garden before they left for church. The jacaranda had lost its flowers and was now a feathery umbrella of cool green. A soft nor-easter came off the harbour. They placed their presents on the parlour hearth and walked through the embarrassing plenty of Whitfield's Farm (all of New South Wales was in the grip of drought, and all the feed between Sydney and Bathhurst was eaten down to the roots) through all the golden grass to church. Oscar said the colours felt wrong for Christmas. Lucinda said the colours in Bethlehem must surely have been like this: this dazzling blue sky, this straw-gold earth, and not the cold and bracken-brown of pagan Britain.

Oscar smiled at her, his eyes glistening.

She thought: He *does* love me. And if his behaviour is always proper, then it is perverse of me to be irritated with him because of it. I could not respect him if he were to act improperly, to place, like Mr d'Abbs or Mr Paxton, his hand upon my knee.

She accepted the glistening fluid that threatened to spill over his lower lids as the exact equivalent of a kiss and she was moved, and excited, and bowed her head and fixed her bonnet although she had not planned to do so until they were amongst the new houses of Balmain.

And then there was the sermon.

She felt herself slapped and spat on and all that landscape which she had smugly celebrated not half an hour before – she had gone on and on, naming trees and birds for her companion – now seemed a hateful place – dry, harsh, a tinder-box with black snakes coiled amongst its deadly grasses.

The urge to cry was so strong she must battle with her body to subdue it. She bit her lip and breathed through her mouth. She ran the gauntlet of the crowded churchyard with her face blazing red. She thought: They *hate* me, and it is not only the men.

Oscar said: "they do not even *know* us," but this voice was high and nervous. This tone was no help. She drew away from him.

"I cannot speak," she managed. She took off her bonnet and, in her agitation, wrapped it around her prayer book while they were still in sight of the church.

"It was a most unchristian sermon," said Oscar to whom had come, in the midst of all this turbulence and upset, the following very simple thought: It is my *duty* to save her name; there is no question but that I must propose marriage to her. This thought was both respectable and gentlemanly, but because it so neatly coincided with his own desires, he could not believe it uncorrupted. "*Most* unchristian," he repeated.

"Oh, do not be so *hurt*," she snapped.

"It is on your behalf I hurt."

"I thank you, but on my behalf it would be best if we did not discuss the matter."

Lucinda did not like herself like this. She knew herself wrong and also in the wrong. She was poisoned by that hateful sermon, by its crudeness, its intolerance, its certainty of its own whisky-and-tobacco-smelling strength. And now she snapped and slapped at the one soul whose goodness and kindness she would not question. She was acting like a spoiled child, like her mother had acted on the days when her daughter hated her, and although she knew all this, she could not stop herself. She was tearing Christmas Day to shreds.

She had put such store in this day, and not merely in the care with which she chose a turkey and a pair of pale blue poplin shirts for her dear friend. In her imagination she had seen all the unspoken things between them come, at last, to be spoken of directly. She had imagined the shirts laid across the faded damask of the parlour armchair, seen crumpled paper and golden ribbon discarded on the blood-red Turkish rug. And other things, like kissing, but not quite so sharp and clear, with furry unfocused edges like a water-colour.

But now she could not bear the way she sounded. She was not a person anyone could love. She drew herself into herself, and when they let themselves into the cottage she could not even look at the table she had set with so many feverish thoughts. She told herself: It does not matter what bigots think of me.

But it did matter. She could not bear to be so hated.

She took down the chipped brown-glaze tea-pot. She put the kettle on the stove and riddled the grate and then, feeling her tears well up inside her, she hurried upstairs to her room.

Oscar saw the tumescent top lip and understood her intention. She was going to her room to cry.

But he was to propose to her.

If he delayed the matter further all courage would depart him. And this is why he went chasing after her, up the clattery uncarpeted stairs, two strides at at time. He caught her on the landing and he dare not ask her to accompany him downstairs to some prettier place—he saw she would almost certainly refuse this for, not understanding his intention, she had a cornered, wild-eyed look. So it was here, in the gloomiest corner of the cottage, the sticky place were Prucilla Twopenny had once spilled a pot of honey from her mistress's breakfast tray, that Oscar put his proposal to Lucinda Leplastrier.

Some peeling wallpaper tickled against Lucinda's neck. She hit at it, imagining a spider. Oscar put his hand in his pocket and jiggled his pennies and threepences together. He wished to be principled. He did not wish to take advantage of a situation where a Christian and gentlemanly act would so benefit his personal desires. He therefore excluded from his breathless speech everything good and noble in his heart. He jiggled his change. He tapped his foot. He offered to marry her to "save your reputation in Balmain."

"Oh, no," she said, "you are too kind to me."

And thus fled to her room. There she wept, bitterly, an ugly sound punctuated by great gulps. She could not stop herself. She could hear his footsteps in the passage outside. He walked up and down, up and down.

"Come in," she prayed. "Oh, dearest, do come it."

But he did not come in. He would not come in. This was the man she had practically contracted to give away her fortune to. He offered to marry her as a favour and then he would not even come into her room.

Later, she could smell him make himself a sweet pancake for his lunch. She thought this a childish thing to eat, and selfish, too. If he were a gentleman he would now come to her room and save her from the prison her foolishness had made for her. He did not come. She heard him pacing in his room.

It was into this environment that Mr Jeffris came with his hock bottle and his meticulously wrapped little gifts. He brought a packet of Eleme raisins for Lucinda and a brass compass for Oscar. And although he was not exactly a jolly man, and was, indeed, for the most part angry and when not angry rather doleful, he was capable of charm when there was sufficient reason for it. He was compact and good-looking with a great deal of lustrous black hair and very white even teeth beneath his big moustache and when he engaged you in conversation he had the trick of holding your eyes—no matter where his obsessive mind was really dwelling—as if what you had to say was of great importance to him. He was, as Mr d'Abbs would later claim, an actor, although not such a good one that he would, in normal circumstances, have deceived Lucinda.

But the circumstances were not normal and it was Mr Jeffris who rescued them from the embarrassment and estrangement of their ruined Christmas Day. His hock was warm and more than a little acid, but they drank it thirstily and ate his raisins and shared their shortbread and laughed gratefully at his jokes and talked about the journey to Boat Harbour in such a shy and tentative way that Mr Jeffris, not understanding the personal aspect of the matter, began to think that his own speech had "put them off."

"You should not pay much heed to my little speech in Sussex Street," he said. He smiled and tugged at his moustache and seemed to be debating as to whether he would continue to take them into his confidence. "I will tell you," he said. "My situation is that I am employed, eh? For the present at any rate. And while I am employed it is a case of he-who-pays-the-fiddler-calls-the-tune, isn't that so, Miss Leplastrier?"

"Mr d'Abbs required you to answer in this way?" Lucinda asked.

Mr Jeffris could see he did not have her full attention. He could not know that her mind was much occupied with the question of the lamp and whether she had turned it down low enough to hide the evidence of her red-rimmed eyes. Mr Jeffris thought the expedition in grave danger of being stillborn.

"He did not specifically tell me to answer as I did, Miss Leplastrier, but I understand my employer well enough. You must have noted how happy the little chap was with the answer I gave." (He said "little chap" on purpose. It was calculated to communicate the complications of their relationship.) "It has been on my conscience ever since. I mean, that I deceived you. I thought I might write you a note, and then there was too much delay involved in such a plan. I never like delay. There is so much of it that can be avoided. It is true in business and in journeys. So I said to myself, this is unnecessary delay, and besides," Mr Jeffris smiled at them, first at Oscar, then at Lucinda, "it was Christmas, so I called in person."

"It is very kind of you," said Oscar, squirming in his seat and hazarding a smile towards Lucinda whose moods and motives were of far more importance to him than Mr Jeffris's; so although he was, indeed, puzzled by the pleasant transformation of the head clerk's character, his interest in the man was of a much lower order than his interest in Lucinda Leplastrier who now, in the lamplight, bestowed such a sweet smile on him that he knew his rude assumption about marriage now to be forgiven. He may not be loved, not yet, but neither was he to be hated as he had feared all through the dreadful afternoon. He would not propose again until he had made the journey which Mr Jeffris was, at this very moment, so enthusiastically discussing. Oscar heard him say that there was, contrary to what he had said in Mr d'Abbs's office, a safe way to Boat Harbour.

"Provided," Mr Jeffris said, spreading butter on his shortbread and thereby causing Lucinda's eyebrow to raise itself, "provided you will gently-gently catchee monkey."

It did not occur to Oscar that this philosophy did not mesh with one that could not tolerate delay. He was more interested in the butter on the shortbread and raised an eyebrow of his own and thereby—ah!—caused Miss Leplastrier to smile.

"You have probably heard about the butchering habits of the northern blacks," said Mr Jeffris.

They had. They did not raise any more eyebrows. Mr Jeffris had their complete attention.

"This is the direct result," said Mr Jeffris, "of rushing. They are incompetents. They go straight through the centre of the niggers' kingdoms. It is like thrusting your bare hand into a beehive and it gets them hopping mad, ma'am, whereas if you took your time, as I should, and went around the boundaries," his whole demeanour changed; you could see his shoulders loosen; his hands soften, "why, as you can imagine, Jacky-Jacky would be pleased to let you be."

The woman was alert and thoughtful. She asked: "Who knows these boundaries?"

He answered: "I do."

He liked that. An answer like a pistol shot.

It was a lie. He had read some thoughts on the matter in the journals of Mrs Burrows's late husband (not a clever man) who had spent his last months like a chap rolling amongst beehives with a blazing torch. Mr Jeffris took these musings (you could not call them theories) and developed them as he spoke. He did not think that he was lying. Neither, had he paused to see what he was doing, would he have denied it to himself. He would now say *anything* which would result in him being put in charge of this expedition. He would write such journals as the colony had never seen. Every peak and saddle surveyed to its precise altitude. Each saw-tooth range exquisitely rendered. His prose would have a spine of steel and descriptions as delicate as violet petals.

Mr Jeffris was a coster's son and although he now despised salesmen he had a salesman's skills and he spoke to Lucinda directly and often, not because he valued the opinions of women (he did not) but because he saw that this one was at least as important as Mr Smudge in deciding whether or not his lovely journals should e'er be born. He did not flirt because he saw this would not be welcome, but if it had been welcome, then he would have flirted without Oscar being aware of it.

Lucinda opened the bottle of claret she had intended for their lunch. And when Mr Jeffris finally departed, sometime in the early hours of Boxing Day, she and Oscar sat at the table in the garden and—midst the heavy perfume of the citronella which they rubbed on their faces and arms to keep away mosquitoes—ate cold dry turkey and drank strong black tea.

They said nothing to each other about the incident on the landing. Yet they thought of little else and all their tender feelings, their shyness, embarrassment, hurt, their edgy, anxious, sometimes angry love, were like loose flecks of precious thread caught in the warp of a sturdy carpet, incorporated in that conversation which concluded with them wondering if it might be (a) possible and (b) ethical to persuade Mr Jeffris to take a leave of absence from Mr d'Abbs so he might lead the expedition to Boat Harbour.

87

Gratitude

Long, scythed sweeps of sunshine ran across the carpet, cutting through dull olive and leaving it a mown and brilliant green. Mr d'Abbs sat with his mustard-checked knees in sunshine, his face in shadow. It was difficult to see his expression, but his voice, no matter what private outrage he might feel about the theft of his head clerk, revealed only his own great satisfaction with himself, and if he was put out by these uninvited visitors, he did not show it.

Lucinda sat on the edge of what was normally "Mr Burrows's chair" facing Mr d'Abbs. She rolled open the plans, but they were not inclined to stay open and so Oscar held one edge for her. The plans were beautiful. Oscar was surprised that anything so light and fanciful had come from the gold-ringed hand of Mr d'Abbs. Fine graphite lines, soft crinkly yellow tissue paper—it was as though he held the map of a thought between thumb and forefinger.

"Mr d'Abbs," said Lucinda, "this plan has taken you eight weeks."

Oscar thought: She is already doing that which, not half an hour before, she has sworn she will not do. She has not even complimented him.

Mr d'Abbs stiffened slightly. He crossed his legs. He had dainty feet and slender ankles. "Rome," he said, "was not built in a day."

Oscar crossed his legs too, in sympathy. His right knee clicked. He worried about his knees. Soon he would have to walk beside the wagons Mr Jeffris was commissioning. He would have to walk day after day, week after week. It was for this reason that he soaked his feet in methylated spirits every night and why, by day, he wore these extraordinary boots which caused his feet such pain.

"And what size sheet have you planned for?" asked Lucinda. She smiled, but she was not an actress and her cheeks—as they always did when she was unhappy—seemed to disappear; the smile was as bleak as a cipher scratched on the wall of a house.

"Oh," Mr d'Abbs's rings fluttered through the sunshine, retreated into shadow) "oh, I'll leave that to your discretion."

"But, Mr d'Abbs," she pronounced it Mis-ter, "I specified a particular sheet size."

Oscar watched with alarm as Lucinda tried to hold her anger in its place. Her sinuses seemed to swell visibly. Her nostrils flared. Her hands were leaving damp stains on the crinkly yellow paper. She said: "That is the whole point."

"Your point." Mr d'Abbs uncrossed his legs and then crossed them the other way.

"My point, yes."

"But not my point."

"It is my life that is involved here, and yours only to the most limited extent. Your point, with respect, Mr d'Abbs, does not matter."

"There is no respect in that at all, Miss Leplastrier, and simply saying 'with respect' does not put it there."

There was an alarming silence. Oscar could hear Lucinda breathing. He was afraid she did herself no credit with this behaviour and, in truth, he did not understand why she should be so very angry. It was a fanciful church, he saw that, and perhaps a little pagan, but that, surely, was not the root of the problem. He prayed: Dear Lord, grant her patience, and charity.

But all Lucinda could see was an irreligious nightmare, a bloated monument to ignorance and tastelessness—curved canopies, Moorish screens, Tudor gables, Japanese "effects." It was a monster, too—one hundred feet across.

"An artist," Mr d'Abbs was saying, "cannot be constrained by blacksmiths."

"But, Mr d'Abbs, don't you see—you have taken six weeks and I cannot build what you have drawn."

"Miss Leplastrier," (Mr d'Abbs's voice had a tremor in it) "eight weeks is nothing." He stepped into the full glare of morning sunshine. His eyes were baleful. His chin was quivering. The hands that had begun by gesturing so freely were now clasped tight, one manacled to the other behind his back. He sat down. He looked around the walls at all his crowded landscapes. He smiled. His eyes pleaded. "Eight weeks is nothing for a building that will last a century."

As Mr d'Abbs spoke and as Lucinda looked at this tawdry church she began to suffer a tight, airless feeling in her chest. The fact that the object of their bet was now made to appear at once so vain and mediocre and that it was, in any case, impossible to build, conspired to act as a catalyst in Lucinda's soul, to make a focus for all the vague unease she harboured about the bet, and fearful thoughts which she had hitherto managed to keep submerged, now bubbled up like marsh gas and burst, malodorous, in the very forefront of her conscious mind. The tight band across her chest was a not unfamiliar feeling. It normally came on her after a night spent at the gaming tables. It was a panic produced by the fear of throwing away her fortune. She pressed her forearms against her abdomen. She looked to Oscar, wishing only that he would dispel her panic with a smile.

Oscar uncrossed his leg. His knee clicked again. He folded his arms which were sore as a result of Mr Jeffris's recommended dumb-bell exercises.

Mr d'Abbs leaned forward. He rubbed at the yellow paper as if he were a salesman in a Manchester department and the plans were fabric he had set his mind on selling. "You may not see the work in this plan."

"Oh," Lucinda sighed, "I see it, Mr d'Abbs, I really do." However she was not looking at Mr d'Abbs, but at the green-eyed man she had allowed herself to believe might love her. She could not see this man. She saw another, a queer stranger who rubbed his hands together like a praying mantis. She had made a bet with him and that was all. You could claim that it was code for a betrothal, a token of love, but not if you were sane. It was a bet, and only a mad woman would imagine anything else.

"With *respect,* Miss—you cannot see it. It is not here, but in all the scraps of paper, all the scribblings, the full-drawn plans that were flawed. I have been up early in the mornings. I have talked to my many artistic friends. I have pursued this most diligently, Miss Leplastrier, and not to make money."

"I am most appreciative," Lucinda said.

"You are *not* appreciative." His voice rose and the tremble could not be ignored. Oscar saw how the brown eyes pleaded, even while they closed down with anger. "I tender no fee, merely the pleasure of doing the job well for you because I care for matters of the spirit . . ."

A small vertical frown mark appeared on Lucinda's high forehead.

". . . more than most men in this town. As you know, as you know. And I take it," his voice rose even more as a flock of white cockatoos rose shrieking from the Moreton Bay fig beside the window, "I take it most uncivilized to be hectored on account of it. Do you see my bill attached?" (Oscar crossed his leg again.) "Do you see an account of my worry? Or my hours? Who protected your interests when you arrived in Sydney? You were lucky you were not robbed blind in daylight. Who invited you into his home, and provided you with friends? Here, in this room. How often you thanked me."

"Please," said Oscar, who could not bear the little man's pain. "Please, Mr d'Abbs . . ."

"You will hold your tongue, sir," said Mr d'Abbs, rising suddenly to his feet. He began to stride around the room picking up leather-bound volumes and banging them together. They gave off a smell like old bacon fat. There seemed to be no sense in the action except the exercise of anger. "I took you in when nobody would touch you. You were not a clerk's bootlace, sir. You were a smudge. A disgraceful, cast-out little smudge. You ruined my journals. I will always be able to look at the pages and remember your untidy habits. So do not," he shrieked, "presume to tell me how to draw a plan."

"I was not," said Oscar.

"Then do not," said Mr d'Abbs, quiet again. He took a breath and then expelled it. He turned to Lucinda, speaking to her even while he continued to pick up the books which last night's party had left abandoned on sideboard, sofa, table, ottoman. "I have not the skill to draw in perspective, miss, and I am not the only architect with this disability. Greenway—so Mr Fig informs me—was the same. But I have commissioned Mr Hill, from my own pocket" (by now he had half a dozen volumes clasped to his chest) "from my own pocket, to provide the perspective you have in front of you. You will see it is signed" (it was an untidy nest of books he held, quite unstable) "and if you do not like it" (a thick brown volume dropped and he kicked it—thwack—against the skirting board) "if you do not like it, you may take it to Lawson's and sell it for ten guineas."

Oscar still held one corner of the plan between thumb and forefinger. He was now crouching awkwardly with his backside hovering above Miss Shaddock's low-slung sewing chair. He looked at Lucinda, expecting to see a sympathetic softening of the face, but saw, if anything, the opposite.

"Mr d'Abbs," she said, relinquishing the plans to Oscar. "You have been complacent about the most serious matter imaginable. Good taste aside, this church cannot be made. You ignored the information I provided you with. The sheets must be three feet long and eighteen inches wide. Did it ever occur to you," she cried, her voice shaking, "you who call yourself my friend, did you ever think what might depend on this?"

Mr d'Abbs was so loaded with his own emotions that he had no space to take on Lucinda's anguish or wonder what might cause it. He looked like an actor stabbed on stage. He opened his mouth and then shut it. He caught a book as it slipped from his grasp.

"There is a wager dependent on this, Mr d'Abbs. I stand to lose my fortune."

In her heart Lucinda expected this revelation to have some effect on Mr d'Abbs. It was an expectation carried from the time when she had placed a cauliflower on the front desk at Petty's Hotel.

But she was not a little girl and Mr d'Abbs was not her protector. "What do you know about stakes?" he hissed.

Lucinda thought: So! He hates me. So be it. Why shouldn't he?

"You little brat. You are playing with money as if it were windfalls in an orchard. What do you know about business?"

This insult had a most salutary effect on Lucinda. It dismissed her panic. It unlocked all those not inconsiderable opinions which told her that she was a better person that Mr d'Abbs. She drew herself up to her full height, unclenched her hands and rubbed their palms together.

"Do not patronize me, Mr d'Abbs," she said. "You are a dabbler. You are all dabblers." She felt herself at one with Oscar Hopkins. They stood together, outside the pale, united. "You are children."

"*We* are children?"

"Oh, yes, indeed," Lucinda said, imagining that the day would come when she would regret this outburst. "Indeed you are."

"*We*?"

"All of you," said Lucinda, indicating with a sweep all the empty chairs, thus summoning and dismissing the images of Miss Malcolm, Mr Calvitto, Mr Fig, Mr Borrodaile, and even—there—Mr Henry Parkes. Thus, with a disdain worthy of Elizabeth Leplastrier, she burned the last of her social bridges in Sydney.

Mr d'Abbs affected spluttering. "And you, I suppose, are adults?"

"We are wagering everything. We place ourselves at risk."

"Oh, how noble you are," cried Mr d'Abbs, his face quite twisted with passion, "how elevated."

"We are *alive*," said Lucinda and at that moment she felt herself to be what she said. "We are alive on the very brink of eternity."

Lucinda took the plans from Oscar and placed them gently on the low walnut table beside her chair.

"You get out of my house," said Mr d'Abbs, snatching up the plans. He looked as if he might cry if not obeyed. "You, sir, Mr Smudge, go now."

"Do not call him Mr Smudge, if you please."

"This is my house and I will call him what I like."

For a moment Oscar thought Lucinda intended to strike Mr d'Abbs with her hand. Mr d'Abbs anticipated the same. He screwed up his face and this gave his hatred a slightly pathetic cast.

Lucinda's cheeks were flushed and her lips, hitherto so tightly tucked away, were now released and slightly parted. She gazed at Mr d'Abbs with an expression related to, but slightly kinder than, contempt. Her passions rushed through her veins declaring their intensity (but not their tangled nature) in lips, nostrils, in those extraordinary large green eyes. Oscar thought: How beautiful she is.

"You have no head for business," said Mr d'Abbs.

Oscar held out his arm. Lucinda took it. Oscar thought: I love her.

"She takes his arm," hissed Mr d'Abbs. "Not that door, unless you wish the sleeping quarters. You have no head for business and no eye either."

They found their way into the hallway. Oscar saw a woman (it was

Mrs d'Abbs) holding the front door open for them. She was apple-cheeked with golden curls and she looked at them both with her eyes bright, her mouth open. As they passed through the door she pressed an orange into Oscar's free hand.

"Thieves walking out the door," announced Mr d'Abbs, running into the passage. "An idea stolen and no thanks given."

He stood beside his pretty wife watching Oscar and Lucinda walk arm in arm up the garden steps to their sulky.

"You are not the maid, Henny," he said. "It is hardly seemly that you open and close our door for riff-raff." But his tone was not as harsh as his words suggest and all the time he spoke, his eyes quizzed hers on quite a different subject which related to how much she had heard and what she thought of him as a result.

And all the while Henny d'Abbs was picturing her orange. She saw it peeled and broken into segments and thought how all that was good in it would soon be incorporated in a completely different world.

88

A Lecture Based upon a Parable

That Mr Ahearn chose to walk four miles from his hotel in Pitt Street all the way to Whitfield's Farm, was partly the result of his habit of early rising, a good habit at home when one could light the stove, feed the hens, study the newspaper, and still be at one's office half an hour before one's clerks, but there was also, in this long slow walk, a kind of conceit. For to soak one's shoes in dew-wet grass, to pick one's way along a foot-wide path of the meandering type more often made by cattle than by humans was, to Mr Ahearn's mind, evidence of a kind of honesty, and this differentiated his advice (the advice he was about to deliver, the advice he carried with him) from that of people who travelled in hansoms at speed, cut a dash in traps, sulkies, broughams, phaetons. He could see himself in his mind's eye, a view from up and looking down— a man with a staff on a road, a traveller in a parable.

Mr Ahearn was aware of how he looked to such a degree that, were he at all good-looking, it would be obvious that he was vain. But he was not good-looking, knew himself not good-looking, and yet he had a knowledge of his appearance so exact that it could only have been obtained by examining himself not with one mirror, but with two, and sometimes—there was a silver-backed one of his wife's he sometimes used—three.

Mr Ahearn's face had become, in the five years since he saw Lucinda on Sol Myer's boat on the Parramatta wharf, more so. It had become more blotched and leathery. The cheeks seemed to have sunken, the Adam's apple to have risen, the long strands of hair across his bald pate to have reduced themselves in number while they increased their thin black definition. The nose craned forward while the belly had swollen, and underneath his cardigan he had permitted himself to leave a button undone. His shoulders were narrow, but his arms were long and powerful and his hips wide. And he did not need you to tell him it was so—he saw it all. He thought himself the tortoise, and from this, unlikely as it may seem, he drew great strength, and he saw, with all this peering at himself with two and three mirrors, not merely imitating the behaviour of a vain man—he was a vain man, although he knew perfectly well that most of the world would class him as downright ugly.

Mr Ahearn believed his adult form was one for which he was personally responsible, that he had made his own face and manner through the habits of his life. He had cultivated goodness and propriety. He had begun as a poor clerk and thought himself lucky to have got that far. His mother was a rag and bone merchant and his father the same, but mostly drunk or absent. When he was twelve years old he had copied down the parable of the talents. He had written it on a small piece of white paper. He had a good hand, mercifully free of fashionable flourishes, and he was able to fit Matthew 25: 14–30 on a piece of paper the size of a postcard. He folded it in four and kept it in his wallet, and he had the parable in his wallet now, fifty years later, as he walked across the rickety wooden plank bridge at the entry of Balmain, where Mullens Street is these days. It was a single plank, and often stolen, and in that respect Balmain has not changed very much, but it was not Balmain which was the subject, but this piece of paper, measuring six inches by four which was not the same piece of paper, of course not, as the original, for it was a piece of paper that received much wear, was taken out, folded, shown, to a child, to a grandchild, to a stranger in a coffee palace, and even the best paper will not withstand this, and so Mr Ahearn had, over the years, got himself into the habit of transcribing the parable on to a new piece of paper on every New Year's Day. He would begin: "For the kingdom of heaven is a man travelling into a far country . . ." and work slowly and painstakingly until, just as his wife was laying the roast potatoes out on a bed of brown paper and popping them back into the kookaburra oven, he would, with much satisfaction, transcribe: "And cast ye the unprofitable servant into outer darkness: there shall be weeping and gnashing of teeth." And thus, as Chas Ahearn folded the piece of paper into four between the thick pincers of his nails, a new year would begin.

What talents he had been given, he had used. He was a man of property but a careful man, a Christian man, and if the Lord had seen fit to bestow on Lucinda Leplastrier an amount of capital equal to the sum of all his lifetime's labour, he had not been resentful of this.

But he had watched her. He had watched her carefully, sometimes from close by, but more normally from a distance, via rumour and hearsay. He watched her as he might have watched a stranger's child playing with a crystal glass. In other words, it was not his right to say anything but he sat, on edge, waiting for the crash, hoping perhaps to catch the glass between the child's hand the the floor, unable to rest or read a newspaper for fear of what might happen.

He had not approved of the purchase of the glassworks. He had thought it impulsive, ill-considered. But when he heard about the glass church, he was beside himself. He was angry. He could not help this anger, but he was now making this journey, not to chide her or vent his spleen, but to avert the crash. It was his Christian duty.

He came, at last, along the rocky ridge past Birchgrove House, a solid enough property which she would have been wise to purchase herself. He had told her so, four years ago. He had directions from a farmhand knee-deep in pig mire. The man pointed down through the orchard to a small half-painted cottage above the western side of the peninsula.

He had burrs caught in his socks and in his trousers. There were burrs caught even in his shoelaces. The pasture was in poor condition, and Chas Ahearn, observing the burrs, the state of the sheds, fences, the piebald cottage, could not help himself valuing the property. If it had been his he would have had surveyor's pegs dotted like cribbage pegs throughout the orchard.

The gate all but fell off the cottage fence. What this gate was meant to keep in or out was not exactly clear. There was a cow tethered in its front garden. Mr Ahearn checked his gold fob watch. It was a gift from the Parramatta Benevolent Society of which he had been chairman for twenty years. He did his jacket up around his cardigan and knocked loudly on the door.

The servant was a fright. He had never seen such a servant, not even at Parramatta where every second one was a murderer. He had coal dust on his hands, and on his face. His hair was unruly, sticking out in all directions and although his beard was not heavy, the early sun, cutting in from the direction of The Heads, showed the orange stubble on his skin. His eyes were red and the left one smudged about with black.

"Is your mistress at home?"

He was informed she was still abed. This information was delivered in a voice so well educated that it confused Mr Ahearn a little, but not for long: he decided he was an actor, and having leapt to this conclusion, he clung to it.

He told the servant he would wait, but if he himself had not made to move towards the passageway, it is doubtful he would have been invited in. He was taken to the kitchen with the explanation it was "cosy." As the day was unpleasantly hot and humid Mr Ahearn could see nothing in this "cosy" but a convict form of clever rudeness. It was chaps like this who allowed Englishmen to write such patronizing accounts of their visits to the colony. And what a feast of sneering could be had here. The house was not clean. The kitchen was practically disemboweled. There were empty pots with burned bottoms and if these appeared to Lucinda as symbols of recklessness and joy, they were not perceived as such by Mr Ahearn. There was an item of female clothing strung across a chair like a fisherman's net. A bottle of brandy sat next to a small potted plant. A single tracery of cobweb ran across a sparkling clean glass window. A drawing board was propped on a workbench, which had, until recently, occupied a space more suited to it, inside the garden shed. On the drawing board he found evidence of the folly he had come to stop.

Mr Ahearn sat heavily, leaning forward, his hat in his left hand, while the right hand wiped and smoothed and patted his head.

When Lucinda came downstairs to receive him, she found that he had taken it upon himself to remove the drawing from the place where she had left it so carefully pinned. He held it against the window pane, and was kneeling on her three-legged stool with his big sweaty nose (on which his wire-rimmed spectacles were precariously perched) pressed close to it. He was caught in *flagrante delicto.* He had no time to rearrange his face. His mouth was open, but his forehead creased, as if wonder and censoriousness were there lined up for battle.

He did not greet her formally. In fact he began as if she had, just a moment before, left him with an invitation to inspect her plan. He made no apology for the early hour but rather held out her plan to her as if it were a table napkin he had finished with, and she a woman with nothing better to do than take it to the laundry.

Oscar stood in the doorway and watched. He was quite insensitive to Mr Ahearn's rudeness. He saw only what he imagined Mr Ahearn must see—that in this room, two hours before, he had kissed Miss Leplastrier on her soft and pliant mouth. Lust was visible. Mr Ahearn should surely see it.

"Where will the vicar change into his vestments?" Mr Ahearn demanded. "Where will he blow his nose in private? When he is late, he will be on show, like a fish in an aquarium. and what will you do," asked Mr Ahearn, seating himself upon the three-legged stool, "about the heat?"

Lucinda knew it impolite to greet the old goose in her gown, and yet she wished him witness to it. She was a free woman, and she dared stand before her visitor, uncorseted, with burnt pots and unwashed plates around her. She had kissed her lodger's mouth and held him hard against her loins. She stood thus before Mr Chas Ahearn and refused to be ashamed.

"A fatal flaw," intoned Mr Ahearn. "A cardinal error."

Lucinda looked at Oscar and pulled a face. Oscar blushed. She knew why he blushed and, in the midst of her growing irritation, was warmed by the heat of it. She smiled at Mr Ahearn who, seeing, but not understanding, the sleepy contentment in the girl's face, was not only puzzled but also, a little, embarrassed.

"It is this which makes this church impossible," he said. He could see that the damned servant was listening to every word he said. "The Australian sun will scorch your congregation as though they were in hell itself."

"It was kind of you to come early to tell me this," said Lucinda.

"And have you become so sarcastic, Miss Leplastrier?"

She was sarcastic, it was true. It was not an attractive quality. But she could not toleraste the satisfaction he had from finding fault in her design. He stood in judgement on her work as passionately as she had so short a time before, stood in judgement on Mr d'Abbs. She could not bear it, even if he were right.

But he could not be right.

It was far too late for him to be right.

Oscar came forward and picked up the brandy bottle, using two fingers like tweezers open its long neck. He carried it from the room. Lucinda opened her mouth as if she would say something in explanation, but then she shut it again.

Mr Ahearn, however, did not seem to notice either Oscar or the bottle.

"Who has ordered this?"

"Ordered?" said Lucinda, anxious that he not attempt to find more faults, fearful that there were many there to find.

"Commissioned, purchased, requested that you manufacture this?"

He knew the answer was "no one." But Lucinda said: "The Lord Jesus Christ."

Mr Ahearn hissed.

"Whose glory it celebrates," said Lucinda, wrapping her gown a little tighter.

"The glory of God is not served by folly."

"There are circumstances where it is called folly to be wise."

"Do not banter with me," said Chas Ahearn. "It is not practical. It is too hot to sit in. No congregation will pay for it."

She looked for Oscar in order that he might come to her defence but he had begun to stack cups and saucers in the scullery. "It is," she decided, "to be built beneath a shady tree."

"Oh, fiddlesticks," said Chas Ahearn, rising to his feet. He buttoned his long grey jacket and retrieved his wallet from the secret pocket where no Sydney footpad would ever find it. He took out his parable which, being late in the year, had become very frayed at the edges.

"The Kingdom of Heaven," said Lucinda, "is a man visiting a foreign country."

"*Travelling* into a *far* country."

"Yes, I know."

Still, she took the piece of paper when it was offered to her. She had read it before. The paper smelled of boring afternoons in Parramatta.

"But you *do not know.* you do not act as if you know."

"Yes, yes. My fortune is unearned. It is the fruit of your clever subdivision, and it was bought by the labour of my mother and my father and the blood of the blacks of the Dharuk. I have no right to it."

"The scripture says no such thing."

"Perhaps that is a lack in the scripture."

"It will be hot," he said, retrieving his parable, "as hot as hell. The congregation will fry inside," he said. "They will curse you. They will curse God's name."

"Mr Ahearn, please do be calm." Lucinda was not calm herself. "Mr Hopkins," she called, "perhaps you would fetch Mr Ahearn a glass of brandy?"

Mr Ahearn thought: "*Mister*? She calls her servant Mister." His lips were showing small small white bubbles at the sides and he was having a great deal of trouble fitting his parable back inside his wallet.

"I have come to tell you this in respect of the wishes of your mother who was my client. You were given such a start in life, young lady. And I have tried my best to steer you right." But this manner was not as his words. His voice was angry. There was something he did not understand at work within him, a rage so great he could not make his hands stay still. He saw himself tear up his parable. It was not symbolic. It was mechanical—the forces of agitation and rage at work. He could not bear this glass church, and yet he could not explain this, or any of his passions to himself. He saw himself, from a great distance, a tortoise-necked man with a quaking voice. He heard himself shout. He saw himself gently escorted from the sloth-house by the man who, he found out later that day, was not a servant at all, but a defrocked priest, the little harlot's lover.

89

Of the Devil

Lust was an insect, a beetle, a worm. It slipped into his belly like the long pink parasites which had thrived in the intestines of the Stratton's pigs, and he had tried to drown it with long clear draughts of tank water, with holy scriptures, with meditations upon hell.

John wrote: "He that committeth sin is of the devil, for the devil sinneth from the beginning."

In Galatians it is said: "If we live in the spirit, we also walk in the spirit."

But the mail from England said that the Reverend Mr Stratton had hanged himself from the rafters of his church while he who had corrupted him, the same Oscar Hopkins, the so-called servant of God, had seduced an honest woman, had pressed his lips against her tea-sweet mouth and felt the soft curve of her stomach against his loins.

It had been three in the morning. He had come out to draw more water and had found here there, in her Chinese gown. His penis was a hard rod against the softness of her stomach. He felt Satan take his soul like an overripe peach with a yielding stalk.

He kissed her dear, soft lips. He nuzzled her long white neck. He touched and broke away, touched and broke away, moaned and begged his God's forgiveness while the clock in the kitchen struck the hour.

He withdrew from her, made patting motions in the air with long outstretched fingers as if their passion was a silky beast between them that could be soothed and patted into docility.

They went into the kitchen and drank tea. They did not discuss this thing, which Oscar, with extraordinary selfcentredness, saw as his responsibility. He did not think, She loves me. He thought, rather, I am seducing her.

They talked earnestly about the glass church, although not of its faults or impracticalities. When his unholy passion rose in him Oscar used fear to still it. He thought of the boat carriage that Mr Jeffris was having built at Mort Bay. Mr Jeffris had described the carriage in the most minute detail, at this very kitchen table and Oscar had listened with a sick feeling in the pit of his stomach as if it were not a vehicle for carrying a boat, but a gallows or a set of stocks. Mr Jeffris was precise and fastidious. He was pleased to demonstrate this in the design of the boat carriage. The two boats were carried one inside the other, like two spoons. Each was suspended on canvas slings and such was the ingenious nature of the design that neither could ever rub against the other.

The thing that made Mr Jeffris so proud served only to paralyze Oscar.

He would be called to travel in a boat.

Dear God, give me hard and difficult things. Give me a rocky path that I may not sin.

Mr Jeffris loved to talk of rivers, mountains, trigonometry. He promised Oscar he would have him delivered to Boat Harbour, and do not fear. There was no risk from drowning.

Oscar had not known about these rivers when he talked about going overland. The Hastings, the Clarence, the Macleay, these rivers now snaked through his dreams. They were miles wide, bruised and swollen by the rain.

He was ill with fear at the thing he had begun. When he woke from sleep it was there to meet him, as cruel as death.

He thought: I will drown.

He thought: Dear God, take my soul into Thy safe-keeping.

He thought: I love her. He thought: I am impure. In the kitchen they bit each other, dragged at their faces. They wedged themselves together against the door jamb like two clothes pegs.

The Reverend Mr Stratton had hanged himself from the rafter above his pulpit. Wardley-Fish must already be in Sydney searching for his friend who was ashamed and hid from him.

He lusted after a woman who loved another.

He thought: God, do not have me lead her into sin.

He thought: There is no God. There is nothing. I do not have to cross these six rivers. I do not have to travel with mad Jeffris with his compasses, his journals, his trained criminals, his dumb-bells, his picks, his carpenter, his saddler, his three brass chronometers. I am someone put backwards on a horse and paraded through the bush for ridicule. He was baggage, carried by Mr Jeffris, his ticket paid by Miss Leplastrier.

But he had promised God he would do this.

Although only because he wished Lucinda to love him.

Did she not love him?

Did she say so?

No, she did not. She kissed his lips and made them as blue as ink, but when he had offered to marry her, on Christmas Day, she had fled, weeping, to her room.

Why was this?

Because she loved Hasset.

Then why go through this danger, this risk, this crippling fear?

So she would love him.

Because he had promised God. So he would not be cast into hell.

If there was no God?

But he had bet there was a God. He had bet on Goodness. He had bet he would be rewarded in paradise. He had bet he would carry this jewel of a church through the horrid bush and have it in Boat Harbour by Easter.

His life was riddled with sin and compromise. Mr Stratton had wrapped a rope around his neck and committed the sin of suicide. God forgive him. He was murdered by Oscar Hopkins's system.

He had posed as a holy man to Wardley-Fish. He had enticed him to Botany Bay and then hidden from him.

He could not love his father enough. He had written "dearest papa" but he had been happiest when he was away from him. He had left this good and godly man to die alone and unloved except by his unlettered flock.

Give me a hard journey, dear God. Deliver me from evil. Lead me not into temptation.

And then, inside the scullery, at breakfast, he offered his bruised and swollen lips to Miss Leplastrier, and the devil played the tune, and then he saw, in the corner of his mind, the possibility that the glass church was just the devil's trick. Mr Ahearn was right. It would be too hot. The congregation would curse Christ's name.

90

A Reconciliation

Mr d'Abbs had been to Miss Leplastrier's office on four occasions before he found her, at last, inside. He had come up those three wide sets of stairs four times, rehearsed his little speech four times, but when he found her, on the fifth, the meeting did not progress as he had rehearsed it.

His first thought was: Consumption.

Her skin was very pale, stretched; it was shining, slightly blue, translucent. Her eyes seemed overly large, the whites not white but that bluish grey you find in certain porcelains. Her manner, in that bright, hot, sun-drenched room – all the windows open and papers smacking each other on a green felt board, and fluttering under glass-bottle paperweights – seemed too fast, too frantic to Mr d'Abbs who immediately forgot his speech, which was all to do with the lasting value of friendship, that it should not be thrown away though one simple misunderstanding, but that friendship was what he valued more than anything in life. Except that one might guess that he was using "friendship" when what he really meant was "companionship," this was spoken truly. He had brought her a cribbage board and a signed edition of his friend Hill's engravings of Pittwater. He had intended to make the speech and then give the gifts, but when he saw how she looked he was overcome by thoughts of her mortality, and he pressed the gifts on her without proper explanation of his feelings.

He had dressed carefully in his splendid cream linen suit and his white straw hat. He had chosen the colours at least half-conscious of their symbolism: the blank page, the clean start, and if he had it in mind to say anything about Mr Jeffris, it was only as a by the by. But now, so disconcerted was he by Miss Leplastrier's over-bright appearance, that he mentioned Jeffris when she was still opening his gifts.

"Oh, by the by, Miss Leplastrier," he said, closing one of her windows without thinking what he did. (He could not bear paper fluttering in a room.) "You do know about Mr Jeffris's passion, do you not? It occurred to me that you might not. It is impertinent to mention it, were we not such old friends."

This was a dangerous tack to take, and he knew it. He could easily give the impression that he wished to sabotage her project and that he had come here, only pretending friendship, in order to assassinate the character of her trusted guide. And yet he could not protest friendship without telling her: Jeffris was a dangerous fellow, and although you could have him in your employ in an office where he might, like a guard dog on a leash, be at once frightening and useful, it would not be the same to entrust your life to his ambitions.

When he mentioned Mr Jeffris's passion he saw Lucinda tense and he feared he had "set her off" again.

"Oh, Mr d'Abbs," Lucinda sighed, then smiled (Mr d'Abbs thought: Her arms are thin, they were not so thin before). "Do tell me about Mr Jeffris, for I see you have come here with his 'passion' most particularly in mind." And smiling very broadly, so broadly that Mr d'Abbs could easily have felt himself quite patronized, she sat herself behind her desk and folded her arms across her bosom.

"Indeed," said Mr d'Abbs, "it is not so." There was no chair for him to sit on. He would have shut the second window, but he judged she would misinterpret it. "Quite the contrary. The reverse. I came here intent on keeping it under my hat. I thought: It is not my business, no more than how many windows you wish to have open.

I really do take it very ill to be so uncharitably interpreted."

"Forgive me."

"You do not wish to be forgiven, you little scallywag. You completely lack the conventional sense of sin, upon my word I swear it is true."

"Indeed?" said Lucinda, quite pleased to be misunderstood in this particular way.

"Indeed, you have no shame. You are pure will, and I noted this in you when you first came into my office. You hold your chin high." (He thought: You can see the blood vessels in her neck; her lower lip is distinctly blue; these are not good signs.) "I said to Fig, it does not matter what the gossips say, she is above gossips."

Oh, that this were true.

"And what," she asked, "do the gossips say about Mr Jeffris?"

"See," said Mr d'Abbs with genuine admiration, "that is the other thing I always said about you—that you would not be diverted."

"So," said Lucinda, knowing herself flattered and surprised to enjoy such falsehood so immensely.

"So it is not gossip, but, please, really." He felt silly standing in front of her. He came to sit on the edge of the desk, but the desk was a trifle taller than the beginning of his bottom, and having attempted, with one or two discreet little hops which made him look a little like a mynah bird in a cage, he contented himself with leaning. "Really, it is *most* important that you know—he will use you."

"And I him," said Lucinda, but felt, even while she professed such certainty, the sort of panic and anger which Mr Ahearn had produced when he called the church a "folly."

"He cares only to make a name for himself with his trigonometry and explorations. He courted Mrs Burrows—what a pair, imagine it, eh?—so Miss Malcolm tells me, until he had everything transcribed from her husband's journals and then he courted her no more."

"I do not imagine Mrs Burrows would be so easily used."

"Mrs Burrows is not the tough old thing she pretends to be. And what do you mean with that little smile, but never mind. The point is: you wish Mr Hopkins to be delivered safely."

It was cruel to speak to her like this. She said: "Mr Jeffris's trigonometry and explorations would seem the perfect qualifications."

"Mr Jeffris," said Mr d'Abbs, finally getting his backside on to the desk, "is a man in love with danger."

"You must realize, Mr d'Abbs, that I have interviewed Mr Jeffris at some length. We are engaged in this project," she gestured towards the sheets of paper which were pinned, as regular as the bricks of a wall, to the green felt board, "together. I find him to be fastidious."

"*You* are fastidious," said Mr D'Abbs. "Therefore he is fastidious. He is an actor. His performance will vary with his audience. If you wish to know him as I do you must hear him speak when he is alone with men. With women he is a different creature entirely. His every story, when he is with his own sex, ends with some chap fainting or hollering in horror when they see how brave old Jeffris had got himself bloodied or broken in some way. And now you have supplied him with the funds and he has a little army and he is out to make a name for himself."

"Mr d'Abbs," Lucinda said, "admit it: you have come to frighten me."

"I swear no."

"It was most ill mannered of me to steal away your clerk. Although I did not steal him. It was not my intention to steal, but still I can understand you might wish to punish me. This is why you speak to me like this."

"No," said Mr d'Abbs, waving his hands violently, "no, no, no. That is the past. I came to say nothing, to patch up our quarrel, and then I thought my silence hypocritical."

"Then what would you have me do?"

"Oh, please," said Mr d'Abbs. "Cancel the whole damn thing. It is too silly for words and you will make yourself a laughing stock."

Then he saw he had gone too far. He saw her face close against him, and he suddenly lacked the courage for the continued assault.

"Of course," he said, "I am a skeptic. It is probably a corollary of my age."

"Yes."

"And I am peeved, of course, to have lost a damn good clerk. You must allow for that."

"I do," said Lucinda with some relief.

"And after that I wish only that our friendship be maintained. My wife says she is sorry not to have made a closer friend of you. She was so taken with you. She begs me to patch up my difference with you."

"It is patched," Lucinda said, and when she bade him goodbye, in a minute or two, she kissed him gently on the cheek. It was not something she had ever done before.

The effect of Mr d'Abbs's visit was that Lucinda chose to believe that

Mr d'Abbs had accused Mr Jeffris falsely. What touched her was the picture she made of Mr d'Abbs grappling with the demons of his own falsehood. She did not know what to make of it, except that she was moved, as it seems she was by almost everything in that month of March as they prepared to make the journey. She was in an emotional state where the smallest thing, the frailness of a twig, the unravelling of a cloud in a blue sky, was filled with poignancy and that bursting love which is the anxious harbinger of loss. She saw goodness everywhere, perhaps attributing much of her own character or longings to others, and thus chose to see Mr d'Abbs's "confession" of his falsehood as the keystone of his character, the main thrust of his speech.

It is curious that Lucinda, while rejecting most of Mr d'Abbs's accusations, chose to believe that Mr Jeffris was in love with danger. Believing this allowed her to like Mr Jeffris more. She imagined she knew the disease he suffered from, that she too was in love with danger, not, of course, as it applied to blood and body wounds, but as it applied to the more general business of life. It was not just risk, but actual loss that quickened her. And on the day Mr d'Abbs found her in her office she had come from a Pitt Street solicitor's where she had, in the face of not inconsiderable resistance, formalized her bet in a document which she placed, that night, in her dusty-smelling cedar secretaire.

She did not tell Oscar what she had done and yet it was through the medium of this document that she believed that Oscar would, magically, triump on his journey. She did not express what she believed, not even to herself. But the confidence she felt when she touched the rolled-up document (which she did often, at least twice each day), could only have its source in this simple superstition: that if she could manage to lose this bet, then Oscar Hopkins would not die.

She was a thorough woman and she had a great capacity for detail, and so she did not trust her beloved's safety solely to this voodoo in a cedar box. She had meetings with Mr Jeffris, far more than Mr Jeffris at first thought necessary. She went through his shopping lists and his accounts and if Mr Jeffris was at first outraged to suffer this from a woman, he soon discovered that his patron—far from being the niggardly boarding-house marm he had at first imagined—would question no expense that might relate to safety. But at first he had not understood her. She had spoken philosophically of the nature of danger. It was hard for him not to smirk at her. He thought her ridiculous, a monkey in a top hat, a woman acting like a man. But when the philosophy had finished he saw she would pay up for any item which might be seen to lessen danger. And she *begged* him to tell her the dangers. He took great pleasure in obliging her. He enjoyed himself. He made her very frightened.

Lucinda was too much in love to think of how masculine hierarchies are created, but it was a mistake to have these meetings with Oscar absent. It encouraged Mr Jeffris in his habit of thinking of Oscar scornfully.

Lucinda thought only that she loved him, that he must be safe.

When she had imagined "love" it had always been with someone broad and square. Even Mr Hasset had been taller than this comforting prototype. When picturing her future husband she had seen strong square hands and a black square beard. She had never imagined the snaky insinuating passion she would feel to hold a thin white man who she called (although not out loud) "my sweet archangel."

"He is a brave man," she told Mr Jeffris, "far braver than you or I."

"He is an extraordinary chap," said Jeffris.

"You will deal with mountains and rivers, but he will do battle with demons."

"One can only respect him, ma'am," said Mr Jeffris.

Mr Jeffris's eyes were soft and sympathetic, but his mind was totally dedicated to the satisfaction of his present ambition: to extract a cheque for twenty pounds for the purchase of three brass chronometers from Mr Dulwich of Observatory Hill.

91

A Man of Authority

Horses and bullocks were scarce in consequence of the long drought and although it was not Mr Jeffris himself who went to Parramatta sales in search of decent beasts, the worry of this item lay heavily on him, for it was no use at all tearing up the road to Wiseman's Ferry with all the finest men, all perfectly kitted out, if all he had to pull them were beasts like you saw everywhere around the colony, with their spines showing like ridgepoles under the baggy canvas of their hides.

He had become a man of authority. He felt himself uncramped at last, free from the petty limitations of Mr d'Abbs's employ. He could say to one man, go, and he went, to another, come, and he came. He was conscious of standing straighter. He could feel the girth of his chest pressing against the buttons of his shirt. He employed tall men he knew he could control with the strength of his eyes. He was stern with them and unsmiling. He dispatched his overseer and bullock driver both with instruction that no beast he bought but that they both be in agreement. They took this order meekly, although they surely found it most distasteful. The bullock driver called him "Captain," Later this misunderstanding was to spread.

Mr Jeffris engaged a storekeeper, two blacksmiths, a medical attendant, a collector of birds and a collector of plants (although these last two were entered on the paybook as "riflemen"), a groom, a trumpeter, two carpenters, a shoemaker, a cook.

Miss Leplastrier did not query him on a single point.

He borrowed two mountain barometers and entrusted one of these to the collector of birds and another to the collector of plants, telling them that it was to be their main duty whilst actually travelling to guard the safety of these barometers for he planned to go about this journey like a trigonometrist, knowing always, exactly, where he was in space, and he would not be, he told the red-necked, Belfast-born plant collector, like some fart-faced Irishman crashing through the undergrowth like a wombat.

They would carry axes and they would be razor-sharp at all times, for there is nothing a surveyor despises more than a tree that obscures his trig point.

Miss Leplastrier made a horse and sulky available to him so he might move about smartly. He was soon a familiar sight on the road out to Mort Bay, standing straight and flaying the poor animal to get a skip on. He was on his way to Harrison's shipyards where old Oliver Crawley, a wide, bow-legged shipwright with a white cataract on his left eye, was constructing two light whale boats, the smaller designed to fit inside the larger when the thwarts of the larger one were removed for travelling. The larger boat was then to be suspended within a frame of belts and canvases and the canvas most in contact with the boat was to be guarded with sheepskin and greased hide, and this whole sling, of course, was to be fitted into the boat carriage, that machine which rolled silently through the tracks of Oscar Hopkins's nightmares.

Mr Jeffris took each man, as he was engaged, to Anthony Hordern's store where they were kitted out, on account of Miss Leplastrier, with a suit of new clothing. There were strong grey twill trousers, a red woollen shirt which, when crossed with white braces, provided a military appearance. This was as Mr Jeffris had calculated it. He would require absolute obedience and he made it clear from the beginning.

It was his intention that Oscar Hopkins also dress in this manner. It was important that he not place himself, as it were, above the law. And yet Mr Jeffris could not come at the matter directly. He could hardly demand it, and yet he could not countenance any exception to his rule. He broached the subject with Miss Leplastrier but she only laughed and said it was something he must discuss with Mr Hopkins. When she laughed like that he would like to put her on her back in bed. He bowed formally and said nothing, but he went to Hordern's, anyway, and bought the correct items of clothing in sizes he guessed would suit the stick-limbed Mr Smudge. He cantered back across the city and out to the Darling Harbour glassworks where he was told Mr Hopkins was "in preparation."

He was amused at the idea of Mr Smudge preparing for anything. He had never, in all his experience, met anyone so mentally and physically unprepared for life. In the world that Mr Jeffris called the "real world," an imaginary place with neither parliaments nor factories, Mr Smudge would simply die. When he heard he was "preparing" he had a vision of him in baggy combinations, with pencil-thin arms, working with his dumbbells. Thus he arrived at the glassworks in an excellent humour, with his handsome dark eyes dancing and his teeth showing beneath the curtain of his moustache. He wore his wide-shouldered, box-pleated coat and a pair of white cotton gloves. If the effect was eccentric, he was unaware of it. At this very moment there were sixteen men in Sydney whose only labour was to make his dream a reality.

For I also am a man of authority, and I say to one man go, and he goeth, I say to another come and he cometh.

But when he entered the glassworks he was not pleased (not *pleased*? He was furious) to see that they were, once again, unpacking the glass church and all the crates, which had been, at six o'clock last night, screwed tightly shut, now had their lids (A, B, C, D, etc.) stacked against the walls, and all the hessian bags, which had been lined up and laced tight, were now as empty as bladders on a slaughterhouse floor. The furnaces were cold and the glass blowers were at the boxes like children on Christmas morning while the biggest child of them all, the pale and excitable Mr Smudge, was calling out instructions in his fluting choirboy's voice.

And they obeyed him! Oh, my God, thought Mr Jeffris, I cannot bear it.

It was against the natural order, that a man like this should give orders to men like these, and not only be obeyed, but be willingly obeyed.

"'No, no, Harry, no," the fool cried to Flood, the foundryman from Leichhardt, "I must do it by myself without instruction."

He was incompetent. You could see he was incompetent. He had a little hessian bag labelled "B1" from which he was removing the pieces of decorative cast-iron cresting, which was to run along the ridge of the roof. Why was he fiddling with this now? Was he not meant to be assembling a wall section?

Jeffris looked towards the one person whom he most reluctantly admitted as "competent." She, who should be disapproving of all this, sat complacently in the glass blower's wooden throne. She was a handsome little woman with dainty feet and slender ankles and it angered Mr Jeffris that she should choose to lie in bed with this extraordinary child.

As for the church itself, it was the silliest thing he had ever heard of. He imagined it was the single-armed foundryman—he who was always cooing over the bits and pieces with a measuring rod and calliper—who had tricked her into it. What a fortune he must be making from her with all his little extra frills, his fiddly crests, his gay little "terminals," his ornate railing, all of them—Mr Jeffris assumed—"specials" and therefore charged out at a premium.

Mr Jeffris did not like the church even when it was packed away. And yet he could not help but admire Miss Leplastrier for the way she looked after the details of her own deception. She was a great woman for lists. He was the same. His whole life now was a series of lists and he saw, in Lucinda Leplastrier, his equal in meticulous order. He also thought this list-making of hers to be demeaning to him. It was he, as expedition leader, who should be in charge of packing the cargo. Yet she stated, very clearly—her eyes meeting his full square while she did so—that the responsibility was hers. She gave him a list of cargo appended to which she had written, all in a strong clear hand, directions on how each wagon was to be packed. The whole damn thing was like a jigsaw puzzle. The long, hessian-wrapped "barley-sugar" columns must lie on the starboard whilst boxes "H" and "B"—being balanced in weight—must lie on the port. No box with a "2" suffix (A2, B2) could be packed over an axle, and so on. It took a full day to load, and now, just when everybody seemed happy, when the embarrassment had been covered with canvas and lashed down securely, the Hooting Boy had decided he must have the whole thing in pieces and go again. He was like a child who cannot leave his toys alone.

He was not wearing combinations as Mr Jeffris had imagined when he thought of him "preparing." But the vision was very close to life. Oscar Hopkins was clad in a workman's boiler suit. His face was streaked with packing grease. He rubbed his hands together and returned Mr Jeffris's actor's smile.

"I am in rehearsal, you see," he said. "There is no doubt I will require some assistance at Boat Harbour, but it need not be skilled. I can glaze, you see. You must admit yourself surprised."

"Indeed," said Mr Jeffris.

"It is a tougher job than Latin verbs, I promise you."

Mr Jeffris had all his spleen. He wedged the parcel containing Oscar's uniform underneath his arm and held his arms behind his back. He rocked on his toes and heels and while Oscar teetered on a ladder, and clambered on the empty spider web of glasshouse roof, he made small talk with Miss Leplastrier about a play he had seen at the Lyceum in Pitt Street. He admired the church, and was able to use his knowledge of trigonometry to flatter the design. And all the way he wished only that they would *pack the thing away*.

Mr Jeffris did not like the church but he was certainly not without a sense of history. Each pane of glass, he thought, would travel through country where glass had never existed before, not once, in all time. These sheets would cut a new path in history. They would slice the white dust-covers of geography and reveal a map beneath, with rivers, mountains, and names, the streets of his birthplace, Bromley, married to the rivers of savage Australia.

There would be pain in this journey, and most likely death. Mr Jeffris knew it now. He felt the axe in his hands, the cut scrub, the harsh saw-teeth of mountains giving up their exact latitude to his theodolites. There would be pain like this wax-skinned girlie boy had never known, and if he was afeared of water he was afeared of the wrong thing entirely.

92

The Lord is My Shepherd

Lucinda thought: Terrible things always happen on beautiful days. Nothing bad has ever happened to me on a rainy day. When they brought my papa home with his socks showing there were butcher-birds singing along the fences and king-fishers with chests like emeralds flying two inches above the surface of the creek. The sky was blue.

The sky was also blue in the week when her mama died, on the day Hasset sailed, and now, here, as they followed the wagons down to Semi-Circular Quay—she in her white hat and veil, he in the silly uniform that Jeffris wished him in—it was a clear blue-skied day.

The uniform was too big around his chest and shoulders. It gathered and rucked. His braces were not tight. She thought of a poor creature she had seen in the street outside the Sydney asylum, a nurse on either side of him; he had a bare white neck so long you could not help but think of knives.

All her passion, all her intelligence, her discipline, her love had gone to produce nothing but a folly. She had not known this until she saw him in his humiliating suit. It would seem that he also knew this. There was a panic in his eyes, but now all these sixteen wagons would not be stopped. They were rolling like tumbrils through the public street of Sydney and urchins ran out of lanes hoorahing the procession. They called Mr Jeffris "Captain" and wanted to know if he was Captain Stuart. Mr Jeffris did not deign to answer them. His back was straight, his lips glistening. His horse was all impatience, eager to over-leap the air. Lucinda felt an animosity towards the handsome chestnut she would not yet permit herself to feel towards the rider.

The Lord is my shepherd
I shall not want
He maketh me to lie down in green pastures
He leadeth me beside the still waters.

There was not a single black in the party, although Lucinda had directed that this be otherwise. Now Jeffris clattered beside her shouting that there was no point recruiting the unhappy souls in the streets of Sydney. He would recruit his niggers when they were up country.

"I am offering a bonus," Lucinda called, digging into her purse.

They were now moving along the bottom end of George Street. The trumpeter—he was riding in the wagon behind—made a loud discordant noise on his instrument.

"No trumpets," roared Jeffris, wheeling and rearing.

Why pay for trumpets then? Lucinda thought. "A bonus," she shouted, having to wave the crumpled white envelope at Mr Jeffris. She knew this was too weak and desperate. She saw how he despised her and she was frightened of what she had done.

She told Jeffris that Mr Hopkins would hand over the money when he had been safely delivered. She then gave Oscar the envelope and as she had offended and humiliated her friend. She saw how patronizing she had been. She could have wept. She thought: They will cut his throat and steal the money from him.

He restoreth my soul: he leadeth me in the paths of righteousness for his name's sake.

"The Lord keep you safe," she said.

She gave him the scroll which was the formal document of their wager. He also pushed an envelope at her. And then he was down on the ground, away from her. She felt the cruel emptiness in her arms and her chest, as if she were nothing but an empty mould—she felt an ache in the places where he had, a moment before, pressed against her. She touched her shoulders with the tips of her fingers. She embraced the echo of his presence. She wrapped a rug around herself although it was not cold.

All around her the navvies swore and cursed the sap-heavy boxes, which contained nothing to equate with the crystal-pure, bat-winged structure of her dreams, but a lead-heavy folly, thirty hundredweight of cast-iron rods, five hundred and sixty-two glass sheets weighing two pounds each, twenty gross of nuts and bolts, sixty pounds of putty, five gallons of linseed oil.

She saw him walk out on to a barge, then be escorted to its neighbour. There was a man on either side of him.

93

Doggerel

The envelope Oscar gave Lucinda was bent in half, and then quarters, and then eighths. It was folded and refolded until, in its tired and grimy state, its simple address smudged, its corners dog-eared, it became a flimsy monument to all her misery.

That she did not open it was not forgetfulness. On the contrary, she was more aware of that envelope than anything else on her slow return to Longnose Point. She placed it on her kitchen table, leaned it against the brown-glazed tea-pot which still contained the cold soggy dregs of their last cup of tea. There were blow-flies in here as well. They crawled around the milky rim of two tea-cups, neither of which was empty. She picked up the envelope, but did not open it.

She did not wish to weep. She dreaded the sound of her howling in an empty house. This noise was a living nightmare in her imagination. And she would not open the envelope because she imagined it contained all of those fine feelings of the heart that they had, both of them, so passionately hinted at.

So this is how it was not until Tuesday 15 March, a full six days after the party's departure, that Lucinda opened it.

In her hand she found this simple doggerel:

I dare not hope,
And yet I must
That through this deed,
I gain your trust.

"Oh, my darling," she cried out loud to the kitchen as she had never done when he stood in it. "You had my trust, always."

She sat down heavily on the rung-backed chair but then, driven by a great shiver of passion, sprang up again, her face contorted, her hands clutching at the loose hair at the nape of her neck.

"My God, you *fool*."

She walked to the window. She took out hairpins. She put them back in. The light from the harbour was as harsh and cold as chips of broken glass. She bit the knuckles of her hand. She screwed up her eyes and grunted: aaaah.

She had not cared about the church. The church had been conceived in a fever. It was not a celebration of sacred love, but of their own. Likewise this wager—she saw now, with her head pressed hard against the window pane, with her eyes tight shut, that she had only made this bet so that she might finally do what she had never managed to do upon a gaming table, that is to slough off the great guilty weight of her inheritance, drop it like a rusty armour she did not need, that she be light as a feather, as uncorrupted as an empty purse, unencumbered, naked, with her face pressed into the soft and secret place at the bottom of his graceful neck.

With this ring I thee wed, with this body I thee worship, and with all my worldly goods I thee endow.

"You knew," she said, walking to the sitting room, up the stairs. "You knew my heart. How could you misunderstand me to such an extent."

That very day she sent a messenger to find the party, but they had already departed from the expected track at Singleton and were pushing into unmapped country with the two blacks from the Wonnarua tribe.

94

Mr Smith

Mr Smith, Mr Percy Smith, he with the sandy hair and mild, blinking eye, Mr Borrodaile's friend, he who was forever removing llama hair from his trousers, Mr Smith had been engaged as a collector of animals for the expedition, and he had purchased, from his own funds, seven octavo volumes of one hundred pages in each in which to record his findings, together with sixteen crates containing empty bottles, cork, paper, wax, etc. He had a barrel of formaldehyde and another of spirits together with other instruments, many of which he had, again purchased especially for this journey, which he understood was to enter that teeming semi-tropical country which the cedar cutters had named, typically, "The Big Scrub."

But he had gone no further than a chain out from Semi-Circular Quay when the leader of the expedition, without being aware of his acquaintance with the Reverend Mr Hopkins, appointed him the latter's keeper and told him, while all the rest of the men were more concerned with a passenger who had leapt from the deck of the berthing *Sobraon* and seemed intent on drowning—it was the pilot boat that saved him in any case—that he should regard all other duties as second to this one. So while the pilot's deckhand forced a boat hook through the swimming man's breeches, Mr Smith assisted Mr Jrffris in inserting a metal funnel between Oscar Hopkins's clenched teeth. The funnel had last seen service inside the jaws of a dying Derby hog. It had not since been sterilized, but Mr Jeffris would not hear of such a nicety—he was laready administering the first dose of laudanum which he had, he claimed, purchased by the gallon jar for this specific purpose. It was then, with the treacly green liquid running down Mr Hopkins's pointed chin, with the shadow of the *Sobraon's* sails falling across his extraordinary passionate face, that Mr Jeffris—he who had been so dedicated, nay *fanatical* about the importance of professionally collecting fauna—coolly, without apology, revised his duties. He put it to him thus: "You are to supervise him at all times. You are not to let him out of your sight. If you wipe your arse-hole, you will have one eye on him. While you have your hand upon your roger, you will have the other hand around his ankle. Where there are rivers to be forded, you will be advised, where possible, of the impending crossing, and you will administer five fluid ounces of the laudanum."

Percy Smith thought: I am a weak man to agree to this. How can they always seek me out, and why do I smile at them and nod my head?

He had looked at Mr Jeffris's face at that moment, on the barge, when he was asked if these orders were acceptable. He had been unable to hold the eyes. His soul had shrivelled like a leech in salt.

At the first night's camp, Mr Jeffris had made a speech around the campfire. He had told the party: "You can be raging boys at night, but, by God, you will be soldiers in the day." And they were.

Now on the second night, at Wiseman's Ferry, the men were shouting raving drunk and Mr Smith half-expected one of them to shoot or hack or slash his way into the lighted tent where the leader worked upon his journals. That they did not was as much due to the type of man Mr Jeffris had selected as the force of his character. They were men who, no matter how they might glower or curse, enjoyed being "soldiers." And Mr Jeffris's leadership was such that you could believe this former clerk would murder a man for disobedience. His hand was never far from pistol and sword, and, indeed, he had drawn the latter at a creek crossing that day—a leafy little place with clear water running six inches deep across a sandy bed—and had sworn he would cut the hand off the carpenter and feed it to the dogs, and this merely because the carpenter had expressed the view that the cargo was "safe enough." Mr Jeffris did not show a different character from the one he had revealed when wearing striped trousers in Mr d'Abbs office. He merely brought himself into keener focus. He drew his antique sword and called the man—he was a boy, really, with sandy hair and a newly sunburnt nose—"a frigging colonial frigging dog, a frigging lemon-sucking incompetent." He would cut his hand off. By God he would. You watch him. He would feed it to him for his dinner. Etc.

Now Mr Smith sat on a log next to the young clergyman and stared into the fire. He had been on several journeys of exploration, and this always was a time of day he enjoyed. There was no shortage of water here, and so he had washed his day's clothes and hung them on a line he had rigged along the wagon where he and Oscar were carried as passengers. This was already dubbed by the overseer the "Ladies' Compartment," on account of the canvas awning provided them. Mr Smith now wore clean clothes. They were cool against the skin and still smelt of his wife's ironing board.

His companion had neither washed nor changed his clothes. He had been too shy to bathe naked in front of the other men and must now, surely, be in a state of some discomfort. So much did Mr Smith enjoy the feeling of clean linen against his skin, that he was made vicariously uncomfortable at that thought of Oscar Hopkins's sweat-sticky garments. It had been hot travelling. The country was still very dry, and where ploughed, dusty. They had travelled half a day along a series of ridges still smouldering from bushfire. Tree roots were still alight and, twice, burning branches crashed dangerously close to the party. He and Mr Hopkins had travelled with wet handkerchiefs on their faces but their skin, of course, was filthy from the smoke and ash. Percy Smith could not bear for his companion to sit in his filth.

"It is a pleasant time for bathing," he said. "The moon up over the water. I think there is nothing so pleasant. In fact I have a mind to bathe again. Old mother night," he said, "throws a modest curtain on us."

Oscar said nothing.

Two Scots were singing somewhere by the boat carriage:

"I wae tae ye a tale o' angel named Beggs,
Came down ta earth, silk purse 'tween ha legs."

Percy Smith was embarrassed on the clergyman's account. He sipped his rum and water and stared at the fire.

"Does your throat still pain you?"

"Oh, it is not so bad."

"I have been thinking," Percy Smith said, taking out his pipe and tobacco pouch, "that if I were to coat the funnel with wax it might not be so painful. But then I fear your fit will make you bite it, and a loose piece of wax could easily choke."

"I had no fit."

"But you have a phobia about the water."

"All my life. Yet when I mounted the barge I had no phobia. I was merely sad to leave one I loved so dearly."

"Mr Hopkins," said Mr Smith, sending great plumes of blue smoke into the night, "Mr Hopkins, has the laudanum removed all memory from you?" And he laughed to show he did not mean it unkindly. "You forget."

"And what do I forget, Mr Smith?" The voice was cool and unfriendly.

Mr Smith thought: He will not easily forgive me for what I must do to him. Yet he, too, is in the maniac's power. We are both in the same boat. He must forgive me. It is intolerable he should not.

Mr Smith said: "You forget I found you in a fit. Your teeth were clenched. Your face was red as butcher's meat. Your eyes had rolled and your veins were like worms lying on your brow."

"You found me thus, on account of that 'person' who we stupidly engaged to deliver this cargo," Oscar hissed. "It was he who assaulted me and pushed me down and forced this 'medicine' upon me."

"He has a great responsibility," said Percy Smith. "He fears you will throw yourself into the water."

"He fears he will lose his bonus. But he will not lose me. I will not allow myself to be lost. I have much to live for."

"Do you forget it was I who introduced her to our table?"

"I am sorry . . ."

"Your 'much-to-live-for.' Do you remember who it was who arranged her invitation to Mr Borrodaile's table?"

"Oh, yes," said Oscar, and Mr Smith was pleased to hear the voice, at last, lighten.

"You have that to thank me for."

"Indeed."

A moment later, Oscar said: "I have never seen men behave like this."

Percy Smith was not sure exactly what he referred to, whether he meant Mr Jeffris himself or the men who wrestled with each other by the edge of the fire or those dancing a drunken jig around the overseer's grey tent. There was also, of course—and this was quite normal—much profanity in the night.

"I fear I am not suited to this life," the clergyman said. "There is a cruel feel to it. Indeed, it is extraordinary that one can go through life and know so little of it. I suppose much of it is like this."

"Oh, aye," said Percy Smith, and sighed. "Oh, aye."

"You need give me no medicine tomorrow. It does not agree with me."

Percy Smith said nothing.

"Strictly speaking," Oscar said, "Mr Jeffris is in my employ." He stood up. For a moment it seemed that he would walk to Mr Jeffris's tent. Indeed he took a step in the direction of that tent, which glowed with the light of three lanterns. But then he stopped and Percy Smith stood to see what it was had halted him: it was the carpenter, he who had been threatened with amputation. He was kneeling in the outer circle of firelight and thus, with his fair hair touching the ground, was allowing himself to be penetrated by the overseer.

"May God save you," said Oscar Hopkins. He said it in a high clear voice. It cut across the campsite with that clean slice you hear in whipbirds in dense bush.

In a moment there would be a general eruption of laughter, an ugly noise which could contain, within its chaos, noises like doors slamming, donkeys braying. But for a moment, everything was very quiet.

95

Arrival of Wardley-Fish (1)

Four weeks out from Home, Ian Wardley-Fish had looked into his silver-backed mirror and seen, above the unblemished white of his clerical collar, a gross and thick-lipped man with weak and watery bloodshot eyes, a buffoon who—even whilst standing in the dock before his Better Self—tried to grin and joke his way to acceptance; but it would not do. Wardley-Fish placed his mirror upon the washstand and, having wedged his bulk between washstand and bed, kneeled upon his cabin floor. He vowed to God that he would henceforth forswear not only cards and alcohol and smutty talk, but also that he would acquit himself with dignity, that he would eschew the company of Messrs Clarkson and Maguire, those two "gentlemen" with whom he had, not three hours previously, been pleased to recite sixteen verses of "Eskimo Nell."

His head hurt terribly. He had drunk a thing which Clarkson, an agent of some type in Sydney, called Squatter's Punch. It was made with grenadine, champagne and a particularly foul colonial rum, which Clarkson, who was addicted to the stuff, had carried with him to London. Maguire, being from Belfast, claimed he could drink anything, but had been defeated by the Squatter's Punch. Wardley-Fish was playing the "Modern Man of God." He had outdone himself last night.

He had also, again, said unflattering things about his exfiancée's knees. He had said these things before. He had said it was the image of these knees—glimpsed accidentally in a moment on the Serpentine—that had made the marriage impossible to him. This was not true. But in his cups he had enjoyed drawing gross pictures for Maguire and Clarkson. They thought him exceedingly modern. But he would do this no more, and with his stomach rebelling against the smell of his own chamber-pot, he promised God he would henceforth behave as both a Christian and a gentleman.

Even as he made the vow he feared he had not the strength to keep it, and yet he did, well past the time when he had the queasiness of his stomach to assist him.

His earlier "shenanigans" had attracted a great deal of attention, and his period of reform was therefore quite luminous in its effect. Indeed, by the time the *Sobraon* heeled over for its last long straight tack into Sydney Harbour, the Powells and Halfsmiths and even Miss Masterson were all beginning to bid him good day and smile in that special fond way one reserves for those who have regained the fold.

And yet you would be surprised at the damage a man can do in the distance between the high wild cliffs that guard the entrance to Sydney harbour and the placid waters at Semi-Circular Quay. The distance is three nautical miles, no more.

The problem was that Wardley-Fish liked to be liked. It was a weakness, he knew, but having cut Clarkson and Maguire without explanation, and having ignored them completely for so many weeks, he wished to make his peace with them.

He could not hope to achieve this reconciliation and then refuse Clarkson's offer of a glass of rum. This rum was a very personal matter with Clarkson. It was not something he would entrust to a steward. It must be dispensed from a silver flask and have a dash of cloves cordial added with an eyedropper. Now Wardley-Fish was a big man and built—with his powerful haunches and hefty backside—not unlike a sturdy pottery jug. In normal circumstances he held his liquor well and yet on this occasion, drinking rum at the rails of the *Sobraon*, it took only two noggins to make his speech quite slurry. Perhaps it was excitement, to be at last in Sydney Harbour on this glorious blue-skied day, or relief, that Clarkson (who had a prim red nose and a small censurious mouth) seemed so ready to accept him, once again, as a friend. But when he remarked that he would soon be dining at the Randwick vicarage, he said "vicarrish."

"You are drunk," said Clarkson, not pleased. "Blow me, I cannot see the point for the life of me. You cut us cold when there is fun to be had, and now you go on a bender when, who knows, maybe your bishop is waiting at the quay."

"I have no bishop."

"You have no Randwick vicarage either," said Clarkson, consulting his gold watch as he always did when he wished to give authority to himself. "the Randwick vicarage is burnt to the ground."

"No," said Wardley-Fish, his mouth wide open.

"We sailed right past it."

"You tease."

"No, I swear," said Clarkson who was already enjoying the power of the Pure Merino over the New Chum. "Surely you saw it." And he pointed back towards Watson's Bay which is a good six miles from Randwick.

"Look at your face," said Maguire.

"Look at your own, you rascal," said Wardley-Fish. "I know when my leg is being pulled." And he accepted more rum—held his glass steady while the little drops of cloves cordial were added—and could not understand why this lie should make his heart beat so wildly. He thought: I wonder *will* I see the dear Odd Bod tonight. He will be all settled in his manse with some old Mrs Williams giving him orders and telling him to sit up straight at table before she serves him. It is Saturday today. I will wait till the morrow. I will wait. I will go to his church and listen to his sermon. He will look down into the faces and see me sitting there. Yes, yes, that is what I will do.

There was plenty of wind in the harbour, but they had half the canvas bound and buttoned and were proceeding slowly. Wardley-Fish was suddenly overcome with impatience. He wished to be ashore. He wished to be asleep. He wished to wake and find it the morrow and be seated in the Randwick congregation. He accepted a fourth glass. The cloves improved the flavour, there was no doubt of that. He looked down over the side and saw the pilot who had joined their ship outside The heads was leaving before he reached the quay. The pilot boat nuzzled alongside to receive him. As the wiry grey-bearded man landed on his own deck again, Wardley-Fish looked up and saw, not twenty yards beyond the pilot boat, a whole series of barges being towed off the wharf. It was set up for an expedition—horses, carts, men dressed up like soldiers, a little Gilbert and Sullivan chappie with a huge dress sword strapped to his belt. And by his side Wardley-Fish saw this horrid puzzle, this vision, of the person he was waiting so impatiently to see—the Odd Bod—his chicken neck sticking out of a horrible red shirt, his narrow chest criss-crossed by silly braces.

"Oh, no," he said. "It is my friend," he said to Clarkson who nodded but did not seem to understand what was being said to him. "My friend," he said to little plump Maguire who rubbed his stomach as if he were being spoken to about a meal, or lack of a meal, but not this: that the man who should be dressed in a black cassock in a pulpit was here standing before them on a raft.

"Hopkins," bellowed Wardley-Fish. He cupped his hands and called again: "Mr Oscar Hopkins."

"What chaps are these?" Maguire said. He had a little brass telescope he always carried with him on to the deck. Now he raised it and pointed it at the barges.

"It is my friend," said Wardley-Fish. "Mr Hopkins from the Randwick vicarage."

"Then wave," said Clarkson, setting the example himself. "Yoo-hoo," he cried in a mocking imitation of a woman. "Yoo-hoo, Mr Randwick." He turned to Wardley-Fish. "Wave," he said. "Your friend is leaving on an expedition to the inland. Wave, Fish, you will not see him for a year."

Wardley-Fish looked at Clarkson and knew that Clarkson did not like him, had not forgiven him, would not forgive him.

"Liar," said Wardley-Fish.

"I beg your pardon, sir?"

"Poppycock," revised Wardley-Fish who could not afford to waste time on this sort of petty discord but must find out, and rapidly at that, whether he was having his leg pulled or no.

"Is it someone famous?" asked Maguire, taking off his spectacles and readjusting the little telescope.

"Is it true?" asked Wardley-Fish, quietly, politely.

Clarkson poured himself rum but offered none. "You see that wagon there," he said, pointing with his eyedropper, "with its two boats fited one inside the other? See that? Then tell me, Fish, why someone has a wagon like that, if they are not setting off to go exploring. And criminee, man, just look at them. Did you ever see such a lot of tin soldiers?"

The barges were being pulled out across the water by a little steamboat. Wardley-Fish removed his jacket and laid it loosely across the rail. He took off his clerical collar and placed this across the jacket. He slipped the studs in his pocket.

No one took any notice of him, not even when he bellowed: "Mr Oscar Hopkins."

Clarkson sipped his rum and cloves. Maguire leaned his belly against the rail and focused his telescope. Wardley-Fish clambered on to the rail and having first removed his shoes in full view of the Halfsmiths, Miss Masterson *et al,* dived head first into Sydney Harbour.

This was the "drowning man" who had a boathook driven into his breeches.

96

Arrival of Wardley-Fish (2)

The man who was saved from drowning had a backside like a horse and a bulk – so claimed Alfred Spinks, the deckhand who had so neatly hooked him – enough to cause a bloke a hernia. The hook got in the breeches without the gentleman's soft white bum getting so much as a scratch on it. The man was saved from drowning but did not want to bestow a reward. He was a New Chum of the lah-di-dah variety, a remittance man no doubt with nothing in his pockets and cheap rum on his breath.

Alfred Spinks, his spot of rescuing now done, stood in the wheel-house with his foot shoved hard to bring the wheel round to the star-board. They would circle now while wall-eyed Captain Simmons – it was the leathery shrunken pilot with the silver beard – did a spot of questioning. It would be a rare old show, for Captain Simmons liked a reward as well as the next chap and he had a great aversion to New Chums and an even greater aversion to taking orders, and he was al-ready turning his wall-eye towards the rescued man and his winking eye towards the appreciative Alfred Spinks.

The rescued man had a gold tooth and a mole on the edge of his fair beard which was easy to mistake for a shell-backed tick. "I will ask you one more time," the pommy said – you would think he was a frigging magistrate – "I will ask you one more time to deliver me to that place where the expedition barges are bound."

He was so bloody proper and dignified. It was a shame you could see his titty through his shirt. It was shocking that he had to cough and spit up all that smelly water.

Captain Simmons lowered himself companionably beside the drip-ping man. Above his head the funnel farted black soot into the sky. "I was not aware," the pilot said, "you had a rank."

"A rank?"

"Yes, sir, a rank. An admiral, a vice-admiral, someone who is entitled – in certain circumstances – to give orders to the captain of a pilot boat."

"I am a gentleman, you knave," said Wardley-Fish.

"You must not call me knave, sir. I am a captain."

This answer made Wardley-Fish narrow his eyes. If all of New South Wales was like this, why then, it was beyond toleration–nothing would get done. You could not argue with a man about whether he was a knave or not.

"I am a gentleman," he said.

"And I am a captain, and it's the other captain I must take you to visit, not go running you across the harbour."

"What other captain, man?"

"The Captain of the *Sobraon,* the Captain from whose authority you have thought to run away."

Wardley-Fish sprang to his feet, but the blessed boat was so small there was nowhere to go. In two paces he was at the wheelhouse where he met the possum-bright eyes of Arthur Spinks. He looked up at the *Sobraon* but its decks were now crowded with faces, all carefully observing his public disgrace.

"I beg you, man," he hissed at Captain Simmons.

A smile stirred in the depths of Captain Simmons's silver beard.

"You do not look like a begging sort of man," said Captain Simmons, and began to tamp his tobacco with a broad black thumb.

Wardley-Fish cast another look towards the decks of the *Sobraon.* He caught the eye of Miss Masterson, she who, not five weeks before, he had imagined he was in love with. She did not avert her gaze, but neither did she smile. She looked down on him as if he were some species of marsupial rat.

The barges were now a quarter of a mile away. Wardley-Fish considered swimming but knew he was too drunk for it.

"Why do you take it to act so uncharitably?" he asked the captain.

Captain Simmons thought that pretty rich: charity. But he said nothing.

"If you are a captain," said the gent, "you must be the slowest-witted captain on the sea. I told you once, I told your man here twice–I only wish to see my friend. He is over there. There he goes. I have travelled all the way from London to see him. And he is there, damn you, and you will not take me. Take me, please, I beg you," cried Wardley-Fish, but his manner, as the Captain had previously observed, was not that of a begging man.

"So he was on his way to see his *friend,*" Captain Simmons exclaimed to his deckhand. "Is *this* the case?"

"You know it is," said Wardley-Fish.

"And yet, you know, I have the damnedest feeling that there is a problem of a friend *behind* you, some problem perhaps, a little debt incurred whilst gambling, or a matter between you and the purser on the *Sobraon*, some little thing like that which made this 'friend' you saw upon the barge seem like a chap you must get in touch with urgently, if you get my meaning."

"Oh, you have a beastly, tricky little mind," roared Wardley-Fish. "Would you like money? I will give you five pounds if you take me where that barge has gone."

Captain Simmons stood slowly. He tucked his pipe in his trouser pocket. "Ten pounds," he said.

Wardley-Fish was caught in the tug of different violent passions—his outrage at being robbed of ten pounds, his realization that he did not have ten pounds, that it was in his jacket aboard the ship, his knowledge that this hawk-nosed little chap would enjoy refusing credit, his mortification at disgracing himself in the eyes of the entire ship, his grief at missing his friend, his anxiety that all as not right with the Odd Bod who had seemed, in that ridiculous shirt and criss-crossed braces, like a poor fowl trussed up for a cooking pot. It was all of this, not his simple dislike of the sly aggressions of the pilot, that led him to pick the man up bodily in his bearlike arms and, with a terrible roar that could be heard by all aboard the *Sobraon*, hurl him into the water.

The incident created complications that kept him a prisoner in Sydney for two days. On the third day he set off in search of Mr Jeffris's expedition.

97

Laudanum

He had accepted the laudanum for three days because Percy Smith had begged him to, but now he was resolved he would accept it no more. The laudanum did not suit him. It gave him unsettling dreams. It made him nauseous and jittery. It also produced severe constipation and now he had haemorrhoids and his anus itched and bled continually. He had no experience of haemorrhoids and imagined a condition far more serious. He had dreams involving shit and blood, the buggered carpenter, and the endless ridge roads out of Sydney, which laced through his imaginings like the stretched intestines of a slaughtered beast.

The others had all washed. He had not washed. He would not stand naked before them. He splashed water on his face and forearms and calves, but the rest of his body felt cased with a grimy viscous film. His modesty was somehow offensive to the party. Mr Jeffris suggested that it would be in his interests "to reassure the men that you have all the correct equipment."

Oscar had never hated anyone before (not even they who made him eat a stone, or those who had let rats loose in his room at Oriel) but he hated Mr Jeffris who was now, on the fourth morning of their journey, strutting around the dead brown dew-wet grass finding fault with his "soldiers" and their wagons.

Oscar and Mr Smith stood beside their wagon. Mr Smith had the laudanum bottle perched on the metal step and the funnel stuck in the pocket of his twill trousers.

"I do not have the strength to defy him," he said, crossing his burly, sandy-haired arms.

"Then we will pretend," said Oscar. "You will pretend to pour. I will pretend to drink."

"No," said Percy Smith. "He will know."

Percy Smith had a kindly, decent face, one you would naturally trust to the end of the world. But Mr Jeffris had such a power over him that when Oscar looked at his face he was reminded of a rabbit on a laboratory bench assaulted by current from a voltaic cell.

"I am employed by him," pleaded Percy Smith, blinking.

"Look at him. He is too busy to know anything."

Mr Jeffris pulled at a rope on the lead wagon in such a way that a vast lumpy canvas swag fell to the earth.

"If you wish to change his orders, you must settle the matter with him."

"Oh, mercy," cried Oscar in despair. "You were there when I attempted it."

"And he said it could only be settled with Miss Leplastrier present. He does not accept your authority. But I must accept his. Dear Mr Hopkins, you are a good man—"

"An angry man."

"A good man, and I must ask you, please," said Percy Smith, sneaking his hand around Oscar's shoulder and suddenly clamping it around his jaw, "you must forgive me."

"No," said Oscar. The back of his head was jammed hard against the buckle of Mr Smith's crossed white braces. He was pulled back and down, out of the shadow of the wagon. The sun laid a stripe across his livid face. A blow-fly settled on his nose. He tried to wave it away. Mr Smith clamped his wrist with his other hand. Two bullocks in the carpenter's team defecated at once. Mr Jeffris was bawling out the cook and threatening to make him walk without his boots. And at this moment, with Percy Smith's hand held around his jaw, Oscar thought: I do not even know where I am.

Percy Smith had found the funnel and pushed it hard against his lips. Oscar opened his mouth. It hit his teeth. He opened more. He had already been cut. He could taste the blood. Percy Smith's breath was bad. He had his knees against the back of Oscar's knees, making him keel over backwards.

"No," Oscar said, or tried to say, for trying to speak made him dry-retch.

Percy Smith lowered him to the ground. Oscar did not struggle. His friend put a knee upon his chest. He had the stone bottle with "Manufacturing Chemists" engraved in brown upon its rotund middle. He pulled the cork with his teeth. And then, before he poured, he put the bottle down. He touched Oscar's cheek with the back of his hand. An odd, gentle, lover's pat. "I would not do this to you," said Percy Smith, "for anything."

And then he poured the muck into the funnel.

Oscar kicked out with his boots. He connected with nothing. He hated Percy Smith.

98

An Explorer

Until he had the ill fortune to imagine a glass church and therefore be obliged to take this journey, Oscar's knowledge of the world had been severely limited. He was, by his nature, a creature suited to burrows and hutches and so even at Oriel—which many would see as a civilized and unthreatening environment—he had his definite tracks beside which there were great unexplored areas he was either frightened of or had no interest in.

His knowledge of Hennacombe was confined to two households and various red-soiled paths no more than one foot wide. And although he had, in the very act of writing home, posed as an authority on Sydney, had been happy to relay the common platitudes (that it was, for instance, a working-man's paradise) he had known nothing of it.

Now he felt himself cast into a morass and little dreamed he was dragging his puffing, saddle-sore friend, the bewildered Wardley-Fish, through the muck behind him. He felt himself a beetle inside the bloody intestines of an alien animal. And any idea he had harboured that the bush was, as the engravings of the *Sydney Mail* might suggest, a pure and pristine place of ferns and waterfalls was soon demonstrated to be quite false. There were ferns, of course, and waterfalls. There were clouds of splendid birds but this was not the point.

At Maitland, Wardley-Fish had been barely a day behind the party, but then there was a game of cards with squatters in a so-called Grand Hotel. He had tried to leave, but he was too far ahead and his companions would not hear of it. By the time this game was finally settled Mr Jeffris's squeaking, whip-rattling convoy was far ahead: passing along burning ridges somewhere north of Singleton. The Odd Bod's eyes streamed. His lungs rebelled. His hard-sprung wagon lurched and banged over rocky tracks or squelched into fart-sour mud. The Odd Bod sat on a wooden bench and buttoned his long-sleeved shirt against the mosquitoes and the sun. He comforted the burly Percy Smith. He assured him that he was forgiven. The air was filled with foul language, such hatred of God as Oscar would have imagined suitable for hell itself. They travelled behind the quartermaster's wagon and thus behind the smell of bad meat which made up their diet. They travelled beside ugly windrows, great forest trees pulled into piles by settlers eager to plant their first crops.

In a pretty clearing beside some white-trunked paper-barks, Oscar saw a man tied to a tree and whipped until there was a shiny red mantle on his white shoulders and brown seeping through his Anthony Horderns' twill trousers. His "mates" all watched. Oscar prayed to Jesus but no prayer could block out the smell of the man's shit.

He forgave Mr Smith. How could he not? He who stood witness to far greater crimes than his. He accepted his laudanum. He lay down on the grass and let the funnel be inserted. He had queer laudanum dreams and other thoughts you could not label so neatly.

If you plucked Sydney from the earth, he thought, like an organ ripped from a man, all these roads and rivers would be pulled out like roots, canals, arteries. He saw the great hairy, flesh-backed tuft, which he saw was Sydney, saw the rivers pushing, the long slippery yellow tracks like things the butcher would use for making sausages.

While he saw all this, he also saw Percy Smith's unhappy, pale, blinking eyes as he handled his blackened short-stemmed pipe.

He saw his father killing moths by driving copper pins into their eyes.

He dreamed of enormous sea-shells, soft, like ladies' quilted jackets—pale pink, lilac, lily green—cast up on a Devon beach.

He had ecstatic dreams involving water in one of which his body assumed the form of a river.

His anus itched. His head was jolted and thrown forward. Through all the physical discomforts, the dreams cam to him, like complicated melodies played by a man lying in a bed of nettles.

He dreamed he was somehow inside his father's aquarium. The cool water was very soothing to his prickling skin. He could see his father's wise and smiling face peering in at him. He could see, dimly, the outside world, the chair and benches of his father's study. Sunlight streamed through a window. He thought: That window faces north. He felt very happy for he knew that the sunlight meant his father was now in the southern hemisphere.

But it was Wardley-Fish who was in the southern hemisphere. He was one day's fast trot behind the wagons. He had a tired horse, but plenty of money for a fresh one. He walked the dark-flanked beast along the flat sandy path above the Macleay. The path was through tea-tree scrub. He came round a bend to find a man with a handkerchief tied across his face. As the man produced his pistol, bright loud birds flew across the path behind his shoulder.

Oscar had dreams in which portions of the real world stumbled, like horses' hooves stuck in drought-cracked clay. These dreams were marked by the filigree of giant trees silhouetted against the sky, by beards, by curses, and the plant collector's German hymns.

But only the longest and most beautiful dream transcended the jolting, jogging rhythms of the wagon. It involved a glass-house shaped like a seamless teardrop; the teardrop suspended in a wire net; the net held by cast-iron rods out from a cliff above the sea. On the sand below was the refuse from his other dreams, those enormous pink shells, his mother's buttons, a sherry bottle.

In his dream he had one thought which turned and turned on itself like a shining steel corkscrew. The thought was this: I am not afraid.

Wardley-Fish returned to Sydney in the company of a travelling draper of exotic extraction. He was indebted to the man for the trousers he wore.

99

An Old Blackfellow

The sand for our glassworks did not come from Bellingen, but from Yellow Rock, which is on the coast, not far from where Mr Jeffris's party finally emerged from the bush.

The sand at Yellow Rock is not as good as the Botany sand which Dennis Hasset, and others before him, tried to promote in London and Sydney, but it is good enough sand. It produces a glass with a faint yellow tinge, the effect of which, in the windows of old Bellinger Valley farmhouses, is to make the kikuyu pastures a particularly dazzling green.

The sand was held in big corrugated-iron hoppers and when these ran low my father would employ a gang of men and we would take three wagons over to Yellow Rock and load them. I say "we" because I went too, even—and I cannot see how this was so, except that it was—ven on a school day. We would stay overnight at the Old Blacks' Camp.

The Old Blacks' Camp consisted of seven weatherboard huts, built in a row. They were constructed after the style of the so-called "shelter sheds" which are still the feature of school playgrounds around Australia. They were bleak palces, each with a single "room," a single door, three steps, one window. In these huts the surviving members of the Kumbaingiri tribe lived, and died.

The only one I remember is the one they called Kumbaingiri Billy. More commonly he was known as Come-and-get-it Billy. I do not know his real name, or even his age.

My father liked Kumbaingiri Billy. He always brought him bacon. I think they were friends, proper friends. They drank tea together. My father never made jokes about him. Once he said: "Kumbaingiri Billy has more brains in his nose than the whole shire council wrapped into one."

When I was ten, Kumbaingiri Billy told the story of "How Jesus come to Bellingen long time-ago." Afterwards I made a patronizing joke about it and my father hit me around the legs with the electric flex from the kettle. I didn't make jokes about it again, although I listened to the story a number of times. Kumbaingiri Billy must have first heard it when he was very young, and now I think about it it seems probable that its source is not amongst the Kumbaingiri but the Narcoo blacks whom Mr Jeffris conscripted at Kempsey to guide the party on the last leg of its journey. But perhaps it is not one story anyway. The assertion that "our people had not seen white people before" suggests a date earlier than 1865 and a more complex parentage than I am able to trace.

100

Glass Cut

The white men came out of the clouds of Mount Darling. Our people had not seen white men before. We thought they were spirits. They came through the tea-trees, dragging their boxes and shouting. The birds set up a chatter. What a noise they all made. Like twenty goannas had come at once to raid their nests. Anyway, it was not nesting time.

We thought they were dead men. They climbed hills and chopped down trees. They did not cut down the trees for sugar bag. There was no sugar bag in the trees they chopped. They left the trees lying on the ground. They cut these trees so they could make a map. They were surveying with chains and theodolites, but we did not understand what they were doing. We saw the dead trees. Soon other white men came and ring-barked the trees. At that time we made a song:

Where are the bees which grew on these plains?
The spirits have removed them.
They are angry with us.
They leave us without firewood when they are angry.
They'll never grow again.
We pine for the top of our woods,
but the dark spirit won't send them back.
The spirit is angry with us.

The white men spoke to two men of the Narcoo tribe. They were young men. They gave the white men a big kangaroo, and some coberra. The white men would not eat the coberra. They told the Narcoo men to show them the way to the Kumbaingiri, although the Narcoo men had never seen anyone from that tribe. They were neighbours, but they did not visit.

The Narcoo men said: "You wait here."

They went back to the tribes and the elders had a big talk and then they told the young men: "You keep them buggers going quick and smart."

So that is what the young men did. They showed them the way, although it was not easy. They had seven wagons. Sometimes the boss would say: "We going to camp here." And then he would gallop off and chop down trees and make more maps. Then he would come back and say: "Right you are, we go now."

It was in these camps the young fellows learned about Jesus. This was the first time they ever heard of such a thing. They were told the story of Jesus nailed to the cross. They were told by the Reverend Mr Hopkins. Whenever they crossed a river this fellow had to lie on his back first. Then he would put a tin funnel in his mouth and then they would fill him up with grog. He must have been drunk, but the young men were never offered the bottle so they did not find out what it was he drank.

The Reverend Mr Hopkins told the Narcoo men the story of St Barnabas eaten by a lion. He told them the story of St Catherine killed with a wheel. He told them the story of St Sebastian killed with spears.

Naturally the Narcoo men misunderstood many things, but many things they understood very well. One thing they did not understand was the boxes on the wagons: they got the idea these boxes were related to the stories. They thought they were sacred. They thought they were the white man's dreaming.

Coming down Mount Leadenhall it was so steep they were lowering wagons on pulleys and ropes. It was a great bloody mess with ropes tied to trees and bullocks pulling up so the wagons would get lowered down. There was an accident. One of the boxes fell. Straight away the white fellows opened up this box. Naturally the Narcoo men were keen to see what was inside.

You know what they saw? It was glass. Up until that time they had not seen glass. There was glass windows down in Kempsey and Port Macquarie, but these fellows had not been to those places. They saw the glass was sharp. This was the first thing they noticed – that it cuts. Cuts trees. Cuts the skin of the tribes.

When the white men wanted to cross Mount Dawson, the Narcoo men did not wish them to. Mount Dawson was sacred. The young men were forbidden to go there. It was against their law. Then the leader of the white men shot one of the Narcoo men with his pistol. The other Narcoo man was named Odalberee. This Odalberee took them up Mount Dawson, and down towards the Bellinger Valley. He made a song.

Glass cuts.
We never saw it before.
Now it is here amongst us.
It is sacred to the strangers.
Glass cuts.
Glass cuts kangaroo.
Glass cuts bandicoot.
Glass cuts the trees and grasses.
Hurry on, strangers.
Hurry on to the Kumbaingiri.
Leave us, good spirits, go, go.

Odalberee led them down towards the coast at Uranga. He thought he should take them towards the sea so they could go away. But on the last night, when they were almost there, the Kumbaingiri knew there were strangers in their country. The Kumbaingiri came with torches at night. They walked through the bush to talk to the strangers. But the strangers got frightened. Odalberee got frightened too. The Kumbaingiri men did not understand him. Then there was a lot of shooting.

The Reverend Mr Hopkins made a big fuss. He shouted. He ran about.

The leader of the white men said: "Tie that fellow up."

They tied him up to a tree down in a gully. There were two men with him to keep him safe. Then they went back and fired more riffes at the Kumbaingiri. You could hear the red-haired man wailing. He was like a ghost in the night.

The next day Odalberee went off and found the Kumbaingiri again. He told the story of everything that had happened to him. He cut himself. He brought glass with him, wrapped in a possum skin. He was sick to have caused such death. He cut himself not only on the chest, but on the arms. He did this with the glass.

In a short time Odalberee was very sick. No one could cure him. Before too long he died.

That glass was kept a long time by the elders of the Kumbaingiri, but it was not kept with the sacred things. It was kept somewhere else, where it would not be found.

101

Oscar at Bellingen Heads

When Oscar Hopkins arrived at the banks of the Bellinger, he had changed. Those limpid eyes, which had once irritated Wardley-Fish with their "holy" pose, now showed a dull, ash-covered anger. His face was burnt a painful vermilion and his nose—due to an illusion created by the peeling skin—seemed to have grown large and slightly hooked. It was a gaunt, scraped-out kind of personality you saw there, scarred by bushfire, incapable of so fat a luxury as tears. He was a red salmon as it enters the waters of its home river where it will spawn and die, no longer plump and silver but with its belly empty, its jaw become long and hooked, its whole body bright red and splendidly, triumphantly ugly.

Mr Jeffris's party found the Bellinger River at a place where the Narcoo man judged they would do the least amount of damage. This was at Urunga, a wounded place in any case.

In those days it was called Bellingen Heads.

As they came down the dry and pebbly ridge towards the high white trees, the Narcoo man slipped away. Mr Jeffris took a pot-shot, but with no real intention of killing—just a shot which threw the white cockatoos into the air like screeching feathers from a burst pillow.

Oscar sat beside Mr Smith under the canvas awning of the "Ladies' Compartment." Mr Smith was sharpening his axe on a stone. The laudanum bottle sat between them, but the humiliating funnel was nowhere in evidence. Since the slaughter at Sandy Creek, Oscar had administered his own laudanum. He kept a small clear-glass bottle in his jacket pocket which he replenished from the large stone demijohn. He sipped on it from time to time, but it was like water on a rock-hot fire—it gave off steam, but did not stop the heat. He sat on the hard wooden seat beside the silent Mr Smith who seemed to have contracted his whole being into the shadow of his hat. Mr Smith honed his axe. He had honed it for a long time now. Oscar Hopkins was drunk on laudanum. He sat with his back to the carefully labelled crates of glass and iron. He rubbed at the brown-stained bandages on his wrist. He knew his rope burns to be infected, but could not bear to speak of this, or any other matter, to Mr Jeffris who, now they were almost arrived at their destination, had begun to change in his manner toward him so that he could, cantering back up the hill towards him, actually smile and, without either apology or irony, ask him was it not sweet to be alive.

Mr Jeffris was content. He had not made a great exploration—you could not have a great exploration with seven wagons in mountainous country—but he had done sound work, which would serve as evidence of his ability to lead other expeditions. He had put names to several largish creeks. He had set the heights of many mountains which had previously been wildly misdescribed. He had established a reputation for courage, having led his party through places inhabited by desperate blacks. His journals recorded that he had "given better than we took" from the "Spitting Tribe." Also: "6 treacherous knaves" from the Yarra-Happini had been "dispatched" by their guns. He had also successfully defended the party from the "murderous Kumbaingiri." He recorded all this in a neat and flowing hand which gave no indication of the peculiarities of his personality. His sketches of the countryside, the long ridges of mountains etc, were as good as anything in Mitchell's journals.

When he cantered up the ridge toward Messrs Smith and Hopkins, he felt as fresh and clean as the morning he had left Port Jackson, felt far better, for on that occasion he had suffered a mild case of jitters, a looseness of the bowels which had been difficult to hide from men with a keen eye for weakness.

Mr Smudge was "not talking" to him. So, he thought, we have our little tiff. And a smile, he could not help it, ruffled the smooth cloak of concern he had arranged on his handsome face. Mr Smudge had still not attended to his toilet. There was a sprinkling of ginger hair upon his chin and some black charcoal marks on his ears here he had been scratching his mosquito bites. He was a contrast to his companion who was, as usual, neatly kitted out in fresh-washed twill and cotton. Yet you could not conclude from this that one had "character" whilst the other had not. They were a pair, in Jeffris eyes, and he thought the "Ladies' Compartment" aptly named.

Mr Jeffris had, perhaps, been to harsh with Mr Smudge. But the man was alive, was he not? He would be delivered as requested. He was not speared or poisoned by serpents. He had seen things no Sydney clerk would ever dream of seeing: life, death, savages. He had eaten snake and played the missionary. And now he should not be sitting on his car with his ramrod back, but should be throwing his hat in the air and offering to shout his protectors' drinks. They had guaranteed his place in history.

It was such a crisp, clear day and the ridge was almost as good as Her Majesty's highway. Mr Jeffris brought his stallion to a trot and rode beside the "Ladies' Compartment" for a piece. The view was splendid: the Bellinger estuary swept beneath them like an illustration to a fairy tale: strokes of aqua, gold, turquoise. Three pelicans thrust out their chests and glided on the air below.

"Well, Mr Hopkins," said Mr Jeffris, as he plucked a blood-bloated tick from his stallion's neck. "What do you say to that?"

"To what?" the clergyman said abruptly, turning his haughty red face briefly towards his questioner before looking back again. Beside him, Mr Smith honed his axe, and hid his anger and self-loathing from no one.

"What do you say," insisted Mr Jeffris, "to this, the countryside?"

"If it was my country, sir, I would be feared to see you coming."

Mr Jeffris laughed, a harsh, impatient laugh.

And I would pray to God to forgive you, and all of us who are of your party."

"It has been an education for you," said Mr Jeffris complacently. "That I can understand."

Oscar said nothing. His anus itched beyond belief. He thought: If

I were a strong man I would leap on him now and commit the sin of murder.

"Churches are not carried by choirboys," said Mr Jeffris. "Neither has the Empire been built by angels," and he would have said more on the subject, for it was one he had a secret passion for, and his hand had just drifted to his broad moustache which he would stroke as he gathered in the strands of his defence, when he was interrupted by that bow-legged gentleman, the plant collector, who was, as usual, wanting to go cantering away from the main party, and wished to take the carpenter as "bodyguard." As it was Mr Jeffris's agreement that he had the rights of sale of all the plant collector's delicate drawings, he was more than pleased to humour him.

The subjects of Empire and angels were forestalled by other calls on his attention, and finally he gave up. "We will drink," he shouted as he trotted back to settle some dispute that his brightly tattooed overseer was in the process of beginning. "We will drink champagne and send a message on the mail boat to Miss Leplastrier."

Oscar made a small noise, a little grunt of pain. In relationship to Miss Leplastrier, he felt only that he was a coward and complicitous in murder. As the wagon banged and thumped down the ridge into Bellingen Heads, its wooden brake squealing on the last steep drop, Oscar made a pair with his hunched and silent companion. He saw, in every blackened stump, every fallen log, in every shadow beneath a she-oak or turpentine, the same crumpled dark bodies, the frail and tender envelopes of human souls. He sought his laudanum. He imagined he could smell blood, and perhaps he could, for his own bandages were caked with it.

There were two taverns at Bellingen Heads and, discounting some grey neglected tents with dull, fat-leaved weeds growing along their perimeter drains, nothing else. The taverns faced each other across a sandy flat in the centre of which was a greenish-coloured waterhole surrounded by a ring of faeces. He and Mr Smith remained in their seat while the teams were unhitched and watered there, but when this lengthy business was at last completed Oscar climbed down.

"Come, Smith."

"Oh, God, man," said Percy Smith. "Surely you are not going to drink with them?"

Oscar said: "I have already travelled with them."

Inside the tavern he placed his injured hands flat on a rough table. There was a smell here which was like a condensation of that slightly off odour, that blocked-drain smell which, mixed with salt air, was the distinctive odour of Sydney. There were small black flies everywhere. They climbed across his bandages, his face, across the lids of his eyes. He felt he had travelled to the very heart of New South Wales.

He did not wear his "uniform," but the shiny, frayed black suit he had worn as both clergyman and clerk. He had a collarless white shirt from which his long white neck sprouted to his staring crimson face and blooming ginger hair. He sat with his back very straight against the wall and held his hands together across his chest. He thought: I will smite them all.

He trembled. He glared around the room at whiskered faces which not only stared back at him, but more often, laughed and pointed.

He said: "The pillars of society."

He thought: What would God have me do? He saw, in his mind, his father's face. He sighed.

He was the subject of much curiosity. He himself felt only that he was in an evil place. He had no curiosity beyond that. Yet the little tavern was filled with curiosities. The bar was made from a single three-foot-wide plank of cedar. The walls had pennies and florins driven into place with six-inch nails. A couple seemed to be having sexual congress on the other side of the torn curtain through which men—short, for the most part, broad and shovel-bearded, none of them too steady on their feet—would occasionally come and go.

While the day outside was clay-white, the inside was as dark and sooty as a painting above a fireplace. There was jostling going on around Mr Jeffris who seemed, in this environment, as white-skinned and genteel as an officer posing for his portrait.

The cedar cutters were insisting Jeffris must play cards with them. They spoke with humour, but if they were ready with a laugh and a wink they were also men whose faces spoke more of their cruelty and selfishness. These were faces that would "turn nasty" in a moment, and this information was, like a pitchfork, only partly hidden in the haystack of their laugh.

Jeffris would be Captain Hackum if he had to, but he would not play them cards. He sent Moët et Chandon to Mr Hopkins's table and the blacksmith and the bugler to go and guard him.

Oscar was unaware of all these currents. He was pressed by a crushing physical weight of evil. Mr Jeffris had been right: the Empire had not been built by choirboys.

At that moment he was his father's son, and he would bring retribution on the wicked. He would burn the tavern down. It was this conflagration that gave his eyes their intensity. He did not wonder why anyone would drive a six-inch nail through the silver and copper images of the Queen but, rather, how one would leave them melted and twisted in the ash. His thoughts were of kindling, ash-buckets, Miss Leplastrier's fireplace. He had left his laudanum aboard the wagon.

The blacksmith had signed the pledge and the bugler (who had only bugled once, as they crossed Sydney Harbour and had, for the rest, been called to obey the diverse and dangerous orders of Mr Jeffris), was of an age when he still cut himself with his razor and diluted his rum with lemonade. He was frightened, although not yet of anything in particular. The blacksmith was also nervous. The three did not speak to each other, but bunched, as you will see cattle in saleyards back their hindquarters against the rail until the auctioneer sends a rouster to prod them with his rod and make them run and skip and shit themselves before the buyers and sellers and those cagey souls who will not sell their stock until next week.

Mr Jeffris then excused his not playing poker on the grounds that, "This gentleman over here is a sky-pilot and it would cause him offence."

It is possible that Mr Jeffris was unaware of the degree to which the cloth was despised in that part of the country. He could not have known that Dennis Hasset's predecessor had drowned after being thrown in the Bellinger.

Oscar sat in the cold sticky envelope of his dirty skin and sipped his tepid champagne. Such was his disturbed state that he was not displeased to feel the heat of the cedar cutters' animus. He watched, and was watched. He had a nagging pain around his eyes that would only be cured by laudanum.

He was invited to step through the torn curtain and "dip your wee white toe in the holy well." Several glasses of dark liquor were delivered by the publican's pale and pimple-faced wife with "the compliments of Sir Roger Rogerer" or "Lord Pupslaughter," each glass being placed on Oscar's table in reverent silence, each announcement of the glass's donor being greeted with inordinate laughing and whistling.

You could feel the atmosphere becoming overloaded and had the tavern been a living organism it would soon have suffered a shiver of retro-peristalsis and spewed its poisonous contents out into the green shit-littered waterhole. But the tavern was inert, constructed from two-foot-diameter posts of Bellinger River turpentine, these being buried four feet down in the sandy soil.

Mr Jeffris had not come this far to die in a tavern brawl. He fiddled with his sword hilt. The publican picked up a claw hammer and was smacking its heavy head into the fleshy palm of his large hand. It was then—at the moment when everyone seemed to have focused on this hammer—that Oscar felt himself rising to his feet. He had not planned to. It was as if the pressure of his outrage could no longer be accommodated by the bent pipe of his body. He rose without a plan, but with the clear knowledge that retribution must be meted out to these blasphemers. He could not stand straight, but at an angle, and thus must prop his long arms out on the table.

There was a silence in the tavern. A woman was crying softly on the other side of the torn curtain.

Oscar thought: What would God have me do?

Everyone seemed to move and breathe very slowly. A freakishly large red-bearded man raised a glass to his glistening lips. Oscar thought: Like the hand of a clock.

He held up his own hand. He watched, as they watched, as his wrist emerged—a living thing—from the frayed shell of his sleeve.

"How thin my wrist is," he told them. "This wrist God made for me."

No one said anything.

"How could I smite you?"

He did not feel afraid. He felt a great clarity. He saw his own hand. He saw it in his mind's eye holding a shining white flower with five petals. The flower became a hand of cards.

"But I will play you poker and I will win. And you may know now, this money will be your gift to God's work in Boat Harbour."

A movement at his own table made him cast his eyes down. He saw the bugler had spilled his drink. The bugler's red lips were moving. The boy was praying. Oscar thought: I am drunk with laudanum. He also thought: I need a little sip. He put his hand to his jacket pocket where his bottle would normally be and then remembered—how disappointing this was; how angry it made him feel—that he had left the blessed thing in the wagon. His fingers found, instead, the crumpled envelope Lucinda had given him with which to reward Mr Jeffris.

God put this in his hand.

He took the envelope out and held it aloft. "I have a pot of one hundred guineas."

"No," cried the loathsome Mr Jeffris from the bar. "I forbid it."

"I would shoot you dead," cried Oscar above the general noise, "and go to hell for it; and I am only saved for want of a weapon." He pushed the table forward so that the blacksmith's glass of seltzer was toppled over and both blacksmith and bugler struggled to free themselves from their tangled chairs. "You murderer," cried Oscar. He put his hand in his pocket. His pocket was empty. Mr Jeffris had drawn his sword and was moving towards him. No one tried to hold him back.

" 'The Lord is my shepherd,' " said Oscar, his eyes bright, his back straight, " 'I shall not want. Thou preparest a table for me in the presence of mine enemies: thou anointest my head with oil.' "

Mr Jeffris's hand grasped Oscar above the elbow and pulled him so hard that he cried out with pain. Mr Jeffris's blue-black hair was carefully brushed. His moustache was waxed. He smelt of the barber's shop.

"Out," shrieked Mr Jeffris. "Out now."

"I warn you," called Oscar. He was yanked from the tavern like a tooth. He left much laughter behind, but he did not hear it. He was aware only of his outrage, of his pain, his impotence, his hatred. He was hurled on to the bare ground. He was kicked. Many times. There were no witnesses to save him. He was afraid. He was a crab scuttling across the grim grey sand. He was a cur. There was a wagon. He crawled beneath its rancid axle. The boot followed him. The sword poked between the spokes of the wheel.

He prayed: Oh God, give me the means to smite Thy enemy.

102

A Christian Man

Percy Smith had always thought himself a good and Christian man. He did not say his prayers by rote. The envelopes he put inside the felt-lined plate in in his parish church were fatter than the custom, not because he was wealthy but because he saw it as his duty.

He was a gentle man. He was gentle with the animals he tended and went to unusual lengths to make sure they suffered as little as possible. He was faithful to his wife, and a loving and tender father to his baby girls.

But what he feared about his character was that all his tenderness was but the visible shadow of his cowardice. When he was gentle and kind to those who might suffer it was because he was one with them, and he was frightened.

He could not bear to hear the stories of Christ's crucifixion. Neither habit nor repetition dulled the pain of that spear in the side, the long, slow, thirsty agony of death. When a preacher held up to him the shining example of the Christian martyrs, he feared that he–in such a moment–would deny his God.

The journey under Mr Jeffris's leadership had confirmed all these fears he had about himself. He was a counterfeit and coward. He had tortured Oscar Hopkins with a funnel. He had not stood up to defend him. He had lowered his eyes and "yes, sirred" the little martinet. He had "gone along." He had persuaded himself it would do no harm. And he had sat there–how damnable this was–while natives were slaughtered. And when Mr Hopkins had protested he had been one of those who tied him to a tree–on Jeffris's orders–so that he would cause no harm.

All his anger and disgust, all that which should have decently gone outwards, was driven inwards and he found himself–this happy, optimistic, loving man–sharpening his axe, honing it, so it would be as sharp as a razor.

He did not think: A razor for my wrists. He thought no actual words. He worked the round whetstone on and on, tasting only the great deep well of evil from which he had drunk.

When he had done the axe he began on the tomahawk.

He was seated thus, in the Ladies' Compartment, when he heard a cry and saw Mr Jeffris, sword raised high, booting Mr Hopkins in the backside and ribs. Mr Hopkins held an envelope which Mr Jeffris tried to snatch.

Mr Hopkins disappeared underneath the wagon. And then he was up beside the Ladies' Compartment, trying to clamber up the steps.

"God help me," said Oscar Hopkins.

Mr Hopkins was almost in the wagon when Mr Jeffris took him by his shoulder.

Percy Smith raised his tomahawk and brought it down on Mr Jeffris's upper arm. The head had not much weight. But Mr Smith was a strong man. He felt the bone cut. He felt the most immense satisfaction, a great shudder of something so close to pleasure you could not give it another name.

As Mr Jeffris stumbled back from the wagon, blood spurting through the fabric of his bright blue coat, Mr Smith saw that

Mr Hopkins had hefted the axe.

Mr Hopkins stood with his feet astride, the axe held incorrectly, the two white hands too close together. His face was blazing red. His mouth open. As the clergyman brought the axe up above his head, Mr Smith thought: He will hurt himself, he does it wrong.

"Hi," screamed Oscar Hopkins.

He brought the hate-bright axe down in the middle of Mr Jeffris's glistening, brilliantined head. And then his hands sprung loose from the handle. They were quivering and clapping. Mr Jeffris slumped to his knees and then tilted forward in the direction indicated by the ash axe handle. The blade was three inches into his skull which split around the orbit of his left eye.

All the drinkers were inside the tavern. Mr Smith noted this before he did a thing. Then he took the blanket from the seat and wrapped it around the quaking Hopkins. He brought him forcefully to the ground and there, without thinking why or what he was doing, he swaddled him as though he were a little child. He stilled the thrashing limbs by force. He held him bodily across his knees and patted him.

103

Did I Not Murder?

"Mr Smith, did I not murder a man?"

"We did, we did."

"Then tell me, pray, why this dreadful levity? And why are we here? And where is our party?"

Oscar had awoken on the morning of the day after the one in which Mr Smith had wrapped him in his blanket. It had taken some time to loosen himself from his sweaty swaddle, but when he was outside the familiar stained canvas walls of the tent, he discovered, not the scene of his nightmare, but a cool blue stretch of the Bellinger River, a wide, still sheet of water at a place where a rough little wharf had been constructed. At the wharf were moored two barges, or rather (because they were long craft with square-sawn bows), lighters. It was here that he found Percy Smith, a clean white shirt upon his back, busily hammering and sawing. He had already constructed an open platform across the two lighters.

"Our 'party' is at this moment going south in pursuit of Mr Jeffris," called Percy Smith, bestowing upon Oscar a cheerful grin and running his hand through his short hair so that it stood up at the back in a cocky's crest. "They now think him nought but an oiler. They want their pay, and so they've gone to relieve him of it."

"Oh, Lord," said Oscar, and groaned, holding his head in his hands.

Mr Smith put his hammer in his belt and sprang up the bound sapling ladder to the wharf.

"Whoa," he said. "Whoa, Neddy."

"Oh, God," said Oscar, unconscious of where he walked, stumbling on piles of bearers which were stacked about his feet. "Oh, dear God, what have we done?"

"Ssh," said Percy Smith, guiding his friend back through the tangle of hessian bags and beams, off the wharf to solid ground.

"Ssh, you must not fear."

"I have killed a man."

"Your Maker will forgive you."

A shudder passed through Oscar's thin white body. Percy Smith felt it, and knew it for what it was. He was not without symptoms of the same variety, and yet what he felt, for the most part—he begged God forgive him—was exhilaration.

He felt so light. When he came across the wharf to Oscar he could have skipped.

"The Lord was his Maker, too," said Oscar severely.

"Look," said Percy Smith, "we are alive. He is dead. Give thanks to God for our deliverance."

Percy Smith held Oscar by the arm and led him to a log beside the smoky campfire. He found some little sticks and leaves and, in a moment, had a blaze going. "They were nice enough to leave us tea and sugar and a billy. For the rest, they were in too much of a hurry."

"My church," cried Oscar, struggling to his feet.

"They did not take your church."

Oscar looked around him wildly and Percy Smith could not help laughing.

"Oh," said Oscar screwing up his white face into a crumpled page of irritation, "you are a madman."

"Your church is here," cooed Mr Smith. "Your church is here, my reverend sir. Indeed it is."

"It is no good to me here, fool," cried Oscar, standing straight up from his log and brandishing the finger-thin stick with which he had been poking into the little fire. "It must be in Boat Harbour. I have murdered the man who might get it there. And you, you–" he sighed. "Oh, dear." He sat down again. "I cannot blame you, Mr Smith, and what does any of this matter now when we are likely to be arrested?"

"Dear Mr Hopkins, please do be more cheerful."

"Cheerful!" shrieked Oscar.

"You are a regular little rosella. Look at you–burnt crimson and shrieking from the treetops. If there were troopers here they would soon know where to find us. But there are no troopers in the district."

"No police?"

"And even if there were a herd of Sydney constables, I bet you your laudanum bottle they would be too slow for Percy Smith. You should be proud to know me."

"Oh," Oscar said, "I am far worse."

"Do not 'worse' me, Hopkins. The knave was buried before a soul came out to see the sunlight. Congratulate me."

"Oh, I am sorry, Mr Smith, I cannot."

"Then have some johnnycake. It is a shame you were not awake to enjoy it hot."

Oscar sipped his tea while Mr Smith watched him. "Who would have known me for a murderer?" he said. "I would not have recognized it in myself. Think of my poor mother, when she suckled me . . ." He stopped and gazed into the smoke.

"Do not stew on it."

Oscar cupped his tea in his hand and looked around their campsite. Percy Smith watched him narrowly.

"You must not dwell on it."

"And where is the church on which account so much blood has been spilt?"

"It is all around you. Do you not recognize a pane of glass?" And indeed there were parts of the iron and glass church–all with their little labels flapping like manila leaves–scattered in neat piles all around the campsite and out on the wharf as well.

"I thought you were going to trip on the mullions."

"Oh," said Oscar softly, "oh dearie me."

"Do not dearie me."

"Oh, Lord."

"Oh, nonsense."

"And where are all the crates? And how will we . . .?"

"'Say not the struggle nought availeth,'" said Percy Smith. "'Our struggles and our hopes are vain.' How does it go? You have seen the crates."

"Smith," said Oscar, "I beg you, I am in no state for silly puzzles."

"Then listen to me, and do not stew. I have rented these two lighters on the wharf. They are not, individually, big enough to carry the church, so I have done the mathematics. Now your church is fifty feet long and twenty-five feet wide."

"Twenty-two feet and six inches."

"Good. And all these bits and pieces weigh twelve tons, as you have told me often enough. And to support twelve tons on the water we will need barges to displace two hundred and forty cubic feet. And these chaps here, these ones will do this. We can take the church upriver on the tide. I have arranged for help in the construction. Two men can pole and row to keep the barge in the centre-stream. I figure we can be there in two days."

"And then we must construct the church."

"Not then," said Percy Smith. He stood up. He began to stride around the fire. "Not then, now, here. On the barge. You see, I have worked it out. We will enter Boat Harbour in glory. Can you imagine it? Can you see the look on their godless faces? A crystal vision. My oh my. Can you see it, Mr Hopkins? What a visitation it would be to see God's temple come to them upon the water."

"Mr Smith, I am tired."

"Do not be tired, my Reverend Jolly-man," said Percy Smith. "Lean on me. I am a practical man. I have the base plate already constructed on the water. It is a simple matter."

"But what will happen at the other end?"

"Why, dear Mr Hopkins, listen to this. I asked myself the same question. It is easy enough, I thought, to bet this glass church built on water, but what will happen at the other end? And the answer is this. I have twelve wooden joists laid across the two barges. You must have seen them. But you did not, of course. You were Macbeth in a dream. I have been busy. I have twelve joists across, you see. When we are at Boat Harbour I will have twenty-four men lift the church by these joists and they can carry it. You should congratulate me."

"Twenty-four would not be enough. They must carry half a ton each."

"Then forty-eight or ninety-six. It doesn't matter. These towns are always full of men wanting to prove their strength. We will have them carry it up the main street like a float in a procession."

"Mr Smith, why are you like this?"

"You would not like the answer, Mr Hopkins."

"Tell me anyway."

"I am like this because we killed an evil man," said Percy Smith. "It has done me a power of good. I cannot tell you."

"And do you feel no shame?"

"Oh, yes, of course. And guilt, but I will tell you, in truth, that I have felt more *sorrow* to have slain a beast. That is something you never become accustomed to. You take care to make your knife sharp and to make the killing quick, but the moment always comes when you look that poor beast in the eye, and you can ask other farmers the same question and if they are honest they will tell you the truth—it is a dreadful thing. But this man was cruel. I am glad we killed him. I could not have borne to be a jellyfish one more day."

"And what of the Commandment we have broken?"

"I am sure the Almighty does not have a mind like a railway clerk."

"By which you mean?"

"He is not a puffed-up little toad in the government offices. He knows you are not a bad man."

Oscar reached his hand into his pocket and found his laudanum was in its proper place.

"You should wash," said Percy Smith. "I have some soap."

"Yes," said Oscar. He did not believe any of the things Percy Smith said about God.

104

Mary Magdalene

Kumbaingiri Billy was not in that tavern or any other tavern, ever. But the woman on the other side of the torn curtain was his father's sister and she had been abducted by cedar cutters about a year before that time and was as reduced and miserable as any human being might ever be. Kumbaingiri Billy's father's sister was about twenty years old. She said the tavern was very quiet when Oscar made his speech. She said he had a face that was torn and peeling like the trunks of the paper-barks which grow in swampy land around the Bellinger. She saw great unhappiness there, said Kumbaingiri Billy, but that unhappiness, he reckoned, was most likely her own.

This young woman was a witness to the murder. It was she who showed Percy Smith the cesspit which was to be Mr Jeffris's final resting place. It was she who took him down along the river to the decaying homestead of H. M. McCracken and stood outside, scratching her long thin legs, while Percy Smith haggled with McCracken about a fair rent for his leaky lighters.

She saw Oscar awake. She heard all the arguments about murder. She was squatting in the bush some five yards from them. She was very taken with Oscar. She thought him a good man. When he finished his damper she came out of the bush and told him there were two men she could get to help them with their building.

She saw the glass church built upon those lighters.

Kumbaingiri Billy knew the story. He said: "He moved fast, that man with the red face and the red hair. My aunty named him 'Bushfire' for the way he leapt from place to place on that barge, burning red, dancing in his own firelight. They got the columns up the first day—they were twisty-curly things like rope, like the corkscrew on a can opener. These columns were black and greasy. The grease was black too. It made the white chaps into blackfellows. They braced these columns off with saplings. They could not use nails, of course. They tied the saplings on with rope. Then they got the trusses assembled on the wharf. There was no fancy stuff in the trusses. There was plenty of fancy stuff, but that came later—all this fancy iron like the houses down in Lawson Street—all this went around the bottom of the walls. There was other stuff along the top, a real cocky's crest it was, but the trusses were dead plain. They assembled them on the wharf and then they waited for the tide to go down. They waited. They had a smoke. Round about lunchtime the tide went down. The top of the walls came level with the wharf and then this Mr Hopkins yelled out: 'Right you are.' They slid the trusses out and fixed them on. Mr Hopkins would not go out on the roof, but, by golly he was not shy to give those fellows orders. He called to them, you do this, you do that, you be careful, better not drop that thing and break it. They started two days before Palm Sunday. They worked on the sabbath too. That was the day they began to cover the iron with glass. They were working for a bet, or so I heard later, and this is why they broke the sabbath. They started at the bottom and moved from left to right, tap-tap. They must have used some metal clips, I reckon, to keep the glass in. This was when my aunty saw glass. My word, she was tickled by it. She had only seen glass in booze bottles until that day. She saw glass could be good. She had not thought this before. When she saw this glass church built she became a Christian. This was the day Jesus first came to the Bellinger. She saw Jesus, Mary, Joseph, Paul, and Jonah—all that mob she never knew before. She saw your great-grandfather was a brave man. She saw he had a halo like one of those saints. She saw that when it was night he shivered—not from cold, but from a sort of holy happiness. He told her: 'You will live in paradise.' He christened her Mary, for Magdalene. It was a damn silly name for a Kumbaingiri and if you want my opinion, Bob, it was ignorant to talk to us Kooris in that way."

105

Miriam

Miriam Chadwick was not in mourning and had, once again, thrown away her widow's weeds although Mrs Trevis, her smudge-lipped employer, had thought, out loud, that this was tempting fate.

"Who have *I* to mourn for any more?" said Miriam Chadwick who was, when this conversation took place, holding Mrs Trevis's newborn babe, a bad-tempered little chap, always "sucky" and given to banging his little head against the governess's shoulder.

"You might mourn for me, or Mr Trevis," suggested Mrs Trevis.

"Oh, there is no likelihood of that," said Miriam Chadwick tossing her hair back off her shoulders—beautiful hair, coal-black hair, raven hair, but who was there to see its dark blue lights out here at Marx Hill? "No likelihood at all," said Miriam, bouncing the babe resentfully, and leaving her comment ambiguous as long as she dare, "with both you and Mr Trevis in such fine health."

"Here," said Mrs Trevis, reaching out for the babe while she gently cuffed her little boy who was reaching for a saucepan on the kitchen table. "Here, I'll take bubba. You try your hand at t'other."

"T'other" was the butter churn which wooden wheel of torture Mrs Trevis now abandoned to her governess.

"If you have nabbed young Reverend Hasset," Mrs Trevis began, an observation that had nothing to do with mourning or widow's weeds, but was intended to bring her uppity governess (she thought herself too good to set the fires or scrub the milk pails) to a proper understanding of her place in this society.

"I did *not* attempt, as you put it, to 'nab' the poor man, although there is no doubting he was properly 'nabbed' without him knowing what had happened."

"Jealousy killed the cat," said Mrs Trevis, dipping her finger in the butter jar and then slipping it into her infant's sucky mouth.

Miriam Chadwick looked on with her handsome nose wrinkled.

"Curiosity."

"Beg yours?"

"It was curiosity that killed the cat."

"Curiosity in the beginning," said Mrs Trevis, "but jealousy in the end. It is bad luck to throw away your widow's weeds."

This conversation was in Miriam Chadwick's mind on the hot Thursday afternoon when, with the Trevises all gone into Boat Harbour to buy provisions for the Easter feast, she was savouring her solitude, sitting on the wooden step, looking down at the curve of the Bellinger river. She was running through her list of unsatisfactory or irritating or boorish suitors when she saw a church made from glass towed into her field of vision by two men in wide straw hats.

Her first thought was disappointment that Mrs Trevis was not here to witness this thing with her, that she must exclaim to nothing but the empty air. "Oh, my," she said, feeling that some subtle victory had been somehow denied her, "just look at what you have missed. Just look. Just *look* at it."

It came up the river, its walls like ice emanating light, as fine and elegant as civilization itself.

"Who?" demanded Miriam Chadwick." "Who? Just answer me that." Who in this valley of muddy boots could be responsible for such a thing? For it was not simply that the little steep-roofed church was made from glass, but that it had all the lovely proportions and grace-notes of a fancy constructed for a prince, say, in Bavaria.

All along its roof ridge there was a decorative edging, a frill—she could not make it out exactly but it would seem, there, to be like a line of fleurs-de-lis. The glass sheets of its walls were not square and dull like window panes, but tall and thin, with a triangulation at the top, and a lovely cast-iron frieze made of medallions (crests?), which repeated in a frieze along the bottom of the walls. This cast-iron frieze must be nearly three feet high—ornate like the rood screen in a cathedral.

She did not see or appreciate Mr Flood's speciality—the cast-iron barley-sugar scrolls of which he had been so proud—and indeed it would not be more than a minute before she forgot the miraculous building entirely—it soon assumed no more importance than a pretty wrapping paper for, as the lighters slewed in the river, the glass regained its transparency, and she saw the black-suited figure sitting on a chair inside the church.

At this moment her sense of wonder was completely swamped by more practical concerns, for if this lovely building was a church—and was that not a cross at the termination of the cresting?—then the black-suited man inside was almost certainly a clergyman.

She had an aqua moiré-silk riding habit, which was thought "unsuitable" in Boat Harbour. She put it on. She had a little hat with a veil. She fastened it with a long pin. There was no time for bathing. She went out into the home paddock and caught the bad-tempered little Shetland which had been left at home, smacked it hard across the nose when it tried to bite her. The beast pulled its head back and its eye, though wild, was less wild than usual. "So," thought Miriam Chadwick, "you are a bully like the rest of them." The pony pulled. Miriam hit it again, refllecting bitterly on the brutalizing effects of life at Fernmount.

The pony would not go slow. It went at speed, cantering, almost galloping down the rutted shale-loose hill towards the river. She lost her pretty little whip at the gate but the pony was hard-mouthed and would not pull up. She came on to the cattle path beside the Bellinger. She came beside the rowing men and the glass church on the barge.

"Oh, dear God," she prayed, "do not let me appear as such a fool." She cried with fright as the pony stumbled on a crumbling piece of riverbank, regained its footing, and continued, leaving the church behind, in the direction of the landing wharf at Boat Harbour.

She thought it obvious to everyone what she was up to and was, in consequence, ashamed.

At Boat Harbour she had to hide an hour or two and not be seen by her employers or their children, who were, it seemed, at every draper's shop and corner. She sat in the prayer room above the cobbler's shop and having begun by pretending to pray, ended by doing it in earnest.

106

The Aisle of a Cathedral

The Bellinger was not like it is now, with wide electric-green fields pushing down on to the river. The banks were like green cliffs of camouflage pierced with giant knitting needles and spun and tangled all about with ferns and creepers. It was a landscape already bleeding from the stabbing and hacking of the cedar cutters, but the wounds were all internal, in the belly of the bush, and although Oscar saw how Percy Smith and his two helpers must jump and poke with their punting poles to keep them clear of floating cedar logs, he did not guess the history of these logs. He saw only the shrieking walls of jungle which threw up wide-winged birds as the church approached.

Laudanum or no, he was not at ease. He called for Percy Smith to lock the door. He placed his hard wooden chair in the very middle of the church. He prayed out loud and his voice had a hard vibrant quality inside the glass. He said: "Oh Lord, I am alive in the midst of Thy dreadful river. All Thy glory surrounds me, but I am afraid."

Outside the walls, he could hear the man named "rumgo" giggling. This had no more importance to him than the cries of savage birds.

My great-grandfather drifted up the Bellinger River like a blind man up the central aisle of Notre Dame. He saw nothing. The country was thick with sacred stories more ancient than the ones he carried in his sweat-slippery leather Bible. He did not even imagine their presence.

Some of these stories were as small as the transparent anthropods that lived in the puddles beneath the river casuarinas. These stroies were like fleas, thrip, so tiny that they might inhabit a place (inside the ears of the seeds of grass) he would later walk across without even seeing. In this landscape every rock had a name, and most names had spirits, ghosts, meanings.

He had given his hat to Kumbaingiri Billy's father's sister. It was the Wednesday before Good Friday, and although it was now cool in Sydney, it was hot at this latitude. Under the canopy of glass it was very hot indeed. Only on the dog-leg bend at Fernmount was the riverbank able to provide any shade.

Kumbaingiri Billy saw the glass church. He was a young boy, initiated only the year before. He was with the men, hunting, at the place which is now named Marx Hill. He saw the glass church in the distance—a prism, a cube, a steeple of light sliding into the green shadows of Fernmount. There were men with blue shirts and wide-brimmed hats. They held long poles. They stood around the perimeter. In the middle was a man. Even in the shadow, so Kumbaingiri Billy told my father, fire danced around this man's head.

Oscar could not see the blacks watching him. He was not frightened of the blacks. He was frightened of other things. The wooden platform beneath his feet was built on H. M. McCracken's two lighters, which remained, in spite of all the nails and planks and lashing that joined them together, two independent entities. Thus when one lighter bobbed it would not be in step with its companion and the result of this was that the foundation of the fragile bird-cage church would shift and twist. Glass, for all its great strength under compression, cannot easily tolerate this sort of twisting.

Three panes of glass had cracked. These panes were in the roof. They crazed and hung like ice-knives. Their jigsaw edges refracted the colours of the rainbow across my great-grandfather's clasped hands. He was gaunt and ugly, with a bright Adam's apple and a bright red hooked nose. He looked like the most fearsome Calvinist. There were white unburnt rings around his eyes. His green irises were set in yellow whites and these were laced with fine red rivers.

Percy Smith drove his pole into the mud. Vectors of force fought with each other for a resolution. The platform beneath Oscar's feet twisted. Another pane splintered and, this time, fell at the foot of the barley-sugar columns in the little chancel. "Oh, Lord," he prayed, as sweat ran down his brow and into his eyes, "I thank Thee for granting me this day."

For answer, three more panes crazed. And while, according to all the laws of science, they should have fallen–there was no wire reinforcing in the glass, nothing but its own splintered edges to hold it there–it stayed in place. It was a blemish on the sky, like something curdled–milky-white, like crinkled Cellophane.

The man inside the church waved his hands, gestures which appeared, from the perspective of Marx Hill, to be mysterious, even magical, but which, inside the crystal furnace of the church, had the simple function of repelling the large and frightening insects which had become imprisoned there.

There were bush-flies inside the church. They did not understand what glass was. There were also three blue-bellied dragonflies. For one hundred thousand years their progenitors had inhabited that valley without once encountering glass. Suddenly the air was hard where it should be soft. Likewise the tawny hard-shelled water beetle and the hang-legged wasp. They flew against the glass in panic. They had the wrong intelligence to grasp the nature of glass. They bashed against "nothing" as if they were created only to demonstrate to Oscar Hopkins the limitations of his own understanding, his ignorance of God, and that the walls of hell itself might be made of something like this, unimaginable, contradictory, impossible.

While the three men worked around him with their long sapling punting poles, Oscar put his hands over his ears or waved them in the air. The fractured glass cast a burning spectrum across his forehead. He said: "Oh, God, I praise Thee. I praise Thy dreadful river. I am not afraid." But his hand sat on the hard lump in his pocket where the sticky laudanum bottle sat.

He thought: It will soon be over.

But the church burnt his already burnt skin and he watched the exquisite jewel-blue dragon-flies crash against the glass. He felt a stab of panic, that he had made his bet on second-rate information. It was not God who had persuaded him, but that "other voice."

He took his jacket off and put it over his head and shoulders, and that is how, when the fractured church was finally towed to the jetty at Boat Harbour, the government inspector mistook him, in the evening light, for a hooded nun.

107

Arrival of Anglican Church at Boat Harbour

The Reverend Dennis Hasset had discovered a leech in his sock. He was trying to walk home to his house so he might remove it. Actually, it was not merely one leech, it was two, although both of them were anchored at almost the one spot with the result that one had grown fat and bloated while the other stayed lean. The sight of this shining black slug with two tails turned his stomach and he would have run, were it not for the likelihood that, being seen to be in flight from something, he would be set upon by drunken bullock drivers or be pelted with potatoes by the snotty-nosed children of the Magneys or the Walls.

When he heard about the glass church his only thought was that he would not now be able to deal with the leech at home. He certainly did not make the connection with Lucinda. In fact he did not strictly believe what he heard. He knew only that there was a structure which his informant, the clerk from the government offices, imagined was a church and which would, eventually, prove to be a steam saw or a lifeboat or a smashed-up phaeton recovered from a shipwreck at The Heads.

To remove the leech, he needed salt. He could buy a ha'penny-worth at Hammond and Wheatley, which he did, favouring one foot a little, resisting the urge to rub ankle against ankle while he waited behind Mrs Trevis who was, between buying flour and bacon, relating the story of her Grandfather Dawson's service as a coach painter to Her Majesty the Queen. The clerk from the government offices ran in twice to fetch him and it was he who begged Mr Hammond please to serve the reverend gentleman because he was required by the government inspector to be at the landing wharf "quick and lively."

The Reverend Dennis Hasset got his salt. He was not accustomed to shopping. He was surprised at how much salt you got for a ha'penny. There was no way you could slip this into your pocket. It was a hefty bag and must be held under the arm. He did so, marching down Hyde Street while the government clerk, a huge fellow with hefty hands and a cowed spirit that made him bend forward and bow his neck, clucked and fussed and postulated this and that about this strange glass church.

The Reverend Mr Hasset was plotting a way to get the salt in contact with the leeches. He was therefore disappointed to see that a crowd had gathered at the wharf. This would make the operation that much more difficult.

He listened to the clerk as they pressed through to the river. As usual, most of the crowd were drunk. They smelt loathsome: unwashed clothing, rum, vomit. Hell itself could smell no worse than this. Dennis Hasset opened his bag of salt and took a fistful.

It was then that he saw the church. He thought so many things at once. That it was a miracle, a spider web, a broken thing, a tragedy, a dream like something constructed for George III and then assaulted in a fit of rage. He thought: It has been hit with hail. He thought: it has been salvaged from a wreck out at The Heads. He thought: it was a mistake to triangulate those tall panes of glass when a Roman arch would be much more graceful. He thought: Lucinda.

It was the latter thought that made the mole on his back turn hot and itchy because he had never, in all his letters, bothered to tell her that he was now a married man and soon to be the father of a child.

In the face of this crazed image of Lucinda's passion, he was numb with panic.

His mole was driving him crazy with its itching. He held his salt. He stood with the most of his weight on the foot that did not have the leeches. He waited for Lucinda to emerge from between the barley-sugar columns. He could not see through the glass itself—it had become, with all the splintering, almost opaque. He tucked the bag of salt under his arm and fixed a smile on his face, but as H. M. McCracken's leaky old lighters were moored to the bollards on the wharf, the figure that emerged from the church's wooden door was not that of Lucinda Leplastrier, but a gaunt collarless burnt-ghost figure who marched towards him carrying a little suitcase like a hat-box.

"Sir," said Oscar and held out his hand.

Dennis Hasset's hand, alas, was filled with salt. He opened it, by way of explanation. The burnt man stared at it and laughed; it was not a normal laugh but a dry noise like a cough.

"The Reverend Mr Hasset?"

There was something very dangerous about this staring man. His green-eyed gaze was too intense. He would not release his hold on Dennis Hasset's eyes, not even for a second.

"Yes," said Dennis Hasset.

"Then I have the pleasure, sir, to present this splendid church to you. It is a gift to the Christians of Boat Harbour from the most wonderful woman in New South Wales." The ghost seemed oblivious to the splintered state of the church. "I tell you now, without reserve," he roared, "I envy you. This woman loves you."

Dennis Hasset felt ill. He wished to withdraw. All the godless of Boat Harbour pressed their thick necks and cauliflower ears forward. He stooped and poured his fistful of salt into his sock.

The madman was now crying. His face was as dirty and tattered as the bandages around his wrists.

"How you can stand there," Oscar said, "when Miss Leplastrier pines in Sydney, why, it is quite beyond my comprehension."

The salt in Dennis Hasset's sock was as painful as ground glass. He thought: When, oh Lord, will my past follies stop returning to torment me?

He put his hand on the shoulder of the weeping man. He intended Christian charity, but felt only an alien body as hard and bony as a suit of armour. It was then, wondering how he could stop the germs of scandal which were already multiplying around him, that he saw Miriam Chadwick's bright green riding costume.

"Mrs Chadwick," he said, "I wonder could you assist us?"

Thus, while Percy Smith was busy shifting his mooring in accordance with the wishes of the government inspector, Dennis Hasset and Miriam Chadwick escorted Oscar Hopkins up the rutted track to Hyde Street. Both men limped a little, one from an injury incurred upon a journey, the other on account of blood-red salt grinding against a naked high-arched foot.

At the Hyde Street corner, Dennis Hasset requested that Oscar excuse them both. He left him standing, still weeping, in the shelter of the post office while he conferred with Mrs Chadwick whose large, dark brown eyes, so obviously filled with charity for the weeping man, moved him greatly.

"Miriam," he said, "you must help me, please. I must hurry to my wife before she hears all this puffed up by gossips. Would you be the good Samaritan? Here is a crown. Buy him bandages and mercurochrome. Here is the key to the meeting room. You can lock the door and keep the busybodies out. Look after him. He is in such a sorry state, poor beggar. Can you manage this? Will Mrs Trevis permit you?"

"Dear Dennis," said Miriam Chadwick, who was at once delighted to have exactly what she wished and outraged that a man who had (not long ago either) cruelly spurned her, should now beg favours of her. "Dear Dennis, you must hurry home to Elizabeth and leave this wounded soul to me."

She accepted the large brass key, the crown piece, and the torn bag of salt which Dennis Hasset thrust into her bosom. And then my great-grandmother took Oscar Hopkins by the arm and walked very slowly, oblivious to the stares, to the meeting hall above the cobbler's shop. There she locked the door and began her ministrations.

108

Oscar and Miriam

When Oscar Hopkins and Miriam Chadwick came down the stairs to the cobbler's shop at last, it was to announce their impending marriage.

There was a small wet stain on the back of my great-grandmother's green silk riding habit. This was remarked on–how could it not be–but nothing was ever said out loud, and, in any case, Miriam had plied the young traveller with Mr Hammond's expensive emollients and creams, with stinging iodine, blue-red mercurochrome, bright yellow "Healing Ointment," had rubbed him with so many healing dyes that he soon looked like a tropical fish in his father's aquarium; with so many wet and greasy substances about, no one could be surprised if Miriam also spilled a wee drop on her clothing.

Oscar, when at last he opened the heavy cedar door at the top of the stairs above the cobbler's, had the stunned and slightly vacant air you might see in some one rescued from a burning house.

As he walked down the loud, uncarpeted stairs, he felt his sin declared to all the world.

I love Lucinda Leplastrier.

The cobbler was working at his bench. Oscar could not meet his gaze. He looked instead at a pair of dancing pumps hanging from the door. To these he nodded.

He had fornicated in God's temple, he who had judged the cedar cutters at Urunga.

All my life, he thought, I have sought the devil's murmuring in my ear, have let him persuade me that it is holy that I bet, that I abandon my father, that I draw poor Stratton into the morass, and all the while I am armoured by conceit. I play the saint. When Miss Leplastrier and I were most passionately engaged, I imagined it was I who restrained us from sin, I who ensured our chastity until that happy day, (today, today I might have written to her in triumph) when she might have seen what I am and accepted my proposal that we stand as bride and bridegroom in God's sight. But it was not I. And the proof is here: that the moment a ministering hand is placed on that part of my anatomy, the minute, the *instant* it is touched, the first time in all its life—why, then, I fail the test. And find my Christianity to be but a spiderweb, so easily it is brushed aside. And I am a dog in the street prepared to be crushed by a waggon's wheel in order to let its beastly nature have its head. I cannot even justify my act by calling out "love, love, I did it for love."

His punishment was that he must marry this woman he had compromised. It did not occur to him that it was she who had compromised him. He must marry her. He took the laudanum from his pocket and sipped it in the deep shadowed doorway of the cobbler's shop. The street was lined with bullock waggons all loaded with logs as thick as four big men. The air was fat and warm and syrupy, sweet with forest sap, urine, brandy. There were yellow dogs and yellow clay earth littered with furry bark.

Oscar's eyes remained focused in the middle distance. He sucked in his cheeks, biting them harder than he knew. He limped beside my great grandmother as they set about this business, each equally determined that the job be done properly, and yet with a definite distance between them, like allies in a business venture, or the captains of opposing cricket teams. They posted the banns. It was done in fifteen minutes. They went to Bernie Lovell and each rewrote their wills. It took half an hour. They went to the offices of the *Courier-Sun* and filled out a little form for the advertisement which announced their engagement.

Only when my great-grandmother saw he did not write "Reverend" in their engagement notice, did she suspect he might not be a clergyman. She certainly had no idea that he was now the owner of a glass church in Sydney and a fortune of ten thousand pounds.

Oscar had forgotten this himself. He was sick at heart, preoccupied by what he had lost, not gained. All he could think was that the glass church was the devil's work, that it had been the agent of murder and fornication. The only clear thing he could think, the only thing he could hear above the raging passions of his beating heart, was how he could destroy the hateful thing.

It was just five o-clock, and the government clerks were already closing their shutters for the day, when he began to bid her goodbye. She had employment to return to, and although he should have seen the word "Governess" on both her will and the marriage banns, he had not; her employment remained a mystery to him. Like two strangers introduced to business partnership by medium of a newspaper advertisement, they agreed to meet at the post office at ten o-clock upon the morrow. He saw her on to her pony which she had tethered in the government paddock. He must have known, already, that he would not commit himself to her in any but a legalistic way, for he felt only mild dismay to see how she treated the animal. He made the motion of doffing his hat to her, although he had no hat, having given the same to Kumbaingiri Billy's father's sister. He held open the gate of the government paddock, and when the pony and its rider had passed through, he walked thoughtfully down towards the river, dragging a stick behind him, scratching a line in the baked clay track and thus – his route marked by this fine erratic line – he disappeared for ever from my great-grandmother's life.

109

A Cheque Amidst Her Petticoat

When Miriam was old, she wore long black dresses and violent-coloured petticoats (crimson, royal purple, blazing yellow) and it was easy enough at that time to see her as an ugly old parrot in a Victorian cage, but when she stood in Dennis Hasset's little study – hardly a study at all for it was what they call, in Bellingen, a sleep-out, a makeshift enclosure of a pleasant back veranda—when she stood there, she was straight and young and strikingly handsome. She had strong features, a straight nose, a long jaw, wide-placed brown eyes above defined cheekbones. She was almost severe, but yet was not severe, and her true obsessive qualities were clouded by her habit of making small flirtatious gestures which she offered—she could not seem to help herself—even when she was in a furry. Thus she might lower her eyes, or lean forward in a certain way or even let some part of her clothing brush against her listener, all this in a soft, yes, even seductive style, while you could see, if you had an eye for these things, the tight and secret clenching of her jaw.

She was in mourning for Oscar, and although she would very soon grow out of her flirtatious habits, she would never abandon this particular style of mourning. It was not a fashion in mourning. It was something she invented herself to cater for all her conflicting needs, and although this style would finally look—as I said before—cranky, Victorian, simply crazy, this was not the effect when Dennis Hasset looked at her.

She wore long black watered silk, cut tight around her well-formed bosom and flowing in expensive folds across her bustle. She wore a black veil and a black hat with feathers in it. Her petticoats showed here and there. They were bright red. They said: To hell with you; I will do what I like.

If Dennis Hasset had ever regretted not marrying her, this was no longer the case. He recognized her as a dangerous woman. He wished her to leave his study. She smiled at him and twice, accidentally he supposed, touched his trouser leg with the toe of her little buttoned boot.

She had never guessed the size of Oscar's estate until Dennis Hasset had come to her, begging her to give it up. It was he, this handsome, educated man who trembled like a girl before the godless cedar cutters, who had tried to trick her into signing a "waiver." It was only then, and very slowly, that she began to understand about the wager which was celebrated in that rolled-up document the dead man had carried in his little case.

It was then that she began her lifetime habit of acting against the dictates of the "best advice." The best advice would have had her still a governess, less than a governess, a target for the milky-white spew of the youngest Trevis. The best advice would have her leave the glassworks in Darling Harbour, and have her believe it quite impractical to remove them to so isolated a post as Boat Harbour. She said (many, many times): "I loved Boat Harbour. It was my home. How could I leave it?" She sold off the land in Darling Harbour and transported what she could, including glass blowers and their families, all of whom she persuaded, by dint of personal visits, gifts, bribes, bonuses, to make the dangerous sea journey north.

She did not love Boat Harbour at all. She loathed it. But now she was rich and she began a lifetime of paying back those whom she felt had slighted her. And she would, in the careful, almost feudal structure she built to hold the hierarchy of offences, place this clergyman near the top of the triangle, the apex of which was occupied by Mrs Trevis.

There was no room in the little study. You sat crammed on a straight-backed chair and looked across the vicar's shoulder to the open-sided veranda where the crates of books his present circumstances made it impossible to unpack stood greying and gathering new watermarks each time the wind came from the south. Or you could, if you cricked your neck a little, look down the long thin block of land, past the vicar's Jersey cow picking what it could from the low winter grass, to where the black bones of the glass church stood, its panes mostly cracked or crazed, with long dried strands of dead water clinging to its roof.

This church belonged to Miriam, or so it had been determined in the court at Sydney. Dennis Hasset had imagined it was his, for it had been intended as a gift and he had taken it upon himself to have it transported on to his back paddock.

Miriam sat on the chair and smoothed her skirts. She placed her hands in her lap, quite so, not attempting to hide – Dennis Hasset thought her intention to be the opposite – the tell-tale roundness of her stomach. She crossed her leg, showed a little petticoat, and looked at him in such a way he could not hold her gaze.

"I have been speaking to Mr Field from Gleniffer," Miriam said, removing a black glove to reveal than an extra wedding ring had found its way on to her pretty hand in Sydney. "He says there are now fifteen Anglican families who would be pleased to fill a plate each Sunday."

Dennis Hasset thought: Fill a plate. She says it so grandly, but she has not seen the coppers and threepences looking so lonely on the green felt base. When Mr Field says he will "fill a plate" he is being a grand man with his thumbs stuck in his braces, but the reality is different. They will have me, Dennis Hasset thought, riding out to Gleniffer twice on a Sunday and expect me to do it for the love of God and twopence ha'penny.

"And that is when it came to me," said Miriam, smiling sweetly, "that we might make a present of my dear little church to them. Mr Field says he has no shortage of corrugated iron, and as for the walls, he explained to me how he would fix weatherboards to it."

"How clever of him," said Dennis Hasset sourly.

"Well," said Miriam, "indeed it is. You cannot just nail a

board on to a cast-iron frame."

"I never thought of it," said Dennis Hasset. This was play-acting. A weatherboard could be secured, just as glass could, on the wooden mullions.

"Spare me your wit then, Mr Vicar, and if you are so wise in these worldly things, tell me how you would fix a weatherboard to the walls of the church."

Dennis Hasset smiled at her in a way which, in any other context, would be taken to be friendly.

"With fencing wire," Miriam said. "Like a stockyard fence. But if you are wise in these country matters, you will know how to do it. But, then again, you will not need to. The Gleniffer Anglicans will be here tomorrow. There has been so much trouble with white ant they are pleased to have a cast-iron frame. But, Mr Hasset you look disappointed."

"As you know," he said, "I had rather hoped I would at last have a church here.

"Then we must get up a fête, and raise some money," Miriam said. "But you cannot ask me to worship in my husband's tomb."

"Still, I am disappointed."

"Your Sundays will certainly be very busy."

"I do not complain about God's work, but rather that the church was intended for me. But, but," he held his hand up as if to hold off her fury, "the courts said otherwise."

"Miss Leplastrier must have been most fond of you."

"We were friends, yes."

"As she was obviously fond of my husband."

Husband? How is he husband?

"She has been in correspondence with me again. I must say I admire her frankness."

"Oh?"

"You are not aware of our correspondence? She does not keep you informed? And yet I understood from her when we met outside the court in Sydney that you had a detailed correspondence. Indeed, she knew so much about our little town."

"Come, Miriam, what has she said." He held out his hand to the letter that Miriam was unfolding.

"It is not gentlemanly to pry into the private correspondence of young ladies. But I will read you little pieces. She writes: 'I made a bet in order that I keep my beloved safe.' I take that ill, Dennis, that she call him 'beloved.' I think that poor taste. What say you?"

"She was fond of him?"

"She seems fond of almost everyone. But let me read some more: 'I beg you, please, as one woman to another, to not do this to me. I am astounded to see these words come off the tip of my own pen, but still they come. Let us not have our fears make us greedy.' Our fears', said Miriam, "make *us* greedy. Really, I can't think what she means. 'When I walk the streets of Sydney I realize I cannot bear to be an impoverished woman here. Please, Mrs Chadwick, if you have any Christian charity at all, you will allow me to keep some small percentage of my fortune.' " Miriam then folded the letter and placed it in her bag.

"So," she said.

Dennis Hasset's lips parted and his eyes narrowed a fraction.

"So," he said, "and what do your reply?"

"I replied sympathetically, of course. How could I not be sympathetic, I who have spent half her life in mourning rags, as I am again. I have an intimate knowledge of the poor woman's situation. It is I, after all, who was brought to this town through ill-fortune, was shipwrecked, and although a governess have had to suffer the indignity of a life better suited to an Irish servant. I know, better than she knows, what her situation must mean to her."

"And your response?"

"I worked as a servant," Miriam repeated. "I set fires. I milked cows when I should be teaching them their Shakespeare and their Milton."

"And you would have her do the same."

"Dennis, you think me hard."

"Mrs Chadwick," he said.

"Hopkins," she corrected.

"Mrs Hopkins," he said, "let us not be enemies."

Mr Hasset, you are in such a rush to be friends you are stamping on my feet. Have I not said I will donate my little church to your Gleniffer Anglicans?"

"Indeed you have."

"Why then, I am dispatching today my cheque to Miss Leplastrier. It is not a fortune, but certainly should be some assistance to her in her present needs."

It was this cheque which occasioned the short letter from Lucinda to Miriam which was unearthed nearly half a century later amongst Miriam's darned and fretted-over petticoats. By the time it was found, her letter was as fragile as the body of a long-dead dragon fly. Its juice was dry. It was history. Lucinda was known for more important things than her passion for a nervous clergyman. She was famous, or famous at least amongst students of the Australian labour movement. One could look at this letter and know that its implicit pain and panic would be but a sharp jab in the long and fruitful journey of her life. One could view it as the last thing before her real life could begin. But in 1865, Lucinda could not be so disengaged and she had written with passionate down-strokes on poor quality paper which was speckled like a plover's egg, and spotted with dark blue patches where the paper drank over thirstily of the ink. It was a letter written by a weary woman with red eyes and scalded arms, an employee of Mr Edward Jason's Druitt Street pickle factory.

"Dear Mrs Chadwick," Lucinda wrote, "There is no disputing that you are a thief, but a thief, I think, made so by fear and weakness and as I too understand the terror you have felt in your soul to contemplate a woman's life alone in New South Wales, then I forgive you."

Miriam's cheque, for ten guineas, was enclosed.

Lucinda wrote no return address upon her envelope, but she was certainly no longer at Longnose Point for when, in June of 1865, Wardley-Fish came out to Whitfield's Farm in search of Odd Bod, he found the little cottage deserted and not so much as a blanket or button to provide a clue as to what passions had brought his friend to inhabit this damp and sorry place. It was a rainy, overcast day with wind driving across Snails Bay from the south. Wardley-Fish stood on the spine of rock. His beard was soaked. His eyes were narrowed against the wind and water. The only brightness on that long peninsula came from Borrodaile's shiny red surveyor's stakes which dotted the earth as regularly as pegs upon a cribbage board.

110

Songs about Thistles

After only one hundred and twenty years this church, the one in which my mother sang "Holy, Holy, Holy," the one of which my father was so jealous, the one my great-grandfather assembled, shining clear, like heaven itself, on the Bellinger River, this church has been carted away. It was not of any use.

Where it stood last Christmas there is now a bare patch of earth, which is joined to the kikuyu grass by two great wheel ruts where the low-loader was temporarily bogged. There are sixteen banks of old cinema chairs which had lately served as pews for the small congregation. But there is no sign here of anything that the church meant to us: Palm Sundays, resurrections, water into wine, loaves and fishes, all those cruel and lofty ideas that Oscar, gaunt, sunburnt, his eyes rimmed with white, brought up the river in 1865.

There are thistles everywhere. They are small and flat now, like prickly sunbathers, but by the end of summer they will be three feet tall, and they will be thickest beside the short fat stumps where the church has stood. No one will slash them because this ground belongs to the church and the church is not here.

There are wheel ruts. There are thistles. By autumn their seeds will be catching in the needles of casuarinas, floating down across the shallow gravel beds of Sweet Water Creek. There are no stories to tell about thistles.

111

A Song for Oscar

When Oscar said goodbye to my great-grandmother he no longer thought that the glass church was a holy thing. He thought it a conceit, a vanity, a product of the deuce's insinuations into the fancy-factory of his mind. He was like a drunk waking after a spree, sour and sick and full of remorse and mixed in with all of this was the sin of fornication, his great fright to discover women have hair in "that place," the throbbing pain of his sunburn, the lesser pain of the infected blister on his heel, his itching, bleeding arsehole, the rope burns on his wrists and the nauseous fluttering feeling that told him he needed more laudanum.

He walked out along the ringing wooden wharf as though the water were no threat to him. The church rode on its mooring, creaking slightly as its ropes stretched against the zenith of high tide. He limped down the steps, grimacing, and entered through the cedar door which he carefully shut behind him. He walked across splintered glass and the bodies of dragonflies and wasps. He sat on the straight-backed chair which Kumbaingiri Billy's father's sister had carried through the bush to give him as a farewell gift. He reached for his laudanum and, having raised it to his lips, found it empty. He dropped the bottle on the deck, and then bent his head to pray.

He begged God forgive him for the murder of the blacks which he, through his vanity, had brought about.

He begged God forgive him for the death of Mr Stratton.

He begged God forgive him for the murder of Mr Jeffris.

He begged God forgive him for the seduction of Mrs Chadwick.

He begged God forgive him for his complacency, his pride, his wilful ignorance. But even as he prayed he felt himself polluted almost beyond redemption.

He prayed as he had prayed in his Bathurst Street boarding house, digging his nails into the backs of his hands, rocking to and fro on his chair until its legs groaned, but somewhere on the inky side of dusk, as the flying foxes began to detach their pegged and ragged forms from the branches of the Moreton Bay fig trees by the Bellinger, he drifted into sleep.

Thus he never reached the final destination of his prayer which was to ask God to destroy the glass church. In the event, no heavenly intervention was necessary, for the lighters belonged to H. M. McCracken whose house stood on sinking stumps, whose wagons had wheels with broken staves. One of the lighters, the one away from the wharf, shipped water, not so much, but enough to have made H. M. McCracken tell Percy Smith to "keep an eye on 'er." It had been taking in just under half an inch of water for every hour and now it was over one hundred hours since anyone had thought to look at it. At ten minutes past eight on Good Friday eve, the old lighter passed the point at which it was buoyant and then, with no fuss—it sank.

The clever platform Percy Smith had built dropped on one side. Water rose into the church. There was nothing to stop it.

Oscar awoke as he hit the floor. He slipped down to the low side, furthest from the door.

He scrabbled up the sloping platform towards the door. He slashed his hands on broken glass. The twisting of the platform had jammed the door.

It was not quite dark. Flying foxes filled the sky above the river. The tilting platform became a ramp and the glass church slid beneath the water and while my great-grandfather kicked and pulled at the jammed door, the fractured panes of glass behind his back opened to let in his ancient enemy.

A great bubble of air broke the surface of the Bellinger and the flying foxes came down close upon the river. When they were close enough for his bad eyes to see, he thought they were like angels with bat wings. He saw it as a sign from God. He shook his head, panicking in the face of eternity. He held the doorknob as it came to be the ceiling of his world. The water rose. Through the bursting gloom he saw a vision of his father's wise and smiling face, peering in at him. He could see, dimly, the outside world, the chair and benches of his father's study. Shining fragments of aquarium glass fell like snow around him. And when the long-awaited white fingers of water tapped and lapped on Oscar's lips, he welcomed them in as he always had, with a scream, like a small boy caught in the sheet-folds of a nightmare.

Glossary

brolga—a large silvery-grey crane found in Northern and Eastern Australia, which performs an elaborate courtship dance.

Coberra—a worm, eaten as a delicacy.

jinker—a light vehicle, designed to carry two people.

kingsman—a large showy handkerchief in fashion in the late eighteenth and early nineteenth centuries.

Mohawk—a colloquial term for a late Regency/early Victorian "Hooray Henry."

the push—colloquial Australian for a gang of vicious hooligans.

shickered—drunk.

swy—a gambling game.